The History of the Devil

As Well Ancient as Modern

Daniel Defoe

The History of the Devil: As Well Ancient as Modern

Contact:
BibliotechPress@gmail.com

The present edition is a reproduction of 1922 publication of this work. Minor typographical errors may have been corrected without note, however, for an authentic reading experience the spelling, punctuation, and capitalization have been retained from the original text.

ISBN: 978-1-61895-158-8

PREFACE

This Second Edition of this Work, notwithstanding a large Impression of the First, is a Certificate from the World of its general Acceptation; so we need not, according to the Custom of Editors, boast of it without Evidence, or tell a F——b in its Favor.

The Subject is singular, and it has been handled after a singular Manner: The wise World has been pleased with it, the merry World has been diverted with it, and the ignorant World has been taught by it; none but the malicious part of the World has been offended at it: Who can wonder, that when the Devil is not pleased, his Friends should be angry?

The strangest thing of it all is, to hear Satan complain that the Story is handled profanely: But who can think it strange that his Advocates should be, what he was from the Beginning?

The Author affirms, and has good Vouchers for it (in the Opinion of such whose Judgment passes with him for an Authority) that the whole Tenor of the Work is solemn, calculated to promote serious Religion, and capable of being improved in a religious manner. But he does not think that we are bound never to speak of the Devil but with an Air of Terror, as if we were always afraid of him.

It's evident the Devil, as subtle and as frightful as he is, has acted the ridiculous and foolish Part, as much as most of God's Creatures, and daily does so. And he cannot believe 'tis any Sin to expose him for a foolish Devil, as he is, or show the World that he may be laughed at.

Those that think the Subject not handled with Gravity enough, have all the Room given them in the World to handle it better; and as the Author professes he is far from thinking his Piece perfect, they ought not to be angry that he gives them leave to mend it. He has had the Satisfaction to please some Readers, and to see good Men approve it; and for the rest, as my Lord Rochester says in another Case,

He counts their Censure Fame

As for a certain Reverend Gentleman, who is pleased gravely to dislike the Work (he hopes, rather for the Author's sake than the Devil's) he only says,

Let the Performance be how it will, and the Author what he will, it is apparent he has not yet preached away all his Hearers.

It is enough to me (says the Author) that the Devil himself is not pleased with my Work, and less with the Design of it; let the Devil and all his fellow Complainers stand on one side, and the honest, well meaning, charitable World, who approve my Work, on the other, and I'll tell Noses with Satan, if he dares.

Table of Contents

PART I

Containing a State of the *Devil*'s Circumstances, and the various Turns of his Affairs; from his Expulsion out of Heaven, to the *Creation* of Man; with Remarks on the Several Mistakes concerning the Reason and Manner of his Fall.

Also his Proceedings with *Mankind* ever since *Adam*, to the first planting of the Christian Religion in the World.

Chapter I

An Introduction to the whole Work

I doubt not but the title of this book will amuse some of my reading friends a little at first; they will make a pause, perhaps, as they do at a witch's prayer, and be some time resolving whether they had best look into it or not, lest they should really raise the *Devil* by reading his story.

Children and old women have told themselves so many frightful things *of the Devil*, and have formed ideas of him in their minds, in so many horrible and monstrous shapes, that really it were enough to fright the *Devil* himself, to meet himself in the dark, dressed up in the several figures which imagination has formed for him in the minds of men; and as for themselves, I cannot think by any means that the *Devil* would terrify them half so much, if they were to converse face to face with him.

It must certainly therefore be a most useful undertaking to give the true history of this *Tyrant of the air*, this *God of the world*, this terror and aversion of mankind, which we call *Devil*; to show what he is, and what he is not, where he is, and where he is not, when he is in us, and when he is not; for I cannot doubt but that the *Devil* is really and *bona fide* in a great many of our honest weak-headed friends, when they themselves know nothing of the matter.

Nor is the work so difficult as some may imagine. The *Devil's history* is not so hard to come at, as it seems to be; His original and the first rise of his family is upon record, and as for his conduct, he has acted indeed in the dark, as to method in many things; but *in general*, as cunning as he is, he has been fool enough to expose himself in some of the most considerable transactions of his Life, and has not shown himself a politician at all: Our old friend *Matchiavel* outdid him in many things, and I may in the process of this work give an account of several of the sons of *Adam*, and some societies of them too, who have out-witted *the Devil*, nay, who have out-sinned *the Devil*, and that I think may be called out-shooting him in his own bow.

It may perhaps be expected of me in this history, that since I seem inclined to speak favorably of *Satan*, to do him justice, and to write his story impartially, I should take some pains to tell you what religion he is of; and even this part may not be so much a jest, as at first sight you may take it to be; for *Satan* has something of religion in him, I assure you; nor is he such an unprofitable *Devil* that way, as some may suppose him to be; for though, in reverence to my brethren, I will not reckon him among the Clergy; No not so much as a gifted Brother, yet I cannot deny, but that he often preaches, and if it be not profitably to his hearers; 'tis as much their fault, as it is out of his design.

It has indeed been suggested that he has taken orders, and that a certain Pope, famous for being an extraordinary favorite of his, gave him both institution and induction; but as this is not upon record, and therefore we have no authentic document for the probation, I shall not affirm it for a truth, for I would not slander the *Devil*.

It is said also, and I am apt to believe it, that he was very familiar with that holy father Pope *Silvester* II. and some charge him with personating Pope *Hildebrand* on an extraordinary occasion, and himself sitting in the chair apostolic, in a full congregation; and you may hear more of this hereafter: But as I do not meet with Pope *Diabolus* among the list; in all father *Platina*'s lives of the Popes, so I am willing to leave it as I find it.

But to speak to the point, and a nice point it is I acknowledge; *namely,* what religion *the Devil* is of; my answer will indeed be general, yet not at all ambiguous, for I love to speak positively and with undoubted evidence.

1. *He is a believer.* And if in saying so it should follow, that even the *Devil* has more religion than some of our men of fame can at this time be charged with, I hope my Lord —— and his Grace the —— of —— and some of the upper class in the red-hot club, will not wear the coat, however well it may sit to their shapes, or challenge the Satyr, as if it were pointed at them, because 'tis due to them: In a word, whatever their Lordships are, I can assure them that the *Devil* is no Infidel.

2. *He fears God.* We have such abundant evidence of this in sacred History, that if I were not at present, in common with a few others, talking to an infidel sort of Gentlemen, with whom those remote things called Scriptures are not allowed in evidence, I might say it was sufficiently proved; but I doubt not in the process of this undertaking to show, that *the Devil* really *fears God*, and that after another manner than ever he feared Saint *Frances* or Saint *Dunstan*; and if that be proved, as I take upon me to advance, I shall leave it to judgment, who's the better Christian, *the Devil* who *believes* and *trembles,* or our modern gentry of —— who believe neither *God nor Devil.*

Having thus brought the *Devil* within the *Pale*, I shall leave him among you for the present; not but that I may examine in its order who has the best claim to his brotherhood, the Papists or the Protestants; and among the latter the Lutherans or the Calvinists; and so descending to all the several denominations of churches, see who has less of *the Devil* in them, and who more; and whether *less* or *more* the Devil has not a seat in every synagogue, a pew in every church, a place in every pulpit, and a vote in every synod; even from the Sanhedrim of the *Jews*, to our friends at the *Bull and Mouth*, etc.. from the greatest to the least.

It will, I confess, come very much within the compass of this part of my discourse, to give an account, *or at least make an essay toward it*, of the share *the Devil* has had in the spreading religion in the world; and especially of dividing and subdividing opinions in religion; perhaps, to eke it out and make it reach the farther; and also to show how far he is or has made himself a missionary of the famous clan *de propaganda fide*; it is true, we find him heartily employed in almost every corner of the world *ad propagandum error*: But that may require a history by itself.

As to his propagating religion, 'tis a little hard indeed, at first sight, to charge *the Devil* with propagating religion, that is to say, if we take it literally, and in the gross; but if you take it as the *Scots* insisted to take the oath of fidelity, *viz.* with an *explanation*, it is plain *Satan* has very often had a share in the method, if not in the design of propagating the *Christian faith*: For example.

I think I do no injury at all to the Devil, to say that he had a great hand in the old *holy war*, as it was ignorantly and enthusiastically called; stirring up the Christian princes and powers of *Europe* to run a madding after the *Turks* and *Saracens*, and make war with those innocent people above a thousand miles off, only because they entered into God's heritage when he had forsaken it; grazed upon his ground when he had fairly turn's it into a common, and laid it open for the next comer; spending their nation's treasure, and embarking their kings and people, (I say) in a war above a thousand miles off, filling their heads with that religious madness, called, in those days, *holy zeal* to recover the *terra sancta*, the sepulchers of Christ and the Saints, and as they called it falsely, the *holy city*, though true religion says it was the accursed city, and not worth spending one drop of blood for.

This religious *Bubble* was certainly of *Satan*, who, as he craftily drew them in, so like a true *Devil* he left them in the lurch when they came there, faced about to the *Saracens*, animated the immortal *Saladin* against them, and managed so dexterously that he left the bones of about thirteen or fourteen hundred thousand Christians there as a trophy of his infernal politics; and after the Christian world had run *a la santa terra*, or in *English* a *saunt'ring*, about a hundred year, he dropped it to play another game less foolish, but ten times wickeder than that which went before it, *namely*, turning the crusades of the Christians one against another; and, as *Hudibras* said in another case,

"Made them fight like mad or drunk
"For dame religion as for punk.

Of this you have a complete account in the history of the Popes decrees against the Count *de Thoulouse*, and the *Waldenses* and *Albigenses*, with the crusades and massacres which followed upon them, wherein to do *the Devil*'s politics some justice, he met with all the success he could desire; the zealots of that day executed his infernal orders most punctually, and planted religion in those countries in a glorious and triumphant manner, upon the destruction of an infinite number of innocent people, whose blood has fattened the soil for the growth of the Catholic faith, in a manner very particular, and to Satan's full satisfaction.

I might, to complete this part of his history, give you the detail of his progress in these first steps of his alliances with *Rome*; and add a long list of massacres, wars, and expeditions in behalf of religion, which he has had the honor to have a visible hand in; such as the *Parisian* massacre, the *Flemish* war under the Duke *d' Alva*, the *Smithfield* fires in the *Marian days* in *England*, and the massacres in *Ireland*; all which would most effectually convince us that *the Devil* has not been idle in his business; but I may meet with these again in my way, 'tis enough, while I am upon the generals only, to mention them thus in a summary way; I say, 'tis enough to prove that *the Devil* has really been as much concerned as anybody, in the methods taken by some people for propagating the Christian religion in the world.

Some have rashly, and I had almost said maliciously charged *the Devil* with the great triumphs of his friends the *Spaniards* in *America*, and would place the conquest of *Mexico* and *Peru* to the credit of his account.

But I cannot join with them in this at all, I must say, I believe *the Devil* was innocent of that matter; my reason is, because, *Satan* was never such a fool as to spend his time, or his politics, or embark his allies to conquer nations who were already his own; that would be *Satan* against *Beelzebub*, making war upon himself, and at least doing nothing to the purpose.

If they should charge him, indeed, with deluding *Philip* II. of *Spain* into that preposterous attempt called *the Armada*, (*anglice*, the *Spanish Invasion*,) I should indeed more readily join with them; but whether he did it weakly, in hope, *which was indeed not likely*, that it should succeed; or wickedly, to destroy that great fleet of the *Spaniards*, and draw them within the reach of his own dominions, the elements; this being a question which authors differ exceedingly about, I shall leave it to decide itself.

But the greatest piece of management, which we find *the Devil* has concerned himself in of late, in the matter of religion, seems to be that of the mission into *China*; and here indeed *Satan* has acted his master-piece:

It was, no doubt, much for his service that *the Chinese* should have no insight into matters of religion, I mean, that we call Christian; and therefore, though *Popery* and the *Devil* are not at so much variance as some may imagine, yet he did not think it safe to let the general system of Christianity be heard of among them in *China*. Hence when the name of the Christian religion had but been received with some seeming approbation in the country of *Japan*, *Satan* immediately, as if alarmed at the thing, and dreading what the consequence of it might be, armed the *Japanese* against it with such fury, that they expelled it at once.

It was much safer to his designs, when, if the story be not a fiction, he put that *Dutch* witticism into the mouths of the States commanders, when they came to *Japan*; who having more wit than to own themselves Christians in such a place as that, when the question was put to them, answered negatively, *That they were not*, but that *they were of another religion called* Hollanders.

However, it seems the diligent *Jesuits* out-witted the Devil in *China*, and, as I said above, over-shot him in his own Bow; for the mission being in danger *by the Devil and the* Chinese *Emperor*'s *joining together*, of being wholly expelled there too, as they had been in *Japan*, they cunningly fell in with the ecclesiastics of the country, and joining the priest craft of both religions together, they brought *Jesus Christ* and *Confucius* to be so reconcilable, that the *Chinese* and the *Roman* idolatry appeared capable of a confederacy, of going on hand in hand together, and consequently of being very good friends.

This was a master-piece indeed, and, *as they say*, almost startled *Satan* out of his wits; but he being a ready manager, and particularly famous for serving himself of the rogueries of the priests, faced about immediately to the mission, and making a virtue of necessity, clapped in, with all possible alacrity, with the proposal [1]; so the *Jesuits* and he formed a *hotch-potch* of *religion* made up of *Popery* and *Paganism* and calculated to leave the latter rather worse than they found it, binding the faith of Christ and the philosophy or morals of *Confucius* together, and formally christening them by the name of *religion*; by which means the politick interest of the mission was preserved; and yet *Satan* lost not one inch of ground with the *Chinese*, no, not by the planting the Gospel itself, *such as it was*, among them.

Nor has it been such disadvantage to him that this plan or scheme of a new modeled religion would not go down at *Rome*, and that the Inquisition damned it with Bell, Book and Candle; distance of place served his new allies, the missionaries, in the stead of a protection from the Inquisition;

---

[1] N. B. He never refused setting his hand to any opinion, which he thought it for his interest to acknowledge.

and now and then a rich present well placed found them friends in the congregation itself; and where any Nuncio with his impudent zeal pretended to take such a long voyage to oppose them, *Satan* took care to get him sent back *re infecta*, or inspired the million to move him off the premises, by methods of their own (that is to say, being interpreted) to *murder him.*

Thus the mission has in itself been truly *devilish*, and the Devil has interested himself in the planting the Christian religion in *China*.

The influence *the Devil* has in the Politics of mankind, is another especial part of his history, and would require, if it were possible, a very exact description; but here we shall necessarily be obliged to inquire so nicely into the Arcane of circumstances, and unlock the cabinets of state in so many courts, canvass the councils of ministers and the conduct of princes so fully, and expose them so much, that it may, perhaps, make a combustion among the great politicians abroad; and in doing that we may come so near home too, that though personal safety and prudential forbid our meddling with our own country, we may be taken in a double entendre, and fall unpitied for being only suspected of touching truths that are so tender, whether we are guilty or no; on these accounts I must meddle the less with that part, at least for the present.

Be it that the Devil has had a share in some of the late councils of *Europe*, influencing them this way or that way, to his own advantage, what is it to us? For example, What if he has had any concern in the late affair of *Thorn*? What need we put it upon him, seeing his confederates the *Jesuits* with the *Assessorial* tribunal of *Poland* take it upon themselves? I shall leave that part to the issue of time. I wish it were as easy to persuade the world that he had no hand in bringing the injured Protestants to leave the justice due to the cries of protestant blood to the arbitrament of a popish power, who dare say that *the Devil* must be in it, if justice should be obtained that way: I should rather say, *the Devil* is in it, or else it would never be expected.

It occurs next to enquire from the premises, whether *the Devil* has more influence or less in the affairs of the world now, than he had in former ages; and this will depend upon comparing, as we go along, his methods and way of working in past times, and the modern politics by which he acts in our days; with the differing reception which he has met with among the men of such distant ages.

But there is so much to enquire of about *the Devil*, before we can bring his story down to our modern times, that we must for the present let them drop, and look a little back to the remoter parts of this history; drawing his picture that people may know him when they meet him, and see who and what he is, and what he has been doing ever since he got leave to act in the high station he now appears in.

In the mean time, if I might obtain leave to present an humble petition to *Satan*, it should be, that he would according to modern usage oblige us all, with writing *the history of his own times*; it would, as well as one that is gone before it, be a Devilish good one; for as to the sincerity of the performance, the authority of the particulars, the justice of the characters, *etc.*. if they were no better vouched, no more consistent with themselves, with charity, with truth, and with the honor of an historian, than the last of that kind which came abroad among us, it must be a reproach to *the Devil* himself to be the author of it.

Were *Satan* to be brought under the least obligation to write truth, and that the matters of fact, which he should write, might be depended upon, he is certainly qualified by his knowledge of things to be a complete historian; nor could the Bishop himself, *who, by the way, has given us already the Devil of a history*, come up to him: *Milton*'s *Pandemonium*, though an excellent dramatic performance, would appear a mere trifling sing-song business, beneath the dignity of *Chevy-chase*: The *Devil* could give us a true account of all the civil wars in Heaven; how and by whom, and in what manner he lost the day there, and was obliged to quit the field: The fiction of his refusing to acknowledge and submit to the *Messiah*, upon his being declared Generalissimo of the Heavenly forces, which Satan expected himself, as the eldest officer; and his not being able to brook another to be put in over his head; I say, that fine-spun thought of Mr. *Milton* would appear to be strained too far, and only serve to convince us that he (*Milton*) knew nothing of the matter. *Satan* knows very well, that the *Messiah* was not *declared to be the Son of God with power* till by and after *the resurrection from the dead*, and that all power was then given him *in Heaven and earth*, and not before; so that *Satan*'s rebellion must derive from other causes, and upon other occasions, as he himself can doubtless give us an account, if he thinks fit, and of which we shall speak further in this work.

What a fine History might this old Gentleman write of the Antediluvian world, and of all the weighty affairs, as well of state as of religion, which happened during the fifteen hundred years of the patriarchal administration!

Who, like him, could give a full and complete account of the Deluge, whether it was a mere vindictive, a blast from Heaven, wrought by a supernatural power in the way of miracle? Or whether, according to Mr. *Burnet*'s *Theory*, it was a consequence following antecedent causes by the mere necessity of nature; seen in constitution, natural position, and unavoidable working of things, as by the Theory published by that learned enthusiast it seems to be?

Satan could easily account for all the difficulties of the *Theory*, and tell us whether, as there was a natural necessity of the Deluge, there is not the like necessity and natural tendency to a Conflagration at last.

Would *the Devil* exert himself as an Historian, for our improvement and diversion, how glorious an account could he give us of *Noah*'s Voyage round the world, in the famous Ark! he could resolve all the difficulties about the building it, the furnishing it, and the laying up provision in it for all the collection of kinds that he had made; He could tell us whether all the creatures came volunteer to him to go into the ark, or whether he went a hunting for several years before, in order to bring them together.

He could give us a true relation how he wheedled the people of the next world into the absurd ridiculous undertaking of building a *Babel*; how far that stupendous stair-case, which was in imagination to reach up to Heaven, was carried, before it was interrupted and the builders confounded; how their speech was altered, how many Tongues it was divided into, or whether they were divided at all; and how many subdivisions or dialects have been made since that, by which means very few of God's creatures, except the Brutes, understand one another, or care one farthing whether they do or no.

In all these things *Satan*, who, no doubt, would make a very good chronologist, could settle every Epoch, correct every Calendar, and bring all our accounts of time to a general agreement; as well the *Grecian Olympiads*, the *Turkish Heghira*, the *Chinese* fictitious account of the world's duration, as our blind *Julian* and *Gregorian* accounts, which have put the world, to this day, into such confusion, that we neither agree in our holy-days or working days, fasts or feasts, nor keep the same Sabbaths in any part of the same globe.

This great Antiquary could bring us to a certainty in all the difficulties of ancient story, and tell us whether the tale of the siege of *Troy*, and the rape of *Helen* was a fable of *Homer* or a history; whether the fictions of the Poets are formed from their own brain, or founded in facts; and whether letters were invented by *Cadmus* the *Phoenician*, or dictated immediately from *Heaven* at mount *Sinai*.

Nay, he could tell us how and in what manner he wheedled *Eve*, deluded *Adam*, put *Cain* into a passion, till he made him murder his own brother; and made *Noah*, who was above 500 years a preacher of righteousness, turn Sot in his old age, dishonor all his ministry, debauch himself with wine, and by getting drunk and exposing himself, become the jest and laughing-stock of his children, and of all his posterity to this day.

And would Satan, according to the modern practice of the late right reverend Historian, enter into the characters of the great men of his age, how should we be diverted with the just history of *Adam*, in paradise and out of it; his character, and how he behaved at and after his expulsion; how *Cain* wandered in the land of *Nod*, what the mark was which *God* set upon him, whose daughter his wife was, and how big the city was he built there, according to a certain Poet of noble extraction,

How *Cain* in the land of *Nod*
When the rascal was alone
Like an owl in an ivy tod
Built a city as big as *Roan*.
Roch

He could have certainly drawn *Eve*'s picture, told us every feature in her face, and every inch in her shape, whether she was a perfect beauty or no, and whether with the fall she did grow crooked, ugly, ill-natured and a scold; as the learned *Valdemar* suggests to be the effects of the curse.

Descending to the character of the Patriarchs in that age, he might, no doubt, give us in particular the characters of *Belus*, worshiped under the name of *Baal*; with *Satan*, and *Jupiter*, his successors; who they were here, and how they behaved; with all the *Pharaohs* of *Egypt*, the *Abimilechs* of *Canaan*, and the great monarchs of *Assyria* and *Babylon*.

Hence also he is able to write the lives of all the Heroes of the world, from *Alexander* of *Macedon* to *Lewis* the XIV. and from *Augustus* to the great King *George*; nor could the Bishop himself go beyond him for flattery, any more than the Devil himself could go beyond the Bishop for falsehood.

I could enlarge with a particular satisfaction upon the many fine things which *Satan*, rummaging his inexhaustible storehouse of slander, could set down to blacken the characters of good men, and load the best Princes of the world with infamy and reproach.

But we shall never prevail with him, I doubt, to do mankind so much service, as resolving all those difficulties would be; for he has an indelible grudge against us; as he believes, and perhaps is assured that men were at first created by his sovereign, to the intent that after a certain state of Probation in life, such of them as shall be approved, are appointed to fill up those vacancies in the Heavenly Host, which were made by the abdication and expulsion of him (*the Devil*) and his Angels; so that man is appointed to come in *Satan*'s stead, to make good the breach, and enjoy all those ineffable Joys and Beatitudes which *Satan* enjoyed before his fall; no wonder then, that *the Devil* swells with envy and rage at mankind in general, and at the best of them in particular; nay, the granting this point is giving an unanswerable reason, why the *Devil* practices with such unwearied and indefatigable application upon the best men, if possible, to disappoint God Almighty's decree, and that he should not find enough among the whole Race, to be proper subjects of his clemency, and qualified to succeed *the Devil* and his host, or fill up the places vacant by the Fall. It is true indeed, *the Devil*, who we have reason to say is no fool, ought to know better than to suppose that if he should seduce the whole race of mankind, and make them as bad as himself, he could, by that success of his wickedness, thwart or disappoint the determined purposes of Heaven; but that those which are appointed to inherit the Thrones, which he and his followers abdicated, and were deposed from, shall certainly be preserved in spite of his Devices for that inheritance, and shall have the possession secured to them, notwithstanding all that *the Devil* and all the Host of *Hell* can do to prevent it.

But, however he knows the certainty of this, and that when he endeavors the seducing the chosen servants of the most High, he fights against God himself, struggles with irresistible grace, and makes war with infinite power; undermining the church of God, and that faith in him which is fortified with the eternal promises of Jesus Christ, that the gates of *Hell*, that is to say, the *Devil* and all his power, shall not prevail against them; I say, however he knows the impossibility there is that he should obtain his ends, yet so blind is his rage, so infatuate his wisdom, that he cannot refrain breaking himself to pieces against this mountain, and splitting against the rock. *qui Jupiter vult perdere hos dementat.*

But to leave this serious part, which is a little too solemn, for the account of this rebel; seeing we are not to expect he will write his own History for our information and diversion, I shall see if I cannot write it for him: In order to this, I shall extract the substance of his whole story, from the beginning to our own times, which I shall collect out of what is come to hand, whether by revelation or inspiration, that's nothing to him; I shall take care so to improve my intelligence, as may make my account of him authentic, and, *in a word*, such as the Devil himself shall not be able to contradict.

In writing this uncouth story I shall be freed from the censures of the Critics, in a more than ordinary manner, upon one account especially; (*viz.*) that my story shall be so just and so well grounded, and, after all the good things I shall say of *Satan*, will be so little to his satisfaction, that *the Devil* himself will not be able to say, I *dealt with the Devil* in writing it: I might, perhaps, give you some account where I had my intelligence, and how all the Arcane of his management have come to my hands; *but pardon me, Gentlemen*, this would be to betray conversation, and to discover my agents, and you know statesmen are very careful to preserve the correspondences they keep in the enemy's country, lest they expose their friends to the resentment of the Power whose councils they betray.

Besides, the learned tell us, that ministers of state make an excellent plea of their not betraying their intelligence, against all party inquiries into the great sums of money pretended to be paid for *secret service*; and whether the secret service was to bribe people to betray things abroad or at home; whether the money was paid to somebody or to no body, employed to establish correspondences abroad, or to establish families and amass treasure at home; in a word, whether it was to serve their country or serve themselves, it has been the same thing, and the same plea has been their protection: Likewise in the important affair which I am upon, it is hoped you will not desire me to betray my Correspondents; for you know *Satan* is naturally cruel and malicious, and who knows what he might do to show his resentment? at least it might endanger a stop of our intelligence for the future.

And yet, before I have done, I shall make it very plain, that however my information may be secret and difficult, that yet I came very honestly by it, and shall make a very good use of it; for 'tis a great mistake in those who think that an acquaintance with the affairs of *the Devil* may not be made very useful to us all: They that know no evil can know no good; and, as the learned tell us, that a stone taken out of the head of a Toad is a good antidote against poison; so a competent knowledge of *the Devil*, and all his ways, may be the best help to make us defy *the Devil* and all his *works*.

Chapter II

Of the word DEVIL, as it is a proper name to the Devil, and any or all his host, Angels, etc.

It is a question, not yet determined by the learned, whether the word *Devil* be a *singular*, that is to say, the *name* of a person standing by himself, or a *noun of multitude*; if it be a singular, and so must be used personally only as *a proper name*, it consequently implies one imperial *Devil*, Monarch or King of the whole clan of Hell; justly distinguished by the term the Devil, or as the *Scots* call him, *the muckle horned Dee'l*, or as others in a wilder dialect, *the Devil of Hell*, that is to say, the *Devil* of a *Devil*; or (better still) as the Scripture expresses it, by way of emphasis, the *great red Dragon*, the *Devil* and *Satan*.

But if we take this word to be, as above, *a noun of multitude*, and so to be used *ambo-dexter*, as occasion presents, singular or plural; then *the Devil* signifies *Satan* by himself, or *Satan with all his Legions* at his heels, as you please, more or less; and this way of understanding the word, as it may be very convenient for my purpose, in the account I am now to give of the infernal Powers, so it is not altogether improper in the nature of the thing: It is thus expressed in Scripture, where the person possessed *Matt.* iv. 24. is first said to be possessed of *the Devil* (singular) and our Saviour asks him, as speaking to a single person, *what is thy name?* and is answered in the plural and singular together, my name is Legion, for *we are many*.

Nor will it be any wrong to *the Devil*, supposing him a single person, seeing entitling him to the conduct of all his inferior Agents, is what he will take rather for an addition to his infernal glory, than a diminution or lessening of him in the extent of his Fame.

Having thus articled with the *Devil* for liberty of speech, I shall talk of him sometimes in the singular, as a person, and sometimes in the plural, as an host of *Devils* or of infernal Spirits, just as occasion requires, and as the history of his affairs makes necessary.

But before I enter upon any part of his history, the nature of the thing calls me back, and my Lord B—— of —— in his late famous orations in defense of liberty, summons me to prove that there is such a thing or such a person as *the Devil*; and in short, unless I can give some evidence of his existence, as my Lord —— said very well, I am talking of *nobody*.

D—m me, Sir, says a graceless comrade of his to a great man, *your Grace* will go to *the Devil*.

D—m ye, Sir, says the D——, then I shall go *nowhere*; I wonder where you intend to go?

Nay, to *the D——l* too I doubt, *says Graceless*, for I am almost as wicked as my *Lord Duke*.

D. Thou ar't a silly empty Dog, says the D—, and if there is such a place as *a Hell*, though I believe nothing of it, 'tis a place for fools, such as thou art.

Gr. I wonder then, what Heaven the great wits go to, such as my *Lord Duke*; I don't care to go there, let it be where it will; they are a tiresome kind of people, there's no bearing them, they'll make *a Hell* wherever they come.

D. Prithee hold thy fool's tongue, I tell thee, if there is any such place as we call nowhere; that's all the Heaven or Hell that I know of, or believe anything about.

Gr. Very good, my Lord—; so that *Heaven* is *nowhere*, and *Hell* is *nowhere*, and the *Devil* is *nobody*, according to my *Lord Duke*!

D. Yes Sir, and what then?

Gr. And you are to go *nowhere* when you die, are you?

D. Yes, you Dog, don't you know what that incomparable noble genius my Lord *Rochester* sings upon the subject, I believe it unfeignedly,

After death nothing is,
And nothing death.

Gr. You believe it, my Lord, you mean, you would fain believe it if you could; but since you put that great genius my Lord *Rochester* upon me, let me play him back upon *your Grace*; I am sure you have read his fine poem upon *nothing*, in one of the stanzas of which is this beautiful thought,

And to be part of thee
The wicked wisely pray.

D. You are a foolish Dog.

Gr. And my *Lord Duke* is a wise Infidel.

D. Why? is it not wiser to believe *no Devil*, than to be always terrified at him?

Gr. But shall I toss another Poet upon you, my Lord?

If it should so fall out, as who can tell
But there may be a God, a *Heaven* and *Hell*?
Mankind had best consider well, for fear
'T should be too late when their mistakes appear.

D. D—m your foolish Poet, that's not my Lord *Rochester*.

Gr. But how must I be damned, if there's *no Devil*? Is not *your Grace* a little inconsistent there? My Lord *Rochester* would not have said that, and't please your Grace.

D. No, *you Dog*, I am not inconsistent at all, and if I had the ordering of you, I'd make you sensible of it; I'd make you think your self damned for want of *a Devil*.

Gr. That's like one of *your Grace*'s paradoxes, such as when you swore *by God* that you did not believe there was any such thing as *a God*, or *Devil*; so you swear by *nothing*, and damn me to *nowhere*.

D. You are a critical Dog, who taught you to believe these solemn trifles? who taught you to say there is a God?

Gr. Nay, I had a better school-master than my *Lord Duke*.

D. Why, who was your school-master pray?

Gr. The Devil, and't please your *Grace*.

D. The Devil! *the Devil he did?* what you're going to quote Scripture, are you? Prithee don't tell me of *Scripture*, I know what you mean, *the Devils believe and tremble*; why then I have the whip-hand of *the Devil*, for I hate trembling; and I am delivered from it effectually, for I never believed anything of it, and therefore I don't tremble.

Gr. And there, indeed, I am a wickeder creature than the *Devil*, or even than my *Lord Duke*, for I believe, and yet don't tremble neither.

D. Nay, if you are come to your penitentials I have done with you.

Gr. And I think I must have done with my *Lord Duke*, for the same reason.

D. *Ay, ay,* pray do, I'll go and enjoy myself; I won't throw away the pleasure of my life, I know the consequence of it.

Gr. And I'll go and reform myself, else I know the consequence too.

This short Dialogue happened between two men of quality, and both men of wit too; and the effect was, that the Lord brought the reality of *the Devil* into the question, and the debate brought the profligate to be a penitent; so in short, *the Devil* was made a preacher of repentance.

The Truth is, *God* and *the Devil,* however opposite in their nature, and remote from one another in their place of abiding, seem to stand pretty much upon a level in our faith: For as to our believing the reality of their existence, he that denies one, generally denies both; and he that believes one, necessarily believes both.

Very few, if any of those who believe there is a God, and acknowledge the debt of homage which mankind owes to the supreme Governor of the World, doubt the existence of *the Devil,* except here and there one, whom we call practical Atheists; and 'tis the character of an Atheist, if there is such a creature on Earth, that like my *Lord Duke,* he believes neither God or *Devil.*

As the belief of both these stands upon a level, and that God and the *Devil* seem to have an equal share in our faith, so the evidence of their existence seems to stand upon a level too, in many things; and as they are known by their Works in the same particular cases, so they are discovered after the same manner of demonstration.

Nay, in some respects 'tis equally criminal to deny the reality of them both, only with this difference, that to believe the existence of a God is a debt to nature, and to believe the existence of *the Devil* is a like debt to reason; one is a demonstration from the reality of visible causes, and the other a deduction from the like reality of their effects.

One demonstration of the existence of God, is from the universal well-guided consent of all nations to worship and adore a supreme Power; One demonstration of the existence of the *Devil,* is from the avowed ill-guided consent of some nations, who knowing no other God, make a God of the *Devil,* for want of a better.

It may be true, that those nations have no other Ideas of the Devil than as of a superior Power; if they thought him a supreme Power it would have other effects on them, and they would submit to and worship him with a different kind of fear.

But 'tis plain they have right notions of him as a Devil or evil Spirit, because the best reason, and in some places the only reason they give for worshiping him is, that he may do them no hurt; having no notions at all of his having any power, much less any inclination to do them good; so that indeed they make a mere *Devil* of him, at the same time that they bow to him as to a God.

All the ages of Paganism in the World have had this notion of *the Devil*: indeed in some parts of the World they had also some Deities which they honored above him, as being supposed to be beneficent, kind and inclined, as well as capable to give them good things; for this reason the more polite Heathens, such as the *Grecians* and the *Romans*, had their *Lares* or household Gods, whom they paid a particular respect to; as being their Protectors from Hobgoblins, Ghosts of the Dead, evil Spirits, frightful Appearances, evil Genius's and other noxious Beings from the invisible World; or to put it into the language of the day we live in, from *the Devil*, in whatever shape or appearance he might come to them, and from whatever might hurt them: and what was all this but setting up *Devils* against *Devils*, supplicating one *Devil* under the notion of a good Spirit, to drive out and protect them from another, whom they called a bad Spirit, the white *Devil* against the black *Devil*?

This proceeds from the natural notions mankind necessarily entertain of things to come; *superior* or *inferior*, God and the *Devil*, fill up all futurity in our thoughts; and 'tis impossible for us to form any images in our minds of an immortality and an invisible World, but under the notions of perfect felicity, or extreme misery.

Now as these two respect the Eternal state of man after life, they are respectively the object of our reverence and affection, or of our horror and aversion; but notwithstanding they are placed thus in a diametrical opposition in our affections and passions, they are on an evident level as to the certainty of their existence, and, as I said above, bear an equal share in our faith.

It being then as certain that there is *a Devil*, as that there is *a God*, I must from this time forward admit no more doubt of his existence, nor take any more pains to convince you of it; but speaking of him as a reality in Being, proceed to enquire who he is, and from whence, in order to enter directly into the detail of his History.

Now not to enter into all the metaphysical trumpery of his Schools, nor wholly to confine myself to the language of the Pulpit; where we are told, that to think of God and of the *Devil*, we must endeavor first to form Ideas of those things which illustrate the description of rewards and punishments; in the one the eternal presence of the highest good, and, as a necessary attendant, the most perfect, consummate, durable bliss and felicity, springing from the presence of that Being in whom all possible Beatitude is inexpressibly present, and that in the highest perfection: On the contrary, to conceive of a sublime fallen Arch-angel, attended with an innumerable host of degenerate, rebel Seraphs or Angels cast out of Heaven together; all guilty of inexpressible rebellion, and all suffering from that time, and to suffer forever the eternal vengeance of the Almighty, in an inconceivable manner; that his presence, though blessed in itself, is to them the most complete article of terror; That they are in themselves perfectly miserable; and to be with whom forever, adds an inexpressible misery to any state as well as place; and fills the minds of those who are to be, or expect to be banished to them with inconceivable horror and amazement.

But when you have gone over all this, and a great deal more of the like, though less intelligible language, which the passions of men collect to amuse one another with; you have said nothing if you omit the main article, namely, the personality of *the Devil*; and till you add to all the rest some description of the company with whom all this is to be suffered, *viz.* the *Devil and his Angels*.

Now who this *Devil and his Angels* are, what share they have either actively or passively in the eternal miseries of a future state, how far they are Agents in or Partners with the sufferings of the place, is a difficulty yet not fully discovered by the most learned; nor do I believe 'tis made less a difficulty by their meddling with it.

But to come to the person and original of *the Devil*, or, as I said before, of *Devils*; I allow him to come of an ancient family, for he is from Heaven, and more truly than the *Romans* could say of their idoliz'd *Numa*, he is of the race of the Gods.

That *Satan* is a fallen Angel, a rebel Seraph, cast out for his Rebellion, is the general opinion, and 'tis not my business to dispute things universally received; as he was tried, condemned, and the sentence of expulsion executed on him in Heaven, he is in this World like a transported Felon never to return; His crime, whatever particular aggravations it might have, 'tis certain, amounted to High-treason against his Lord and Governor, who was also his Maker; against whom he rose in rebellion, took up arms, and in a word, raised a horrid and unnatural war in his dominions; but being overcome in battle, and made prisoner, he and all his Host, whose numbers were infinite, all glorious Angels like himself, lost at once their beauty and glory with their Innocence, and commenced *Devils*, being transformed by crime into monsters and frightful objects; such as to describe, human fancy is obliged to draw pictures and descriptions in such forms as are most hateful and frightful to the imagination.

These notions, I doubt not, gave birth to all the beauteous Images and sublime expressions in Mr. *Milton*'s majestic Poem; where, though he has played the Poet in a most luxuriant manner, he has sinned against *Satan* most egregiously, and done the *Devil* a manifest injury in a great many particulars, as I shall show in its place. And as I shall be obliged to do *Satan* justice when I come to that part of his History, Mr. *Milton*'s admirers must pardon me, if I let them see, that though I admire Mr. *Milton* as a Poet, yet that he was greatly out in matters of History, and especially the History of the *Devil*; in short, That he has charged *Satan* falsely in several particulars; and so he has *Adam* and *Eve* too: But that I shall leave till I come to the History of the Royal Family of *Eden*; which I resolve to present you with when the *Devil* and I have done with one another.

But not to run down Mr. *Milton* neither, whose poetry, or his judgment, cannot be reproached without injury to our own; all those bright Ideas of his, which make his poem so justly valued, whether they are capable of proof as to the fact, are notwithstanding, confirmations of my hypothesis; and are taken from a supposition of the Personality of the *Devil*, placing him at the head of the infernal host, as a sovereign elevated Spirit and Monarch of Hell; and as such it is that I undertake to write his history.

By the word Hell I do not suppose, or at least not determine, that his residence, or that of the whole army of *Devils*, is yet in the same local Hell, to which the Divines tell us he shall be at last chained down; or at least that he is yet confined to it, for we shall find he is at present a prisoner at large: of both which circumstances of Satan I shall take occasion to speak in its course.

But when I call the Devil the Monarch of *Hell*, I am to be understood as suits to the present purpose; that he is the Sovereign of all the race of Hell, that is to say of all the Devils or Spirits of the infernal Clan, let their numbers, quality and powers be what they will.

Upon this supposed personality and superiority of *Satan*, or, as I call it, the sovereignty and government of one Devil above all the rest; I say, upon this notion are formed all the systems of the dark side of futurity, that we can form in our minds: And so general is the opinion of it, that it will hardly bear to be opposed by any other argument, at least that will bear to be reasoned upon: All the notions of a parity of Devils, or making a commonwealth among the black Divan, seem to be enthusiastic and visionary, but with no consistency or certainty, and is so generally exploded, that we must not venture so much as to debate the point.

Taking it then as the generality of mankind do, that there is a Grand Devil, a superior of the whole black race; that they all fell, together with their General, *Satan*, at the head of them; that though he, *Satan*, could not maintain his high station in Heaven, yet that he did continue his dignity among the rest, who are called his servants, *in Scripture his Angels*; that he has a kind of dominion or authority over the rest, and that they were all, how many millions so ever in number, at his command; employed by him in all his hellish designs, and in all his wicked contrivances for the destruction of man, and for the setting up his own kingdom in the world.

Supposing then that there is such a superior Master-Devil over all the rest, it remains that we enquire into his character, and something of his History; in which, though we cannot perhaps produce such authentic documents as in the story of other great Monarchs, Tyrants, and Furies of the World; yet I shall endeavor to speak some things which the experience of mankind may be apt to confirm, and which the Devil himself will hardly be able to contradict.

It being then granted that there is such a thing or person, call him which we will, as a Master-Devil; that he is thus superior to all the rest in power and in authority, and that all the other evil Spirits are his Angels, or Ministers, or Officers to execute his commands, and are employed in his business; it remains to enquire, whence he came? how he got hither, into this World? what that business is which he is employed about? what his present state is, and where and to what part of the creation of God he is limited and restrained? what the liberties are he takes or is allowed to take? in what manner he works, and how his instruments are likewise allowed to work? what he has done ever since he commenced Devil, what he is now doing, and what he may yet do before his last and closer confinement? as also what he cannot do, and how far we may or may not be said to be exposed to him, or have or have no reason to be afraid of him? These, and whatever else occurs in the History and conduct of this Arch-devil and his Agents, that may be useful for information, caution, or diversion, you may expect in the process of this work.

I know it has been questioned by some, with more face than fear, how it consists with a complete victory of the Devil, which they say was at first obtained by the Heavenly Powers over *Satan* and his apostate army in *Heaven*, that when he was cast out of his holy place, and dashed down into the abyss of eternal darkness, as into a place of punishment, a condemned hold, or place of confinement, to be reserved there to the judgment of the great Day; *I say*, how it consists with that entire victory, to let him loose again, and give him liberty, like a thief that has broken prison, to range about God's creation, and there to continue his rebellion, commit new ravages, and acts of hostility against God, make new efforts at dethroning the almighty Creator; and in particular to fall upon the weakest of his creatures, Man? how *Satan* being so entirely vanquished, he should be permitted to recover any of his wicked powers, and find room to do mischief to mankind.

Nay they go farther, and suggest bold things against the wisdom of

Heaven, in exposing mankind, weak in comparison of the immense extent of the *Devil*'s power, to so manifest an overthrow, to so unequal a fight, in which he is sure, if alone in the conflict, to be worsted; to leave him such a dreadful enemy to engage with, and so ill furnished with weapons to assist him.

These objections I shall give as good an answer to as the case will admit in this course, but must adjourn them for the present.

That the Devil is not yet a close prisoner, we have evidence enough to confirm; I will not suggest, that like our *Newgate* Thieves, (to bring little Devils and great Devils together) he is let out by connivance, and has some little latitudes and advantages for mischief, by that means; returning at certain seasons to his confinement again. This might hold, were it not, that the comparison must suggest, that the power which has cast him down could be deluded, and the under-keepers or jailors, under whose charge he was in custody, could wink at his excursions, and the Lord of the place know nothing of the matter. But this wants farther explanation.

Chapter III

Of the original of the Devil, who he is, and what he was before his expulsion out of Heaven, and in what state he was from that time to the creation of Man

To come to a regular enquiry into Satan's affairs, 'tis needful we should go back to his original, as far as history and the opinion of the learned World will give us leave.

It is agreed by all Writers, as well sacred as prophane, that this creature we now call a Devil, was originally an Angel of light, a glorious Seraph; perhaps the choicest of all the glorious Seraphs. See how *Milton* describes his original glory:

Satan, so call him now, his former name
Is heard no more in Heaven: He of the first,
If not *the first Archangel*; great in power,
In favor and preeminence.
                                        lib. v. *fol.* 140.

And again the same author, and upon the same subject:

———Brighter once amidst the host
Of Angels, than that star the stars among.
                                        lib. vii. *fol.* 189.

The glorious figure which Satan is supposed to make among the *Thrones* and *Dominions* in Heaven is such, as we might suppose the highest Angel in that exalted train could make; and some think, *as above*, that he was the chief of the Arch-angels.

Hence that notion, (and not ill founded) *namely*, that the first cause of his disgrace, and on which ensued his rebellion, was occasioned upon God's proclaiming his Son Generalissimo, and with himself supreme ruler in heaven; giving the dominion of all his works of creation, as well already finished, as not then begun, to him; which post of honor (say they) *Satan* expected to be conferred on himself, as next in honor, majesty and power to God the Supreme.

This opinion is followed by Mr. *Milton* too, as appears in the following lines, where he makes all the Angels attending all a general summons, and God the Father making the following declaration to them.

"Here, all ye Angels, prodigy of light,
"Thrones, dominions, princedoms, virtues, powers!
"Hear my decree, which unrevoked shall stand.
"This day I have begot whom I declare
"My only Son, and on this hill
"Him have anointed, whom you now behold
"At my right hand; your Head I Him appoint:
"And myself have sworn to him shall bow
"All knees in Heav'n, and shall confess him Lord,
 "Under his great vice-gerent reign abide
"United, as one individual soul,
"Forever happy: Him who disobeys,
"Me disobeys, breaks union, and that day
"Cast out from God, and blessed vision, falls
"Into utter darkness, deep engulfed, his place
"Ordained without redemption, without end.

 Satan, affronted at the appearance of a new Essence or Being in Heaven, called the Son of God; for God, says Mr. *Milton*, (though erroneously) declared himself at that time, saying, *This day have I begotten him*, and that he should be set up, above all the former Powers of Heaven, of whom Satan (as above) was the Chief and expecting, if any higher post could be granted, it might be his due; I say, affronted at this he resolved

"With all his Legions to dislodge, and leave
"Unworshiped, unobeyed, the throne supreme
"Contemptuous. ———
                          Par. lost, lib. v. fo. 140.

But Mr. *Milton* is grossly erroneous in ascribing those words, *This day have I begotten thee*, to that declaration of the Father before Satan fell, and consequently to a time before the creation; whereas, it is by Interpreters agreed to be understood of the Incarnation of the Son of God, or at least of the Resurrection: [2]see *Pool* upon *Acts* xiii. 33.

---

[2] *Mr.* Pool's *words are these*: Some refer the words, *This day have I begotten thee*, to the incarnation of the Son of God, others to the Resurrection: our Translators lay the stress on the preposition of which the verb is compounded, and by adding *again*, (viz.) *raised up Jesus again*, Acts xiii. 33. intend it to be understood of the Resurrection; and there is ground for it, in the context, for the Resurrection of Christ, is that which St. *Paul* had propounded in v. 30. of the same Chapter, as his theme or argument to preach upon.

In a word, Satan withdrew with all his followers malcontent and chagrine, resolved to disobey this new command, and not yield obedience to the Son.

But Mr. *Milton* agrees in that opinion, that the number of Angels which rebelled with *Satan* was infinite, and suggests in one place, that they were the greatest half of all the angelic Body or seraphic Host.

"But Satan with his Power,
"An host
"Innumerable as the stars of night,
"Or stars of morning, dew drops, which the Sun
"Impearls on every leaf and every flower.
ib. lib. v. fo. 142.

Be their number as it is, numberless millions and legions of millions, that is no part of my present enquiry; Satan the leader, guide and superior, as he was author of the celestial rebellion, is still the great Head and Master-Devil as before; under his authority they still act, not obeying but carrying on the same insurrection against God, which they begun in Heaven; making war still against Heaven, in the person of his Image and Creature man; and though vanquished by the thunder of the Son of God, and cast down headlong from Heaven, they have yet reassumed, or rather not lost either the will or the power of doing evil.

This fall of the Angels, with the war in Heaven which preceded it, is finely described by *Ovid*, in his war of the *Titans* against *Jupiter*; casting mountain upon mountain, and hill upon hill (*Pelion* upon *Ossa*) in order to scale the Adamantine walls, and break open the gates of *Heaven*; till *Jupiter* struck them with his thunder-bolts and overwhelmed them in the abyss: *Vide Ovid Metam.* new translation, lib. i. p. 19.

"Nor were the Gods themselves secure on high,
"For now the *Gyants* strove to storm *the sky*,
"The lawless brood with bold attempt invade
"The Gods, and mountains upon mountains *laid*.
"But now the *bolt*, enrag'd *the Father* took,
"*Olympus* from her deep foundations shook,
"Their structure nodded at the mighty stroke,
"And *Ossa*'s shatter'd top o'er *Pelion* broke,
"They're in their own ungodly ruines slain.—

Then again speaking of *Jupiter*, resolving in council to destroy mankind by a deluge, and giving the reasons of it to the heavenly Host, say thus, speaking of the demy-Gods alluding to good men below.

"Think you that they in safety can remain,
"When I myself who o'er Immortals reign,
"Who send the lightning, and Heaven's empire sway,
"The stern 3 Lycaon practiced to betray.

ib. p. 10.

 Since then so much poetic liberty is taken with the Devil, relating to his most early state, and the time before his fall, give me leave to make an excursion of the like kind, relating to his History immediately after the fall, and till the creation of man; an interval which I think much of the Devil's story is to be seen in, and which Mr. *Milton* has taken little notice of, at least it does not seem completely filled up; after which I shall return to honest Prose again, and pursue the duty of an Historian.

Satan, with hideous ruin thus supprest
Expelled the seat of blessedness and rest,
Looked back and saw the *high eternal mound*,
Where all *his rebel host* their *outlet* found
Restored impregnable: The breach made up,
And garrisons of Angels ranged a top;
In front a hundred thousand thunders roll,
And lightnings tempered to transfix a soul,
Terror of *Devils*. *Satan* and his host,
Now to themselves *as well as station lost*,
Unable to support the hated sight,
Expand *seraphic wings*, and swift as light
Seek for new safety in *eternal Night*.

In the remotest gulps *of dark* they land,
Here vengeance gives them leave to make their stand,
Not that to *steps* and *measures* they pretend,
Councils and *schemes* their station to defend;
But broken, disconcerted and *dismayed*,
By guilt and fright to guilt and fright *betrayed*;
Rage and confusion every Spirit possessed,
And *shame* and *horror* swelled in every breast;
Transforming envy to their essentials burns,
And *the bright* Angel to a *frightful Devil* turns.
Thus Hell began; the fire of conscious rage
No years can quench, no length of time assuage.
Material Fire, with its intensest flame,
Compared *with this* can scarce deserve a Name;
How should it up to *immaterials* rise,
When we're *all flame*, we shall *all fire* despise.
This fire outrageous and its heat intense
Turns all the pain *of loss* to pain *of sense*.

---

3 Satan.

The folding flames *concave* and *inward* roll,
Act *upon spirit* and penetrate *the soul*:
Not force of *Devils* can its new powers repel,
Wherever it burns *it finds* or *makes* a Hell;
For *Satan* flaming with unquenched desire
Forms *his own Hell*, and kindles *his own fire*,
Vanquished, *not humbled*, not in will brought low,
But as *his powers* decline *his passions* grow:
The malice, *Viper like*, takes vent within,
Gnaws its own bowels, and bursts in *its own sin*:
Impatient of the change *he scorns to bow*,
And never *impotent* in power *till now*;
Ardent with hate, and *with revenge* distract,
A will to new attempts, *but none* to act;
Yet all *seraphic*, and in just degree,
Suited *to Spirits high sense* of misery,
Derived from *loss* which *nothing* can repair,
And *room for nothing left* but mere despair.
Here's finished Hell! what fiercer fire *can burn*?
Enough ten thousand Worlds to over-turn.
Hell's but the frenzy of defeated pride,
Seraphic Treason's strong impetuous tide,
Where vile ambition *disappointed* first,
To its *own rage* and *boundless hatred* curst;
The hate's *fanned up to fury*, that to *flame*,
For *fire* and *fury* are in kind the same;
These burn unquenchable in every face,
And the word Endless constitutes the place.

O *state of Being!* where being's the only grief,
And the *chief torture*'s to be damned to life;
O life! the only thing they have to hate;
The *finished torment* of a future state,
Complete in all the parts of endless misery,
And worse ten thousand times than *not to Be!*
Could but the Damned *the immortal law* repeal,
And *Devils dye*, there'd be *an end of Hell*;
Could they that thing called *Being* annihilate,
There'd be *no sorrows* in a future state;
The Wretch, whose crimes had shut him out *on high*,
Could be revenged on God himself *and die*;
Job's Wife was in the right, and always we
Might end *by death* all human misery,
Might have it in our choice, *to be* or not to be.

Chapter IV

Of the name of the Devil, his original, and the nature of his circumstances since he has been called by that name

The Scripture is the first writing on earth where we find the *Devil* called by his own proper distinguishing denomination, DEVIL, or the [4] *Destroyer*; nor indeed is there any other author of antiquity or of sufficient authority which says anything of that kind about him.

Here he makes his first appearance in the world, and on that occasion he is called the *Serpent*; but the *Serpent* however since made to signify the *Devil*, when spoken of in general terms, was but the Devil's representative, or the Devil *in quo vis vehiculo*, for that time, clothed in a bodily shape, acting under cover and in disguise, or if you will the *Devil* in *masquerade*: Nay, if we believe Mr. *Milton*, the *Angel Gabriel's* spear had such a secret powerful influence, as to make him strip of a sudden, and with a touch to unmask, and stand upright in his naked original shape, mere *Devil*, without any disguises whatsoever.

Now as we go to the Scripture for much of his history, so we must go there also for some of his names; and he has a great variety of names indeed, as his several mischievous doings guide us to conceive of him. The truth is, all the ancient names given him, of which the Scripture is full, seems to be originals derived from and adapted to the several steps he has taken, and the several shapes he has appeared in to do mischief in the world.

Here he is called the *Serpent*, Gen. iii. 1.
> The *old Serpent*, Rev. xii. 9.
> The *great red Dragon*, Rev. xii. 3.
> The *Accuser of the Brethren*, Rev. xii. 10.
> The *Enemy*, Matt. xxiii. 29.
> *Satan*, Job i. Zech. iii. 1, 2.
> *Belial*, 2 Cor. vi. 15.
> *Beelzebub*, Matt. xii. 24.
> *Mammon*, Matt. vi. 24.
> The *Angel of light*, 2 Cor. xi. 14.
> The *Angel of the bottomless pit*, Rev. ix. 11.

---

4 The meaning of the word Devil is Destroyer. See *Pool* upon *Acts* xiii. 10.

The *Prince of the power of the air*, Eph. ii. 2.
Lucifer, Isa. xiv. 12.
Abbaddon or *Apollion*, Rev. ix. 11.
Legion, Mark v. 9.
The *God of this world*, 2 Cor. iv. 4.
The *Foul Spirit*, Mark ix. 5.
The *Unclean Spirit*, Mark i. 27.
The *Lying Spirit*, 2 Chron. xxx.
The *Tempter*, Matt. iv. 3.
The *Son of the morning*, Isa. xiv. 12.

But to sum them all up in one, he is called in the new Testament *plain* Devil; all his other names are varied according to the custom of speech, and the dialects of the several nations where he is spoken of; But in a word, *Devil* is the common name of the *Devil* in all the known languages of the earth. Nay, all the mischiefs he is empowered to do, are in Scripture placed to his account, under the particular title of the *Devil*, not of *Devils* in the plural number, though they are sometimes mentioned too; but in the singular it is the identical individual *Devil*, in and under whom all the little *Devils*, and all the great *Devils*, if such there be, are supposed to act; nay, they are supposed to be governed and directed by him. Thus we are told in Scripture of the works of *the Devil*, 1 John iii. 8. of casting out *the Devil*, Mark i. 34. of resisting *the Devil*, James iv. 5. of our Saviour being tempted of *the Devil*, Mat. iv. 1. of *Simon Magus*, a child of the *Devil*, Acts xiii. 10. The *Devil* came down in a great wrath, *Rev.* xii. 12. *and the like.* According to this usage in speech we go on to this day, and all the infernal things we converse with in the world, are fathered upon the *Devil*, as one undivided simple essence, by how many agents so ever working: Everything evil, frightful in appearance, wicked in its actings, horrible in its manner, monstrous in its effects, is called the *Devil*; in a word, *Devil* is the common name for all *Devils*; that is to say, for all evil Spirits, all evil Powers, all evil Works, and even all evil things: Yet 'tis remarkable *the Devil* is no old Testament word, and we never find it used in all that part of the Bible but four times, and then not once in the singular number, and not once to signify *Satan* as 'tis now understood.

It is true, the Learned give a great many differing interpretations of the word *Devil*; the *English* Commentators tell us, it means *a destroyer*, others that it signifies a deceiver, and the *Greeks* derive it from a *Calumniator* or false witness; for we find that *Calumny* was a *Goddess*, to whom the *Athenians* built altars and offered Sacrifices upon some solemn occasions, and they call her Διαβολὴ from whence came the masculine Διάβολος which we translate *Devil*.

Thus we take the name of *Devil* to signify not persons only, but actions and habits; making imaginary Devils, and transforming that substantial creature called Devil into everything noxious and offensive: Thus St. *Francis* being tempted by the *Devil* in the shape of a bag of money lying in the highway, *the Saint* having discovered the fraud, whether seeing his *Cloven-foot* hang out of the purse, or whether he distinguished him by his smell of *sulfur*, or how otherwise, authors are not agreed; but, I say, the Saint having discovered the cheat, and out-witted the *Devil*, took occasion to preach that eminent sermon to his disciples, where his Text was, *Money is* the Devil.

Nor, upon the whole, is any wrong done to *the Devil* by this kind of treatment, it only gives him the sovereignty of the whole army of Hell, and making all the numberless legions of the bottomless pit servants; or, *as the Scripture calls them*, Angels to *Satan* the grand *Devil*; all their actions, performances and achievements are justly attributed to him, not as the prince of *Devils* only, but the Emperor of *Devils*; the prince of all the princes of *Devils*.

Under this denomination then of Devil, all the Powers of Hell, all the Princes of the air, all the black armies of *Satan* are comprehended, and in such manner they are to be understood in this whole work; *mutatis mutandis*, according to the several circumstances of which we are to speak of them.

This being premised, and my authority being so good, *Satan* must not take it ill, if I treat him *after the manner of men*, and give him those titles which he is best known by among us; for indeed having so many, 'tis not very easy to call him out of his name.

However, as I am obliged by the duty of an Historian to decency as well as impartiality, so I thought it necessary, before I used too much freedom with *Satan*, to produce authentic Documents, and bring antiquity upon the stage, to justify the manner of my writing, and let you see I shall describe him in no colors, nor call him by any name, but what he has been known by for many ages before me.

And now, though writing to the common understanding of my Readers, I am obliged to treat *Satan* very coarsely, and to speak of him in the common acceptation, calling him plain *Devil*, a word which in this mannerly age is not so *sonorous* as others might be, and which by the error of the Times is apt to prejudice us against his Person; yet it must be acknowledged he has a great many other names and surnames which he might be known by, of a less obnoxious import than that of *Devil*, or *Destroyer*, etc..

Mr. *Milton*, indeed, wanting titles of honor to give to the Leaders of Satan's Host, is obliged to borrow several of his Scripture names, and bestow them upon his infernal *Heroes*, whom he makes the Generals and Leaders of the armies of Hell; and so he makes *Beelzebub, Lucifer, Belial, Mammon*, and some others, to be the names of particular Devils, members of *Satan's upper house* or *Pandemonium*; whereas indeed, these are all names proper and peculiar to *Satan* himself.

The Scripture also has some names of a coarser kind, by which *the Devil* is understood, as particularly, which is noted already, in the Apocalypse he is called the *Great Red Dragon*, the *Beast*, the *Old Serpent*, and the like: But take it in the Scripture, or where you will in History sacred or prophane, you will find that in general the *Devil* is, as I have said above, his ordinary name in all languages and in all nations; the name by which he and his works are principally distinguished: Also the Scripture, besides that it often gives him this name, speaks of the works of *the Devil*, of the subtlety of *the Devil*, of casting out *Devils*, of being tempted of the *Devil*, of being possessed with a *Devil*, and so many other expressions of that kind, as I have said already, are made use of for us to understand the evil Spirit by, that in a word, *Devil* is the common name of all wicked Spirits: For *Satan* is no more *the Devil*, as if he alone was so, and all the rest were a diminutive species who did not go by that name; But, I say, even in Scripture, every Spirit, whether under his Dominion or out of his Dominion, is called the *Devil*, and is as much a real *Devil*, that is to say, a condemned Spirit, and employed in the same wicked work as *Satan* himself.

His Name then being thus ascertained, and his Existence acknowledged, it should be a little enquired *what he is*; we believe there is such a thing, such a creature as *the Devil*, and that he has been, and may still with propriety of speech, and without injustice to his Character be called by his ancient name *Devil*.

But who is he? what is his original? whence came he? and what is his present station and condition? for these things and these enquiries are very necessary to his History, nor indeed can any part of his History be complete without them.

That he is of an ancient and noble original must be acknowledged, for he is *Heaven-born*, and of *Angelic Race*, as has been touched already: If Scripture-evidence may be of any weight in the question, there is no room to doubt the genealogy of the *Devil*; he is not only spoken of as an *Angel*, but as a *fallen Angel*, one that had been in *Heaven*, had beheld the face of God in his full effulgence of glory, and had surrounded the Throne of the most High; from whence, commencing rebel and being expelled, he was cast down, down, down, God and the *Devil* himself only knows where; for indeed we cannot say that any man on Earth knows it; and wherever it is, he has ever since man's creation been a plague to him, been a tempter, a deluder, a calumniator, an enemy and the object of man's horror and aversion.

As his original is *Heaven-born*, and his Race *Angelic*, so the Angelic nature is evidently placed in a class superior to the human, and this the Scripture is express in also; when speaking of man, it says, he made him a little lower than the Angels.

Thus *the Devil*, as mean thoughts as you may have of him, is of a better family than any of you, nay than the best Gentleman of you all; what he may be fallen to, is *one thing*, but what he is fallen from, *is another*; and therefore I must tell my learned and reverend friend *J. W.* LL. D. when he spoke so rudely of *the Devil* lately, That in my opinion he abused his Betters.

Nor is the Scripture more a help to us in the search after *the Devil's* Original, than it is in our search after his Nature: it is true, Authors are not agreed about his age, what time he was created, how many years he enjoyed his state of blessedness before he fell; or how many years he continued with his whole army in a state of darkness, and before the creation of man. It's supposed it might be a considerable space, and that it was a part of his punishment too, being all the while inactive, unemployed, having no business, nothing to do but gnawing his own Bowels, and rolling in the agony of his own self-approaches, being a Hell to himself in reflecting on the glorious state from whence he was fallen.

How long he remained thus, 'tis true, we have no light into from History, and but little from Tradition; *Rabbi Judah* says, the *Jews* were of the opinion, that he remained twenty thousand years in that condition, and that the World shall continue twenty thousand more, in which he shall find work enough to satisfy his mischievous desires; but he shows no authority for his opinion.

Indeed let the *Devil* have been as idle as they think he was before, it must be acknowledged that now he is the most busy, vigilant and diligent, of all God's creatures, and very full of employment too, *such as it is*.

Scripture indeed, gives us light into the enmity there is between the two natures, the Diabolical and the Human; the reason of it, and how and by what means the power of *the Devil* is restrained by the *Messiahs*; and to those who are willing to trust to Gospel-light, and believe what the Scripture says of *the Devil*, there may much of his History be discovered, and therefore those that list may go there for a fuller account of the matter.

But to reserve all Scripture-evidence of these things, as a Magazine in store for the use of those with whom Scripture-testimony is of force, I must for the present turn to other enquiries, being now directing my story to an age, wherein to be driven to Revelation and Scripture-assertions is esteemed giving up the dispute; people now-a-days must have demonstration; and in a word, nothing will satisfy the age, but such evidence as perhaps the nature of the question will not admit.

It is hard, indeed, to bring demonstrations in such a case as this: *No man has seen* God *at any time*, says the scripture, 1 *John* iv. 12. So *the Devil* being a spirit incorporeal, an Angel of light, and consequently not visible in his own substance, nature and form, it may in some sense be said, *no man has seen the Devil at any time*; all those pretences of phrenziful and fanciful people, who tell us, they have seen *the Devil*, I shall examine, and perhaps expose by themselves.

It might take up a great deal of our time here, to enquire whether *the Devil* has any particular shape or personality of substance, which can be visible to us, felt, heard, or understood; and which he cannot alter, and then, what shapes or appearances *the Devil* has at any time taken upon him; and whether he can really appear in a body which might be handled and seen, and yet so as to know it to have been *the Devil* at the time of his appearing; but this also I defer as not of weight in the present enquiry.

We have divers accounts of Witches conversing with *the Devil*; the *Devil* in a real body, with all the appearance of a body of a man or woman appearing to them; also of having a *Familiar*, as they call it, an *Incubus* or *little Devil*, which sucks their bodies, runs away with them into the air, *and the like*: Much of this is said, but much more than it is easy to prove, and we ought to give but a just proportion of credit to those things.

As to his borrowed shapes and his subtle transformings, that we have such open testimony of, that there is no room for any question about it; and when I come to that part, I shall be obliged rather to give a history of the fact, than enter into any dissertation upon the nature and reason of it.

I do not find in any author, whom we can call creditable, that even in those countries where the dominion of *Satan* is more particularly established, and where they may be said to worship him in a more particular manner, as *a Devil*; which some tell us the *Indians* in *America* did, who worshipped the *Devil* that he might not hurt them; yet, *I say*, I do not find that even there the *Devil* appeared to them in any particular constant shape or personality peculiar to himself.

Scripture and History therefore, giving us no light into that part of the question, I conclude and lay it down, not as my opinion only, but as what all ages seem to concur in, that the *Devil* has no particular body; that he is a spirit, and that though he may, *Proteus* like, assume the appearance of either man or beast, yet it must be some borrowed shape, some assumed figure, *pro hac vice*, and that he has no visible body of his own.

I thought it needful to discuss this as a preliminary, and that the next discourse might go upon a certainty in this grand point; namely, that the Devil, however, he may for his particular occasions put himself into a great many shapes, and clothe himself, perhaps, with what appearances he pleases, yet that he is himself still a mere Spirit, that he retains the seraphic Nature, is not visible by our eyes, which are human and Organic, neither can he act with the ordinary Powers, or in the ordinary manner as bodies do; and therefore, when he has thought fit to descend to the meannesses of disturbing and frightening children and old women, by noises and knockings, dislocating the chairs and stools, breaking windows, and such like little ambulatory things, which would seem to be below the dignity of his character, and which in particular, is ordinarily performed by organic Powers; yet even then he has thought fit not to be seen, and rather to make the poor people believe he had a real shape and body, with hands to act, mouth to speak, *and the like*, than to give proof of it in common to the whole World, by showing himself, and acting visibly and openly, as a body usually and ordinarily does.

Nor is it any disadvantage to the Devil, that his Seraphic nature is not confined or imprisoned in a body or shape, suppose that shape to be what monstrous thing we would; for this would, indeed, confine his actings within the narrow sphere of the organ or body to which he was limited; and though you were to suppose the body to have wings for a velocity of Motion equal to spirit, yet if it had not a power of invisibility too, and a capacity of conveying itself, undiscovered, into all the secret recesses of mankind, and the same secret art or capacity of insinuation, suggestion, accusation, *etc.*. by which his wicked designs are now propagated, and all his other devices assisted, by which he deludes and betrays mankind; I say, he would be no more a Devil, that is a Destroyer, no more a Deceiver, and, no more a Satan, that is, a dangerous Arch enemy to the souls of men; nor would it be any difficulty to mankind to shun and avoid him, as I shall make plain in the other part of his History.

Had the Devil from the beginning been embodied, as he could not have been invisible to us, whose souls equally seraphic are only prescribed by being embodied and encased in flesh and blood as we are; so he would have been no more a Devil to anybody but himself: The imprisonment in a body, had the powers of that body been all that we can conceive to make him formidable to us, would yet have been a Hell to him; consider him as a conquered exasperated Rebel, retaining all that fury and swelling ambition, that hatred of God, and envy at his creatures which dwells now in his enraged spirit as a *Devil*: yet suppose him to have been condemned to organic Powers, confined to corporeal motion, and restrained as a Body must be supposed to restrain a Spirit; it must, at the same time, suppose him to be effectually disabled from all the methods he is now allowed to make use of, for exerting his rage and enmity against God, any farther than as he might suppose it to affect his Maker at second hand, by wounding his Glory thro' the sides of his weakest creature, Man.

He must, certainly, be thus confined, because Body can only act upon Body, not upon Spirit; no species being empowered to act out of the compass of its own sphere: He might have been empowered, indeed, to have acted terrible and even destructive things upon mankind, especially if this body had any powers given it which mankind had not, by which man would be overmatched and not be in a condition of self-defense; for example, suppose him to have had wings to have flown in the air; Or to be invulnerable, and that no human invention, art, or engine could hurt, ensnare, captivate, or restrain him.

But this is to suppose the righteous and wise Creator to have made a creature and not be able to defend and preserve him; or to have left him defenseless to the mercy of another of his own creatures, whom he had given power to destroy him; This indeed, might have occasioned a general idolatry, and made mankind, as the *Americans* do to this day, worship the *Devil*, that he might not hurt them; but it could not have prevented the destruction of mankind, supposing the Devil to have had malice equal to his power: and he must put on a new nature, be compassionate, generous, beneficent, and steadily good in sparing the rival enemy he was able to destroy, or he must have ruined mankind: *In short*, he must have ceased to have been a Devil, and must have re-assumed his original, Angelic, heavenly nature; been filled with the principles of love to, and delight in the Works of his Creator, and bent to propagate his Glory and Interest; or he must have put an end to the race of man, whom it would be in his Power to destroy, and oblige his Maker to create a new species, or fortify the old with some kind of defense, which must be invulnerable, and which his fiery darts could not penetrate.

On this occasion suffer me to make an excursion from the usual stile of this Work, and with some solemnity to express my Thoughts thus:

How glorious is the wisdom and goodness of the great Creator of the World! in thus restraining these seraphic outcasts from the power of assuming human or organic bodies! which could they do, invigorating them with the supernatural Powers, which, as Seraphs and Angels, they now possess and might exert, they would be able even to fright mankind from the face of the Earth, and to destroy and confound God's Creation; nay, *even as they are*, were not their power limited, they might destroy the Creation itself, reverse and over-turn nature, and put the World into a general conflagration: But were those immortal Spirits embodied, though they were not permitted to confound nature, they would be able to harass poor weak and defenseless man out of his wits, and render him perfectly useless, either to his Maker or himself.

But the Dragon is chained, the Devil's Power is limited; he has indeed a vastly extended Empire, being Prince of the Air, having, at least, the whole Atmosphere to range in, and how far that Atmosphere is extended, is not yet ascertained by the nicest observations; *I say at least*, because we do not yet know how far he may be allowed to make excursions beyond the Atmosphere of this Globe into the planetary Worlds, and what power he may exercise in all the habitable parts of the *solar system*; nay, of all the other *solar systems*, which, for ought we know, may exist in the mighty extent of created space, and of which you may hear farther in its order.

But let his power be what it will there, we are sure 'tis limited here, and that in two particulars; first, he is limited as above, from assuming body or bodily shapes with substance; and secondly, from exerting seraphic Powers, and acting with that supernatural force, which, as an Angel, he was certainly vested with before the fall, and which we are not certain is yet taken from him; or at most, we do not know how much it may or may not be diminished by his degeneracy, and by the blow given him at his expulsion: this we are certain, that be his Power greater or less, he is restrained from the exercise of it in this World; and he, who was one equal to the Angel who killed 180000 men in one night, is not able now, without a new commission, to take away the life of one *Job*, nor to touch anything he had.

But let us consider him then limited and restrained as he is, yet he remains a mighty, a terrible, an immortal Being; infinitely superior to man, as well in the dignity of his nature, as in the dreadful powers he retains still about him; it is true the brain-sick heads of our Enthusiastic paint him blacker than he is, and, as I have said, wickedly represent him clothed with terrors that do not really belong to him; as if the power of good and evil was wholly vested in him, and that he was placed in the Throne of his Maker, to distribute both punishments and rewards; In this they are much wrong, terrifying and deluding fanciful people about him, till they turn their heads, and fright them into a belief that the *Devil* will let them alone, if they do such and such good things; or carry them away with him they know not whither, if they do not; as if the *Devil*, whose proper business is mischief, seducing and deluding mankind, and drawing them in to be rebels like himself, should threaten to seize upon them, carry them away, and in a word, fall upon them to hurt them, if they did evil, and on the contrary, be favorable and civil to them, if they did well.

Thus a poor deluded country fellow in our Town, that had lived a wicked, abominable, debauched life, was startled with an Apparition, as he called it, of the *Devil*; He fancied that he spoke to him, and telling his tale to a good honest Christian Gentleman his neighbor, that had a little more sense than himself; the Gentleman asked him if he was sure he really saw the *Devil*? yes, yes, Sir, *says he*, I saw him very plain, and so they began the following discourse.

Gent. See him! See the Devil! art thou sure of it, *Thomas*?

Tho. Yes, yes, I am sure enough of it, *Master*; to be sure 'twas the *Devil*.

Gent. And how do you know 'twas the *Devil*, *Thomas*? had you ever seen the *Devil* before?

Tho. No, no, I had never seen him before, *to be sure*; but, for all that, I know 'twas the *Devil*.

Gent. Well, if you're sure, *Thomas*, there's no contradicting you; pray what clothes had he on?

Tho. Nay, Sir, don't jest with me, he had no clothes on, he was clothed with fire and brimstone.

Gent. Was it dark or day light when you saw him?

Tho. O! it was very dark, for it was midnight.

Gent. How could you see him then? did you see by the light of the fire you speak of?

Tho. No, no, he gave no light himself; but I saw him, for all that.

Gent. But was it within doors, or out in the street?

Tho. It was within, it was in my own Chamber, when I was just going into bed, that I saw him.

Gent. Well then, you had a candle, hadn't you?

Tho. Yes, I had a candle, but it burnt as blue! and as dim!

Gent. Well, but if the Devil was clothed with fire and brimstone, he must give you some light, there can't be such a fire as you speak of, but it must give a light with it.

Tho. No, no, He gave no light, but I smelt his fire and brimstone; he left a smell of it behind him, when he was gone.

Gent. Well, so you say he had fire, but gave no light, it was a devilish fire indeed; did it feel warm? was the room hot while he was in it?

Tho. No, no, but I was hot enough without it, for it put me into a great sweat with the fright.

Gent. Very well, he was all in fire, you say, but without light or heat, only, it seems, he stunk of brimstone; pray what shapes was he in, what was he like; for you say you saw him?

Tho. O! Sir, I saw two great staring saucer eyes, enough to fright anybody out of their wits.

Gent. And was that all you saw?

Tho. No, I saw his *cloven-foot* very plain, 'twas as big as one of our bullocks that goes to plow.

Gent. So you saw none of his body, but his eyes and his feet? a fine vision indeed!

Tho. Sir, that was enough to send me going.

Gent. Going! what did you run away from him?

Tho. No, but I fled into bed at one jump, and sunk down and pulled the bed-clothes quite over me.

Gent. And what did you do that for?

Tho. To hide myself from such a frightful creature.

Gent. Why, if it had really been the Devil, do you think the bed-clothes would have secured you from him?

Tho. Nay, I don't know, but in a fright it was all I could do.

Gent. Nay, 'twas as wise as all the rest; but come, *Thomas*, to be a little serious, pray did he speak to you?

Tho. Yes, yes, I heard a voice, but who it was the Lord knows.

Gent. What kind of voice was it, was it like a man's voice?

Tho. No, it was a hoarse ugly noise, like the croaking of a Frog, and it called me by my name twice, *Thomas Dawson, Thomas Dawson.*

Gent. Well, did you answer?

Tho. No, not I, I could not have spoke a word for my life; why, I was startled to death.

Gent. Did it say anything else?

Tho. Yes, when it saw that I did not speak, it said, *Thomas Dawson, Thomas Dawson, you are a wicked wretch, you lay with* Jenny S—— *last night; if you don't repent, I will take you away alive and carry you to Hell, and you shall be damned, you wretch.*

Gent. And was it true, *Thomas*, did you lye with *Jenny S——* the night before?

Tho. Indeed Master, why yes it was true, but I was very sorry afterwards.

Gent. But how should the Devil know it, *Thomas*?

Tho. Nay, he knows it to be sure; why, they say he knows everything.

Gent. Well, but why should he be angry at that? he would rather did you lye with her again, and encourage you to lye with forty whores, than hinder you: This can't be the Devil, *Thomas*.

Tho. Yes, yes. Sir, 'twas the *Devil* to be sure.

Gent. But he bid you repent too, you say?

Tho. Yes, he threatened me if I did not.

Gent. Why, *Thomas*, do you think the Devil would have you repent?

Tho. Why no, that's true too, I don't know what to say to that; but what could it be? 'twas the Devil to be sure, it could be nobody else?

Gent. No, no, 'twas neither the Devil, *Thomas*, nor anybody else, but your own startled imagination; you had lain with that wench, and being a young sinner of that kind, your Conscience terrified you, told you the Devil would fetch you away, and you would be damned; and you were so persuaded it would be so, that you at last imagined he was come for you indeed; that you saw him and heard him; whereas, you may depend upon it, if *Jenny S——* will let you lye with her every night, the Devil will hold the candle, or do anything to forward it, but will never disturb you; he's too much a friend to your wickedness, it could never be the Devil, *Thomas*; 'twas only your own guilt startled you, and that was *Devil* enough too, if you knew the worst of it, you need no other enemy.

Tho. Why that's true, Master, one would think the *Devil* should not bid me repent, that's true; but certainly 'twas the Devil for all that.

Now *Thomas* was not the only man that having committed a flagitious crime had been deluded by his own imagination, and the power of fancy, to think the Devil was come for him; whereas the Devil, to give him his due, is too honest to pretend to such things; 'tis his business to persuade men to offend, not to repent; and he professes no other; he may press men to this or that action, by telling them 'tis no sin, no offence, no breach of God's Law, and the like, when really 'tis both; but to press them to repent, when they have offended, that's quite out of his way; 'tis none of his business, nor does he pretend to it; therefore, let no man charge the Devil with what he is not concerned in.

But to return to his Person, he is, as I have said, notwithstanding his lost glory, a mighty, a terrible and an immortal Spirit; he is himself called a Prince, *the Prince of the Power of the Air*; the Prince of Darkness, the Prince of *Devils*, and the like, and his attending Spirits are called *his Angels*: so that however *Satan* has lost the glory and rectitude of his Nature, by his apostate state, yet he retains a greatness and magnificence, which places him above our rank, and indeed above our conception; for we know not what he is, any more than we know what the blessed Angels are; of whom we can say no more than that they are *ministering Spirits*, etc.. as the Scripture has described them.

Two things, however, may give us some insight into the nature of the Devil, in the present state he is in; and these we have a clear discovery of in the whole series of his Conduct from the Beginning.

1. That he is the vanquished but implacable enemy of God his Creator, who has conquered him, and expelled him from the habitations of bliss; on which account he is filled with envy, rage, malice, and all uncharitableness; would dethrone God and overturn the thrones of Heaven, if it was in his power.

2. That he is man's irreconcilable Enemy; not as he is a man, nor on his own account simply, nor for any advantage he (the Devil) can make by the ruin and destruction of man; but in mere envy at the felicity he is supposed to enjoy as Satan's rival; and as he is appointed to succeed Satan and his Angels in the possession of those glories from which they are fallen.

And here I must take upon me to say, Mr. *Milton* makes a wrong judgment of the reason of *Satan*'s resolution to disturb the felicity of man; He tells us it was merely to affront God his Maker, rob him of the glory designed in his new work of creations and to disappoint him in his main design, namely, the creating a new species of creatures in a perfect rectitude of soul, and after his own image, from whom he might expect a new Fund of glory should be raised, and who was to appear as the triumph of the Messiah's victory over the Devil. In all which Satan could not be fool enough not to know that he should be disappointed by the same Power which had so eminently counter-acted his rage before.

But, I believe, the Devil went upon a much more probable design; and though he may be said to act upon a meaner principle than that of pointing his rage at the personal glory of his Creator; yet I own, that in my opinion, it was by much the more rational undertaking, and more likely to succeed; and that was, that whereas he perceived this new species of creatures had a sublime as well as a human part, and were made capable of possessing the mansions of eternal Beatitude, from whence, he (*Satan*) and his Angels were expelled and irretrievably banished; envy at such a rival moved him by all possible artifice, *for he saw him deprived of capacity to do it by force*, to render him unworthy like himself; that bringing him to fall into rebellion and disobedience, he might see his Rival damned with him; and those who were intended to fill up the empty spaces in Heaven, made so by the absence of so many millions of fallen Angels, be cast out into the same darkness with them.

How he came to know that this new species of creatures were liable to such imperfection, is best explained by the *Devil*'s prying, vigilant disposition, judging or leading him to judge by himself; (for he was as near being infallible as any of God's creatures had been) and then inclining him to try whether it was so or no.

Modern Naturalists, especially some who have not so large a charity for the fair sex, as I have, tell us, that as soon as ever Satan saw the woman, and looked in her face, he saw evidently that she was the best formed creature to make a Tool of, and the best to make a hypocrite of, that could be made, and therefore the most fitted for his purpose.

1. He saw by some thwart lines in her face, (legible, perhaps, to himself only) that there was a throne ready prepared for the sin of pride to sit in state upon, especially if it took an early possession: Eve you may suppose was a perfect Beauty, if ever such a thing may be supposed in the human frame; her figure being so extraordinary, was the groundwork of his project; there needed no more than to bring her to be vain of it, and to conceit that it either was so, or was infinitely more sublime and beautiful than it really was; and having thus tackled her vanity, to introduce Pride gradually, till at last he might persuade her, that she was really Angelic, or of heavenly Race, and wanted nothing but to eat the forbidden fruit, and that would make her something more excellent still.

2. Looking farther into her Frame, and with a nearer view to her imperfections, he saw room to conclude that she was of a constitution easy to be seduced, and especially by flattering her; raising a commotion in her Soul, and a disturbance among her passions; and accordingly he set himself to work, to disturb her repose, and put dreams of great things into

her head; together with something of a nameless Kind, which (however, some have been ill-natured enough to suggest) I shall not injure the Devil so much as to mention, without better evidence.

3. But, besides this, he found, upon the very first survey of her outside, something so very charming in her mien and behavior, so engaging as well as agreeable in the whole texture of her person, and withal such a sprightly wit, such a vivacity of parts, such a fluency of tongue, and above all, such a winning prevailing whine in her smiles, or at least in her tears, that he made no doubt if he could but once delude her, she would easily be brought to delude *Adam*, whom he found set not only a great value upon her person, but was perfectly captivated by her charms; in a word, he saw plainly, that if he could but ruin her, he should easily make a Devil of her, to ruin her husband, and draw him into any gulp of mischief, were it ever so black and dreadful, that she should first fall into herself; how far some may be wicked enough, from hence, to suggest of the *fair sex*, that they have been Devils to their husbands ever since, I cannot say; I hope they will not be so unmerciful to discover truths of such fatal consequence, though they should come to their knowledge.

Thus subtle and penetrating has Satan been from the beginning; and who can wonder that upon these discoveries made into the woman's inside, he went immediately to work with her, rather than with *Adam*? not but that one would think, if *Adam* was fool enough to be deluded by his wife, the Devil might have seen so much of it in his countenance, as to have encouraged him to make his attack directly upon him, and not go round about, beating the bush, and ploughing with the Heifer; setting upon the woman first, and then setting her upon her husband, who might as easily have been imposed upon as she.

Other Commentators upon this critical Text suggest to us, that *Eve* was not so pleased with the hopes of being made a Goddess; That the pride of a Seraphic Knowledge did not so much work upon her imagination to bring her to consent, as a certain secret Notion infused into her head by the same wicked instrument, that she should be wiser than *Adam*, and should by the superiority of her understanding, necessarily have the government over him; which, at present, she was sensible she had not, he being master of a particular air of gravity and majesty, as well as of strength, infinitely superior to her.

This is an ill-natured suggestion; but it must be confessed the impatient desire of government, which (since that) appears in the general Behavior of the sex, and particularly of governing husbands, leaves too much room to legitimate the supposition.

The Expositors, who are of this opinion, add to it, that this being her original crime, or the particular temptation to that crime; Heaven thought

41

fit to show his justice, in making her more entire subjection to her husband be a part of the Curse, that she might read her sin in the punishment, (*viz.*) *he shall rule over thee.*

I only give the general hint of these things as they appear recorded in the annals of *Satan's* first Tyranny, and at the beginning of his government in the World; those that would be more particularly informed, may enquire of him *and know farther.*

I cannot however, but observe here *with some regret,* how it appears by the consequence, that the Devil was not mistaken when he made an early judgment of Mrs. *Eve*; and how *Satan* really went the right way to work, to judge of her; 'tis certain the Devil had nothing to do but to look in her face, and upon a near steady view he might easily see there, an instrument for his Turn; nor has he failed to make her a Tool ever since, by the very methods which he at first proposed; to which, perhaps, he has made some additions in the corrupting her composition, as well as her understanding; qualifying her to be a complete snare to the poor *weaker vessel* Man; to wheedle him with her *Syren's* voice, abuse him with her smiles, delude him with her crocodile tears, and sometimes cock her crown at him, and terrify him with the thunder of her Treble; making the effeminated *Male Apple-eater* tremble at the noise of that very Tongue, which at first commanded him to Sin. For it is yet a debate which the Learned have not decided, whether she persuaded and entreated him, or like a true she-tyrant, exercised her authority and obliged him to eat the forbidden fruit.

And therefore a certain author, whose name, *for fear of the Sex's resentment* I conceal, brings her in, calling to *Adam* at a great distance, in an imperious haughty manner, beckoning to him with her hand, thus; *Here,* says she, *you cowardly faint-hearted wretch, take this branch of heavenly fruit, eat and be a stupid fool no longer; eat and be wise; eat and be a God; and know, to your eternal shame, that your wife has been made an enlightened Goddess before you.*

He tells you *Adam* hung back a little at first, and trembled, *afraid to trespass: What ails the* Sot, says the new Termagant? *what are you afraid of? did God forbid you! yes, and why? that we might not be knowing and wise like himself! What reason can there be that we, who have capacious souls, able to receive knowledge, should have it withheld? take it, you Fool, and eat; don't you see how I am exalted in soul by it, and am quite another Creature? Take it,* I say, *or, if you don't, I'll go and cut down the Tree, and you shall never eat any of it at all, and you shall be still a fool, and be governed by your wife forever.*

Thus, if this interpretation of the thing be just, she Scolded him into it; Rated him, and brought him to it by the terror of her voice; a thing that has retained a dreadful influence over him ever since; nor have the greatest of

Adam's Successors, how light so ever some husbands make of it in this age, been ever able, since that, to conceal their terror, at the very Sound; nay, if we may believe history, it prevailed even among the Gods; not all the noise of *Vulcan*'s hammers could silence the clamors of that outrageous whore his Goddess; nay, even *Jupiter* himself led such a life with a termagant wife, that once, they say, *Juno* out-scolded the noise of all his Thunders, and was within an ace of brawling him out of Heaven. But to return to the Devil.

With these views he resolved, it seems, to attack the woman; and if you consider him as a Devil, and what he aimed at, and consider the fair prospect he had of success, I must confess, I do not see who can blame him, or at least, how anything less could be expected from him; But we shall meet with it again by and by.

Chapter V

Of the station Satan had in Heaven before he fell; the nature and original of his crime, and some of Mr. Milton's mistakes about it

Thus far I have gone upon general observation, in this great affair of *Satan* and his Empire in the World; I now come to *my Title*, and shall enter upon the historical part, as the main work before me.

Besides what has been said Poetically, relating to the fall and wandering condition of the *Devil* and his Host, which poetical part I offer only as an excursion, and desire it should be taken so; I shall give you what I think is deduced from good originals on the part of *Satan*'s story in a few words.

He was one of the created Angels, formed by the same omnipotent hand and glorious power, who created the Heavens and the Earth, and all that is therein: This innumerable heavenly host, as we have reason to believe, contained Angels of higher and lower stations, of greater and of lesser degree, expressed in the Scripture by *Thrones, Dominions,* and *Principalities*: This, I think, we have as much reason to believe, as we have, that there are Stars in the Firmament (or starry Heavens) of greater and of lesser magnitude.

What particular station among the immortal Choir of Angels, this Arch-seraph, this Prince of *Devils*, called *Satan*, was placed in before his expulsion, that indeed, we cannot come at the knowledge of, at least, not with such an Authority as may be depended upon; but as from Scripture authority, he is placed at the head of all the Apostate armies, after he was fallen, we cannot think it in the least assuming to say, that he might be supposed to be one of the principal Agents in the *Rebellion* which happened in Heaven, and consequently that he might be one of the highest in dignity there, before that Rebellion.

The higher his station, the lower, and with the greater precipitation, was his overthrow; and therefore, those words, though taken in another sense, may very well be applied to him: *How art thou fallen*, O Lucifer! *Son of the Morning!*

Having granted the dignity of his Person, and the high station in which he was placed among the heavenly Host; it would come then necessarily to inquire into the nature of his fall, and *above all*, a little into the reason of it; certain it is, *he did fall*, was guilty of Rebellion and Disobedience, the just effect of Pride; sins, which, in that holy place, might well be called wonderful.

But what to me is more wonderful, and which, I think, will be very ill accounted for, is, how came seeds of crime to rise in the Angelic Nature? created in a state of perfect, unspotted holiness? how was it first found in a place where no unclean thing can enter? how came ambition, pride, or envy to generate there? could there be offence where there was no crime? could untainted purity breed corruption? could that nature contaminate and infect, which was always Drinking in principles of perfection?

Happy 'tis to me, *that* writing the History, *not* solving the Difficulties of *Satan*'s Affairs, is my province in this Work; that I am to relate the Fact, not give reasons for it, or sign causes; if it was otherwise, I should break off at this difficulty, for I acknowledge I do not see thro' it; neither do I think that the great *Milton*, after all his fine Images and lofty Excursions upon the Subject, has left it one jot clearer than he found it: Some are of opinion, and among them the great Dr. *B——s*, that crime broke in upon them at some interval, when they omitted but one moment fixing their eyes and thoughts on the glories of the divine face, to admire and adore, which is the full employment of Angels; but even this, though it goes as high as imagination can carry us, does not reach it, nor, to me, make it one jot more comprehensible than it was before; all I can say to it here, is, that *so it was*, the fact was upon Record, and the rejected Troop are in being, whose circumstances confess the Guilt, and still groan under the Punishment.

If you will bear with a poetic excursion upon the subject, not to solve but to illustrate the difficulty; take it in a few lines, thus,

Thou sin of Witchcraft! firstborn child of Crime!
Produced before the bloom of Time;
Ambition's maiden Sin, in Heaven conceived,
And who could have believed
Defilement could in purity begin,
And bright eternal Day be soiled with Sin?
Tell us, sly penetrating Crime,
How cam'st thou there, thou fault sublime?
How didst thou pass the Adamantine Gate;
And into Spirit thy self insinuate?
From what dark state? from what deep place?
From what strange uncreated race?
Where was thy ancient habitation found
Before void Chaos heard the forming sound?

45

Wast thou a Substance, or an airy Ghost,
A Vapor flying in the fluid waste
Of unconcocted air?
And how at first didst thou come there?
Sure there was once a time when thou wert not,
By whom wast thou created? and for what?
Art thou a steam from some contagious damp exhaled?
How should contagion be entailed,
On bright seraphic Spirits, and in a place
Where all's supreme, and Glory fills the Space?
No noxious vapor there could rise,
For there no noxious matter lies;
Nothing that's evil could appear,
Sin never could Seraphic Glory bear;
The brightness of the eternal Face,
Which fills as well as constitutes the place,
Would be a fire too hot for crime to bear,
it would calcine Sin, or melt it into air.
How then did first defilement enter in?
Ambition, thou first vital seed of Sin!
Thou Life of Death, how cam'st thou there?
In what bright form didst thou appear?
In what Seraphic Orb didst thou arise?
Surely that place admits of no disguise,
Eternal Sight must know thee there,
And being known, thou soon must disappear.
But since the fatal Truth we know,
Without the matter whence or manner how:
Thou high superlative of Sin,
Tell us thy nature, where thou didst begin?
The first degree of thy increase,
Debauched the Regions of eternal Peace,
And filled the breasts of loyal Angels there
With the first Treason and infernal War.

Thou art the high extreme of pride,
And dost o'er lesser crimes preside;
Not for the mean attempt of Vice designed,
But to embroil the World, and damn Mankind.
Transforming mischief, now hast thou procured
That loss that ne'er to be restored,
And made the bright Seraphic Morning-star
In horrid monstrous shapes appear?
Satan, that while he dwelt in glorious light,
Was always then as pure as he was bright,
That in effulgent rays of glory shone,
Excelled by eternal Light, by him alone,
Distorted now, and stripped of Innocence,

And banished with thee from the high Pre-eminence,
How has the splendid Seraph changed his face,
Transformed by thee, and like thy monstrous race?
Ugly as is the crime, for which he fell,
Fitted by thee to make a local Hell,
For such must be the place where either of you dwell.

Thus, as I told you, I only moralize upon the subject, but as to the difficulty, I must leave it as I find it, unless, *as I hinted at first*, I could prevail with Satan to set pen to paper, and write this part of his own History: No question, but he could let us into the secret; but to be plain, I doubt I shall tell so many plain truths of the *Devil*, in this History, and discover so many of his secrets, which it is not for his interest to have discovered, that before I have done, the *Devil* and I may not be so good friends as you may suppose we are; at least, not friends enough to obtain such a favor of him, though it be for public good; so we must be content till we come onto' other side the *Blue-Blanket*, and then we shall know the whole Story.

But now, though as I said, I will not attempt to solve the difficulty, I may, I hope, venture to tell you, that there is not so much difficulty in it, as at first sight appears: and especially not so much as some people would make us believe; let us see how others are mistaken in it, perhaps, that may help us a little in the enquiry; for to know *what it is not*, is one help towards knowing *what it is*.

Mr. *Milton* has indeed told us a great many merry things of the Devil, in a most formal, solemn manner; till in short he has made a good Play of *Heaven* and *Hell*; and no doubt if he had lived in our times, he might have had it acted with our *Pluto* and *Proserpine*. He has made fine Speeches both for *God* and the *Devil*, and a little addition might have turned it *a la modern* into a *Harlequin Dieu & Diable*.

I confess I don't well know how far the dominion of Poetry extends itself; it seems the Buts and Bounds of *Parnassus* are not yet ascertained; so that for ought I know, by virtue of their ancient privileges called *Licentia Poetarum*, there can be no *Blasphemy* in *Verse*; as some of our Divines say there can be no *Treason* in the *Pulpit*. But they that will venture to write that way, ought to be better satisfied about that Point than I am.

Upon this foot Mr. *Milton*, to grace his Poem, and give room for his Towering Fancy, has gone a length beyond all that ever went before him, since *Ovid* in his *Metamorphosis*. He has indeed complimented God *Almighty* with a flux of lofty words, and great sounds; and has made a very fine Story of the *Devil*, but he has made a mere *je ne scay Quoi* of *Jesus Christ*. In one line he has him riding on a *Cherub*, and in another sitting on a Throne, both in the very same moment of action. In another place he has

47

brought him in making a Speech to his *Saints*, when 'tis evident he had none there; for we all know *Man was not created till a long while after*; and nobody can be so dull as to say the *Angels* may be called *Saints*, without the greatest absurdity in nature. Besides, he makes Christ himself distinguish them, as in two several Bands, and of differing Persons and Species, as to be sure they are.

Stand still in bright array, *ye Saints*———
—— ——— ———— ———— Here stand,
Ye Angels. ———
        Par. Lost. lib. vi. *fo.* 174.

So that Christ here is brought in drawing up his Army before the last Battle, and making a Speech to them, to tell them they shall only stand by in warlike order, but that they shall have no occasion to fight, for he alone will engage the Rebels. Then in embattling his Legions, he places the Saints here, and the Angels there, as if one were the main Battle of Infantry, and the other the Wings of Cavalry. But who are those Saints? they are indeed all of *Milton*'s own making; 'tis certain there were no Saints at all in *Heaven* or *Earth* at that time; God and his *Angels* filled up the place; and till some of the *Angels* fell, and Men were created, had lived, and were dead, there could have been no *Saints* there. Saint *Abel* was certainly the *Proto-Saint* of all that ever were seen in *Heaven*, as well as the Proto-martyr of all that have been upon *Earth*.

Just such another Mistake, not to call it a Blunder, he makes about *Hell*; which he not only makes local, but gives it a being before the Fall of the *Angels*; and brings it in opening its mouth to receive them. This is so contrary to the nature of the thing, and so great an absurdity, that no Poetic License can account for it; for though Poesie may form Stories, as Idea and Fancy may furnish Materials, yet Poesy must not break in upon Chronology, and make things which in time were to exist, act before they existed.

Thus a Painter may make a fine piece of Work, the fancy may be good, the strokes masterly, and the beauty of the Workmanship inimitably curious and fine, and yet have some unpardonable improprieties which marr the whole Work. So the famous Painter of *Toledo* painted the story of the three Wiseman of the *East* coming to worship, and bring their presents to our Lord upon his birth at *Bethlehem*, where he represents them as three *Arabian* or *Indian* Kings; two of them are white, and one black; But unhappily when he drew the latter part of them kneeling, which to be sure was done after their faces; their legs being necessarily a little intermixed, he made three black feet for the *Negroe* King, and but three white feet for the two white Kings, and yet never discovered the mistake till the piece was presented to the King, and hung up in the great Church. As this is an unpardonable error in Sculpture or Limning, it must be much more so in

Poetry, where the Images must have no improprieties, much less inconsistencies.

In a word, Mr. *Milton* has indeed made a fine Poem, but it is *the Devil of a History*. I can easily allow Mr. *Milton* to make Hills and Dales, flowery Meadows and Plains (and the like) in Heaven; and places of Retreat and Contemplation in *Hell*; though I must add, that it can be allowed to no Poet on Earth but Mr. *Milton*. Nay, I will allow Mr. *Milton*, if you please, to set the *Angels* a dancing in *Heaven, lib.* v. *fo.* 138. and the *Devils* a singing in Hell, *lib.* i. *fo.* 44. though they are in short, especially the last, most horrid Absurdities. But I cannot allow him to make their Music in *Hell* to be harmonious and charming as he does; such Images being incongruous, and indeed shocking to Nature. Neither can I think we should allow things to be placed out of time in Poetry, any more than in History; 'tis a confusion of Images which is allowed to be disallowed by all the Critics of what tribe or species so ever in the world, and is indeed unpardonable. But we shall find so many more of these things in Mr. *Milton*, that really taking notice of them all, would carry me quite out of my way, I being at this time not writing the History of Mr. *Milton*, but of the *Devil*: besides, Mr. *Milton* is such a celebrated Man, that who but he that can write the History of the *Devil* dare meddle with him?

But to come back to the business. As I had cautioned you against running to Scripture for shelter in cases of difficulty, Scripture weighing very little among the people I am directing my Speech to; so indeed Scripture gives but very little light into anything of the *Devil's* Story before his Fall, and but *to very little* of it for some time after.

Nor has Mr. *Milton* said one word to solve the main difficulty (*viz.*) How the *Devil* came to fall, and how Sin came into Heaven; how the spotless Seraphic Nature could receive infection, whence the contagion proceeded, what noxious matter could emit corruption there, how and whence any vapor to poison the Angelic Frame could rise up, or how it increased and grew up to crime. But all this he passes over, and hurrying up that part in two or three words, only tells us,

——— his Pride,
Had cast him out of Heaven with all his Host
Of rebel Angels, by whose aid aspiring
He trusted to have equaled the most High.
lib. i. *fo.* 3.

His pride! but how came *Satan* while an Arch-angel to be proud? How did it consist, that Pride and perfect Holiness should meet in the same Person? Here we must bid Mr. *Milton* good night; for, in plain terms, he is in the dark about it, and so we are all; and the most that can be said, is, that we know the fact is so, but nothing of the nature or reason of it.

But to come to the History: The Angels fell, they sinned (wonderful!) in Heaven, and God cast them out; what their sin was is not explicit, but in general 'tis called a Rebellion against God; all sin must be so.

Mr. *Milton* here takes upon him to give the History of it, as particularly as if he had been born there, and came down hither on purpose to give us an account of it; (I hope he is better informed by this time;) but this he does in such a manner, as jostles with Religion, and shocks our Faith in so many points necessary to be believed, that we must forbear to give up to Mr. *Milton*, or must set aside part of the sacred Text, in such a manner, as will assist some people to set it all aside.

I mean by this, his invented Scheme of the Son's being declared in Heaven to be begotten then, and then to be declared Generalissimo of all the Armies of Heaven; and of the Father's Summoning all the Angels of the heavenly Host to submit to him, and pay him homage. The words are quoted already, page 32.

I must own the Invention, indeed, is very fine; the Images exceeding magnificent, the Thought rich and bright, and, in some respect, truly sublime: But the Authorities fail most wretchedly, and the miss-timing of it, is insufferably gross, as is noted in the Introduction to this Work; for Christ is not declared the Son of God but on Earth; 'tis true, 'tis spoken from Heaven, but then 'tis spoken as perfected on Earth; if it was at all to be assigned to Heaven, it was from Eternity, and there, indeed, his eternal Generation is allowed; but to take upon us to say, that *On a day, a certain day,* for so our Poet assumes, lib. v. fol. 137.

——— 'When on a day,
——— 'On such a day
'As Heaven's great Year brings forth, the empyreal Host
'Of Angels by imperial Summons called,
'Forthwith from all the ends of Heaven appeared.

This is, indeed, too gross; at this meeting he makes God declare the Son to be *that day begotten,* as before; had he made him not begotten that day, but declared General that day, it would be reconcilable with Scripture and with sense; for either the begetting is meant of ordaining to an office, or else the eternal Generation falls to the ground; and if it was to the office (Mediator) then Mr. *Milton* is out in ascribing another fixed day to the Work; see lib. x. fo. 194. But then the declaring him *that day,* is wrong chronology too, for Christ is declared *the Son of God with power,* only *by the Resurrection of the dead,* and this is both a Declaration in Heaven and in Earth. *Rom.* i. 4. And *Milton* can have no authority to tell us, there was any Declaration of it in Heaven before this, except it be that dull authority called *poetic License*, which will not pass in so solemn an affair as that.

But the thing was necessary to *Milton*, who wanted to assign some cause or original of the *Devil's* Rebellion; and so, *as I said above*, the design is well laid, it only wants two Trifles called *Truth* and *History*; so I leave it to struggle for itself.

This Ground-plot being laid, he has a fair field for the *Devil* to play the Rebel in, for he immediately brings him in, not satisfied with the Exaltation of the Son of God. The case must be thus; *Satan* being an eminent *Arch-angel*, and perhaps, the highest of all the Angelic Train, hearing this Sovereign Declaration, that the *Son of God* was declared to be Head or Generalissimo of all the heavenly Host, took it ill to see another put into the high station *over his head*, as the Soldiers call it; he, perhaps, thinking himself the senior Officer, and disdaining to submit to any but to his former immediate Sovereign; in short, he threw up his Commission, and, in order not to be compelled to obey, revolted and broke out in open Rebellion.

All this part is a Decoration noble and great, nor is there any objection to be made against the invention, because a deduction of probable Events; but the Plot is wrong laid, as is observed above, because contradicted by the Scripture account, according to which Christ was declared in Heaven, not then, but from Eternity, and not declared with power, but on Earth, (*viz.*) in his victory over Sin and Death, by the Resurrection from the dead: so that Mr. *Milton* is not orthodox in this part, but lays an avowed foundation for the corrupt Doctrine of *Arius*, which says, there was a time when Christ *was not* the Son of God.

But to leave Mr. *Milton* to his flights, I agree with him in this part, *viz.* that the wicked or sinning Angels, with the great Arch-angel at the head of them, revolted from their obedience, even in Heaven itself; that *Satan* began the wicked defection, and being a Chief among the heavenly Host, consequently carried over a great party with him, who all together rebelled against God; that upon this Rebellion they were sentenced, by the righteous judgment of God, to be expelled the holy Habitation; this, besides the authority of Scripture, we have visible testimonies of, from the Devils themselves; their influences and operations among us every day, of which Mankind are witnesses; in all the merry things they do in his name, and under his protection, in almost every scene of life they pass thro', whether we talk of things done openly or in Masquerade, things done in— or out of it, things done in earnest or in jest.

But then, what comes of the long and bloody War that Mr. *Milton* gives such a full and particular account of, and the terrible Battles in Heaven between *Michael* with the royal Army of Angels on one hand, and *Satan* with his rebel Host on the other; in which he supposes the numbers and strength to be pretty near equal? but at length brings in the *Devil's* Army, upon doubling their rage and bringing new engines of war into the field, putting *Michael* and all the faithful Army to the worst; and, in a word, defeats them? For though they were not put to a plain flight, in which case he must, at least, have given an account of two or three thousand millions of Angels cut in pieces and wounded, yet he allows them to give over the fight, and make a kind of retreat; so making way for the complete victory of the Son of God: Now this is all invention, or at least, a borrowed thought from the old Poets, and the Fight of the *Giants* against *Jupiter*, so nobly designed by *Ovid*, almost two thousand years ago; and there 'twas well enough; but whether Poetic Fancy should be allowed to fable upon *Heaven*, or no, and upon the King of Heaven too, that I leave to the Sages.

By this expulsion of the *Devils*, it is allowed by most Authors, they are, *ipso facto*, stripped of the Rectitude and Holiness of their Nature, which was their Beauty and Perfection; and being engulfed in the abyss of irrecoverable ruin, *'tis no matter where*, from that very time they lost their Angelic beautiful Form, commenced ugly frightful Monsters and *Devils*, and became evil doers, as well as evil Spirits; filled with a horrid malignity and enmity against their Maker, and armed with a hellish resolution to show and exert it on all occasions; retaining however their exalted spirituous Nature, and having a vast extensive power of Action, all which they can exert in nothing else but doing evil, for they are entirely divested of either Power or will to do good; and even in doing evil, they are under restraints and limitations of a superior Power, which it is their Torment, and, perhaps, a great part of their Hell that they cannot break thro'.

Chapter VI

What became of the Devil and his Host of fallen Spirits after their being expelled from Heaven, and his wandering condition till the Creation; with some more of Mr. Milton's absurdities on that subject

Having thus brought the *Devil* and his innumerable Legions to the edge of the Bottomless-pit, it remains, before I bring them to action, that some enquiry should be made into the posture of their affairs immediately after their precipitate Fall, and into the place of their immediate Residence; for this will appear to be very necessary to *Satan*'s History, and indeed, so as that without it, all the farther account we have to give of him, will be inconsistent and imperfect.

And first, I take upon me to lay down some Fundamentals, which I believe I shall be able to make out Historically, though, perhaps, not so Geographically as some have pretended to do.

1. That *Satan* was not immediately, nor is yet locked down into the Abyss of a *local Hell*, such as is supposed by some, and such as he shall be at last; or that,

2. If he was, he has certain liberties allowed him for excursions into the Regions of this Air, and certain spheres of action, in which he can, and does move, to do, *like a very Devil as he is*, all the mischief he can, and of which we see so many examples both about us and in us; in the inquiry after which, I shall take occasion to examine whether the Devil is not in most of us, sometimes, if not in all of us one time or other.

3. That *Satan* has no particular residence in this Globe or Earth where we live; that he rambles about among us, and marches over and over our whole country, he and his Devils in *Camps volant*; but that he pitches his grand Army or chief Encampment in our Adjacencies or Frontiers, which the Philosophers call *Atmosphere*; and whence he is called the Prince of the Power of that Element or part of the World we call *Air*; from whence he sends out his Spies, his Agents and Emissaries, to get intelligence, and to carry his Commissions to his trusty and well beloved Cousins and Counselors on Earth, by which his business is done, and his affairs carried on in the World.

Here, again, I meet Mr. *Milton* full in my face, who will have it, that *the Devil*, immediately at his expulsion, rolled down directly into a Hell proper and local; nay, he measures the very distance, at least gives the length of the journey by the time they were passing or falling, which, he says, was *nine days*; a good Poetical flight, but neither founded on Scripture or Philosophy; he might every jot as well have brought *Hell* up to the Walls of *Heaven*, advanced to receive them, or he ought to have considered the space which is to be allowed to any locality, let him take what part of infinite distance between *Heaven* and a created Hell he pleases.

But let that be as Mr. *Milton*'s extraordinary genius pleases to place it; the passage, it seems, is just *nine days* betwixt Heaven and Hell; well might *Dives* then see father *Abraham*, and talk to him too; but then the great Gulph which *Abraham* tells him was fixed between them, does not seem to be so large, as according to Sir *Isaac Newton*, Dr. *Halley*, Mr. *Whiston*, and the rest of our Men of Science, we take it to be.

But suppose the passage to be nine Days, according to Mr. *Milton*, what followed? why Hell gaped wide, opened its frightful mouth, and received them all at once; millions and thousands of millions as they were, it received them all at a gulp, *as we call it*, they had no difficulty to go in, no, none at all.

Facilis desensus averni, sed revocare gradum
Hoc opus hic labor est.——   Virg.

All this, as Poetical, we may receive, but not at all as Historical; for then come difficulties insuperable in our way, some of which may be as follow: (1.) Hell is here supposed to be a place; nay a place created for the punishment of Angels and Men, and likewise created long before those had fallen, or these had Being; this makes me say, Mr. *Milton* was a good Poet, but a bad Historian: *Tophet* was prepared of old, indeed, but it was for the King, that is to say, it was prepared for those whose lot it should be to come there; but this does not at all suppose it was prepared before it was resolved whether there should be subjects for it, or no; else we must suppose both Men and Angels were made by the glorious and upright Maker of all things, on purpose for destruction, which would be incongruous and absurd.

But there is worse yet to come; in the next place he adds, that *Hell* having received them, closed upon them; that is to say, took them in, closed or shut its Mouth; and in a word, they were locked in, as it was said in another place, they were locked in, and the Key is carried up to Heaven and kept there; for *we know* the Angel came down from Heaven, having the Key of the Bottomless-pit; but first, see Mr. *Milton*.

'Nine days they fell, confounded chaos roared

'And felt ten-fold confusion in their fall:
'——Hell at last
'Yawning received them all, and on them closed;
'Down from the verge of Heaven, eternal wrath
'Burnt after them ——
'Unquenchable.

This Scheme is certainly deficient, if not absurd, and I think is more so than any other he has laid; 'tis evident, neither *Satan* or his Host of *Devils* are, *no not any of them*, yet, even now, confined in the eternal Prison, where the Scripture says, he shall be *reserved in chains of darkness*. They must have mean thoughts of *Hell*, as a Prison, a *local* Confinement, that can suppose the *Devil* able to break Goal, knock off his Fetters, and come abroad, if he had been once locked in there, as Mr. *Milton* says he was: Now we know that he is abroad again, he presented himself before *God*, among his neighbors, when *Job*'s case came to be discoursed of; and more than that, it's plain he was a prisoner at large, by his answer to God's question, which was, *whence comest thou?* to which he answered, *from going to and fro thro' the Earth*, etc.. this, I say, is plain, and if it be as certain that Hell closed upon them, I demand then, how got he out? and why was there not a Proclamation for apprehending him, as there usually is, after such Rogues as break prison?

In short, the true Account of the *Devil*'s Circumstances, since his Fall from *Heaven*, is much more likely to be thus: That he is more of a Vagrant than a Prisoner, that he is a Wanderer in the wild unbounded Wast, where he and his Legions, like the Hoards of *Tartary*, who, in the wild Countries of *Karakathay*, the Desarts of *Barkan*, *Kassan*, and *Astracan*, live up and down where they find proper; so Satan and his innumerable Legions rove about *hic & oblique*, pitching their Camps (being Beasts of prey) where they find the most Spoil; watching over this World, (and all the other Worlds for ought we know, and if there are any such,) I say watching, and seeking who they may devour, *that is*, who they may deceive and delude, and so destroy, for devour they cannot.

Satan being thus confined to a vagabond, wandering, unsettled Condition, is without any certain Abode; For though he has, in consequence of his Angelic Nature, a kind of Empire in the liquid Wast or *Air*; yet, this is certainly part of his punishment, that he is continually hovering over this inhabited Globe of Earth; swelling with the Rage of Envy, at the Felicity of his Rival, Man; and studying all the means possible to injure and ruin him; but extremely limited in Power, to his unspeakable Mortification: This is his present State, without any fixed Abode, Place, or Space, allowed him to rest the Sole of his Foot upon.

From his Expulsion, I take his first View of Horror to be that, of looking back towards the Heaven which he had lost; there to see the Chasm or

Opening made up, out at which, as at a Breach in the Wall of the holy Place, he was thrust Head-long by the Power which expelled him; I say, to see the Breach repaired, the Mounds built up, the Walls garrisoned with millions of Angels, and armed with Thunders; and, above all, made terrible by that Glory from whose Presence they were expelled, as is Poetically hinted at before.

Upon this sight, 'tis no wonder (if there was such a Place) that they fled till the Darkness might cover them, and that they might be out of the View of so hated a Sight.

Wherever they found it, you may be sure they pitched their first Camp, and began, after many a sour Reflection upon what was passed, to consider and think a little, upon what was to come.

If I had as much personal Acquaintance with the *Devil*, as would admit it, and could depend upon the Truth of what Answer he would give me, the first Question I would ask him, should be, what Measures they resolved on at their first Assembly? and the next should be, how they were employed in all that space of Time, between their so flying the Face of their almighty Conqueror, and the Creation of Man? as for the Length of the Time, which, according to the Learned, was twenty thousand Years, and according to the more Learned, not half a Quarter so much, I would not concern my Curiosity much about it; 'tis most certain, there was a considerable time between, but of that immediately; first let me enquire what they were doing all that time.

The Devil and his Host, being thus, I say, cast out of Heaven, and not yet confined strictly to *Hell*, 'tis plain they must be *somewhere*. Satan and all his Legions did not lose their Existence, no, nor the Existence of *Devils* neither; God was so far from annihilating him, that he still preserved his Being; and this not Mr. *Milton* only, but God himself has made known to us, having left his History so far upon record; several expressions in Scripture also make it evident, as particularly the story of *Job*, mentioned before; the like in our Saviour's time, and several others.

If Hell did not immediately ingulph them, as *Milton* suggests, 'tis certain, I say, that they fled Somewhere, from the anger of Heaven, from the face of the Avenger; and his absence, and their own guilt, *wonder not at it*, would make Hell enough for them wherever they went.

Nor need we fly to the Dreams of our *Astronomers*, who take a great deal of pains to fill up the vast Spaces of the starry Heavens with innumerable habitable Worlds; allowing as many *solar Systems* as there are fixed Stars, and that not only in the known Constellations, but even in *Galaxy* itself; who, to every such System allow a certain number of Planets, and to every one of those Planets so many *Satellites* or *Moons*, and all these Planets and

Moons to be Worlds; solid, dark, opaque Bodies, habitable, and (as they would have us believe) inhabited by the like Animals and rational Creatures as on this Earth; so that they may, at this rate, find room enough for the *Devil* and all his Angels, without making a Hell on purpose; nay they may, for ought I know, find a World for every *Devil* in all the *Devil's Host*, and so everyone may be a Monarch or *Master-Devil*, separately in his own Sphere or World, and play the *Devil* there by himself.

And even if this were so, it cannot be denied but that one *Devil* in a place would be enough for a whole systemary World, and be able, if not restrained, to do mischief enough there too, and even to ruin and overthrow the whole body of People contained in it.

But, I say, we need not fly to these shifts, or consult the Astronomers in the decision of this point; for wherever *Satan* and his defeated Host went, at their expulsion from *Heaven*, we think we are certain, none of all these Beautiful Worlds, or be they Worlds or no, I mean the fixed Stars, Planets, *etc.*. had then any existence; for the Beginning, as the Scripture calls it, was not yet Begun.

But to speak a little by the rules of Philosophy, that is to say, so as to be understood by others, even when we speak of things we cannot fully understand ourselves: Though in the Beginning of Time all this glorious Creation was formed, the Earth, the starry Heavens, and all the Furniture thereof, and there was a Time when they were not; yet we cannot say so of the Void, or that nameless *no-where*, as I called it before, which now appears to be a *some-where*, in which these glorious Bodies are placed. That immense Space which those take up, and which they move in at this Time, must be supposed, before they had Being, to be placed there: As God himself was, and existed before all Being, Time, or Place, so the Heaven of Heavens, or the Place, where the Thrones and Dominions of his Kingdom then existed, inconceivable and ineffable, had an existence before the glorious Seraphs, the innumerable company of Angels which attended about the Throne of God existed; these all had a Being long before, as the Eternal Creator of them all had before them.

Into this void or abyss of Nothing, however immeasurable, infinite, and even to those Spirits, themselves Inconceivable, they certainly launched from the bright Precipice which they fell from, and here they shifted as well as they could.

Here expanding those Wings which Fear, and Horror at their Defeat furnished them, as I hinted before, they hurried away to the utmost Distance possible, from the Face of God their Conqueror, and then most dreaded Enemy; formerly their Joy and Glory.

Be this utmost removed Distance *where it will*, Here, certainly, *Satan* and all his *Gang of Devils*, his numberless, though routed Armies retired. Here *Milton* might, with some good Ground, have formed his *Pandemonium*, and have brought them in, consulting what was next to be done, and whether there was any room left to renew the War, or to carry on the Rebellion; but had they been cast immediately into *Hell*, closed up there, the Bottomless pit locked upon them, and the Key carried up to *Heaven* to be kept there, as Mr. *Milton* himself in part confesses, and the Scripture affirms; I say, had this been so, the *Devil* himself could not have been so ignorant as to think of any future Steps to be taken, to retrieve his Affairs, and therefore a *Pandemonium* or Divan in Hell, to consult of it, was ridiculous.

All Mr. *Milton*'s Scheme of *Satan*'s future Conduct, and all the Scripture Expressions about *the Devil* and his numerous Attendants, and of his actings since that time, make it not reasonable to suggest that the *Devils* were confined to their eternal Prison, at their Expulsion out of *Heaven*; But that they were in a State of Liberty to act, though limited in acting, of which I shall also speak in its place.

Chapter VII

Of the Number of Satan's Host; how they came first to know of the new created Worlds, now in being, and their Measures with Mankind upon the Discovery

Several things have been suggested to set us a calculating the number of this frightful throng of *Devils*, who with Satan, the *Master-Devil*, was thus cast out of *Heaven*; I cannot say, I am so much Master of Political Arithmetic as to cast up the Number of the Beast, no, nor the Number of the Beasts *or Devils*, who make up this Throng. St. *Francis*, they tell us, or some other Saint, they do not say who, asked the *Devil* once, how strong he was? for St. *Francis*, you must know, was very familiar with him; *The Devil*, it seems, did not tell him, but presently raised a great Cloud of Dust, by the help, I suppose, of a Gust of Wind, and bid that Saint count it; He was, I suppose, a Calculator, that would be called grave, who dividing *Satan*'s Troops into three Lines, cast up the Number of the *Devils* of all sorts in each Battalion, at ten hundred times a hundred thousand millions of the first Line, fifty millions of times as many in the second Line, and three hundred thousand times as many as both in the third Line.

The Impertinence of this account would hardly have given it a place here, only to hint that it has always been the Opinion, that *Satan*'s Name may well be called a Noun of Multitude, and that *the Devil* and his *Angels* are certainly no inconsiderable Number: It was a smart Repartee that a *Venetian* Nobleman made to a Priest who rallied him upon his refusing to give something to the Church, which the Priest demanded for the delivering him from Purgatory; when the Priest asking him, *if he knew what an innumerable Number of* Devils *there were to take him*? he answered, *yes, he knew how many* Devils *there were in all*: How many? says the Priest, his curiosity, I suppose, being raised by the novelty of the answer. *Why ten millions five hundred and eleven thousand, six hundred and seventy five Devils and a half*, says the Nobleman: *A half!* says the Priest, *pray what kind of a Devil is that? yourself*, says the Nobleman, *for you are half a Devil already (and will be a whole one when you come there) for you are for deluding all you deal with, and bringing us Soul and Body into your Hands, that you may be paid for letting us go again.* So much for their Number.

Here also it would come in very aptly, to consider the state of that long interval between the Time of their Expulsion from *Heaven*, and the Creation of the World; and what the Posture of the Devil's Affairs might be, during that Time. The horror of their Condition can only be conceived of at a Distance, and especially by us, who being embodied Creatures, cannot fully judge of what is, or is not a Punishment to *Seraphs* and *Spirits*; But 'tis just to suppose they suffered all that Spirits of a Seraphic Nature were capable to sustain, consistent with their Existence; notwithstanding which they retained still the *Hellishness* of their rebellious Principles; namely, their Hatred and Rage against God, and their Envy at the Felicity of his Creatures.

As to how long their time might be, I shall leave that Search; no lights being given me that are either probable or rational, and we have so little room to make a Judgment of it, that we may as well believe Father *M——*, who supposes it to be a hundred thousand Years, as those who judge it one thousand Years; 'tis enough that we are sure, it was before the Creation, how long before is not material to *the Devil's History*, unless we had some Records of what happened to him, or was done by him in the Interval.

During the wandering Condition the Devil was in at that Time, we may suppose, he and his whole Clan to be employed in exerting their Hatred and Rage at the Almighty, and at the Happiness of the remaining faithful Angels, by all the ways they had power to show it.

From this determined stated Enmity of *Satan* and his Host against *God*, and at everything that brought Glory to his Name, Mr. *Milton* brings in *Satan*, (when first he saw *Adam* in *Paradise*, and the Felicity of his Station there) swelling with Rage and Envy, and taking up a dreadful Resolution to ruin *Adam* and all his Posterity, merely to disappoint his Maker of the Glory of his Creation; I shall come to speak of that in its Place.

How *Satan*, in his remote Situation, got Intelligence of the Place where to find *Adam* out, or that any such thing as a Man was created, is Matter of just Speculation, and there might be many rational Schemes laid for it: Mr. *Milton* does not undertake to tell us the Particulars, nor indeed could he find room for it; perhaps, the *Devil* having, *as I have said*, a Liberty to range over the whole Void or Abyss, which we want as well a Name for, as indeed Powers to conceive of; might have discovered that the Almighty Creator had formed a new and glorious Work, with infinite Beauty and Variety, filling up the immense Wast of Space, in which he, (the *Devil*) and his *Angels*, had roved for so long a time, without finding anything to work on, or to exert their Apostate Rage in against their Maker.

That at length they found the infinite distinct Space, on a sudden spread full with glorious Bodies, shining in self-existing Beauty, with a new, and to them unknown Luster, called Light: They found these luminous Bodies, though immense in Bulk, and infinite in Number, yet fixed in their wondrous Stations, regular and exact in their Motions, confined in their proper Orbits, tending to their particular Centers, and enjoying every one their peculiar Systems, within which was contained innumerable Planets with their Satellites or Moons, in which (*again*) a reciprocal Influence, Motion and Revolution conspired to Form the most admirable Uniformity of the whole.

Surprised, to be sure, with this sudden and yet glorious Work of the Almighty; for the Creation was enough, with its Luster, even to surprise *the Devils*; they might reasonably be supposed to start out of their dark Retreat, and with a Curiosity not below the Seraphic Dignity; for *these are* some of *the things which the Angels desire to look into*, to take a flight thro' all the amazing Systems of the fixed Suns or Stars, which we see now but at a Distance, and only make Astronomical Guesses at.

Here the Devil found not subject of Wonder only, but matter to swell his revolted Spirit with more Rage, and to revive the Malignity of his Mind against his Maker, and especially against this new increase of Glory, which to his infinite Regret was extended over the whole Wast, and which he looked upon, as we say in human Affairs, as a *Pays conquis*, or, if you will have it in the Language of the *Devil*, as an invasion upon his Kingdom.

Here it naturally occurred to them, in their State of Envy and Rebellion, that though they could not assault the impregnable Walls of Heaven, and could no more pretend to raise War in the Place of Blessedness and Peace; yet that perhaps they might find Room in this new, and however glorious, yet inferior Kingdom or Creation, to work some despite to their great Creator, or to affront his Majesty in the Person of some of his new made Creatures; and upon this they may be justly supposed to double their Vigilance, in the survey they resolve to take of these new Worlds, however great, numberless and wonderful.

What Discoveries they may have made in the other and greater Worlds, than this Earth, we have not yet had an account; possibly they are conversant with other Parts of God's Creation, besides this little Globe, which is but as a Point in comparison of the Rest; and with other of God's Creatures besides Man, who may, according to the Opinion of our Philosophers, inhabit those Worlds; but as nobody knows that Part but the *Devil*, we shall not trouble ourselves with the Enquiry.

But 'tis very reasonable, and indeed probable, that *the Devils* were more than ordinarily surprised at the Nature and Reason of all this glorious Creation, after they had, with the utmost Curiosity, viewed all the parts of it; The Glories of the several Systems; the immense spaces in which those glorious Bodies that were created and made part of it, were allowed respectively to move; the innumerable fixed Stars, as so many Suns in the Center of so many distant *Solar Systems*; the (likewise innumerable) dark opaque Bodies receiving light, and depending upon those Suns respectively for such light, and then reflecting that light again upon and for the Use of one another; To see the Beauty and Splendor of their Forms, the Regularity of their Position, the Order and Exactness, and yet inconceivable Velocity of their Motions, the certainty of their Revolutions, and the Variety and Virtue of their Influences; and then, which was even to the Devils themselves most astonishing, That after all the rest of their Observations they should find this whole immense Work was adapted for, and made subservient to the Use, Delight and Blessing only of one poor Species, in itself small, and in Appearance contemptible; the meanest of all the Kinds supposed to inhabit so many glorious Worlds, as appeared now to be formed; I mean, that Moon called the Earth, and the Creature called Man; that all was made for him, upheld by the wise Creator, on his account only, and would necessarily end and cease whenever that Species should end and be determined.

That this Creature was to be found nowhere but (as above) in one little individual *Moon*; a Spot less than almost any of the Moons, which were in such great Numbers to be found attendant upon, and prescribed with in every System of the whole created Heavens; This was astonishing even to the *Devil* himself, nay the whole Clan of *Devils* could scarce entertain any just Ideas of the thing; Till at last *Satan*, indefatigable in his Search or Enquiry into the Nature and Reason of this new Work, and particularly searching into the Species of Man, whom he found God had thus placed in the little Globe, called *Earth*; he soon came to an *Eclairicissement*, or a clear Understanding of the whole. *For Example,*

First, He found this Creature, called Man, was however mean and small in his Appearance, a kind of a Seraphic Species; that he was made in the very Image of God, endowed with reasonable Faculties to know Good and Evil, and possessed of a certain thing till then unknown and unheard of even in Hell itself; that is, in the Habitation of Devils, let that be where it would, (*viz.*)

2. That God had made him indeed of the lowest and coarsest Materials, but that he had breathed into him the Breath of Life, and that he became a living thing called Soul, being a kind of an extraordinary heavenly and divine Emanation; and consequently that Man, however mean and Terrestrial his Body might be, was yet, Heaven-born, in his spirituous Part completely Seraphic; and after a Space of Life here, (determined to be a state of probation) he should be translated thro' the Regions of Death into a Life purely and truly Heavenly, and which should remain so for ever; being capable of knowing and enjoying God his Maker, and standing in his Presence, as the glorified Angels do.

3. That he had the most sublime Faculties infused into him; was capable not only of knowing and contemplating God, and which was still more, of

enjoying him, as above; but (which the *Devil* now was not) capable of honoring and glorifying his Maker; who also had condescended to accept of Honor from him.

4. And which was still more, that being of an Angelic Nature, though mixed with, and confined for the present in a Case of mortal Flesh; he was intended to be removed from this Earth after a certain time of Life here, to inhabit that Heaven, and enjoy that very Glory and Felicity, from which Satan and his Angels had been expelled.

When he found all this, it presently occurred to him, that God had done it all as an act of Triumph over him (Satan,) and that these Creatures were only created to people Heaven, depopulated or stripped of its inhabitants by his Expulsion, and that these were all to be made *Angels* in the *Devil's* stead.

If this thought increased his Fury and Envy, as far as *Rage of Devils* can be capable of being made greater; it doubtless set him on work to give a Vent to that Rage and Envy, by searching into the Nature and Constitution of this Creature, called *Man*; and to find out whether he was invulnerable, and could by no means be hurt by the Power of Hell, or deluded by his Subtlety; or whether he might be beguiled and deluded, and so, instead of being preserved in Holiness and Purity, wherein he was certainly created, be brought to fall and rebel as he (*Satan*) had done before him; by which, instead of being transplanted into a glorious State, after this Life in Heaven, as his Maker had designed him to be, to fill up the Angelic Choir, and supply the Place from whence he (*Satan*) had fallen, he might be made to fall also like him, and in a Word, be made a *Devil* like himself.

This convinces us that the *Devil* has not lost his natural Powers by his Fall; and our learned Commentator Mr. *Pool* is of the same Opinion; though he grants that the *Devil* has lost his moral Power, or his Power of doing Good, which he can never recover. *Vide* Mr. *Pool* upon *Acts* xix. 17. where we may particularly observe, when the Man possessed with an evil Spirit flew upon the seven Sons of *Scaeva* the *Jew*, who would have Exorcised them in the Name of *Jesus*, without the Authority of *Jesus*, or without Faith in him; He flew on them and mastered them, so that they fled out of the House from the Devil conquered, naked and wounded: But of this Power of the Devil I shall speak by itself.

In a Word, and to sum up all the *Devil's* Story from his first Expulsion, it stands thus: For so many Years as were between his Fall and the Creation of Man, though we have no *Memoirs* of his particular Affairs, we have Reason to believe he was without any Manner of Employment; but a certain tormenting Endeavour to be always expressing his Rage and Enmity against Heaven; I call it tormenting, Because ever disappointed; every thought about it proving empty; every attempt towards it abortive;

Leaving him only Light enough to see still more and more Reason to despair of Success; and that this made his Condition still more and more a Hell than it was before.

After a Space of Duration in this Misery, which we have no light given us to measure or judge of, He at length discovered the new Creation of Man, as above, upon which he soon found Matter to set himself to work upon, and has been busily employed ever since.

And now indeed there may be room to suggest a Local *Hell*, and the Confinement of Souls (made corrupt and degenerate by him) to it, as a Place; though he himself, as is still apparent by his Actings, is not yet confined to it; of this Hell, its Locality, Extent, Dimensions, Continuance and Nature, as it does not belong to Satan's History, I have a good excuse for saying nothing, and so put off my meddling with that, which if I would meddle with, I could say nothing of to the Purpose.

Chapter VIII

Of the Power of the Devil at the Time of the Creation of this World; whether it has not been farther strained and limited since that Time, and what Shifts and Stratagems he is obliged to make use of to compass his Designs upon Mankind

Cunning Men have fabled, and though it be without either Religion, Authority or physical Foundation, it may be we may like it ne'er the worse for that; that when God made the Stars and all the Heavenly Luminaries, the *Devil*, to mimic his Maker and insult his new Creation, made Comets, in Imitation of the fixed Stars; but that the Composition of them being combustible, when they came to wander in the Abyss, rolling by an irregular ill-grounded Motion, they took Fire, in their Approach to some of those great Bodies of Flame, *the fixed Stars*; and being thus kindled (like a Fire-work unskillfully let off) they then took wild and eccentric, as also different Motions of their own, out of Satan's Direction, and beyond his Power to regulate ever after.

Let this Thought stand by itself, it matters not to our purpose whether we believe anything of it, or no; 'tis enough to our Case, that if Satan had any such Power then, he has no such Power now, and that leads me to enquire into his more recent Limitations.

I am to suppose, he and all his Accomplices being confounded at the Discovery of the new Creation, and racking their Wits to find out the meaning of it, had at last (*no matter how*) discovered the whole System, and concluded, *as I have said*, that the Creature, *called Man*, was to be their Successor in the Heavenly Mansions; upon which I suggest that the first Motion of Hell was to destroy this new Work, and, if possible, to overwhelm it.

But when they came to make the Attempt, they found their Chains were not long enough, and that they could not reach to the Extremes of the System: They had no Power either to break the Order, or stop the Motion, dislocate the Parts, or confound the Situation of Things; they traversed, no doubt, the whole Work, visited every Star, landed upon every Solid, and sailed upon every Fluid in the whole Scheme, to see what Mischief they could do.

Upon a long and full Survey, they came to this Point in their Enquiry, that in short they could do nothing by Force; that they could not displace any Part, annihilate any Atom, or destroy any Life in the whole Creation; but that as Omnipotence had created it, so the same Omnipotence had armed it at all Points against the utmost Power of Hell, had made the smallest Creature in it invulnerable, as to *Satan*; so that without the Permission of the same Power which had made *Heaven*, and conquered the *Devil*, he could do nothing at all, as to destroying anything that God had made, no, not the little diminutive thing called Man, who *Satan* saw so much reason to hate, as being created to succeed him in Happiness in *Heaven*.

Satan found him placed out of his Power to hurt, or out of his Reach to touch; and here, by the way, appears the second Conquest of *Heaven* over the *Devil*; that having placed his Rival, as it were, just before his Face, and showed the hateful sight to him, he saw written upon his Image, *Touch him if you dare*.

It cannot be doubted, but, had it not been thus, Man is so far from being a Match for the *Devil*, that one of Satan's least Imps or *Angels* could destroy all the Race of them in the World, ay World and all in a moment;

As he is Prince of the Power of the Air, taking the Air for *the Elementary World*, how easily could he, at one Blast, sweep all the Surface of the Earth into the Sea, or drive weighty immense Surges of the Ocean over the whole Plane of the Earth, and deluge the Globe at once with a Storm? Or how easily could he, who, by the Situation of the Empire, must be supposed able to manage the Clouds, draw them up, in such Position as should naturally produce Thunders and Lightnings, cause those Lightnings to blast the Earth, dash in Pieces all the Buildings, burn all the populous Towns and Cities, and lay wast the World;

At the same time he might command suited Quantities of sublimated Air to burst out of the Bowels of the Earth, and overwhelm and swallow up, in the opening Chasms, all the Inhabitants of the Globe?

In a Word, *Satan* left to himself as a Devil, and to the Power, which by virtue of his Seraphic Original he must be vested with, was able to have made Devilish Work in the World, if by a superior Power he was not restrained.

But there is no doubt, *at least to me*, but that with his fall from Heaven, as he lost the Rectitude and Glory of his Angelic Nature, I mean his Innocence, so he lost the Power too that he had before; and that when he first commenced Devil, he received the Chains of Restraint too, as the Badge of his Apostasy, *viz.* a general Prohibition, to do anything to the Prejudice of this Creation, or to act anything by Force or Violence without special Permission.

This Prohibition was not sent him by a Messenger, or by an Order in Writing, or proclaimed from Heaven by a Law; but *Satan*, by a strange, invisible and unaccountable Impression felt the Restraint within him; and at the same time that his moral Capacity was not taken away, yet his Power of exerting that Capacity felt the Restraint, and left him unable to do, even what he was able to do at the same time.

I make no question, but the Devil is sensible of this Restraint, that is to say, *not* as it is a restraint only, or as an effect of his Expulsion from *Heaven*; But as it prevents his Capital Design against Man, who, for the Reason I have given already, he entertains a mortal Hatred of, and would destroy with all his Heart, if he might; and therefore, like a chained Mastiff, we find him oftentimes making a horrid hellish Clamor and Noise, barking and howling, and freighting the People, letting them know, that if he was loose he would tear them in pieces; but at the same time his very Fury shakes his Chain, which lets them know, to their Satisfaction, he can only Bark, but cannot Bite.

Some are of Opinion that the Devil is not restrained so much by the superior Power of his Sovereign and Maker; but that all his milder Measures with Man are the effect of a political Scheme, and done upon mature Deliberation; that it was resolved to act thus, in the great Council or P——t of Devils, called upon this very Occasion, when they first were informed of the Creation of Man; and especially when they considered what kind of Creature he was, and what might probably be the Reason of making him, (*viz.*) to fill up the Vacancies in Heaven; I say, that then the *Devils* resolved, that it was not for their Interest to fall upon him with Fury and Rage, and so destroy the Species, for that this would be no Benefit at all to them, and would only cause another original Man to be created; for that they knew God could, by the same Omnipotence, form as many new Species of Creatures as he pleased; and, if he thought fit, create them in Heaven too, out of the Reach of *Devils* or evil Spirits, and that therefore, to destroy Man would no way answer their End.

On the other hand, examining strictly the Mould of this new made Creature, and of what Materials he was formed; how mixed up of a Nature convertible and pervertible, capable indeed of infinite Excellence, and consequently of eternal Felicity; but subject likewise to Corruption and Degeneracy, and consequently to eternal Misery; That instead of being fit to supply the Places of Satan and his rejected Tribe (the expelled Angels) in Heaven, and filling up the Thrones or Stalls in the Celestial Choir, they might, if they could but be brought into Crime, become a Race of Rebels and Traitors like the rest; and so come at last to keep them Company, as well in the Place of eternal Misery, as in the Merit of it, and in a Word, become Devils instead of Angels.

Upon this Discovery, I say, they found it infinitely more for the Interest of

Satan's infernal Kingdom, to go another way to work with Mankind, and see if it were possible, by the strength of all their infernal Wit and Counsels, to lay some Snare for him, and by some Stratagem to bring him to eternal Ruin and Misery.

This being then approved as their only Method, (and the *Devil* showed he was no Fool in the Choice) he next resolved that there was no time to be lost; that it was to be set about immediately, before the Race was Multiplied, and by that means the Work be not made greater only, but perhaps the more difficult too; accordingly the diligent Devil went instantly about it, agreeably to all the Story of *Eve* and the serpent, as before; the belief of which, whether historically or allegorically, is not at all obstructed by this Hypothesis.

I do not affirm that this was the Case at first, because being not present in that black *Divan*, at least not that I know of, *for who knows where he was or was not in his pre-existent State?* I cannot be positive in the Resolve that past there; but except for some very little Contradiction, which we find in the sacred Writings, I should, I confess, incline to believe it Historically; and I shall speak of those things which I call Contradictions to it more largely hereafter.

In the mean time, be it one way or other, *that is to say*, either that Satan had no Power to have proceeded with Man by Violence, and to have destroyed him as soon as he was made; or that he had the Power, but chose rather to proceed by other Methods to deceive and debauch him; *I say*, be it which you please, I am still of the Opinion that it really was not the *Devil*'s Business to destroy the Species; that it would have been nothing to the purpose, and no Advantage at all to him, if he had done it; for that, as above, God could immediately have created another Species to the same end, whom he either could have made invulnerable, and not subject to the Devil's Power, or removed him out of *Satan*'s Reach, placed him out of the *Devil*'s Ken, in Heaven or some other Place, where the Devil could not come to hurt him; and that therefore it is infinitely more his Advantage, and more suited to his real Design of defeating the End of Man's Creation, to debauch him and make a *Devil* of him, that he may be rejected like himself, and increase the infernal Kingdom and Company in the Lake of Misery *in aeternum*.

It may be true, for ought I know, that Satan has not the Power of Destruction put into his Hand, and that he cannot take away the Life of a Man: and it seems probable to be so, from the Story of *Satan* and *Job*, when *Satan* appeared among the Sons of God, as the Text says, *Job* i. 6. Now when God gave such a Character of *Job* to him, and asked him *if he had considered his Servant Job*, v. 8. why did not the Devil go immediately and exert his Malice against the good Man at once, to let his Maker see what would become of his Servant *Job* in his Distress? On the contrary, we see he only answers by showing the Reason of *Job*'s good Behavior; that it was but common Gratitude for the Blessing and Protection he enjoyed, and pleading that if his Estate was taken away, and he was exposed as he (Satan) was, to be a beggar and a Vagabond, going *to and fro in the Earth, and walking up and down therein*, he should be a very Devil too, like himself, and curse God to his Face.

Upon this, the Text says, that God answered v. 11. *Behold all that he hath is in thy Power*; now 'tis plain here, that God gave up *Job*'s Wealth and Estate, nay his Family, and the Lives of his Children and Servants into the Devil's Power; and accordingly, like a true merciless Devil, *as he is*, he destroyed them all; he moved the *Sabeans* to fall upon the Oxen and the Asses, and carry them off; he moved the *Chaldeans* to fall upon the Camels and the Servants, to carry off the first, and murder the last; he made Lightning flash upon the poor Sheep, and kill them all; and he blew his House down upon his poor Children, and buried them all in the Ruins.

Now here is (1.) a Specimen of Satan's good Will to Mankind, and what Havoc the *Devil* would make in the World, if he might; and here is a Testimony too, that he could not do this without leave; so that I cannot but be of the Opinion he has some Limitations, some Bounds set to his natural Fury; a certain Number of Links in his Chain, which he cannot exceed, or, in a Word, that he cannot go a Foot beyond his *Tether*.

The same kind of Evidence we have in the Gospel, *Matth.* viii. 31. where Satan could not so much as possess the filthiest and meanest of all Creatures, *the Swine*, till he had asked leave; and that still, to show his good Will, as soon as he had gotten leave, he hurried them all into the Sea and choked them; these, I say, are some of the Reasons why I am not willing to say, the *Devil* is not restrained in Power; but on the other side, we are told of so many mischievous things the Devil has done in the World, by virtue of his Dominion over the Elements, and by other Testimonies of his Power, that I don't know what to think of it; though, upon the whole, the first is the safest Opinion; for if we should believe the last, we might, for ought I know, be brought, like the *American Indians*, to worship him *at last*, that he may do us no Harm.

And now I have named those People in *America*, I confess it would go a great way in favor of Satan's Generosity, as well as in Testimony of his Power, if we might believe all the Accounts, which indeed Authors are pretty well agreed in the Truth of, namely, of the Mischief's the *Devil* does in those Countries, where his Dominion seems to be established; how he uses them when they deny him the Homage he claims of them as his Due; what Havoc and Combustion he makes among them; and how Beneficent he is (or at least negative in his Mischiefs) when they Appease him by their hellish Sacrifices.

Likewise we see a Test of his wicked Subtlety in his Management of those dark Nations, when he was more immediately worshipped by them; namely, the making them believe that all their good Weather, Rains, Dews, and kind Influences upon the Earth, to make it fruitful, was from Him; whereas they really were the common Blessings of a higher Hand, and came not from him, the *Devil*, but from him that made the *Devil*, and made him a Devil or fallen Angel by his Curse.

But to go back to the Method the Devil took with the first of Mankind; 'tis plain the Policy of Hell was right, though the Execution of the Resolves they took did not fully answer their End neither; For *Satan* fastening upon poor, proud, ridiculous Mother *Eve*, as I have said before, made presently a true Judgment of her Capacities, and of her Temper; took her by the right Handle, and soothing her Vanity (which is to this Day the softest Place in the Head of all the Sex) wheedled her out of her Senses, by praising her Beauty, and promising to make her a Goddess.

The foolish Woman yielded presently, and that we are told is the Reason why the same Method so strangely takes with all her Posterity (*viz.*) that you are sure to prevail with them, if you can but once persuade them that you believe they are Witty and Handsome; for the Devil, you may observe, never quits any Hold he gets, and having once found a way into the Heart, always takes care to keep the Door open, that any of his Agents may enter after him without any more Difficulty: Hence the same Argument, especially the last, has so bewitching an Influence on the Sex, that they rarely deny you anything, after they are but weak enough and vain enough to accept of the Praises you offer them on that Head; on the other hand you are sure they never forgive you the unpardonable Crime of saying they are Ugly or Disagreeable: It is suggested that the first Method the Devil took to insinuate all those fine things into *Eve*'s giddy Head, was by creeping close to her *one Night*, when she was asleep, and laying his Mouth to her *Ear*, whispering all the fine things to her, which he knew would set her Fancy a Tip-toe, and so made her receive them involuntarily into her Mind; knowing well enough that when she had formed such Ideas in her Soul, however they came there, she would never be quiet till she had worked them up to some extraordinary thing or other.

It was evident what the *Devil* aimed at, *namely*, that she should break in upon the Command of God, and so having corrupted herself, bring the Curse upon herself and all her Race, as God had threatened; but why the Pride of *Eve* should be so easily tickled by the Motion of her exquisite Beauty, when there then was no prospect of the use or want of those Charms? that indeed makes a kind of Difficulty here, which the learned have not determined. For,

1. If she had been as Ugly as the *Devil*, she had no body to rival her, so that she need not fear *Adam* should leave her and get another Mistress.

2. If she had been Bright and Beautiful as an Angel, she had no other Admirer but poor *Adam*, and he could have no room to be jealous of her, or afraid she should cuckold him; so that in short, *Eve* had no such Occasion for her Beauty, nor could she make any use of it either to a bad purpose or to a good, and therefore I believe the *Devil*, who is too cunning to do anything that signifies Nothing, rather tempted her by the Hope of increasing her Wit, than her Beauty.

But to come back to the Method of Satan's tempting her, *viz.* by whispering to her in her sleep; 'twas a cunning Trick, that's the Truth of it, and by that means he certainly set her Head a madding after *Deism*, and to be made a Goddess, and then backed it by the subtle talk he had with her afterward.

I am the more particular upon this Part, because, however the Devil may have been the first that ever practiced it, yet I can assure him the Experiment has been tried upon many a Woman since, to the wheedling her out of her Modesty, as well as her Simplicity; and the Cunning Men tell us still, that if you can come at a Woman when she is in a deep sleep, and Whisper to her close to her Ear, she will certainly Dream of the Thing you say to her, and so will a Man too.

Well, be this so to her Race or not, it was it seems so to her; for she walked with her Head filled with pleasing Ideas, and as some will have it, unlawful Desires; such, as to be sure she never had entertained before; These are supposed to be fatally infused in her Dream, and suggested to her waking Soul, when the Organ Ear which conveyed them was dozed and insensible; strange Fate of sleeping in *Paradise*! that whereas we have Notice but of two Sleeps there, that in one a *Woman* should go out of him, and in the other, the *Devil* should come into her.

Certainly, when Satan first made the Attempt upon *Eve*, he did not think he should have so easily conquered her, or have brought his Business about so soon; the *Devil* himself could not have imagined she should have been so soon brought to forget the Command given, or at least who gave it, and have ventured to transgress against him, and made her forget that God had told her, it should be Death to her to touch it; and above all, that she should aspire to be as wise as him, who was so ignorant before, as to believe it was for fear of her being like himself, that he had forbid it her.

Well might she be said to be the weaker Vessel, though *Adam* himself had little enough to say for his being the stronger of the two, when he was over-persuaded (if it were done by Persuasion) by his Wife to do the same thing.

And mark how wise they were after they had Eaten, and what Fools they both acted like, even to one another; nay, even all the Knowledge they attained to by it was, for ought I see, only to know that they were Fools, and to be sensible both of *Sin* and *Shame*; and see how simply they acted, I say, upon their having committed the Crime, and being detected in it.

'View them to Day conversing with their God,
'His Image both enjoyed and understood,
'*To Morrow* skulking with a sordid Flight,
'Among the Bushes from the *Infinite*,
'As if that Power *was blind*, which gave them *Sight*;
'With senseless Labor Tagging Fig-Leaf Vests,
'To hide their Bodies from the sight of Beasts.
'Hark! how the Fool pleads faint, for forfeit Life,
'First he reproaches Heaven, and then his Wife;
'*The Woman which thou gav'st* as if the Gift
'Could rob him of the little Reason left,
'A weak Pretence to shift his early Crime,
'As if accusing her would excuse him;
'But thus encroaching Crime dethrones the Sense,
'And intercepts the Heavenly Influence,
'Debauches Reason, makes the Man a Fool,
'And turns his active Light to Ridicule.

It must be confessed that it was unaccountable Degeneracy, even of their common Reasoning, which *Adam* and *Eve* both fell into upon the first committing the Offence of taking the forbidden Fruit: If that was their being made as Gods, it made but a poor Appearance in its first coming, to hide their Nakedness when there was no body to see them, and cover themselves among the Bushes from their Maker; but thus it was, and this the Devil had brought them to, and well might he, and all the Clan of Hell, as Mr. *Milton* brings them in, laugh and triumph over the Man after the Blow was given, as having so egregiously abused and deluded them both.

But here, to be sure, began the *Devil*'s new Kingdom; as he had now seduced the two first Creatures, he was pretty sure of Success upon all the Race, and therefore prepared to attack them also, as soon as they came on; nor was their increasing Multitude any Discouragement to his Attempt, but just the contrary; for he had Agents enough to employ, if every Man and Woman that should be born was to want a *Devil* to wait upon them, separately and singly to seduce them; whereas some whole Nations have been such willing subjects to him, that one of his Seraphic Imps may, *for ought we know*, have been enough to guide a whole Country; the People being entirely subjected to his Government for many Ages; as in *America*, *for example*, where some will have it, that he conveyed the first Inhabitants, at least if he did not, we don't well know who did, or how they got thither.

And how came all the Communication to be so entirely cut off between the Nations of *Europe* and *Africa*, from whence *America* must certainly have been peopled, or else the *Devil* must have done it indeed? I say, how came the Communication to be so entirely cut off between them, that except the time, *whenever it was*, that People did at first reach from one to the other, none ever came back to give their Friends any account of their Success, or invite them to follow? Nor did they hear of one another afterwards, as we have Reason to think: Did *Satan* politically keep them thus asunder, lest News from Heaven should reach them, and so they should be recovered out of his Government? We cannot tell how to give any other rational Account of it, that a Nation, nay a Quarter of the World, or as some will have it be, half the Globe, should be peopled from *Europe* or *Africa*, or both, and nobody ever go after them, or come back from them in above three thousand years after.

Nay, that those Countries should be peopled when there was no Navigation in use in these Parts of the World, no Ships made that could carry Provisions enough to support the People that failed in them, but that they must have been starved to death before they could reach the Shore of *America*; the Ferry from *Europe* or *Africa*, in any Part (which we have known Navigation to be practiced in) being at least 1000 Miles, and in most Places much more.

But as to the *Americans*, let the *Devil* and they alone to account for their coming Thither, this we are certain of, that we knew nothing of them for many hundred Years; and when we did, when the Discovery was made, they that went from Hence found *Satan* in a full and quiet Possession of them, ruling them with an arbitrary Government, particular to himself; He had led them into a blind Subjection to himself, nay, I might call it Devotion, for it was all of Religion that was to be found among them) worshipping horrible Idols in his Name, to whom he directed human Sacrifices continually to be made, till he deluged the Country with Blood, and ripened them up for the Destruction that followed, from the Invasion of the *Spaniards*, who he knew would hurry them all out of the World as fast as he (*the Devil*) himself could desire of them.

But to go back a little to the Original of Things, It is evident that *Satan* has made a much better Market of Mankind, by thus subtly attacking them, and bringing them to break with their Maker as he had done before them, than he could have done by fulminating upon them at first, and sending them all out of the World at once; for now he has peopled his own Dominions with them, and though a Remnant are snatched as it were out of his Clutches, by the Agency of Invincible Grace, of which I am not to discourse in this Place; yet this may be said of the *Devil*, without Offence, that he has in some Sense carried his Point, and as it were forced his Maker to be satisfied with a Part of Mankind, and the least Part too, instead of the great Glory he would have brought to himself by keeping them all in his Service.

Mr. *Milton*, as I have noted above, brings in the *Devil* and all Hell with him, making a *Feu de Joye* for the Victory *Satan* obtained over one silly Woman; indeed it was a Piece of Success greater in its Consequence than in the immediate Appearance; nor was the Conquest so complete as Satan himself imagined to make, since the Promise of a Redemption out of his Hands, which was immediately made to the Man, in behalf of himself and his believing Posterity, was a great Disappointment to Satan, and as it were snatched the best Part of his Victory out of his Hands.

It is certain the *Devils* knew what the meaning of that Promise was, and who was to be the *Seed of the Woman*, namely, the incarnate *Son of God*, and that it was a second Blow to the whole infernal Body; but as if they had resolved to let that alone, *Satan* went on with his Business; and as he had introduced Crime into the common Parent of Mankind, and thereby secured the Contamination of Blood, and the Descent or Propagation of the corrupt Seed, he had nothing to do but to assist Nature in time to come, to carry on its own Rebellion, and act itself in the Breasts of *Eve*'s tainted Posterity; and that indeed has been the Devil's Business ever since his first Victory upon the Kind, to this Day.

His Success in this Part has been such, that we see upon innumerable Occasions a general Defection has followed; a kind of a Taint upon Nature, *call it what you will*, a Blast upon the Race of Mankind; and were it not for one thing, he had ruined the whole Family; *I say*, were it not for one thing, namely, a selected Company or Number, which his Maker has resolved he shall not be able to corrupt, or if he does, the sending the promised Seed shall recover back again from him, by the Power of irresistible Grace; which Number thus selected or elected, call it which we will, are still to supply the Vacancies in Heaven, which *Satan*'s Defection left open; and what was before filled up with created Seraphs, is now to be restored by recovered Saints, by whom infinite Glory is to accrue to the Kingdom of the Redeemer.

This glorious Establishment has robbed Satan of all the Joy of his Victory, and left him just where he was, defeated and disappointed; nor does the Possession of all the Myriads of the Sons of Perdition, who yet some are of the Opinion will be snatched from him too at last; I say, the Possession of all these makes no amends to him, for he is such a *Devil* in his Nature, that the Envy at those he cannot seduce, eats out all the Satisfaction of the Mischief he has done in seducing all the rest; but *I must not preach*, so I return to things as much needful to know, though less solemn.

Chapter IX

Of the Progress of Satan in carrying on his Conquest over Mankind, from the Fall of Eve to the Deluge

I doubt if the Devil was asked the Question plainly, he would confess, that after he had conquered *Eve* by his own wicked Contrivance, and then by her Assistance had brought *Adam* too (like a Fool as he was) into the same Gulp of Misery, he thought he had done his Work, compassed the whole Race, that they were now his own, and that he had put an End to the grand Design of their Creation; namely, of Peopling Heaven with a new Angelic Race of Souls, who when glorified, should make up the Defection of the Host of Hell, that had been expunged by their Crime; in a Word, that he had gotten a better Conquest than if he had destroyed them all.

But in the midst of his Conquest, he found a Check put to the Advantages he expected to reap from his Victory, by the immediate Promise of Grace to a Part of the Posterity of *Adam*, who, notwithstanding the Fall, were to be purchased by the *Messiah*, and snatched out of his (*Satan's*) Hands, and over whom he could make no final Conquest; so that his Power met with a new Limitation, and that such, as indeed fully disappointed him in the main thing he aimed at, (*viz.*) preventing the Beatitudes of Mankind, which were thus secured; (And what if the Numbers of Mankind were upon this account increased in such a manner, that the selected Number should, by Length of Time, amount to just as many as the whole Race, had they not fallen, would have amounted to in all?) And thus, indeed, the World may be said to be upheld and continued for the Sake of those few, since till their Number can be completed, the Creation cannot fall, any more than, that without them, or but for them it would not have stood.

But leaving this Speculation, and not having enquired of Satan what he has to say on that Subject, let us go back to the Antediluvian World: The *Devil* to be sure, gained his Point upon *Eve*, and in her upon all her Race: He drew her into Sin; got her turned out of *Paradise*, and the Man with her: The next Thing was to go to work with her Posterity, and particularly with her two Sons *Cain* and *Abel*.

Adam having, notwithstanding his Fall, repented very sincerely of his Sin; received the Promise of Redemption and Pardon, with an humble but believing Heart; Charity bids us suppose that he led a very religious and sober Life ever after; and especially in the first Part of his Time, That he brought up his Children very soberly, and gave them all the necessary

Advantages of a Religious Education, and a good Introduction into the World, that he was capable of; and that *Eve* likewise assisted to both in her Place and Degree.

Their two eldest Sons *Cain* and *Abel*; The one Heir apparent to the Patriarchal Empire, and the other Heir presumptive, I suppose also, lived very sober and religious Lives; and as the Principles of natural Religion dictated a Homage and Subjection due to the Almighty Maker, as an Acknowledgment of his Mercies, and a Recognition of their Obedience; so the received Usage of Religion dictating at that Time that this Homage was to be paid by a Sacrifice, they either of them brought a Free-will-offering to be dedicated to God respectively for themselves and Families.

How it was, and for what Reason that God had respect to the Offering of *Abel*, which the Learned say, was *a Lamb* of the Firstlings of the Flock, and did not give any Testimony of the like Respect to *Cain* and his Offering, which was of the first Fruits of the Earth, the Offerings being equally suited to the respective Employment of the Men, that is not my present Business; but this we find made Heart-burnings, and raised Envy and Jealousy in the Mind of *Cain*; and at that Door the *Devil* immediately entered; for he, who from the Beginning, was very diligent in his way, never slipped any Opportunity, or missed any Advantages that the Circumstances of Mankind offered him to do Mischief.

What Shape or Appearance the Devil took up to enter into a Conversation with *Cain* upon the Subject, that Authors do not take upon them to determine; but 'tis generally supposed he personated some of *Cain*'s Sons or Grandsons to begin the Discourse, who attacked their Father, or perhaps Grandfather, upon this Occasion, in the following manner, or to that Purpose.

D. Sir, I perceive *your Majesty* (for the first Race were certainly all Monarchs as great as Kings, to their immediate Posterity) to be greatly disturbed of late, your Countenance is changed, your noble Cheerfulness (the Glories of your Face) are strangely sunk and gone, and you are not the Man you used to be; please your Majesty to communicate your Griefs to us your Children, you may be sure, that if it be possible, we would procure you Relief, and restore your Delights, the Loss of which, if thus you go on to subject yourself to too much Melancholy, will be very hurtful to you, and in the End destroy you.

Cain. It is very kind, my dear Children, to show your Respect thus to your true Progenitor, and to offer your Assistance: I confess, as you say, my Mind is oppressed and displeased; but though 'tis very heavy, yet I know not which way to look for Relief, for the Distemper is above our Reach, no Cure can be found for it on Earth.

D. Do not say so, Sir; there can be no Disease sure on Earth but may be cured on Earth; if it be a mental Evil, we have heard that your great Ancestor, the first Father of us all, who lives still on the great western Plains towards the Sea, is the Oracle to which all his Children fly for Direction in such Cases as are out of the Reach of the ordinary understanding of Mankind; please you to give leave, we will take a Journey to him, and representing your Case to him, we will hear his Advice, and bring it to you with all Speed, for the Ease of your Mind.

Cain. I know not whether he can reach my Case or no.

D. Doubtless he may, and if not, the Labor of our Journey is nothing when placed in Competition with the Ease of your Mind; 'tis but a few Days travel lost, and you will not be the worse if we fail of the desired Success.

Cain. The offer is filial, and I accept your affectionate Concern for me, with a just Sense of an obliged Parent; go then, and my Blessing be upon you; but alas! why do I bless? can he bless whom God has not blessed!

D. O! Sir, do not say so, has not God blessed you? are you not the second Sovereign of the Earth? and does he not converse with you Face to Face? are not you the Oracle to all your growing Posterity, and next after his Sovereign Imperial Majesty Lord *Adam*, Patriarch of the World?

Cain. But has not God rejected me, and refused to converse any more with me, while he daily Favors and Countenances my younger Brother *Abel*, as if he resolved to set him up to rule over me?

D. No, Sir, that cannot be, you cannot be disturbed at such a thing; is not the Right of Sovereignty yours by Primogeniture? can God himself take that away, when 'tis once given? are not you Lord *Adam*'s eldest Son? are you not the firstborn Glory of the Creation? and does not the Government descend to you by the divine Right of Birth and Blood?

Cain. But what does all that signify to me, while God appears to favor and caress my younger Brother, and to shine upon him, while a black Dejection and token of Displeasure surrounds me every Day, and he does not appear to me as he used to do?

D. And what need your Majesty be concerned at that, if it be so? if he does not appear pleased, you have the whole World to enjoy yourself in, and all your numerous and rising Posterity Adore and Honor you; what need those remote Things be any disturbance to you?

Cain. How! my Children, not the Favor of God be valued! yes, yes, in his favor is Life; what can all the World avail without the Smiles and Countenance of him that made it?

D. Doubtless, Sir, he that made the World and placed you at the Head of it all, to govern and direct it, has made it agreeable, and it is able to give you a full Satisfaction and Enjoyment, if you please to consider it well, though you were never to converse with him all the while you live in it.

Cain. You are *quite wrong* there, my Children, *quite wrong.*

D. But do you not, great Sir, see all your Children as well as us rejoicing in the Plenty of all Things, and are they not completely happy, and yet they know little of this great God? He seldom converses among us, we hear of him indeed by your sage Advices, and we bring our Offerings to you for him, as you direct, and when that's done, we enjoy whatever our Hearts desire; and so doubtless may you in an abundant manner, if you please.

Cain. But your Felicity is wrong placed then, or you suppose that God is pleased and satisfied in that your Offerings are brought to me; but what would you say, if you knew that God is displeased? that he does not accept your Offerings? that when I sacrificed to him in behalf of you all, he rejected my Offerings, though I brought a princely Gift, being of the finest of the Wheat, the choicest and earliest Fruits, and the sweetest of the Oil, an Offering suited to the Giver of them all?

D. But if you offered them, Sir, how are you sure they were not accepted?

Cain. Yes, yes, I am sure; did not my Brother *Abel* offer at the same Time a Lamb of his Flock, for he, you know, delights in Cattle, and covers the Mountains with his Herds? over him, all the while he was sacrificing, a bright Emanation shone cheering and enlivening; a Pledge of Favor, and light ambient Flames played hovering in the lower Air, as if attending his Sacrifice; and when ready prepared, immediately descended and burnt up the Flesh, a Sweet odoriferous Savor ascending to him, who thus testified his Acceptance; whereas, over my Head a black Cloud, misty, and distilling Vapor, hung dripping upon the humble Altar I had raised, and wetting the finest and choicest Things I had prepared, spoiled and defaced them; the Wood unapt to burn by the Moisture which fell, scarce received the Fire I brought to kindle it, and even then, rather smothered and choked, than kindled into a Flame; in a Word, it went quite out, without consuming what was brought to be offered up.

D. Let not our truly reverenced Lord and Father be disquieted at all this; if he accepts not what you bring, you are discharged of the Debt, and need bring no more; nor have the Trouble of such labored Collections of Rarities anymore; when he thinks fit to require it again, you will have Notice, no

Question, and then it being called for, will be accepted or else why should it be required?

Cain. That may indeed be the Case, nor do I think of attempting any more to bring an Offering, for I rather take it, that I am forbidden for the present; but then, what is it that my younger Brother Triumphs in? and how am I insulted, in that he and his House are all Joy and Triumph, as if they had some great Advantage over me, in that their Offering was accepted when mine was not?

D. Does he Triumph over your Majesty, our Lord and Sovereign? give us but your Order, and we will go and pull him and all his Generation in pieces; for to triumph over you who are his elder Brother, is a horrid Rebellion and Treason, and he ought to be expelled the Society of Mankind.

Cain. I think so too, indeed; however, my dear Children and faithful Subjects, though I accept your Offer of Duty and Service, yet I will consider very well, before I take up Arms against my Brother; besides, our Sovereign Father and patriarchal Lord, *Adam*, being yet alive, it is not in my Right to act offensively without his Command.

D. We are ready therefore to carry your Petition to him, and doubt not to obtain his License and Commission too, to empower you to do yourself Justice upon your younger Brother; who being your Vassal, or at least inferior, as he is junior in Birth, insults you upon the fancied Opinion of having a larger Share in the Divine Favor, and receiving a Blessing on his Sacrifices, on Pretence of the same Favor being denied you.

Cain. I am content, go then, and give a just Account of the State of our Affairs.

D. We shall soon return with the agreeable answer; let not our Lord and Father continue sad and dejected, but depend upon a speedy Relief, by the Assistance of thy numerous Issue, all devoted to thy Interest and Felicity.

Cain. My Blessing be with you in your Way, and give you a favorable Reception at the venerable Tent of our universal Lord and Father.

Note, Here the cursed Race being fully given up to the Direction of the Evil-Spirit, which so early possessed them, and swelling with Rage at the innocent *Abel* and his whole Family, they resolved upon forming a most wicked and detestable lie, to bring about the Advice which they had already given their Father *Cain* a touch of; and to pretend that *Adam* being justly provoked at the undutiful Behavior of *Abel*, had given *Cain* a Commission to chastise him, and by Force to cut him off and all his Family, as guilty of Rebellion and Pride.

Filled with this mischievous and bloody Resolution, they came back to their Father *Cain*, after staying a few Days, such as were Sufficient to make *Cain* believe they had been at the spacious Plains, where *Adam* dwelt; the same which are now called the blessed Valleys, or the Plains of *Mecca* in *Arabia Fælix*, near the Banks of the *Red-Sea*.

Note here also, that *Cain* having received a wicked Hint from these Men, his Children and Subjects, as before, intimating that *Abel* had broken the Laws of Primogeniture in his Behavior towards him, (*Cain*) and that he might be justly punished for it; Satan, that cunning Manager of all our wayward Passions, fanned the Fire of Envy and Jealousy with his utmost Skill all the while his other Agents were absent; and by the Time they came back had blown it up into such a Heat of Fury and Rage, that it wanted nothing but Air to make it burn out, as it soon afterwards did in a furious Flame of Wrath and Revenge, even to Blood and Destruction.

Just in the very critical Moment, while Things stood thus with *Cain*, Satan brings in his wicked Instruments, as if just arrived with the Return of his Message from *Adam*, at whose Court they had been for Orders; and thus they, that is the *Devil* assuming to speak by them, approach their Father with an Air of solemn but cheerful Satisfaction at the Success of their Embassy.

D. Hail Sovereign, Reverend, Patriarchal Lord! we come with Joy to render thee an Account of the Success of our Message.

Cain. Have you then seen the venerable Tents where dwell the Heaven-born, the Angelic Pair, to whom all human Reverence highly due, is and ought always to be humbly paid?

D. We have.

Cain. Did you, together with my grand Request, a just, a humble Homage for me pay, to the great Sire and Mother of Mankind?

D. We did.

Cain. Did you in humble Language represent the Griefs and Anguish which oppress my Soul?

D. We did, and back their Blessing to thee bring.

Cain. I hope with humblest Signs of filial Duty you took it for me on your bending Knees?

D. We did, and had our Share; the Patriarch lifting his Hands to Heaven expressed his Joy to see his spreading Race, and blessed us all.

Cain. Did you my solemn Message too deliver, my Injuries impartially lay down, and due Assistance and Direction crave?

D. We did.

Cain. What spoke the Oracle? he's God to me; what just Command do you bring, what's to be done? am I to bear the insulting Junior's Rage? and meekly suffer what unjustly he, affronting Primogeniture and Laws of God and Man, imposes by his Pride insufferable! Am I to be crushed, and be no more the firstborn Son on Earth, but bow and kneel to him?

D. Forbid it Heaven! as *Adam* too forbids, who with a justice God-like and peculiar to injured Parents, *Abel*'s Pride resents, and gives his high Command to thee to punish.

Cain. To punish? say you, did he use the Word, the very Word? am I commissioned then to punish *Abel*?

D. Not *Abel* only, but his rebel Race, as they alike in Crime alike are joined in Punishment.

Cain. The Race indeed have shared the Merit with him; how did they all insult, and with a Shout of Triumph mock my Sorrow, when they saw me from my Sacrifice dejected come, as if my Disappointment was their Joy?

D. This too the venerable Prince resents, and to preserve the Race in Bounds of Laws subordinate and limited to Duty, Commands that this first Breach be not passed by, lest the Precedent upon Record stand to future Times to encourage like Rebellion.

Cain. And is it then my Sovereign Parent's Will?

D. It is his Will, that thou his eldest Son, his Image, his beloved, should be maintained in all the Rights of Sovereignty derived to thee from him; and not be left exposed to injury and Power usurped, but should do thy self Justice on the rebel Race.

Cain. And so I will; *Abel* shall quickly know what 'tis to trample on his elder Brother; shall know that he's thus sentenced by his Father, and I'm commissioned but to execute his high Command, his Sentence, which is God's, and that he falls by the Hand of Heavenly Justice.

So now Satan had done his Work, he had deluded the Mother to a Breach against the first and only Command, he had drawn *Adam* to the same Snare, and now he brings in *Cain* prompted by his own Rage, and deluded by his, (Satan's,) Craft, to commit Murder, nay a Fratricide, an aggravated Murder.

Upon this he sends out *Cain*, while the bloody Rage was in its Ferment, and wickedly at the same Time bringing *Abel*, innocent and fearing no ill, just in his Way, he suggests to his Thoughts such Words as these.

Look you *Cain*, see how Divine Justice concurs with your Father's righteous Sentence, see there's thy Brother *Abel* directed by Heaven to fall into thy Hands unarmed, unguarded, that thou may'st do thy self Justice upon him without Fear; see thou may'st kill him, and if thou hast a Mind to conceal it, no Eyes can see, or will the World ever know it, so that no Resentment or Revenge upon thee, or thy Posterity, can be apprehended, but it may be said some wild Beast had rent him; nor will any one suggest that thou, his Brother, and Superior, could possibly be the Person.

Cain prepared for the Fact, by his former avowed Rage and Resolution of Revenge, was so much the less prepared to avoid the Snare thus artfully contrived by the Master of all Subtlety, the *Devil*; so he immediately runs upon his Brother *Abel*, and after a little unarmed Resistance, the innocent poor Man expecting no such Mischief, was conquered and murdered; after which, as is to be supposed, the exasperated Crew of *Cain*'s outrageous Race, over-run all his Family and Household, killing Man, Woman and Child.

It is objected here that we have no Authority in Scripture to prove this Part of the Story; but I answer, 'tis not likely but that *Abel*, as well as *Cain*, being at Man's Estate long before this, had several Children by their own Sisters, for they were the only Men in the World who were allowed the Marrying their own Sisters, there being no other Women then in the World; and as we never read of any of *Abel*'s Posterity, 'tis likewise as probable they were all murdered, as that they should kill *Abel* only, whose Sons might immediately fall upon *Cain* for the Blood of their Father, and so the World have been involved in a Civil War as soon as there were two Families in it.

But be it so or not, 'tis not doubted the Devil wrought with *Cain* in the horrid Murder, or he had never done it; whether it was directly or by Agents is not material, nor is the Latter unlikely; and if the Latter, then there is no Improbability in the Story, for why might not he that made Use of the Serpent to tempt *Eve*, be as well supposed to make a Tool of some of

Cain's Sons or Grandsons to prompt him in the wicked Attempt of murdering his Brother? and why must we be obliged to bring in a Miracle or an Apparition into the Story, to make it probable that the *Devil* had any Hand in it, when 'twas so natural to a degenerate Race to act in such a Manner?

However it was, and by whatever Tool the *Devil* wrought, 'tis certain that this was the Consequence, poor *Abel* was butchered, and thus the *Devil* made a second Conquest in God's Creation; for *Adam* was now, as may be said, really Childless, for his two Sons were thus far lost, *Abel* was killed, and *Cain* was curst and driven out from the Presence of the Lord, and his Race blasted with him.

It would be a useful enquiry here, and worthy our giving an Account of, could we come to a Certainty in it, namely, what was the Mark that God set upon *Cain*, by which he was kept from being fallen upon by *Abel's* Friends or Relations? but as this does not belong to the *Devil's* History, and it was God's Mark, not the *Devil's*, I have nothing to do with it here.

The *Devil* had now gained his Point, the Kingdom of Grace, so newly erected, had been as it were extinct without a new Creation, had not *Adam* and *Eve* been alive, and had not *Eve*, though now 130 Years of Age, been a breeding young Lady, for we must suppose the Woman, in that State of Longevity, bare Children till they were seven or eight hundred Year old: This Teeming of *Eve* peopled not the World so much as it restored the blessed Race; for though *Abel* was killed *Cain* had a numerous Offspring presently, which had *Seth*, (*Adam's* third Son) never been born, would soon have replenished the World with People, such as they were; the Seed of a Murderer, cursed of God, branded with a Mark of Infamy, and who afterwards fell all together in the universal Ruine of the Race by the Deluge.

But after the Murder of *Abel*, *Adam* had another Son born, namely, *Seth*, the Father of *Enos*, and indeed the Father of the holy Race; for during his Time and his Son *Enos*, the Text says that Men began to call on the Name of the Lord; that is to say, they began to look back upon *Cain* and his wicked Race, and being convinced of the Wickedness they had committed, and led their whole Posterity into, they began to sue to Heaven for Pardon of what was past, and to lead a new sort of Life.

But the *Devil* had met with too much Success in his first Attempts, not to go on with his general Resolution of debauching the Minds of Men, and bringing them off from God; and therefore as he kept his Hold upon *Cain's* cursed Race, embroiled already in Blood and Murder; so he proceeded with his degenerate Offspring, till in a Word he brought both the holy Seed and the degenerate Race to join in one universal Consent of Crime, and to go on in it with such aggravating Circumstances, as that it repented the

Lord that he had made Man, and he resolved to overwhelm them again with a general Destruction, and clear the World of them.

The Succession of Blood in the royal original Line of *Adam*, is preserved in the sacred Histories and brought down as low as *Noah* and his three Sons, for a continued series of 1450 Years, say some, 1640 say others; in which Time Sin spread itself so generally thro' the whole Race, and *the Sons of God*, so the Scripture calls the Men of the righteous Seed, the Progeny of *Seth*, came in unto the *Daughters of Men*, that is, joined themselves to the cursed Race of *Cain*, and married promiscuously with them, according to their Fancies, the Women it seems being beautiful and tempting; and though the Devil could not make the Women handsome or ugly in one or other Families, yet he might work up the Gust of wicked Inclination on either Side, so as to make both the Men and Women tempting and agreeable to one another, where they ought not to have been so; and perhaps, as it is often seen to this Day, the more tempting for being under legal Restraint.

It is objected here, that we do not find in the Scripture that the Men and Women of either Race were at that Time forbidden intermarrying with one another; and it is true, that literally it is not forbid; but if we did not search rather to make doubts than to explain them, we might suppose it was forbidden by some particular Command at that Time; seeing we may reasonably allow every Thing to be forbidden, which they are taxed with a Crime in committing; and as the Sons of God taking them Wives as they thought fit to choose, though from among the Daughters of the cursed Race, is there charged upon them as a general Depravation, and a great Crime; and for which, 'tis said, God even repented that he had made them, we need go no farther to satisfy our selves that it was certainly forbidden.

Satan no doubt too had a Hand in this Wickedness; for as it was his Business to prompt Men to do every Thing which God had prohibited, so the Reason given why the Men of those Days did this Thing was, they saw the Daughters of Men, that is of the wicked Race or forbidden Sort, *were fair*, he tempted them by the Lust of the Eye; in a word, the Ladies were beautiful and agreeable, and the *Devil* knew how to make use of the Allurement; the Men liked and took them by the mere Direction of their Fancy and Appetite, without regarding the supreme Prohibition; *They took them Wives of all which they chose*, or such as they liked to choose.

But the Text adds, that this promiscuous Generation went farther than the mere outward Crime of it, for it showed that the Wickedness of the Heart of Man was great before God, and that he resented it; In short, God perceived a Degeneracy or Defect of Virtue had seized upon the whole Race, that there was a general Corruption of Manners, a Depravity of Nature upon them, that even the holy Seed was tainted with it, that the Devil had broken in upon them, and prevailed to a great Degree; that not only the Practice of the Age was corrupt, for that God could easily have restrained, but that the very Heart of Man was debauched, his Desires wholly vitiated, and his Senses engaged in it; so that in a Word, it became necessary to show the divine Displeasure, not in the ordinary Manner, by Judgment and Reproofs of such kind as usually reclaim Men, but by a general Destruction to sweep them away, clear the Earth of them, and put an End to the Wickedness at once, removing the Offence and the Offenders all together; this is signified at large, Gen. vi. 5. *God saw that the Wickedness of Man was great in the Earth, and that every Imagination of the Thoughts of his Heart was only evil continually.* And again v. 11, 12. *The Earth also was corrupt before God; and the Earth was filled with Violence. And God looked upon the Earth and behold it was corrupt; for all Flesh had corrupted his Way upon the Earth.*

It must be confessed it was a strange Conquest the *Devil* had made in the Antediluvian World, that he had, as I may say, brought the whole Race of Mankind into a general Revolt from God; *Noah* was indeed a Preacher of Righteousness, and he had preached about 500 Years to as little Purpose as most of the good Ministers ever did; for we do not read there was one Man converted by him, or at least not one of them left, for that at the Deluge there was either none of them alive, or none spared but *Noah* and his three Sons, and their Wives; and even they are ('tis evident) recorded, not so much to be saved for their own Goodness, but because they were his Sons; Nay, without Breach of Charity we may conclude, that at least one went to the *Devil* even of those three, namely, *Ham* or *Cham* for triumphing in a brutal Manner over his Father's Drunkenness; for we find the Special Curse reached to him and his Posterity for many Ages; and whether it went no farther than the present State of Life with them, we cannot tell.

We will suppose now that thro' this whole 1500 Years the Devil having so effectually debauched Mankind, had advanced his infernal Kingdom to a prodigious Height; for the Text says, *the whole Earth was filled with violence*; in a Word, Blood, Murder, Rape, Robbery, Oppression and Injustice prevailed everywhere, and Man, like the wild Bear in the Forest, lived by Prey, biting and devouring one another.

At this Time *Noah* begins to preach a new Doctrine to them, for as he had before been a Preacher of Righteousness, now he becomes a Preacher of Vengeance; first he tells them they shall be all overwhelmed with a Deluge, that for their Sins God repented they were made, and that he would destroy them all, adding, that to prevent the Ruin of himself and Family, he resolved to build him a Ship to have recourse to when the Water should come over the Rest of the World.

What Jesting, what Scorn, what Contempt did this Work expose the good old Man to for above a 100 Years? for so long the Work was building, as ancient Authors say; let us represent to ourselves in the most lively Manner how the witty World at that Time behaved to poor old *Noah*; how they took their Evening Walks to see what he was doing, and passed their Judgment upon it, and upon the Progress of it; I say, to represent this to ourselves, we need go no farther than to our own Witticisms upon Religion, and upon the most solemn Mysteries of Divine Worship; how we damn the Serious for Enthusiasts, think the Grave mad, and the Sober melancholy; call Religion itself Flatus and Hypo; make the Devout ignorant, the Divine mercenary, and the whole Scheme of Divinity a Frame of Priest craft; and thus no doubt the building an Ark or Boat, or whatever they called it, to float over the Mountains, and dance over the Plains, what could it be but a religious Frenzy, and the Man that so busied himself, a Lunatic? and all this in an Age when divine Things came by immediate Revelation into the Minds of Men! the *Devil* must therefore have made a strange Conquest upon Mankind to obliterate all the Reverence, which but a little before was so strangely impressed upon them concerning their Maker.

This was certainly the Height of the *Devil's* Kingdom, and we shall never find him arrive to such a Pitch again; he was then truly and literally the universal Monarch, nay the God of this World; and as all Tyrants do, he governs them with an arbitrary absolute sway; and had not God thought fit to give him a Writ of Ejectment, and afterwards drown him out of Possession I know not what would have been the Case, he might have kept his Hold for ought I know till the Seed of the Woman came to bruise his Head, that is to say, cripple his Government, Dethrone him and Depose his Power, as has been fulfilled in the Messiah.

But as he was, I say, drowned out of the World, his Kingdom for the present was at an End; at least, if he had a Dominion he had no Subjects, and as the Creation was in a Manner renewed, so the *Devil* had all his Work to do over again: Unhappy Man! how has he, by his weak Resistance, made the *Devil*, recovering his Hold too easy to him, and given him all the Advantages, except as before excepted, which he had before? Now whether he retired in the mean Time, and how he got footing again after *Noah* and his Family were landed upon the New Surface, that we come next to enquire.

Chapter X

Of the Devil's second Kingdom, and how he got footing in the renewed World by his Victory over Noah and his Race

The Story of *Noah*, his building the Ark, his embarking himself and all Nature's Stock for a new World on board it; the long Voyage they took, and the bad Weather they met with, though it would embellish this Work very well, and come in very much to the Purpose in this Place, yet as it does not belong to the *Devil*'s Story, for I cannot prove what some suggest (*viz.*) that he was in the Ark among the Rest, I say, for that Reason I must omit it.

And now having mentioned Satan's being in the Ark; as I say, I cannot prove it, so there are, I think, some good Reasons to believe he was not there: *First*, I know no Business he had there; *secondly*, we read of no Mischief done there, and these joined together make me conclude he was absent; the last I chiefly insist upon, that we read of no Mischief done there, which if he had been in the Ark, would certainly have happened; and therefore I suppose rather, that when he saw his Kingdom dissolved, his Subjects all engulfed in an inevitable Ruin and Desolation, a Sight suitable enough to him, except as it might unking him for a Time; *I say*, when he saw this, he took care to speed himself away as well as he could, and make his Retreat to a Place of Safety, where that was, is no more difficult to us, than it was to him.

It is suggested that as he is Prince of the Power of the Air, he retired only into that Region. It is most rational to suppose he went no further on many Accounts, of which I shall speak by and by: Here he stayed hovering in the Earth's Atmosphere, as he has often done since, and perhaps now does; or if the Atmosphere of this Globe was affected by the In draft of the Absorption, as some think, then he kept himself upon the Watch, to see what the Event of the new Phenomenon would be, and this Watch, wherever it was, I doubt not, was as near the Earth as he could place himself, perhaps in the Atmosphere of the Moon, or in a Word, the next Place of Retreat he could find.

From hence I took upon me to insist, that *Satan* has not a more certain Knowledge of Events than we; I say, he has not a *more certain Knowledge*; that he may be able to make stronger Conjectures and more rational Conclusions from that he sees, I will not deny; and that which he most outdoes us in is, that he sees more to conclude from than we can, but I am satisfied he knows nothing of Futurity more than we can see by Observation and Inference; nor, *for Example*, did he know whether God would repeople the World any more or no.

I must therefore allow that he only waited to see what would be the Event of this strange Eruption of Water, and what God proposed to do with the Ark, and all that was in it.

Some Philosophers tell us, besides what I hinted above, that the *Devil* could have no Retreat in the Earth's Atmosphere, for that the Air being wholly condensed into Water, and having continually poured down its Streams to deluge the Earth, that Body was become so small, and had suffered such Convulsions, that there was but just enough Air left to surround the Water, or as might serve by its Pressure to preserve the natural Position of Things, and supply the Creatures in the Ark with a Part to breath in.

The Atmosphere indeed might suffer some strange and unnatural Motions at that Time, but not (I believe) to that Degree, however, I will not affirm that there could be room in it, or is now for the Devil, much less for all the numberless Legions of Satan's Host; but there was, and now certainly is, sufficient Space to receive him, and a sufficient Body of his Troops for the Business he had for them at that time, and that's enough to the Purpose; or if the Earth's Atmosphere did suffer any particular Convulsion on that Occasion, he might make his Retreat to the Atmosphere of the Moon, or of *Mars*, or of *Venus*, or of any of the other Planets; or to any other Place, for he that is Prince of the Air could not want Retreats in such a Case, from whence he might watch for the issue of Things; certainly he did not go far, because his Business lay here, and he never goes out of his Way of doing Mischief.

In particular, his more than ordinary Concern was, to see what would become of the Ark; he was wise enough doubtless to see, that God, who had directed its making, nay even the very Structure of it, would certainly take Care of it, preserve it upon the Water, and bring it to some Place of Safety or other; though where it should be, the *Devil* with all his Cunning could not resolve, whether on the same Surface the Waters drawing off, or in any other created or to be created Place; and this State of Uncertainty being evidently his Case, and which proves his Ignorance of Futurity, it was his Business, *I say*, to watch with the utmost vigilance for the Event.

If the Ark was (as Mr. *Burnet* thinks) guided by two Angels, they not only held it from foundering or being swallowed up in the Water, but certainly kept the Waters calm about it, especially when the Lord brought a strong Wind to blow over the whole Globe, which by the Way was the first, and, I suppose, the only universal Storm that ever blew, for to be sure it blew over the whole Surface at once; I say, if it was thus guided, to be sure the *Devil* saw it, and that with Envy and Regret that he could do it no Injury, for doubtless had it been in the Devil's Power, as God had drowned the whole Race of Man, except what was in the Ark, he would have taken care to have dispatched them too, and so made an End of the Creation at once; but either he was not empowered to go to the Ark, or it was so well guarded by Angels, that when he came near it he could do it no harm: So it rested at length, the Waters abating on the Mountains of *Ararat* in *Armenia*, or somewhere else that Way, and where they say a Piece of the Keel is remaining to this Day; of which, however with Dr. ——— I say, I believe not one Word.

The Ark being safe landed, 'tis reasonable to believe *Noah* prepared to go on Shore, as the Seamen call it, as soon as the dry Land began to appear; and here you must allow me to suppose Satan, though himself clothed with a Cloud, so as not to be seen, came immediately, and perching on the Roof, saw all the Heaven-kept Household safely landed, and all the Host of living Creatures dispersing themselves down the Sides of the Mountain, as the Search of their Food or other proper Occasions directed them.

This Sight was enough; Satan was at no Loss to conclude from hence that the Design of God was to repeople the World by the Way of ordinary Generation, from the Posterity of these eight Persons, without creating any new Species.

Very well, says the *Devil*, then my Advantage over them, by the Snare I laid for poor *Eve*, is good still; and I am now just where I was after *Adam*'s Expulsion from the Garden, and when I had *Cain* and his Race to go to work with; for here is the old expunged Corrupted Race still, as *Cain* was the Object then, so *Noah* is my Man now, and if I do not master him one way or another, I am mistaken in my Mark. *Pardon me for making a Speech for* the Devil.

Noah big with a Sense of his late Condition, and while the Wonders of the Deluge were fresh in his Mind, spent his first Days in the Ecstasies of his Soul, giving Thanks, and praising the Power that had been his Protection, in and thro' the Flood of Waters, and which had in so miraculous a Manner, safely landed him on the Surface of the newly discovered Land; and the Text tells us, as one of the first Things he was employed in, *He built an Altar unto the Lord, and offered Burnt-Offerings upon the Altar.* Gen. viii. 20.

While *Noah* was thus employed he was safe, the *Devil* himself could no where break in upon him; and we may suppose very reasonably, as he found the old Father invulnerable, he left him for some Years, watching notwithstanding all possible Advantages against his Sons and their Children; for now the Family began to increase, and *Noah*'s Sons had several Children; whether himself had any more Children after the Flood or not, that we are not arrived to any Certainty about.

Among his Sons the *Devil* found *Japhet* and *Shem*, good, pious, religious, and very devout Persons; serving God daily, after the Example of their good old Father *Noah*, and he could make nothing of them or of any of their Posterity; but *Ham* the second, or according to some, the younger Son of *Noah*, had a Son who was named *Canaan*, a loose young profligate Fellow, his Education was probably but cursory and superficial, his Father *Ham* not being near so religious and serious a Man as his Brothers *Shem* and *Japhet* were; and as *Canaan*'s Education was defective, so he proved, as untaught Youth generally do, a wild, and in short a very wicked Fellow, and consequently a fit Tool for the *Devil* to go to work with.

Noah, a diligent industrious Man, being with all his Family thus planted in the rich fruitful Plains of *Armenia*, or wherever you please, let it be near the Mountains of *Caucasus* or *Ararat*; went immediately to work, cultivating and improving the Soil, increasing his Cattle and Pastures, sowing Corn, and among other Things planting Trees for Food, and among the Fruit Trees he planted Vines, of the Grapes thereof he made no doubt, as they still in the same Country do make, most excellent Wine, rich, luscious, strong, and pleasant.

I cannot come into the Notion of our Critics, who to excuse *Noah* from the guilt of what followed, or at least from the Censure, tell us, he knew not the Strength or the Nature of Wine, but that gathering the heavy Clusters of the Grapes, and their own weight crushing out their balmy Juices into his Hand, he tasted the tempting Liquor, and that the *Devil* assisting he was charmed with the delicious Fragrance, and tasted again and again, pressing it out into a Bowl or Dish, that he might take a larger Quantity; till at length the heady Froth ascended and seizing his Brain, he became intoxicate and drunk, not in the least imagining there was any such Strength in the Juice of that excellent Fruit.

But to make out this Story, which is indeed very favorable for *Noah*, but in itself extremely ridiculous, you must necessarily fall into some Absurdities, and beg the Question most egregiously in some particular Cases, which way of arguing will by no means suppose what is suggested; at first you must support there was no such Thing as Wine made before the Deluge, and that no Body had been ever made drunk with the Juice of the Grape before *Noah*, which, I say, is begging the Question in the grossest Manner.

If the Contrary is true, as I see no Reason to question, if, *I say*, it was true that there was Wine drank, and that Men were or had been drunk with it before, they cannot then but suppose that *Noah*, who was a wise, a great and a good Man, and *a Preacher of Righteousness*, both knew of it, and without doubt had in his preaching against their Crimes, preached against this among the rest, upbraided them with it, reproved them for it, and exhorted them against it.

Again, 'tis highly probable they had Grapes growing, and consequently Wines made from them, in the Antediluvian World, how else did *Noah* come by the Vines which he planted? For we are to suppose, he could plant no Trees or Shrubs, but such as he found the Roots of in the Earth, and which no doubt had been there before in their highest Perfection, and had consequently grown up and brought forth the same luscious Fruit before.

Besides, as he found the Roots of the Vines, so he understood what they were, and what Fruit they bore, or else it may be supposed also he would not have planted them; for he planted them for their Fruit, as he did it in the Provision he was making for his Subsistence, and the Subsistence of his Family: and if he did not know what they were, he would not have set them, for he was not planting for Diversion but for Profit.

Upon the whole it seems plain to me he knew what he did, as well when he planted the Vines as when he pressed out the Grapes; and also when he drank the Juice that he knew it was Wine, was strong and would make him drunk if he took enough of it: He knew that other Men had been drunk with such Liquor before the Flood, and that he had reprehended them for it; and therefore it was not his Ignorance, but the *Devil* took him at some Advantage, when his Appetite was eager, or he thirsty, and the Liquor cooling and pleasant; and in short, as *Eve* said, *the Serpent beguilded her*, and she did eat, so the Devil beguiled *Noah*, and *he* did drink; the Temptation was too strong for *Noah*, not the Wine; he knew well enough what he did, but as the Drunkards say to this Day, it was so good he could not forbear it, and so he got drunk before he was aware; or as our ordinary Speech expresses it, *he was overtaken with drink*; and Mr. *Pool* and other Expositors are partly of the same Mind.

No sooner was the poor old Man conquered, and the Wine had lightened his Head, but it may be supposed he falls off from the Chair or Bench where he sate, and tumbling backward his Clothes, which in those hot Countries were only loose open Robes, like the Vests which the *Armenians* wear to this Day, flying abroad, or the *Devil* so assisting on purpose to expose him, he lay there in a naked indecent Posture not fit to be seen.

In this juncture who should come by but young *Canaan*, say some; or as others think, this young Fellow first attacked him by way of Kindness and pretended Affection; prompted his Grandfather to drink, on Pretence of the Wine being good for him, and proper for the Support of his old Age, and subtly set upon him, drinking also with him, and so (his Head being too strong for the old Man's) drank him down, and then, *Devil* like, triumphed over him; boasted of his Conquest, insulted the Body as it were dead, uncovered him on purpose to expose him, and leaving him in that

91

indecent Posture, went and made Sport with it to his Father *Ham*, who in that Part, wicked like himself, did the same to his Brethren *Japhet* and *Shem*; but they like modest and good Men, far from carrying on the wicked Insult on their Parent, went and covered him, as the Scripture expresses it, and as may be supposed informed him how he had been abused, and by whom.

Why else should *Noah*, when he came to himself, show his Resentment so much against *Canaan* his Grandson, rather than against *Ham* his Father, and who 'tis supposed in the Story the guilt chiefly lay upon? we see the Curse is (as it were) laid wholly upon *Canaan* the Grandson, and not a Word of the Father is mentioned, Gen. ix. 25, 26, 27, *Cursed be* Canaan, *a Servant of Servants shall he be*, etc..

That *Ham* was Guilty, that's certain from the History of Fact, but I cannot but suppose his Grandson was the Occasion of it; and in this Case the Devil seems to have made *Canaan* the Instrument or Tool to delude *Noah*, and draw him in to Drunkenness, as he made the Serpent the Tool to beguile *Eve*, and draw her into Disobedience.

Possibly *Canaan* might do it without Design at first, but might be brought in to ridicule and make a Jest of the old Patriarch afterward, as is too frequent since in the Practice of our Days; but I rather believe he did it really with a wicked Design, and on Purpose to expose and insult his Reverend old Parent; and this seems more likely too, because of the great Bitterness with which *Noah* resented it, after he came to be informed of it.

But be that as it will, the *Devil* certainly made a great Conquest here, and as to outward Appearance no less than that which he gained before over *Adam*; nor did the *Devil*'s Victory consist barely in his having drawn in the only righteous Man of the whole Antediluvian World, and so beginning or initiating the new young Progeny with a Crime; but here was the great Oracle silenced at once; the Preacher of Righteousness, for such no doubt he would have been to the new World, as he was to the old, I say, the Preacher was turned out of Office, or his Mouth stopped, which was worse; nay, it was a stopping of his Mouth in the worst kind, far worse than stopping his Breath, for had he died, the Office had descended to his sons *Shem* and *Japhet*, but he was dead to the Office of an Instructor, though alive as to his Being; For of what Force could his Preachings be, who had thus fallen himself into the most shameful and beastly Excess?

Besides some are of the Opinion, though I hope without Ground, that *Noah* was not only overtaken once in his Drink, but that being fallen into that Sin it became habitual, and he continued in it a great while, and that it was this which is the meaning of his being uncovered in his Tent, and that his Son saw his Nakedness; that is, he continually exposed himself for a long Time, a hundred Years, say they, and that his Son *Ham*, and his

Grandson *Canaan* having drawn him into it, kept him in it, encouraged and prompted it, and all the while Satan still prompting them, joined their Scoffs and contempt of him, with their wicked Endeavors to promote the Wickedness; and both with as much Success as the Devil himself could wish for.

Then as for his two Sons modestly and decently covering their Father, they tell us, that Represents *Shem* and *Japhet* applying themselves in an humble and dutiful Manner to their Father, to entreat and beseech him to consider his ancient Glory, his own pious Exhortations to the late drowned World, and to consider the Offence which he gave by his evil Courses to God, and the Scandal to his whole Family, and also that they are brought in effectually prevailing upon him; and that then *Noah* cursed the Wickedness of *Ham*'s degenerate Race, in Testimony of his sincere Repentance after the Fact.

The Story is not so very unlikely as it is certain that it is not to be proved, and therefore we had better take it as we find it (*viz.*) for one single Act; but suppose it was so, 'tis still certain that *Noah*'s Preaching was sadly interrupted, the Energy of his Words flattered, and the Force of his Persuasions enervated and abated, by this shameful Fall; that he was effectually silenced for an Instructor ever after, and this was as much as the Devil had Occasion for; and therefore indeed we read little more of him, except that he lived three hundred and fifty Years after the Flood; nay, we do not so much as read that he had any more Children, but the contrary, nor indeed could *Noah* have any more Children, except by his old and perhaps super-annuated Wife, who it was very likely he had had four or five hundred Year, unless you will suppose he was allowed to marry some of his own Progeny, Daughters or Granddaughters, which we do not suppose was allowed, no not to *Adam* himself.

This was certainly a Master-piece of the *Devil*'s Policy, and a fatal Instance of his unhappy Diligence, (*viz.*) that the Door of the Ark was no sooner open, and the Face of the World hardly dry from the universal Destruction of Mankind, but he was at work among them; and that not only to form a general Defection among the Race, upon the Foot of the original Taint of Nature, but like a bold *Devil* he strikes at the very Root, and flies at the next general Representative of Mankind, attacks the Head of the Family, that in his Miscarriage the Rise and Progress of a Reformation of the new World should receive an early Check, and should be at once prevented; I say, like a bold Devil, he strikes at the Root, and *alas!* poor unhappy *Noah*, he proved too weak for him, *Satan* prevailed in his very first Attempt, and got the Victory over him at once.

Noah thus overcome, and Satan's Conquest carried on to the utmost of his own Wishes, the *Devil* had little more to do in the World for some Ages, than to carry on an universal Degeneracy among Mankind, and to finish it by a like diligent Application, in deluding the Generality of the Race, and them as they came on gradually into Life; this he found the less difficult, because of the first Defection which spread like a Contagion upon the Earth immediately after.

The first Evidence we have of his Success in this mischievous Design was in the Building that great stupendous Stair-case, for such it seems it was intended, called *Babel*, which if the whole World had not been drunk, or otherwise infatuated, they would never have undertaken; even Satan himself could never have prevailed with them to undertake such a preposterous Piece of Work, for it had neither End or Means, Possibility or Probability in it.

I must confess I am sometimes apt to vindicate our old Ancestors, in my Thoughts, from the Charge itself, as we generally understand it, namely, that they really designed to build a Tower which should reach up to Heaven, or that it should secure them in case of another Flood; and Father *Casaubon* is of my Opinion, whether I am of his or no, is a Question by itself; his opinion is that the Confusion was nothing but a Breach among the Undertakers and Directors of the Work, and that the Building was designed chiefly for a Store-house for Provisions, in Case of a second Deluge; as to their Notion of its reaching up to Heaven, he takes the Expression to be allegorical rather than little, and only to mean that it should be exceeding high; perhaps they might not be Astronomers enough to measure the Distance of Space between the Earth and Heaven, as we pretend to do now; but as *Noah* was then alive, and as we believe all his three Sons were so too, they were able to have informed them how absurd it was to suppose either the one or the other (*viz.*) (1.) that they could build up to Heaven, or (2.) that they could build firm enough to resist, or high enough to overtop the Waters, supposing such another Flood should happen; I would rather think it was only that they intended to build a most glorious and magnificent City, where they might all inhabit together; and that this Tower was to be built for Ornament and also for Strength, or as above, and for a Store-house to lay up vast Magazines of Provisions, in Case of extraordinary Floods or other Events, the City being built in a great Plain, namely, the Plains of *Shimar* near the River *Euphrates*.

But the Story, as it is recorded, suits better with Satan's Measures at that Time; and as he was from the Beginning prompting them to every Thing that was contrary to the Happiness of Man, so the more preposterous it was, and the more inconsistent with common Sense, the more to his Purpose; and it showed the more what a complete Conquest he had gained over the Reason as well as the Religion of Mankind at that Time.

Again, 'tis evident in this Case, they were not only acting contrary to the Nature of Things, but contrary to the Design and to the Command of Heaven; for God's Command was that they should replenish the Earth, that is, that they should spread their Habitations over it, and People the whole Globe; whereas they were pitching in one Place, as if they were not to multiply sufficient to take up any more.

But what cared the Devil for that, or to put it a little handsomer, that was what *Satan* aimed at; for it was enough to him, to bring Mankind to act just contrary to what *Heaven* had directed or commanded them in anything, and if possible in every Thing.

But God himself put a stop to this foolish Piece of Work, and it was time indeed to do so, for a madder thing the Devil himself never proposed to them; I say, God himself put a stop to this new Undertaking, and disappointed the Devil; and how was it done? not in Judgment and Anger, as perhaps the Devil expected and hoped for, but as pitying the Simplicity of that dreaming Creature Man, he confused their Speech, or as some say, divided and confused their Councils, so that they could not agree with one another, which would be the same Thing as not to understand one another; or he put a new Shibboleth upon their Tongues, thereby separating them into Tribes or Families, for by this every Family found themselves under a Necessity of keeping together, and this naturally increased that Differing Jargons of Language, for at first it might be no more.

What a Confusion this was to them we all know, by their being obliged to leave off their building, and immediately separating one from another; but what a Surprise it was to the old Serpent, that remains to be considered of, for indeed it belongs to his History.

Satan had never met with any Disappointment in all his wicked Attempts till now; for first, he succeeded even to triumph upon *Eve*, he did the like upon *Cain*, and in short upon the whole World, *one Man* (Noah) *excepted*; when he blended the Sons of God, and the Daughters of Hell, for so the Word is understood, together, in promiscuous voluptuous Living as well as Generation.

As to the Deluge, Authors are not agreed whether it was a Disappointment to the Devil or no, it might be indeed a Surprise to him, for though *Noah* had preached of it for a hundred Year together, yet as he (*Satan*) daily prompted the People not to heed or believe what that old Fellow *Noah* said to them, and to ridicule his whimsical Building a monstrous Tub to swim or float in, when the said Deluge should come; so I am of the Opinion he did not believe it himself, and am positive he could not foresee it, by any insight into Futurity that he was Master of.

It's true the Astronomers tell us, there was a very terrible Comet seen in the Air, that it appeared for 180 Days before the Flood continually; and that as it approached nearer and nearer every Day all the while, so that at last it burst and fell down in a continual Spout or Stream of Water, being of a watery Substance, and the Quantity so great, that it was forty Days a falling; so that this Comet not only foretold the Deluge or drowning of the Earth, but actually performed it, and drowned it from itself.

But to leave this Tale to them that told it, let us consider the Devil, surprised, and a little amazed at the Absorption or Inundation, or whatever we are to call it, of the Earth in the Deluge, not, I say, that he was much concerned at it, perhaps just the Contrary; and if God would drown it again, and as often as he thought fit, I do not see by anything I meet with in Satan's History, or in the Nature of him, that he would be at all disturbed at it; all that I can see in it, that could give Satan any Concern, would be that all his Favorites were gone, and he had his Work to do over again, to lay a Foundation for a new Conquest in the Generation that was to come; But in this his Prospect was fair enough, for why should he be discouraged, when he had now eight People to work upon, who met with such Success when he had but two? and why should he question breaking in now where Nature was already vitiated and corrupted, when he had before conquered the same Nature, when in its primitive Rectitude and Purity, just come out of the Hands of its Maker, and fortified with the Awe of his high and solemn Command just given them, and the threatening of Death also annexed to it, if broken?

But I go back to the Affair of *Babel*: This Confusion of Language or of Councils, take it which way you will, as the first Disappointment that I find the Devil met with, in all his Attempts and Practices upon Mankind, or upon the new Creature, which I mentioned above; for now he foresaw what would follow; namely, that the People would separate and spread themselves over the whole Surface of the Earth, and a thousand new Scenes of Actions would appear, in which he therefore prepares himself to behave as he should see Occasion.

How the Devil learned to speak all the Languages that were now to be used, and how many languages they were, the several ancient Writers of the *Devil*'s Story have not yet determined; some tell us they were divided only into fifteen, some into seventy two, others into one hundred and eighty, and others again into several Thousands.

It also remains a doubt with me, and, I suppose, will be so with others also, whether Satan has yet found out a Method to converse with Mankind, without the Help of Language and Words, or not: Seeing Man has no other Medium of Conversing, no not with himself: This I have not time to enter upon here; however, this seems plain to me (*viz.*) that the *Devil* soon learned to make Mankind understand him, whatever Language he spoke, and no doubt but he found Ways and Means to understand them, whatever Language they spoke.

After the Confusion of Languages, the People necessarily sorted themselves into Families and Tribes, every Family understanding their own particular Speech, and that only; and these Families multiplying grew into Nations, and those Nations wanting Room, and seeking out Habitations wandered some this Way, some that, till they found out Countries respectively proper for their settling, and there they became a Kingdom, spreading and possessing still more and more Land as their People increased, till at last the whole Earth was scarce big enough for them: This presented *Satan* with an Opportunity to break in upon their Morals at another Door, (*viz.*) their Pride; for Men being naturally Proud and Envious, Nations and Tribes began to jostle with one another for Room; either one Nation enjoyed better Accommodations, or had a better Soil or a more favorable Climate than another; and these being numerous and strong thrust the other out, and encroached upon their Land; the other liking their Situation, prepare for their Defense, and so began Oppression, Invasion, War, Battle and Blood, Satan all the while beating the Drums, and his Attendants clapping their Hands, as Men do when they set Dogs on upon one another.

The bringing Mankind thus to *War* and *Confusion*, as it was the first Game the Devil played after the confounding of Languages and Divisions at *Babel* so it was a Conquest upon Mankind, purely devilish, born from Hell, and so exactly tinctured with Satan's original Sin *Ambition*, that it really transformed Men into mere Devils; for when is Man transformed into the very Image of Satan himself, when is he turned into a mere Devil, if it is not when he is fighting with his fellow Creatures and dipping his Hands in the Blood of his own Kind? Let his Picture be considered, the Fire of Hell flames or sparkles in his Eyes, a voracious Grin sits upon his Countenance; Rage and Fury distort the Muscles of his Face; his Passions agitate his whole Body, and he is metamorphosed from a comely Beauteous angelic Creature into a *Fury*, a *Satyr*, a terrible and frightful Monster, nay, into a *Devil*; for *Satan* himself is described by the same Word which on his very Account is changed into a Substantive, and the Devils are called *Furies*.

This sowing the Seeds of Strife in the World, and bringing Nations to fight and make War upon one another, would take up a great Part of the *Devil's* History, and abundance of extraordinary Things would occur in relating the particulars; for there have been very great Conflagrations kindled in the World, by the Artifice of Hell, under this Head, (*viz.*) of making War; in which it has been the *Devil's* Master-piece, and he has indeed shown himself a Workman in it, that he has wheedled Mankind into strange unnatural Notions of things, in order to propagate and support the fighting Principle in the World; such as Laws of War, fair Fighting, behaving like Men of Honor, fighting at the last Drop, and the like, by which killing and murdering is understood to be justifiable. Virtue and a true Greatness in Spirit is rated now by Rules which God never appointed, and the Standard of Honor is quite different from that of Reason and of Nature: Bravery is denominated not from a fearless undaunted Spirit in the just Defense of Life and Liberty, but from a daring Defiance of God and Man, fighting, killing and treading under Foot his fellow Creatures, at the ordinary Command of the Officer, whether it be right or wrong, and whether it be in a just Defense of Life, and our Country's Life, that is Liberty, or whether it be for the Support of Injury and Oppression.

A prudent avoiding causeless Quarrels is called Cowardice, and to take an affront Baseness, and Meanness of Spirit; to refuse fighting, and putting Life at a Cast on the Point of a Sword, a Practice forbid by the Laws of God and of all good Government, is yet called Cowardice; and a Man is bound to die dueling, or live and be laughed at.

This trumping up these imaginary Things called Bravery and Gallantry, naming them Virtue and Honor, is all from the *Devil*'s new Management, and his subtle influencing the Minds of Men to fly in the Face of God and Nature, and to act against his Senses; nor but for his Artifice in the Management, could it be possible that such Inconsistencies could go down with Mankind, or they could pass such absurd Things among them for reasoning; for Example, A is found in Bed with B's Wife, B is the Person injured, and therefore offended, and coming into the Chamber with his Sword in his Hand, A exclaims loudly, *Why Sir, you won't murder me, will you? as you are a Man of Honor let me rise and take my Sword.*

A very good Story indeed! fit for nobody but the Devil to put into any Man's Head; But so it is, B being put in mind, forsooth, that he is *a Man of Honor*, starts back and must act the honorable Part; so he lets A get up, put on his Clothes and take his Sword; then they fight, and B is killed for his Honor; whereas had the Laws of God, of Nature and of Reason taken Place, the Adulterer and the Adulteress should have been taken Prisoners and carried before the Judge, and being taken in the Fact, should have been immediately sentenced, he to the Block and she to the Stake, and the innocent abused Husband had no Reason to have run any Risque of his Life for being made a Cuckold.

But thus has *Satan* abused the Reason of Man; and if a Man does me the greatest Injury in the World, I must do myself Justice upon him, by venturing my life upon an even Lay with him, and must fight him upon equal Hazard, in which the injured Person is as often killed as the Person offering the Injury: Suppose now it be in the same Case *as above*, a Man abuses my Wife, and then to give me Satisfaction, tells me, he will fight me, which the *French* call *doing me Reason*; *No Sir*, say I, *let me lie with your Wife too, and then if you desire it, I may fight you; then I am upon even Terms with you*; but this indeed is the Reasoning which the *Devil* has brought Mankind too at this Day: But to go back to the Subject, *viz.* the Devil bringing the Nations to fall out, and to quarrel for Room in the World, and so to fight in order to dispossess one another of their Settlements: This began at a Time when certainly there were Places enough in the World for everyone to choose in, and therefore the *Devil*, not the want of Elbow-room, must be the Occasion of it; and 'tis carried on ever since, as apparently from the same Interest, and by the same original.

But we shall meet with this Part again very often in the *Devil's* Story, and as we bring him farther on in the Management of Mankind, I therefore lay it by for the Present, and come to the next Steps the *Devil* took with Mankind after the Confusion of Languages, and this was in the Affair of Worship; It does not appear yet that ever the *Devil* was so bold, as either,

1. To set himself up to be worshipped as a God, or which was still worse,

2. To persuade Man to believe there was no God at all to worship.

Both these are introduced since the Deluge, *one* indeed by the *Devil*, who soon found Means to set himself up for a God in many Parts of the World, and holds it to this Day; but the *last* is brought in by the Invention of Man, in which it must be confessed Man has out-sinned the Devil; for to do Satan justice, he never thought it could ever pass upon Mankind, or that any Thing so gross would go down with them; so that, *in short*, these modern Casuists, in the Reach of our Days, have, *I say*, out-sinned the *Devil*.

As then both these are modern Inventions, *Satan* went on gradually, and being to work upon human Nature by Stratagem, not by Force, it would have been too gross to have set himself up as an Object of Worship at first, it was to be done Step by Step; *for Example*.

1. It was sufficient to bring Mankind to a Neglect of God, to worship him by halves, and give little or no Regard to his Laws, and so grow loose and immoral, in direct Contradiction to his Commands; this would not go down with them at first, so the Devil went on gradually.

2. From a Negligence in worshiping the true God, he by Degrees introduced the worship of false Gods; and to introduce this he began with the *Sun*, *Moon*, and *Stars*, called in the holy Text the Host of Heaven; these had greater Majesty upon them, and seemed fitter to command the Homage of Mankind; so it was not the hardest Thing in the World, to bring Men, when they had once forgotten the true God, to embrace the Worship of such Gods as those.

3. Having thus debauched their Principles in Worship, and led them from the true and only Object of Worship to a false, it was the easier to carry them on; so in a few Gradations more he brought them to downright Idolatry, and even in that Idolatry he proceeded gradually too; for he began with awful Names, such as were venerable in the Thoughts of Men, as Baal or Bell, which, in *Chaldaick* and *Hebrew*, signifies Lord or

Sovereign, or Mighty and Magnificent, and this was therefore a Name ascribed at first to the true God; but afterwards they descended to make Images and Figures to represent him, and then they were called by the same Name, as *Baal*, *Baalim*, and afterwards *Bell*; from which, by a hellish Degeneracy, Saturn brought Mankind to adore every Block of their own hewing, and to worshipping Stocks, Stones, Monsters, Hobgoblins, and every sordid frightful Thing, and at last the *Devil* himself.

What Notions some People may entertain of the Forwardness of the first Ages of the World, to run into Idolatry, I do not enquire here; I know they tell us strange Things, of its being the Product of mere Nature, one remove from its primitive State; but I, who pretend to have so critically enquired into *Satan*'s History, can assure you, and that from very good Authority, that the *Devil* did not find it so easy a task to obliterate the Knowledge of the true God, in the Minds and Consciences of Men, as those People suggest.

It is true he carried Things a great Length under the Patriarchal Government of the first Ages, but still he was sixteen hundred Years bringing it to pass; and though we have Reason to believe the old World, before the Flood was arrived to a very great Height of Wickedness, and *Ovid* very nobly describes it by the War of the *Titans* against *Jupiter*, yet we do not read that ever Satan was come to such a Length as to bring them to Idolatry; indeed we do read of Wars carried on among them, whether it was one Nation against another, or only Personal, we cannot tell; But the World seemed to be swallowed up in a Life of Wickedness, that is to say, of Luxury and Lewdness, Rapine and Violence, and there were *Giants* among them, and Men of Renown, that is to say, Men famed for their mighty Velour, great Actions of War we may suppose, and their Strength, who personally opposed others. We read of no considerable Wars indeed, but 'tis not to be doubted but there was such Wars, or else it is to be understood that they lived (in common) a Life somewhat like the Brutes, the Strong devouring the Weak; for the Text says, *the whole Earth was filled with Violence*, hunting and tearing one another in Pieces, either for Dominion or for Wealth, either for Ambition or for Avarice, we know not well which.

Thus far the old Antediluvian World went, and very wicked they were, there is no doubt of that; but we have Reason to believe that was no Idolatry, the *Devil* had not brought them to that Length yet: perhaps it would soon have followed, but the Deluge intervened.

After the Deluge, *as I have said*, he had all his Work to do over again, and he went on by the same Steps; *first* he brought them to Violence and War, then to Oppression and Tyranny, then to neglect of true Worship, then to false worship, and then Idolatry by the mere natural Consequence of the Thing; who were the first Nation or People that fell from the Worship of the true God, is something hard to determine; the *Devil*, who certainly of all *God*'s Creatures is best able to inform us, having left us nothing upon Record upon that Subject, but we have Reason to believe it was thus introduced.

Nimrod was the Grandson of *Ham*, *Noah*'s second Son, the same who was cursed by his Father for exposing him in his Drunkenness: This *Nimrod* was the first who it seems *Satan* picked out for a Hero: Here he inspired him with ambitious Thoughts, dreams of Empire, and having the Government of all the Rest, *that is to say*, universal Monarchy; the very same Bait with which he has plaid upon the Frailty of Princes, and ensnared the greatest of them ever since, even from his most August Imperial Majesty King *Nimrod* the first, to his most Christian Majesty *Louis* the XIV. and many a mighty Monarch between.

When these mighty Monarchs and Men of Fame went off the Stage, the World had their Memories in esteem many Ages after; and as their great Actions were no otherwise recorded than by oral Tradition, and the Tongues and Memories of fallible Men, Time and the Custom of magnifying the past Actions of Kings, Men soon fabled up their Histories, *Satan assisting*, into Miracle and Wonder: Hence their Names were had in Veneration more and more; Statues and Bustoes representing their Persons and great Actions were set up in public Places, till from Heroes and Champions they made Gods of them, and thus (*Satan* prompting) the World was quickly filled with Idols.

This *Nimrod* is he, who according to the received Opinion, though I do not find Satan's History exactly concurring with it, was first called *Belus*, then *Baal*, and worshipped in most of the eastern Countries under those Names; sometimes with Additions of Sir-names, according to the several countries, or People, or Towns where he was particularly set up, as *Baal Peor, Baal Zephon, Baal Phegor*, and in other Places plain *Baal*, as *Jupiter* in after Times had the like Additions; as *Jupiter Ammon, Jupiter Capitolinus, Jupiter Pistor, Jupiter Feretrius*, and about ten or twelve *Jupiters* more.

I must acknowledge, that I think it was a Master-piece of Hell to bring the World to Idolatry so soon after they had had such an eminent Example of the infinite Power of the true God, as was seen in the Deluge, and particularly in the Escape of *Noah* in the Ark, to bring them (even before *Noah* or his Sons were dead) to forget whose Hand it was, and give the Homage of the World to a Name, and that a Name of a mortal Man dead and rotten, who was famous for nothing when he was alive but Blood and War; I say, to bring the World to set up this Nothing, this mere Name, nay the very Image and Picture of him for *a God*, it was *first* a Mark of most prodigious Stupidity in the whole Race of Men, a monstrous Degeneracy from Nature, and even from common Sense; and in the next Place 'twas a token of an inexpressible Craft and Subtlety in the *Devil*, who had now gotten the People into so full and complete a Management, that in short, he could have brought them, by the same Rule, to have worshipped any thing; and in a little while more, did bring many of them to worship himself, *plain Devil as he was*, and knowing him to be such.

As to the Antiquity of this horrible Defection of Mankind, though we do not find the beginning of it particularly recorded, yet we are certain it was not long after the Confusion of *Babel*; for *Nimrod*, as is said, was no more than *Noah*'s great Grandson and *Noah* himself, I suppose, might be alive some Years after *Nimrod* was born; and as *Nimrod* was not long dead, before they forgot that he was a Tyrant and a Murderer, and made a *Baal*, that is a Lord or Idol of him, I say, he was not long dead, for *Nimrod* was born in the Year of the World 1847, and built *Babylon* the Year 1879; and we find *Terah* the Father of *Abraham*, who lived from the Year 1879 was an Idolater, as was doubtless *Bethuel*, who was *Terah*'s Grandson; for we find *Laban*, who was *Bethuel*'s Son, was so, and all this was during the Life of the first Post-Diluvian Family, for *Terah* was born within one hundred ninety three Years after the Flood, and one hundred fifty seven Years before *Noah* was dead; and even *Abram* himself was eight and fifty Years old before *Noah* died, and yet Idolatry had been then, in all probability, above an hundred Years practiced in the World.

> N. B. It is worth Remark here, what a terrible Advantage the Devil gained by the debauching poor *Noah*, and drawing him into the Sin of Drunkenness; for by this, as I said, he silenced and stopped the Mouth of the great Preacher of Righteousness, that Father and Patriarch of the whole World, who not being able for the Shame of his own foul Miscarriage, to pretend to instruct or reprove the World any more, the *Devil* took hold of them immediately, and for want of a Prophet to warn and admonish, ran that little of Religion which there might be left in *Shem* and *Japhet*, quite out of the World, and deluged them all in Idolatry.

How long the whole World may be said to be thus overwhelmed in Ignorance and Idolatry, we may make some tolerable guess at by the History of *Abraham*; for it was not till God called him from his Father's House, that any such Thing as a Church was established in the World; nor even then, except in his own Family and Successors for almost four hundred Years after that Call; and till God brought the *Israelites* back out of *Egypt*, the whole World may be said to be involved in Idolatry and *Devil* worship.

So absolute a Conquest had the *Devil* made over Mankind immediately after the Flood, and all taking its Rise and Beginning at the fatal Defeat of *Noah*, who had he lived untainted and invulnerable, as he had done for six hundred Years before, would have gone a great way to have stemmed the

Torrent of Wickedness which broke in upon Mankind; and therefore the *Devil*, I say, was very cunning and very much in the Right of it, take him as he is a mere *Devil*, to attack *Noah* personally, and give him a Blow so soon.

It is true, the *Devil* did not immediately raze out the Notion of Religion and of a God from the Minds of Men, nor could he easily suppress the Principle of Worship and Homage to be paid to a Sovereign Being, the Author of Nature and Guide of the World; the *Devil* saw this clearly in the first Ages of the new World, and therefore, as I have said, he proceeded politically and by Degrees: That it was so, is evident from the Story of *Job* and his three Friends, who, if we may take it for a History, not a Fable, and may judge of the Time of it by the Length of *Job*'s Life, and by the Family of *Eliphaz* the *Temanite*, who it is manifest was at least Grandson or Great Grandson to *Esau Isaac*'s eldest Son, and by the Language of *Abimilech* King of *Gerar* to *Abraham*, and of *Laban* to *Jacob*, both the Latter being at the same Time Idolaters; I say, if we may judge of it by all these, there were still very sound Notions of Religion in the Minds of Men; nor could Satan with all his Cunning and Policy deface those *Ideas*, and root them out of the Minds of the People.

And this put him upon taking new Measures to keep up his Interest and preserve the Hold he got upon Mankind; and his Method was like himself, subtle and politick to the last Degree, as his whole History makes appear; for seeing he found they could not but believe the Being of a God, and that they would needs worship something, it is evident, he had no Game left him to play but this, namely, to set up wrong Notions of Worship, and bring them to a false Worship instead of a True, supposing the Object worshipped to be still the same.

To finish this Stratagem, he first insinuates that the true God was a terrible, a dreadful, unapproachable Being; that to see him was so frightful, that it would be present Death; that to worship him immediately, was a Presumption which would provoke his Wrath; and that as he was a *consuming Fire* in himself, so he would burn up those in his Anger that dared to offer up any Sacrifice to him, but by the Interposition of some Medium which might receive their Adorations in his Name.

Hence it occurred presently, that subordinate Gods were to be found out and set up, to whom the People might pay the Homage due to the supreme God, and who they might worship in his Name; this I take from the most ancient Account of Idolatry in the World; nor indeed could the Devil himself find out any other Reason why Men should Canonize or rather Deify their Princes and Men of Fame, and worship them after they were dead, as if they could save them from Death and Calamity, who were not able to save themselves when they were alive; much less could *Satan* bring Men to swallow so gross, so absurd a Thing as the bowing the Knee to a Stock or a Stone, a Calf, an Ox, a Lion, nay the Image or Figure of a Calf, such as the *Israelites* made at Mount *Sinai*, and say, *These be thy Gods, O Israel, who brought thee out of the Land of* Egypt.

Having thus, I say, brought them to satisfy themselves that they worshipped the true God and no other, under the Figures and Appearances which they made to represent him, it was easy after that to worship anything for the true God; and thus in a few Ages they worshipped nothing but Idols, even throughout the whole World; nor has the *Devil* lost this hold in some Parts of the World, nay not in most Parts of the World to this Day; He holds still all the Eastern Parts of *Asia*, and the Southern Parts of *Africa*, and the Northern Parts of *Europe*, and in them the vast Countries of *China* and *Tartary*, *Persia* and *India*, *Guinea*, *Ethiopia*, *Zanquebar*, *Congo*, *Angola*, *Monomotapa*, etc.. in all which, *except Ethiopia*, we find no Vestiges of any other worship but that of Idols, Monsters, and even the *Devil* himself; till after the very coming of our Saviour, and even then, if it be true that the Gospel was preached in the *Indies* and *China* by St. *Thomas*, and in other remote Countries by other of the Apostles; we see that whatever Ground *Satan* lost, he seems to have recovered it again; and all *Asia* and *Africa* is at present overrun with Paganism or Mahometanism, which I think of the two is rather the worst; Besides all *America*, a Part of the World, as some say, equal in Bigness to all the other, in which the *Devil's* Kingdom was never interrupted from its first being inhabited, *whenever it was*, to the first Discovery of it by the *European* Nations in the sixteenth Century.

In a Word, the *Devil* got what we may call an entire Victory over Mankind, and drove the Worship of the true God, in a Manner quite out of the World, forcing, *as it were*, his Maker in a new kind of Creation, the old one proving thus ineffectual to recover a certain Number by Force and mere Omnipotence to return to their Duty, serve him and worship him; *But of that hereafter.*

Chapter XI

Of God's calling a Church out of the midst of a degenerate World, and of Satan's new Measures upon that Incident: How he attacked them immediately, and his Success in those Attacks

Satan having, as I have said in the preceding Chapter, made, as it were, a full Conquest of Mankind, debauched them all to Idolatry, and brought them at least to worshiping the true God by the wretched Medium of corrupt and idolatrous Representations; God seemed to have no true Servants or Worshippers left in the World, but if I may be allowed to speak so, was obliged, in order to restore the World to their Senses again, to call a select Number out from among the rest, who he himself undertook should own his Godhead or supreme Authority, and worship him as he required to be worshipped; this, *I say*, God was obliged to do, because 'tis evident it has not been done so much by the Choice and Council of Men, *for Satan would have over-ruled that Part*, as by the Power and Energy of some irresistible and invincible Operation, and this our Divines give high Names to; but be it what they will, it is the second Defeat or Disappointment that the *Devil* he met with in his Progress in the World; the first I have spoken of already.

It is true, Satan very well understood what was threatened to him in the original Promise to the Woman, immediately after the Fall, namely, *thou shalt bruise his Head*, etc.. but he did not expect it so suddenly, but thought himself sure of Mankind, till the Fullness of Time when the Messiah should come; and therefore it was a great Surprise to him, to see that *Abraham* being called was so immediately received and established, though he did not so immediately follow the Voice that directed him, yet in him, in his Loins was all God's Church at that time contained.

In the calling *Abraham*, it is easy to see that there was no other way for God to form a Church, that is to say, to single out a People to himself, as the World was then stated, but by immediate Revelation and a Voice from Heaven: All Mankind were gone over to the Enemy, overwhelmed in Idolatry, in a Word, were engaged to the *Devil*; God Almighty, or as the Scripture distinguishes him, *the Lord*, the true God, was out of the Question; Mankind knew little or nothing of him, much less did they know anything of his Worship, or that there was such a Being in the World.

Well might it be said the *Lord* appeared to *Abraham*, Gen. xii. 7. for if God had not appeared himself, he must have sent a Messenger from Heaven, *and perhaps it was so too*, for he had not one true Servant or Worshiper that we know of then on Earth, to send on that Errand; no Prophet, no Preacher of Righteousness, *Noah* was dead, and had been so above seventeen Year; and if he had not, his preaching, as I observed after his great Miscarriage, had but little Effect; we are indeed told, that *Noah* left behind him certain Rules and Orders for the true Worship of God, which were called the Precepts of *Noah*, and remained in the World for a long Time; though how written, when neither any Letters, much less Writing were known in the World, is a Difficulty which Remains to be solved; and this makes me look upon those Laws called the Precepts of *Noah* to be a modern Invention, as I do also the *Alphabetum Noachi*, which *Bochart* pretends to give an Account of.

But to leave that Fiction, and come back to *Abraham*; God called him, whether at first by Voice without any Vision, whether in a Dream or Night Vision, which was very Significant in those Days, or whether by some awful Appearance, we know not; the second Time, 'tis indeed said expressly God appeared to him; Be it which Way it will, God himself called him, showed him the Land of *Canaan*, gave him the Promise of it for his Posterity, and withal gave him such a Faith, that the *Devil* soon found there was no room for him to meddle with *Abraham*. This is certain, we do not read that the *Devil* ever so much as attempted *Abraham* at all; some will suggest that the Command to *Abraham* to go and offer up his Son *Isaac*, was a Temptation of the *Devil*, if possible to defeat the glorious Work of God's calling a holy Seed into the World; for the *first*, if *Abraham* had disobeyed that Call, the new Favorite had been overcome and made a Rebel of, or *secondly*, if he had *obeyed*, then the promised Seed had been cut off, and *Abraham* defeated; but as the Text is express that God himself proposed it to *Abraham*, I shall not start the Suggestions of the Critics, in Bar of the sacred Oracle.

Be it one way or other, *Abraham* showed a Hero-like Faith and Courage, and if the *Devil* had been the Author of it, he had seen himself disappointed in both his Views; (1.) by *Abraham*'s ready and bold Compliance, as believing it to be God's Command; and (2.) by the divine Countermand of the Execution, just as the fatal Knife was lifted up.

But if the *Devil* left *Abraham*, and made no attack upon him, seeing him invulnerable, he made himself amends upon the other Branch of his Family, his poor *Nephew* Lot; who, notwithstanding he was so immediately under the particular Care of Heaven, as that the Angel who was sent to destroy *Sodom*, could do nothing till he was out of it; and who, though after he had left *Zoar*, and was retired into a Cave to dwell, yet the subtle *Devil* found him out, deluded his two Daughters, took an Advantage of the Fright they had been in about *Sodom* and *Gomorrah*, made them believe the whole World was burnt too, as well as those Cities, and that in short, they could never have any *Husbands*, etc.. and so in their abundant Concern to repeople the World, and that the Race of Mankind might not be destroyed, they go and lie with their own *Father*; the *Devil* telling them doubtless how to do it, by intoxicating his Head with Wine; in all which Story, whether they were not as drunk as their Father, seems to be a Question, or else they could not have supposed all the Men in the Earth were consumed, when they knew that the little City *Zoar* had been preserved for their Sakes.

This now was the third Conquest *Satan* obtained by the Gust of humane Appetite; that is to say, once by Eating and twice by Drinking, or Drunkenness, and still the last was the worst and most shameful; for *Lot*, however his Daughters managed him, could not pretend he did not understand what the Strength of Wine was; and one would have thought after so terrible a Judgment as that of *Sodom* was, which was, as we may say, executed before his Face, his Thoughts should have been too solemnly engaged in praising God for sparing his Life, to be made drunk, and that two Nights together.

But the *Devil* played his Game sure, he set his two Daughters to work, and as the *Devil's* Instruments seldom fail, so he secured his by that hellish Stratagem of deluding the Daughters, to think all the World was consumed but they two and their Father: To be sure the old Man could not suspect that his Daughters Design was so wicked as indeed it was, or that they intended to debauch him with Wine, and make him drink till he knew not what he did.

Now the *Devil* having carried his Game here, gained a great Point; for as there were but two religious Families in the World before, from whence a twofold Generation might be supposed to rise religious and righteous like their Parents, (*viz.*) that of *Abraham* and this of *Lot*; this Crime ruined the Hopes of one of them; it could no more be said that just *Lot* was in Being, who vexed his *righteous Soul* from Day to Day with the wicked Behavior of the People of *Sodom*; righteous *Lot* was degenerated into drunken incestuous *Lot*, Lot fallen from what he was, to be a wicked and unrighteous Man; no pattern of Virtue, no Reprover of the Age, but a poor fallen Degenerate Patriarch, who could now no more reprove or exhort, but look down and be ashamed, and nothing to do but to repent; and see the poor mean Excuses of all the three.

Eve says, *The Serpent beguiled me, and I did eat.*

Noah says, —— *My Grandson beguiled me, or the Wine beguiled me, and I did drink.*

Lot says, *My Daughters beguiled me, and I also did drink.*

It is observable, that as I said above, *Noah* was silenced, and his Preaching at an End, after that one Action, so the like may be said of *Lot*; and in short, you never hear one Word more of either of them after it; as for Mankind, both were useless to them, and as to themselves, we never read of any of their Repentance, nor have we much Reason to believe they did repent.

From this Attack of the *Devil* upon *Lot*, we hear no more of the *Devil* being so busily employed as he had been before in the World; he had indeed but little to do, for all the rest of the World was his own, lulled asleep under the Witchcraft of Idolatry, and are so still.

But it could not be long that the *Devil* lay idle; as soon as God called himself a People, the *Devil* could not be at Rest; till he attacked them.

'Wherever God sets up a House of Prayer,
'The Devil always builds a Chapel there.

Abraham indeed went off the Stage free, and so did *Isaac* too, they were a Kind of first Rate Saints; we do not so much as read of any failing they had, or of any Thing the *Devil* had ever the Face to offer to them; no, or with *Jacob* either, if you will excuse him for beguiling his Brother *Esau*, of both his Birthright and his Blessing, but he was busy enough with all his Children; for Example,

He sent *Judah* to his Sheep-shearing, and placed a Whore (*Tamar*) in his Way, in the Posture of Temptation, so made him commit Incest and Whoredom both together.

He sent incestuous *Reuben* to lie with his Father's Concubine *Billah*.

He sent *Dinah* to the Ball, to dance with the *Sichemite* Ladies, and play the Whore with their Master.

He enraged *Simeon* and *Levi*, at the supposed Injury, and then prompted them to Revenge, for which their Father heartily cursed them.

He set them all together to fall upon poor *Joseph*, first to murder him intentionally, and then actually sell him to the *Midianites*.

He made them show the Party-colored Coat, and tell a lie to their Father, to make the poor old Man believe *Joseph* was killed by a Lion, *etc.*.

He sent *Potiphar*'s Wife to attack *Joseph*'s Chastity, and filled her with Rage at the Disappointment.

He taught *Joseph* to swear by the Life of *Pharaoh*.

In a Word, he debauched the whole Race, except *Benjamin*, and never Man had such a Set of Sons, so wicked and so notorious, after so good an Introduction into the World as they all of them had, *to be sure*; for *Jacob*, no doubt, gave them as good Instruction as the Circumstances of his wandering Condition would allow him to do.

We must now consider the *Devil* and his Affairs in a quite differing Situation: When the World first appeared peopled by the creating Power of God, he had only *Adam* and *Eve* to take care of, and I think he played his Time with them to purpose enough: After the Deluge he had *Noah* only to pitch upon, and he quickly conquered him by the Instigation of his *Grandson*.

At the Building of *Babel* he guided them by their acting all in a Body as one Man; so that in short he managed them with ease, taking them as a Body politic; and we find they came into his Snare as one Man; but Now, the Children of *Israel* multiplying in the Land of their Bondage, and God seeming to show a particular Concern for them, the *Devil* was obliged to new Measures, stand at a Distance, and look on for some Time.

The *Egyptians* were plagued even without his Help, nor though the cunning Artist, as I said, stood and looked on, yet he durst not meddle; nor could he make a few Lice, the least and meanest of the Armies of Insects raised to afflict the *Egyptians*.

However, when he perceived that God resolved to bring the *Israelites* out, he prepared to attend them, to watch them, and be at Hand upon all the wicked Occasions that might offer, as if he had been fully satisfied such Occasions would offer, and that he should not fail to have an Opportunity to draw them into some Snare or another, and that therefore it was his Business not to be out of the Way, but to be ready (as we say) to make his Market of them in the best Manner he could: How many Ways he attempted them, nay, how many Times he conquered them in their Journey, we shall see presently.

First he put them in a fright at *Baal-Zephon*, where he thought he had drawn them into a Noose, and where he sent *Pharaoh* and his Army to block them up between the Mountains of *Piahiroth* and the *Red Sea*; but there indeed *Satan* was outwitted by *Moses*, so far as it appeared to be a humane Action, for he little thought of their going dry footed *thro' the Sea*, but depended upon having them all cut in Pieces the next Morning by the *Egyptians*; an eminent Proof, *by the Way*, that the *Devil* has *no Knowledge of Events*, or any Insight into Futurity; nay that he has not so much as a second Sight, or knows to Day what his Maker intends to do to Morrow; for had *Satan* known that God intended to Ford them over the

Sea, if he had not been able to have prevented the Miracle, he would certainly have prevented the Escape, by sending out *Pharaoh* and his Army time enough to have taken the Strand before them, and so have driven them to the Necessity of travelling on Foot round the North Point of that Sea, by the Wilderness of *Etan*, where he would have pursued and harassed them with his Cavalry, and in all Probability have destroyed them: But the blind short-sighted Devil, perfectly in the Dark, and unacquainted with Futurity, knew nothing of the Matter, was as much deceived as *Pharaoh* himself, stood still flattering himself with the Hopes of his Booty, and the Revenge he should take upon them the next Morning; till he saw the startled Waves in an Uproar, and to his utter Astonishment and Confusion saw the Passage laid open, and *Moses* leading his vast Army in full March over the dry Space; nay even then 'tis very probable Satan did not know that if the *Egyptians* followed them, the Sea would return upon and overwhelm them; for I can hardly think so hard of the *Devil* himself, that if he had, he would have suffered, much less prompted *Pharaoh* to follow the Chase at such an Expense; so that either he must be an ignorant unforeseeing Devil, or a very ungrateful false *Devil* to his Friends the *Egyptians*.

I am inclined also to the more charitable Opinion of Satan too, because the Escape of the *Israelites* was really a Triumph over himself; for the War was certainly his, or at least he was auxiliary to *Pharaoh*, it was a Victory over *Hell* and *Egypt* together, and he would never have suffered the Disgrace, if he had known it beforehand; that is to say, though he could not have prevented the Escape of *Israel*, or the dividing the Water, yet he might have warned the *Egyptians*, and cautioned them not to venture in after them.

But we shall see a great many weak Steps taken by the Devil in the Affair of this very People and their forty Years Wandering in the Wilderness; and though he was in some things successful, and wheedled them into many foolish and miserable Murmurings and Wrangling against God, and Mutinies against poor *Moses*, yet the *Devil* was oftentimes baulked and disappointed; and 'tis for this Reason that I choose to finish the first Part of his History with the particular Relation of his Behavior among the *Jews*, because also, we do not find any extraordinary Things happening anywhere else in the World for above one thousand five hundred Years, no Variety, no Revolutions; all the Rest of Mankind lay still under his Yoke, quietly submitted to his Government, did just as he bad them, worshipped every Idol he set up, and in a Word, he had no Difficulty with any Body but the *Jews*, and for this Reason, I say, this Part of his Story will be the more useful and instructing.

To return therefore to *Moses* and his dividing the *Red Sea*; that the People went over or thro' it, that we have the sacred History for; but how the Devil behaved, that you must come to me for, or I know not where you will find a true Account of it, at least not in Print.

1. It was in the Night they marched thro', whether the *Devil* saw it in the Dark or no, that's not my Business.

But when he had Day-Light for it, and viewed the next Day's Work, I make no Question but *all Hell felt the Surprise*, the Prey being thus snatched out of their Hands unexpectedly. It's true the *Egyptians* Host was sent to him in their Room, but that was not what he aimed at; for he was sure enough of them his own Way, and if it was not *just at that Time*, yet he knew what and who they were; but as he had devoured the whole *Israelites* Host in his Imagination, to the Tune of at least a Million and a half of Souls; Men, Women and Children; it was, no doubt, a great Disappointment to the Devil to miss of his Prey, and to see them all triumphing on the other Side in Safety.

It is true, *Satan's* Annals do not mention this Defeat, for Historians are generally backward to register their own Misfortunes; but as we have an Account of the Fact from other Hands, so as we cannot question the Truth of it; the Nature of the Thing will tell us it was a Disappointment to the *Devil*, and a very great one too.

I cannot but observe here, that I think this Part of the *Devil's* Story very entertaining, because of the great Variety of Incidents which appear in every Part of it; sometimes he is like a hunted Fox, curveting and counter-running to avoid his being pursued and found out, while at the same time he is carrying on his secret Designs to draw the People he pretends to manage, into some Snare or other to their Hurt; at another time, though the Comparison is a little too low for his Dignity, like a Monkey that has done Mischief, and who making his own Escape sits and chatters at a Distance, as if he had trumped in what he had done; so Satan, when he had drawn them in to worship a Calf, to offer strange Fire, to set up a Schism, and the like; and so to bring the Divine Vengeance upon themselves, leaving them in their Distress, kept at a Distance, as if he looked on with Satisfaction to see them Burnt, swallowed up, swept away, and the like; as the several Stories relate.

His indefatigable Vigilance is, on the other hand, a useful Caveat, as well as an improving View to us; no sooner is he routed and exposed, defeated and disappointed in one Enterprise, but he begins another, and, like a cunning Gladiator, warily defends himself, and boldly attacks his Enemy at the same time. Thus we see him, up and down, conquering and conquered, thro' this whole Part of his Story, till at last he receives a total Defeat; of which you shall hear in its place: In the mean time, let us take up his Story again at the *Red Sea*, where he received a great Blow, instead of which he expected a complete Victory; for doubtless the Devil and the King of *Egypt* too, thought of nothing but Conquest at *Piahiroth*.

However, though the Triumph of the *Israelites* over the *Egyptians* must needs be a great Mortification to the *Devil*, and exasperated him very much, yet the Consequence was only this, *viz.* that *Satan*, like an Enemy who is baulked and defeated, but not overcome, redoubles his Rage, and reinforces his Army, and what the *Egyptians* could not do for him, he resolves to do for himself; in order then to take his Opportunity for what Mischief might offer, being defeated, and provoked, I say, at the Slur that was put upon him, he resolves to follow them into the Wilderness, and many a vile Prank he plaid them there; as first, he straitens them for Water, and makes them murmur against God, and against *Moses*, within a very few Days, nay, Hours, of their great Deliverance of all.

Nor was this all, but in less than one Year more we find them, (at his Instigation too) setting up a *golden Calf*, and making all the People dance about it at Mount *Sinai*; even when God himself had but just before appeared to them in the Terrors of a burning Fire upon the Top of the Mountain; *and what was the Pretence?* Truly, nothing but that they had lost *Moses*, who used to be their Guide, and he had hid himself in the Mount, and had not been seen in forty Days, so that they could not tell what was become of him. This put them all into Confusion; a poor Pretence indeed, to turn them all back to Idolatry! but the *watchful Devil* took the Hint, pushed the Advantage, and insinuated that they should never see *Moses* again, that he was certainly devoured by venturing too near the Flashes of Fire in the Mount, and presuming upon the Liberty he had taken before; in a word, that God had destroyed *Moses*, or he was starved to Death for want of Food, having been forty Days and forty Nights absent.

All these were, it's true, in themselves most foolish Suggestions, considering *Moses* was admitted to the Vision of God, and that God had been pleased to appear to him in the most intimate manner; that as they might depend God would not destroy his faithful Servant, so they might have concluded he was able to support his Being without Food as long as he thought fit; but to a People so easy to believe anything, what could be too gross for the *Devil* to persuade them to?

A People who could dance round a Calf, and call it their God, might do anything; that could say to one another, that this was the Great Jehovah, *that brought them out of the Land of Egypt*; and that within so few Days after God's miraculous Appearance to them, and for them; I say, such a People were really fitted to be imposed upon, nothing could be too gross for them.

This was indeed his first considerable Experiment upon them as *a People*, or as a body; and the Truth is, his Affairs required it, for *Satan*, who had been a Successful Devil in most of his Attempts upon Mankind, could hardly doubt of Success in anything after he had carried his Point at Mount *Sinai*: To bring them to Idolatry in the very Face of their Deliverer, and just after their Deliverance! It was more astonishing in the main than even their passing *the Red Sea*: In a Word, the *Devil*'s whole History does not furnish us with a Story equally surprising.

And how was poor *Aaron* bewildered in it too? He that was *Moses*'s Partner in all the great Things that *Moses* did in *Pharaoh*'s Sight, and that was appointed to be his Assistant and Oracle, *or Orator rather*, upon all public Occasions; that he, above all the rest, should come into this absurd and ridiculous Proposal, he that was singled out for the sacred Priesthood, for him to defile his holy Hands with a polluted abominable Sacrifice, and with making the Idol for them too, (for 'tis plain that he made it,) how monstrous it was!

And see what an Answer he gives to his Brother *Moses*, how weak! how simple! *I did so and so, indeed*, I bad them bring the Ear-rings, *etc.*. and I cast the Gold into the Fire, and *it came out this Calf*. Ridiculous! as if the Calf came out by mere fortuitous Adventure, without a Mould to cast it in; which could not be supposed: And if it had not come out so without a Mould, *Moses* would certainly have known of it; had *Aaron* been innocent, he would have answered after quite another manner, and told *Moses* honestly that the whole Body of the People came to him in a Fright, that they forced him to make them an Idol; which he did, by making first a proper Mould to cast it in, and then taking the proper Metal to cast it from: That indeed he had sinned in so doing, but that he was mobbed into it, and the People terrified him, perhaps they threatened to kill him; and if he had added, that the *Devil* prompting his Fear beguiled him, he had said nothing but what was certainly true; for if it was in Satan's Power to make the People insolent and outrageous enough to threaten and bully the old venerable Prophet (*for he was not yet a Priest*) who was the Brother of their Oracle *Moses*, and had been Partner with him in so many of his Commissions; I say, if he could bring up the Passions of the People to a Height to be rude and unmannerly to him (*Aaron*) and perhaps to threaten and insult him, he may be easily supposed to be able to intimidate *Aaron*, and terrify him into a Compliance.

See this cunning Agent, when he has Man's Destruction in his View, how securely he acts! he never wants a handle; the best of Men have one weak place or other, and he always finds it out, takes the Advantage of it, and conquers them by one Artifice or another; only take it with you as you go, 'tis always *by Stratagem*, never *by Force*; a Proof that he is not empowered to use Violence: He may tempt, and he does prevail; but 'tis all *Legerdemain*, 'tis all Craft and Artifice, he is still Διαβολή, the *Calumniator* and Deceiver, that is, the Misrepresenter; he misrepresents *Man* to God, and misrepresents God to *Man*, also he misrepresents Things; he puts false Colors, and then manages the Eye to see them with an imperfect View, raising Clouds and Fogs to intercept our Sight; in short, he deceives all our Senses, and imposes upon us in Things which otherwise would be the easiest to discern and judge of.

This indeed is in part the Benefit of the *Devil's* History, to let us see that he has used the same Method all along; and that ever since he has had anything to do with Mankind, he has practiced upon them with Stratagem and Cunning; also 'tis observable that he has carried his Point better that way than he would have done by Fury and Violence, if he had been allowed to make use of it; for by his Power indeed he might have laid the World desolate, and made a Heap of Rubbish of it long ago; but, as I have observed before, that would not have answered his Ends half so well, for by destroying Men he would have made Martyrs, and sent abundance of good Men to Heaven, who would much rather have died, than yielded to serve him, and, as he aimed to have it, to fall down and worship him; I say, he would have made Martyrs, and that not a few: But this was none of *Satan's* Business; his Design lies quite another Way; his Business is to make Men *sin*, not to make them *suffer*; to make *Devils* of them, not *Saints*; to delude them, and draw them away from their Maker, not send them away to him; and therefore he works by Stratagem, not by Force.

We are now come to his Story, as it relates to the *Jewish* Church in the Wilderness, and to the Children of *Israel* in their travelling Circumstances; and this was the first Scene of public Management that the Devil had upon his Hands in the World; for, as I have said, *till now*, he dealt with Mankind either in their separate Condition, one by one, or else carried all before him, engrossing whole Nations in his Systems of Idolatry, and overwhelming them in an ignorant Destruction.

But having now a whole People as it were snatched away from him, taken out of his Government, and, which was still worse, having a View of a Kingdom being set up independent of him, and superior to his Authority, it is not to be wondered at if he endeavored to overthrow them in the Infancy of their Constitution, and tried all possible Arts to bring them back into his own Hands again.

He found them not only carried away from the Country where they were even in his Clutches, surrounded with Idols, and where we have Reason to believe the greatest part of them were polluted with the Idolatry of the *Egyptians*; for we do not read of any stated Worship which they had of their own, or if they did worship the true God, we scarce know in what manner they did it; they had no Law given them, nothing but the Covenant of Circumcision, and even *Moses* himself had not strictly observed that, till he was startled into it; we read of no Sacrifices among them, no Feasts were ordained, no solemn Worship appointed, and how, or in what manner they performed their Homage, we know not; the Passover was not ordained till just at their coming away; so that there was not much Religion among them, at least that we have any Account of; and we may suppose the *Devil* was pretty easy with them all the while they were in the House of their Bondage.

But now, to have a Million of People fetched out of his Hands, as it were all at once, and to have the immediate Power of Heaven engaged in it, and that *Satan* saw evidently God had singled them out in a miraculous manner to favor them, and call them *his own*; this alarmed him at once, and therefore he resolves to follow them, lay close Siege to them, and take all the Measures possible to bring them to rebel against, and disobey God, that he might be provoked to destroy them; and how near he went to bring it to pass, we shall see presently.

This making a Calf, and paying an idolatrous Worship to it (for they acted the Heathens and Idolaters, not in the setting up the Calf only, but in the manner of their Worshiping, *viz. Dancing* and *Music*, Things they had not been acquainted with in the Worship of the true God) I mention here, to observe how the Devil not only imposed upon their Principles, but upon their Senses too; as if the awful Majesty of Heaven, whose Glory they had seen in Mount *Sinai*, where they stood, and whose Pillar of Cloud and Fire was their Guide and Protection, would be worshipped by dancing round a Calf! and that not a living Creature, or a real Calf, but the mere Image of a *Calf* cast in Gold, or, as some think, in Brass gilded over.

But this was the *Devil's* Way with Mankind, namely, to impose upon their Senses, and bring them into the grossest Follies and Absurdities; and then, having first made them Fools, it was much the easier to make them Offenders.

In this very manner he acted with them thro' all the Course of their Wilderness Travels; for as they were led by the Hand like Children, defended by Omnipotence, fed by Miracles, instructed immediately from Heaven, and in all things had *Moses* for their Guide; they had no room to miscarry, but by acting the greatest Absurdities, and committing the greatest Follies in Nature; and even these, the *Devil* brought them to be guilty of, in a surprising manner: 1. As God himself relieved them in every Exigency, and supplied them in every Want, one would think 'twas impossible they should be ever brought to question either his Willingness or his Ability, and yet they really objected against both; which was indeed very provoking, and I doubt not, that when the *Devil* had brought them to act in such a preposterous Manner, he really hoped and believed God would be provoked effectually: The Testimonies of his Care of them, and Ability to supply them, were miraculous and undeniable; he gave them Water from the Rock, Bread from the Air, sent the Fowls to feed them with Flesh, and supported them all the Way by Miracles; their Health was preserved, none were sick among them, their clothes did not wear out, nor their Shoes grow old upon their Feet; could anything be more absurd, than to doubt whether he could provide for them who had never let them want for so many Years?

But the *Devil* managed them in spite of Miracles; nor did he ever give them over till he had brought six hundred thousand of them to provoke God so highly that he would not suffer above two of them to go into the Land of Promise; so that in short, Satan gained his Point as to that Generation, for all their Carcasses fell in the Wilderness. Let us take but a short View to what a Height he brought them, and in what a rude, absurd Manner they acted; how he set them upon murmuring upon every Occasion, now for Water, then for Bread; nay, they murmured *at their Bread* when they had it; *Our Soul loathes this light Bread.*

He sowed the Seeds of Church-Rebellion in the Sons of *Aaron*, and made *Nadab* and *Abihu* offer strange Fire till they were strangely consumed by Fire for the doing it.

He set them a complaining at *Taberah*, and a lusting for Flesh at the first three Days Journey from Mount *Sinai.*

He planted Envy in the Hearts of *Miriam* and *Aaron*, against the Authority of *Moses*, to pretend God had spoke by them as well as by him, till he humbled the Father, and made a Leper of the Daughter.

He debauched ten of the Spies, startled them with sham Appearances of Things, when they went out to search the Land; and made them fright the whole People out of their Understanding as well as Duty, for which six hundred thousand of their Carcasses fell in the Wilderness.

He raised the Rebellion of *Korah*, and the two hundred and fifty Princes, till he brought them to be swallowed up alive.

He put *Moses* into a Passion at *Meribah*, and ruffled the Temper of the meekest Man upon Earth, by which he made both him and *Aaron* forfeit their Share of the Promise, and be shut out from the *Holy Land.*

He raised a Mutiny among them when they travelled from Mount *Hor*, till they brought fiery Serpents among them to destroy them.

He tried to make *Baalim* the Prophet curse them, but there the *Devil* was disappointed: However, he brought the *Midianites* to debauch them with Women, as in the Case of *Zimri* and *Cosbi.*

He tempted *Achan* with the Wedge of Gold, and the *Babylonish* Garment, that he might take of the accursed thing, and be destroyed.

He tempted the whole People, not effectually to drive out the cursed Inhabitants of the Land of Promise, that they might remain, and be Goads in their Sides, till at last they often oppressed them for their Idolatry; and, which was worse, debauched them to Idolatry.

He prompted the *Benjamites* to refuse Satisfaction to the People, in the Case of the Wickedness of the Men of *Gibeah*, to the Destruction of the whole Tribe, four hundred Men excepted in the Rock *Rimmon*.

At last he tempted them to reject the Theocracy of their Maker, and call upon *Samuel* to make them a King; and most of those Kings he made Plagues and Sorrows to them in their time, as you shall hear in their Order.

Thus he plagued the whole Body of the People continually, making them sin against God, and bring Judgments upon themselves, to the consuming some Millions of them, first and last, by the Vengeance of their Maker.

As he did with the whole Congregation, so he did with their Rulers, and several of the Judges, who were made Instruments to deliver the People, yet were drawn into snares by this *subtle Serpent*, to ruin themselves or the People they had delivered.

He tempted *Gideon* to make an *Ephod*, contrary to the Law of the Tabernacle, and made the Children of *Israel* go a whoring (that is, a worshiping) after it.

He tempted *Sampson* to debauch himself with a Harlot, and betray his own happy Secret to a Whore, at the Expense of both his Eyes, and at last of his Life.

He tempted *Eli*'s Sons to lie with the Women, in the very Doors of the Tabernacle, when they came to bring their Offerings to the Priest; and he tempted poor *Eli* to connive at them, or not sufficiently reprove them.

He tempted the People to carry the Ark of God into the Camp, that it might fall into the Hands of the *Philistines*. And

He tempted *Uzzi* to reach out his Hand to hold it up; as if he that had preserved it in the House of *Dagon* the Idol of the *Philistines*, could not keep it from falling out of the Cart.

When the People had gotten a King, he immediately set to work in diverse Ways to bring that King to load them with Plagues and Calamities not a few.

He tempted *Saul* to spare the King of *Amaliek*, contrary to God's express Command.

He not tempted *Saul* only, but possessed him with an evil Spirit, by which he was left to wayward Dispositions, and was forced to have it fiddled out of him with a Minstrel.

He tempted *Saul* with a Spirit of Discontent, and with a Spirit of Envy at poor *David*, to hunt him like a Partridge upon the Mountains.

He tempted *Saul* with a Spirit of Divination, and sent him to a Witch to enquire of *Samuel* for him; as if God would help him when he was dead, that had forsaken him when he was alive.

After that, he tempted him to kill himself, on a Pretence that he might not fall into the Hands of the Uncircumcised; as if *Self-Murder* was not half so bad, either for Sin against God, or Disgrace among Men, as being taken Prisoner by *a Philistine*! A Piece of Madness none but the *Devil* could have brought Mankind to submit to, though some Ages after that, he made it a Fashion among the *Romans*.

After *Saul* was dead, and *David* came to the Throne, by how much he was a Man chosen and particularly savored by Heaven, the *Devil* fell upon him with the more Vigor, attacked him so many Ways, and conquered him so very often, that as no Man was so good a King, so hardly any good King was ever a worse Man; in many Cases one would have almost thought the *Devil* had made Sport with *David*, to show how easily he could overthrow the best Man *God* could choose of the whole Congregation.

He made him distrust his Benefactor so much as to feign himself mad before the King of *Gath*, when he had fled to him for Shelter.

He made him march with his four hundred Cut-throats, to cut off poor *Nabal*, and all his Household, only because he would not send him the good Cheer he had provided for his honest Sheep-shearers.

He made him, for his Word's sake, give *Ziba* half his Master's Estate for his Treachery, after he knew he had been the Traitor, and betrayed poor *Mephibosheth* for the sake of it; in which

'The good old King, it seems, was very loath
'To break his Word, and therefore broke his Oath.

Then he tempted him to the ridiculous Project of numbering the People, though against God's express Command; a Thing *Joab* himself was not wicked enough to do, till *David* and the *Devil* forced him to it.

And to make him completely wicked, he carried him to the Top of his House, and showed him a naked Lady bathing herself in her Garden, in which it appeared that the *Devil* knew *David* too well, and what was the particular Sin of his Inclination; and so took him by the Right Handle; drawing him at once into the Sins of *Murder* and *Adultery*.

Then, that he might not quite give him over, (though *David*'s Repentance for the last Sin kept the *Devil* off for a while) when he could attack him no farther personally he fell upon him in his Family, and made him as miserable as he could desire him to be, in his Children, three of whom he brought to Destruction before his Face, and another after his Death.

First, he tempted *Ammon* to ravish his Sister *Tamar*; so, there was an End of her (*poor Girl!*) as to this World, for we never hear any more of her.

Then he tempted *Absalom* to murder his Brother *Amnon*, in Revenge for *Tamar*'s Maidenhead.

Then he made *Joab* run *Absalom* thro' the Body, contrary to *David*'s Command.

And after *David*'s Death he brought *Adonija* (weak Man!) to the Block, for usurping King *Solomon*'s Throne.

As to *Absalom*, he tempted him to Rebellion, and raising War against his Father, to the turning him shamefully out of *Jerusalem*, and almost out of the Kingdom.

He tempted him, for *David*'s farther Mortification, to lie with his Father's Wives, in the Face of the whole City; and had *Achitophel*'s honest Council been followed, he had certainly sent him to Sleep with his Fathers, long before his time—But there *Satan* and *Achitophel* were both out-witted together.

Thro' all the Reigns of the several Successors of *David*, the *Devil* took care to carry on his own Game, to the continual insulting the Measures which God himself had taken for the establishing his People in the World, and especially as a Church; till at last he so effectually debauched them to Idolatry; that Crime which of all others was most provoking to God, as it was carrying the People away from their Allegiance, and transposing the Homage they owed God their Maker, to a contemptible Block of Wood, or an Image of a brute Beast; and this how sordid and brutish so ever it was in itself, yet so did his Artifice prevail among them, that, first or last, he brought them all into it, the ten Tribes as well as the two Tribes; till at last God himself was provoked to unchurch them, gave them up to their Enemies, and the few that were left of them, after incredible Slaughters and Desolation, were hurried away, some into *Tartary*, and others into *Babylon*, from whence very few, of that few that were carried away, ever found their Way Home again; and some, when they might have come, would not accept of it, but continued there to the very coming of the Messiah. See Epistles of St. *James* and of St. *Peter*, at the Beginning.

But to look a little back upon this Part (for it cannot be omitted, it makes so considerable a Part of the *Devil*'s History) I mean his drawing God's People, Kings and all, into all the Sins and Mischiefs which gradually contributed to their Destruction.

First, (*for he began immediately with the very best and wisest of the Race*) he drew in King *Solomon*, in the midst of all his Zeal for the building God's House, and for the making the most glorious and magnificent Appearance for God's Worship that ever the World saw; I say, in the middle of all this, he drew him into such immoderate and insatiable an Appetite for Women, as to set up the first, and perhaps the greatest *Seraglio* of Whores that ever any Prince in the World had, or pretended to before; nay, and to bring whoring so much into Reputation, that, as the Text says, seven hundred of them were Princesses; that is to say, Ladies of Quality: Not as the Grand Seigniors, and Great Moguls, (other Princes of the Eastern World) have since practiced, namely, to pick up their most beautiful Slaves; but these, it seems, were Women of Rank, King's Daughters, as *Pharaoh*'s Daughter, and the Daughters of the Princes and prime Men among the *Moabites, Ammonites, Zidonians, Hittites*, etc.. 1 *Kings* xi. 1.

Nor was this all; but as he drew him into the Love of these forbidden Women (*for such they were, as to their Nation, as well as Number*) so he ensnared him by those Women to a Familiarity with their Worship; and by degrees brought that famous Prince (famous for his Wisdom) to be the greatest and most-imposed-upon old Fool in the World; Bowing down to those Idols by the Enticing of his Whores, whom he had abhorred and detested in his Youth, as dishonoring that God for whom, and for whose Worship he had finished and dedicated the most magnificent Building and Temple in the World: Nothing but the invincible Subtlety of this *Arch Devil* could ever have brought such a Man as *Solomon* to such a Degeneracy of Manners, and to such Meannesses; no, not the *Devil* himself, without the Assistance of his Whores, nor the Whores themselves, without the *Devil* to help them.

As to *Solomon*, *Satan* had made Conquest enough there, we need hear no more of him; the next Advance he made, was in the Person of his Son *Rehoboam*; had not the *Devil* prompted his Pride and tyrannical Humor, he would never have given the People such an Answer as he did; and when he saw a Fellow at the Head of them too whom he knew wanted and waited for an Occasion to raise a Rebellion, and had ripened up the people's Humor to the Occasion: Well might the Text call it *listening to the Council of the young Heads*; that it was indeed with a Vengeance! but those young Heads too were acted by an old *Devil*, who for his Craft is called, as I have observed, the *Old Serpent*.

Having thus paved the Way, *Jeroboam* revolts. So far God had directed him; for the Text says expressly, speaking in the first Person of God himself, *This Thing is of Me*.

But though God might appoint *Jeroboam* to be King, (that is to say, often Tribes,) yet God did not appoint him to set up the *two Calves* in the two extreme Parts of the Land, *viz.* in *Dan*, and in *Bethel*; that was *Jeroboam*'s own doing, and done on purpose to keep the People from falling back to *Rehoboam*, by being obliged to go to *Jerusalem* to the public Worship: And the Text adds, *Jeroboam made Israel to sin*. This was indeed a Master-piece of the *Devil*'s Policy, and it was effectual to answer the End, nothing could have been more to the Purpose; what Reason he had to expect the People would so universally come into it, and be so well satisfied with a couple of Calves, instead of the true Worship of God at *Jerusalem*; or what Arts and Management he (*Satan*) made use of afterwards, to bring the People in, to join with such a Delusion, that we find but little of in all the Annals of *Satan*; nor is it much to the Case: It's certain the *Devil* found a strange kind of Propensity to worshiping Idols rooted in the Temper of that whole People, even from their first breaking away from the *Egyptian* Bondage; so that he had nothing to do but to work upon the old Stock, and propagate the Crime that he found was so natural to them. And this is *Satan*'s general Way of working, not with them only, but with us also, and with all the World, even then, and ever since.

When he had thus secured *Jeroboam*'s Revolt, we need not trace him among his Successors; for the same Reason of State that held for the setting up the Calves at *Bethel* and *Dan*, held good for the keeping them up, to all *Jeroboam*'s Posterity; nor had they one good King ever after; even *Jehu*, who called his Friends to come and see his *Zeal for the Lord*, and who fulfilled the Threatnings of God upon *Ahab* and his Family, and upon Queen *Jezabel* and her Offspring, and knew all the while that he was executing the Judgment of the true God upon an idolatrous Race; yet he would not part with his Calves, but would have thought it to have been parting with his Kingdom, and that as the People would have gone up to *Jerusalem* to worship, so they would at the same Time have transferred their civil Obedience to the King of *Judah*, (whose Right it really was, as far as they could claim by Birth and right Line); so that by the way, *Satan* any more than other Politicians, is not for the *jus divinum* of lineal Succession, or what we call hereditary Right, any farther than serves for his Purpose.

Thus Satan ridded his Hands of ten of the twelve Tribes; let us now see how he went on with the rest, for his Work was now brought into a narrower Compass; the Church of God was now reduced to two Tribes, except a few religious People, who separated from the Schism of *Jeroboam*, and came and planted themselves among the Tribes of *Judah* and *Benjamin*: The first thing the Devil did after this, was to foment a War between the two Kings, while *Judah* was governed by a Boy or Youth, *Abija* by Name, and he none of the best neither; but God's Time was not come, and the Devil received a great Disappointment; when *Jeroboam* was so entirely overthrown; that if the Records of those Ages do not mistake, no less than 500000 Men of *Israel* were killed, such a Slaughter, that one would think the Army of *Judah*, had they known how to improve as well as gain a Victory, might have brought all the rest back again, and have entirely reduced the House of *Jeroboam* and the ten Tribes that followed him to their Obedience; nay they did take a great deal of the Country from them, and among the rest *Bethel* itself; and yet so cunningly did *Satan* manage, that the King of *Judah*, who was himself a wicked King, and perhaps an Idolater in his Heart, did not take down the golden Calf that *Jeroboam* had there, no nor destroy the Idolatry itself, so that in short, his Victory signified nothing.

From hence to the Captivity, we find the *Devil* busy with the Kings of *Judah*, especially the best of them; as for such as *Manasseth*, and those who transgressed by the general Tenor of their Lives, those he had no great trouble with.

But such as *Asa, Jehoshaphat, Hezekiah*, and *Josiah*, he hung about them and their Courts, till he brought every one of them into some Mischief or another.

As first, good King *Asa*, of whom the Scripture says, his Heart was perfect all his Days, yet this subtle Spirit, that could break in upon him nowhere else, tempted him when the King of *Israel* came out against him, to send to hire *Benhadad* the King of *Syria* to help him; as if God who had before enabled him to conquer the *Ethiopians*, with an Army of ten hundred thousand Men, could not have saved him from the King of the ten Tribes.

In the same manner he tempted *Jehoshaphat* to join with that wicked King *Ahab* against the King of *Syria*, and also to marry his Son to *Ahab*'s Daughter, which was fatal to *Jehoshaphat*, and to his Posterity.

Again, He tempted *Hezekiah* to show all his Riches to the King of *Babylon*'s Messengers; and who can doubt, but that he (*Satan*) is to be understood by the wicked Spirit which stood before the Lord, 2 *Chron.* xviii. 20. and offered his Service to entice *Ahab* the King of *Israel* to come out to Battle to his Ruin, by being a lying Spirit in the Mouths of all his Prophets; and who for that Time had a special Commission, as he had another Time in the Case of *Job*? and indeed it was a Commission fit for nobody but the *Devil*: *Thou shalt entice* him, *and thou shalt* also *prevail: Go out and do* even *so*, V. 21.

Even good *Josiah* himself, of whom it is recorded, that *like him there was no King before him, neither after him arose there any like him*, 2 Kings xxiii. 26. yet the *Devil* never left him with his Machinations, till finding he could not tempt him to any Thing wicked in his Government, he tempted or moved him to a needless War with the King of *Egypt*, in which he lost his Life.

From the Death of this good King, the *Devil* prevailed so with the whole Nation of the *Jews*, and brought them to such an incorrigible Pitch of Wickedness, that *God* gave them up, forsook his Habitation of Glory, the Temple, which he suffered to be spoiled first, then burnt and demolished; destroying the whole Nation of the *Jews*, except a small Number that were left, and those the Enemy carried away into Captivity.

Nor was he satisfied with this general Destruction of the whole People of *Israel*, for the ten Tribes were gone before; but he followed them even into their Captivity; those that fled away to *Egypt*, which they tell us were seventy thousand, he first corrupted, and then they were destroyed thereupon the Overthrow of *Egypt*, by the same King of *Babylon*.

Also he went very near to have them rooted out, young and old, Man, Woman and Child, who were in Captivity in *Babylon*, by the Ministry of that true Agent of Hell, *Haman* the *Agagite*; but there *Satan* met with a Disappointment too, as in the Story of *Hester*, which was but the fourth that he had met with, in all his Management since the Creation; I say, there he was disappointed, and his prime Minister *Haman* was exalted, as he deserved.

Having thus far traced the Government and Dominion of the *Devil*, from the Creation of Man to the Captivity; I think I may call upon him to set up his Standard of universal Empire, at that Period; it seemed just then as if God had really forsaken the Earth, and given the entire Dominion of Mankind up to his outrageous Enemy the *Devil*; for excepting the few *Israelites* which were left in the Territories of the King of *Babylon*, and they were but a few; I say, except among them, there was not one Corner of the World left where the true God was called upon, or his Dominion so much as acknowledged; all the World was buried in Idolatry, and that of so many horrid Kinds, that one would think, the Light of Reason should have convinced Mankind, that he who exacted such bloody Sacrifices as that of *Moloch*, and such a bloody cutting themselves with Knives, as the Priests of *Baal* did, could not be a God, a good and beneficent Being, but must be a cruel, voracious and devouring Devil, whose End was not the Good, but the Destruction of his Creatures: But to such a Height was the blind demented World arrived to at that Time, that in these sordid and corrupt Ways, they went on worshiping dumb Idols, and offering human Sacrifices to them, and in a Word, committing all the most horrid and absurd Abominations that they were capable of, or that the *Devil* could prompt them to, till Heaven was again put, as it were, to the Necessity of bringing about a Revolution, in favor of his own forsaken People, by Miracle and Surprise, as he had done before.

We come therefore to the Restoration or Return of the Captivity: Had *Satan* been able to have acted anything by Force, *as I have observed before*, all the Princes and Powers of the World, having been, as they really were, at his Devotion, he might easily have made use of them, armed all the World against the *Jews*, and prevented the Rebuilding the Temple, and even the Return of the Captivity.

But now the *Devil's* Power manifestly received a Check, and the Hand of God appeared in it, and that he was resolved to reestablish his People the *Jews*, and to have a second Temple built: the *Devil*, who knew the Extent of his own Power too well, and what Limitations were laid upon him, stood still as it were looking on, and not daring to oppose the Return of the Captivity, which he very well knew had been prophesied, and would come to pass.

He did indeed make some little Opposition to the Building, and to the fortifying the City, but as it was to no Purpose, so he was soon obliged to give it over; and thus the Captivity being returned, and the Temple rebuilt, the People of the *Jews* increased and multiplied to an infinite Number and Strength; and from this Time we may say, the Power of the *Devil* rather declined and decreased, than went on with Success, as it had done before; It is true the *Jews* fell into Sects and Errors, and Divisions of many Kinds, after the Return from the Captivity, and no doubt the *Devil* had a great Hand in those Divisions; but he could never bring them back to Idolatry, and his not being able to do that, made him turn his Hand so many Ways to plague and oppress them; as particularly by *Antiochus* the Great, who brought the Abomination of Desolation into the holy Place; and there the Devil triumphed over them for some Time; but they were delivered many Ways, till at last they came peaceably under the Protection rather than the Dominion of the *Roman* Empire: When *Herod* the Great governed them as a King, and redefined, nay almost rebuilt their Temple, with so great an Expense and Magnificence, that he made it, as some say, greater and more glorious than that of *Solomon's*, though that I take to be a great —— Fable, to say no worse of it.

In this Condition the *Jewish* Church stood, when the Fullness of Time, as 'tis called in Scripture, was come; and the *Devil* was kept at Bay, though he had made some Encroachments upon them as above; for there was a glorious Remnant of Saints among *them*, such as old *Zacharias* the Father of *John* the Baptist, and old *Simeon*, who waited for the Salvation of *Israel*; I say, in this Condition the *Jewish* Church stood when the *Messiah* came into the World, which was such another mortal Stab to the Thrones and Principalities infernal, as that of which I have spoken already in Chap. III. at the Creation of Man; and therefore with this I break off the Antiquities of the *Devil's* History, or the ancient Part of his Kingdom; for from hence downward we shall find his Empire has declined gradually; and though by his wonderful Address, his prodigious Application, and the Vigilance and Fidelity of his Instruments, as well human as infernal and diabolical, and of the Human as well the Ecclesiastic as the Secular; he has many Times retrieved what he has lost, and sometimes bid fair for recovering the universal Empire he once possessed over Mankind; yet he has been still defeated again, repulsed and beaten back, and his Kingdom has greatly declined in many Parts of the World; and especially in the Northern Parts, except *Great Britain*; and how he has politically maintained his Interest and increased his Dominion among the wise and righteous Generation that we cohabit with and among, will be the Subject of the *modern* Part of *Satan's History*, and of which we are next to give an Account.

PART II

**OF THE
MODERN History
OF THE
DEVIL**

Chapter I

The Introduction

I have examined the Antiquities of Satan's History in the former Part of this Work, and brought his Affairs down from the Creation, as far as to our blessed Christian Times; especially to the Coming of the *Messiah*, when one would think the *Devil* could have nothing to do among us. I have indeed but touched at some Things which might have admitted of a farther Description of Satan's Affairs, and the Particulars of which we may all come to a farther Knowledge of hereafter; yet I think I have spoken to the material Part of his Conduct, as it relates to his Empire in this World: What has happened to his more sublimated Government, and his Angelic Capacities, I shall have an Occasion to touch at in several solid Particulars as we go along.

The *Messiah* was now born, *the Fullness of Time was come*, that the old Serpent was to have his *Head broken*, that is to say, his Empire or Dominion over Man, which he gained by the Fall of our first Father and Mother in *Paradise*, received a Downfall or Overthrow.

It is worth observing, in order to confirm what I have already mentioned of the Limitation of Satan's Power, that not only his Angelic Strength seems to have received a farther Blow upon the Coming of the Son of God into the World, but he seems to have had a Blow upon his Intellects; his Serpentine Craft and *Devil-like* Subtlety seems to have been circumscribed and cut short; and instead of his being so cunning a Fellow as before, when, *as I said*, 'tis evident he outwitted all Mankind, not only *Eve, Cain, Noah, Lot*, and all the Patriarchs, but even Nations of Men, and that in their public Capacity; and thereby led them into absurd and ridiculous Things, such as the Building of *Babel*, and deifying and worshiping their Kings, when dead and rotten; idolizing *Beasts, Stocks, Stones, any Thing*, and even *Nothing*; and in a Word, when he managed Mankind just as he pleased.

Now and from this Time forward he appeared a weak, foolish, ignorant *Devil*, compared to what he was before; He was upon almost every Occasion resisted, disappointed, baulked and defeated, especially in all his Attempts to thwart or cross the Mission and Ministry of the *Messiah*, while he was upon Earth, and sometimes upon other and very mean Occasions too.

And first, how foolish a Project was it, and how below Satan's celebrated Artifice in like Cases, to put *Herod* upon sending to kill the poor innocent Children in *Bethlehem*, in hopes to destroy the Infant? for I take it for granted, it was the *Devil* put into *Herod*'s Thoughts that Execution, how simple and foolish so ever; now we must allow him to be very ignorant of the Nativity himself, or else he might easily have guided his Friend *Herod* to the Place where the Infant was.

This shows that *either* the *Devil* is in general ignorant as we are, of what is to come in the World, before it is really come to pass; and consequently can foretell nothing, no not so much as our famous old *Merlin* or *Mother Shipton* did, *or else* that great Event was hid from him by an immediate Power superior to his, which I cannot think neither, considering how much he was concerned in it, and how certainly he knew that it was once to come to pass.

But be that as it will, 'tis certain the *Devil* knew nothing where Christ was born, or when; nor was he able to direct *Herod* to find him out, and therefore put him upon that foolish, as well as cruel Order, to kill all the Children, that he might be sure to destroy the *Messiah* among the rest.

The next simple Step that the *Devil* took, and indeed the most foolish one that he could ever be charged with, unworthy the very Dignity of a *Devil*, and below the Understanding that he always was allowed to act with, was that of coming to tempt the *Messiah* in the Wilderness; it is certain, and he owned it himself afterwards, upon many Occasions, that the *Devil* knew our Saviour to be the Son of God; and 'tis as certain that he knew, that *as such* he could have no Power or Advantage over him; how foolish then was it in him to attack him in that Manner, *if thou beest the Son of* God? why he knew him to be the *Son of* God well enough; he said so afterwards, *I know thee who thou art, the holy One of* God; how then could he be so weak a Devil as to say, *if thou art*, then do *so* and *so*?

The Case is plain, the *Devil*, though he knew him to be the Son of God, did not fully know the Mystery of the Incarnation; nor did he know how far the *Inanition* of Christ extended, and whether, *as Man*, he was not subject to fall as *Adam* was, though his reserved Godhead might be still immaculate and pure; and upon this Foot, as he would leave no Method untried, he attempts him three Times, one immediately after another; but then, finding himself disappointed he fled.

This evidently proves that the *Devil* was ignorant of the great Mystery of Godliness, *as the Text calls it*, God manifest in the Flesh, and therefore made that foolish Attempt upon Christ, thinking to have conquered his human Nature as capable of Sin, which it was not; and at this Repulse *Hell* groaned, the whole Army of regimented *Devils* received a Wound, and felt the Shock of it; 'twas a second Overthrow to them, they had had a long

Chain of Success, carried a *devilish* Conquest over the greatest Part of the Creation of God; but now they were cut short, *the Seed of the Woman* was now come *to break the Serpent's Head*, that is, to cut short his Power, to contract the Limits of his Kingdom, and in a Word, to dethrone him in the World: No doubt the *Devil* received a Shock, for you find him always afterward, crying out in a horrible Manner, whenever Christ met with him, or else very humble and submissive, as when he begged leave to go into the Herd of Swine, a Thing he has often done since.

Defeated here, the first Stratagem I find him concerned in after it, was his entering into *Judas*, and putting him upon betraying Christ to the Chief Priest; but here again he was entirely mistaken, for he did not see, *as much a Devil as he was*, what the Event would be; but when he came to know, that if Christ was put to Death, he would become a Propitiatory and be the great Sacrifice of Mankind, so to rescue the fallen Race from that Death they had incurred the Penalty of, by the Fall, that this was the fulfilling of all Scripture Prophesy, and that thus it was that Christ was to be *the End of the Law*, I say, as soon as he perceived this, he strove all he could to prevent it, and disturbed *Pilate*'s Wife in her Sleep, in order to set her upon her Husband to hinder his delivering him up to the *Jews*; for then, and not till then, he knew how Christ was to vanquish Hell by the Power of his Cross.

Thus the *Devil* was disappointed and exposed in every Step he took, and as he now plainly saw his Kingdom declining, and even the temporal Kingdom of Christ, rising up upon the Ruins of his (*Satan*'s) Power; he seemed to retreat into his own Region the Air, and to consult there with his fellow *Devils*, what Measures he should take next to preserve his Dominion among Men; Here it was that he resolved upon that truly hellish Thing called Persecution, by which, *though he proved a foolish Devil in that too*, he flattered himself he should be able to destroy God's Church, and root out its Professors from the Earth, even almost as soon as it was established; whereas on the contrary, Heaven counter-acted him there too, and though he armed the whole *Roman* Empire against the Christians, *that is say*, the whole World, and they were fallen upon everywhere, with all the Fury and Rage of some of the most flaming Tyrants that the World ever saw, of whom *Nero* was the first; yet in spite of Hell, God made all the Blood, which the Devil caused to be spilt, to be *semen Ecclesia*, and the Devil had the Mortification to see, that the Number of Christians increased even under the very Means he made use of to root them out and destroy them: This was the Case thro' the Reign of all the *Roman* Emperors, for the first three hundred Years after Christ.

Having thus tried all the Methods that best suited his Inclination, I mean those of Blood and Death, complicated with Tortures and all Kinds of Cruelty, and that for so long a Stage of Time as above; the *Devil* all on a sudden, as if glutted with Blood, and satiated with Destruction, sits still and becomes a peaceable Spectator for a good while; as if he either found

129

himself unable, or had no Disposition to hinder the Progress of Christianity in the first Ages of its Settlement in the World: In this interval the Christian Church was established under *Constantine*, Religion flourished in Peace, and under the most perfect Tranquility: The *Devil* seemed to be at a Loss what he should do next, and Things began to look as if Satan's Kingdom was at an End; but he soon let them see that he was the same indefatigable *Devil* that ever he was, and the Prosperity of the Church gave him a large Field of Action; for knowing the Disposition of Mankind to Quarrel and Dispute, the universal Passion rooted in Nature, especially among the Church-Men for Presidency and Dominion, he fell to work with them immediately; so that turning the Tables, and reassuming the Subtlety and Craft, which, I say, he seemed to have lost in the former four hundred Years, he gained more Ground in the next Ages of the Church, and went farther towards restoring his Power and Empire in the World, and towards overthrowing that very Church which was so lately established, than all he had done by Fire and Blood before.

His Policy now seemed to be edged with Resentment for the Mistakes he had made; as if the Devil looking back with Anger at himself, to see what a Fool he had been to expect to crush Religion by Persecution, rejoiced for having discovered that Liberty and Dominion was the only way to ruin the Church, not Fire and Faggot; and that he had nothing to do but to give the zealous People their utmost Liberty in Religion, only sowing Error and Variety of Opinion among them, and they would bring Fire and Faggot in fast enough among themselves.

It must be confessed these were devilish Politics; and so sure was the Aim, and so certain was the *Devil* to hit his Mark by them, that we find he not only did not fail then, but the same hellish Methods have prevailed still, and will do so to the End of the World. Nor had the Devil ever a better Game to play than this, for the Ruin of Religion, as we shall have room to show in many Examples, besides that of the Dissenters in *England*, who are evidently weakened by the late Toleration: Whether the *Devil* had any hand in baiting his Hook with an A— of Parliament or no, History is silent, but 'tis too evident he has cached the Fish by it; and if the honest Church of *England* does not in Pity and Christian Charity to the Dissenters, straighten her Hand a little, I cannot but fear the *Devil* will gain his Point, and the Dissenter will be undone by it.

Upon this new foot of Politics the *Devil* began with the Emperors themselves: *Arius*, the Father of the Heretics of that Age, having broached his Opinions, and *Athanasius* the orthodox Bishop of the East opposing him, the *Devil* no sooner saw the Door open to Strife and Imposition, but he thrust himself in, and raising the Quarrel up to a suited Degree of Rage and Spleen, he involved the good Emperor himself in it first and *Athanasius* was banished and recalled, and banished and recalled again, several times, as Error ran high, and as the *Devil* either got or lost Ground: After *Constantine*, the next Emperor was a Child of his own, (*Arian*) and then the Court came all into the Quarrel, as Courts often do, and then the *Arians* and the *Orthodox* persecuted one another as furiously as the Pagans persecuted them all before. To such a Height the *Devil* brought his Conquest in the very Infancy of the Question, and so much did he prevail over the true Christianity of the Primitive Church, even before they had enjoyed the Liberty of the pure Worship twenty Years.

Flushed with this Success, the *Devil* made one Push for the restoring *Paganism*, and bringing on the old Worship of the Heathen Idols and Temples; but like our King *James* II. he drove too hard, and *Julian* had so provoked the whole *Roman* Empire, which was generally at that time become Christian, that had the Apostate lived, he would not have been able to have held the Throne; and as he was cut off in his Beginning, Paganism expired with him, and the *Devil* himself might have cried out, as *Julian* did, and with much more Propriety, *Vicisti Galileane*.

Jovian, the next Emperor, being a glorious Christian, and a very good and great Man, the *Devil* abdicated for a while, and left the Christian Armies to re-establish the Orthodox Faith; nor could he bring the Christians to a Breach again among themselves a great while after.

However, Time and a diligent *Devil* did the Work at last, and when the Emperors concerning themselves one way or other, did not appear sufficient to answer his End, he changed Hands again, and went to work with the Clergy: To set the Doctors effectually together by the Ears, he threw in the new Notion of *Primacy* among them, for a Bone of Contention; the Bait took, the Priests swallowed it eagerly down, and the *Devil*, a cunninger Fisherman than ever St. *Peter* was, *struck them* (as the Anglers call it) with a quick Hand, and hung them fast upon the Hook.

Having them thus in his Clutches, and they being now, as we may say, his own, they took their Measures afterwards from him, and most obediently followed his Directions; nay, I will not say but he may have had pretty much the Management of the whole Society ever since, of what Profession or Party so ever they may have been, with Exception only to the Reverend and Right Reverend among ourselves.

The Sacred, as above, being thus hooked in, and the Devil being at the Head of their Affairs, Matters went on most gloriously his own way; first, the Bishops fell to bandying and Party-making for the Superiority, as heartily as ever Temporal Tyrants did for Dominion, and took as black and devilish Methods to carry it on, as the worst of those Tyrants ever had done before them.

At last Satan declared for the *Roman* Pontiff, and that upon excellent Conditions, in the Reign of the Emperor *Mauritius*; for *Boniface*, who had long contended for the Title of Supreme, fell into a Treaty with *Phocas*,

Captain of the Emperor's Guards; whether the Bargain was from Hell or not, let any one judge, the Conditions absolutely entitle the *Devil* to the Honor of making the Contract, *viz.* That *Phocas* first murdering his Master (the Emperor) and his Sons, *Boniface* should countenance the Treason, and declare him Emperor; and in Return, *Phocas* should acknowledge the Primacy of the Church of *Rome*, and declare *Boniface* universal Bishop. A blessed Compact! which at once set the *Devil* at the Head of Affairs in the Christian World, as well Spiritual as Temporal, Ecclesiastic and Civil. Since the Conquest over *Eve* in Paradise, by which Death and the Devil, Hand in Hand, established their first Empire upon Earth, the *Devil* never gained a more important Point than he gained at this time.

He had indeed prospered in his Affairs tolerably well for some time before this, and his Interest among the Clergy had got Ground for some Ages; but that was indeed a secret Management, was carried on privately, and with Difficulty; as in sowing Discord and Faction among the People, perplexing the Councils of their Princes, and secretly wheedling in with the dignified Clergy.

Also he had raised abundance of little Church-Rebellions, by setting up Heretics of several Kinds, and raising them Favorers among the Clergy, such as *Ebion*, *Cerinthius*, *Pelagius*, and others.

He had drawn in the Bishops of *Rome* to set up the ridiculous Pageantry of the Key; and while he, the Devil, set open the Gates of Hell to them all, set them upon locking up the Gates of Heaven, and giving the Bishop the Key; a Cheat which, as gross as it was, the Devil so gilded over, or so blinded the Age to receive it, that like *Gideon's Ephod*, all the Catholic World went a whoring after the Idol; and the Bishop of *Rome sent* more Fools to the *Devil* by it than ever he pretended to let into Heaven, though he opened the Door as wide as his Key was able to do.

The Story of this Key being given to the Bishop of *Rome* by St. *Peter*, (who, by the way, never had it himself,) and of its being lost by Somebody or other, (the *Devil* it seems did not tell them who) and its being found again by a *Lombard* Soldier in the Army of King *Antharis*, who attempting to cut it with his Knife, was miraculously forced to direct the Wound to himself, and cut his own Throat; that King *Antharis* and his Nobles happened to see the Fellow do it, and were converted to Christianity by it, and that the King sent the Key, with another made like it, to Pope *Pelagius*, then Bishop of *Rome*, who thereupon assumed the Power of opening and shutting Heaven's Gates; and he afterwards setting a Price or Toll upon the Entrance, as we do here at passing a Turn-pike; these fine things, I say, were successfully managed for some Years before this I am now speaking of, and the Devil got a great deal of Ground by it too; but now he triumphed openly, and having set up a Murderer upon the temporal Throne, and a Church Emperor upon the Ecclesiastic Throne, and both of

132

his own choosing, the *Devil* may be said to begin his new Kingdom from this Epoch, and call it the *Restoration*.

Since this time indeed the Devil's Affairs went very merrily on, and the Clergy brought so many Gewgaws into their Worship, and such devilish Principles were mixed with that which we called the Christian Faith, that in a Word, from this Time the Bishop of *Rome* commenced *Whore of Babylon*, in all the most express Terms that could be imagined: Tyranny of the worst sort crept into the Pontificate, Errors of all sorts into the Profession, and they proceeded from one thing to another, till the very Popes, for so the Bishop of *Rome* was now called, by way of Distinction; I say, the Popes themselves, their spiritual Guides, professed openly to confederate with the *Devil*, and to carry on a personal and private Correspondence with him at the same time, taking upon them the Title of Christ's Vicar, and the infallible Guide of the Consciences of Christians.

This we have sundry Instances of in some merry Popes, who, *if Fame lies not*, were Sorcerers, Magicians, had familiar Spirits, and immediate Conversation with the Devil, as well visibly as invisibly, and by this means became what we call *Devils incarnate*: Upon this account it is that I have left the Conversation that passes between *Devils and Men* to this Place, as well because I believe it differs much now in his modern State, from what it was in his ancient State, and therefore that which most concerns us belongs rather to this part of his History; as also because, as I am now writing to the present Age, I choose to bring the most significant Parts of his History, especially as they relate to our selves, into that Part of Time that we are most concerned in.

The *Devil* had once, as I observed before, the universal Monarchy or Government of Mankind in himself, and I doubt not but in that flourishing State of his Affairs, he governed them like what he is (*viz.*) an absolute Tyrant; during this *Theocracy* of his, *for* Satan *is called the God of this World*, he did not familiarize himself to Mankind so much, as he finds Occasion to do now, there was not then so much need of it; he governed then with an absolute Sway; he had his Oracles, where he gave Audience to his Votaries like a Deity, and he had his Sub-Gods, who under his several Dispositions received the Homage of Mankind in their Names; such were all the Rabble of the Heathen Deities, from *Jupiter* the Supreme, to the *Lares* or Household Gods of every Family; these, I say, like Residents, received the Prostrations, but the Homage was all Satan's; the Devil had the Substance of it all, which was the Idolatry.

During this Administration of *Hell*, there was less Witchcraft, less true literal Magic than there has been since; there was indeed no need of it, the Devil did not stoop to the Mechanism of his more modern Operations, but ruled as a Deity, and received the Vows and the Bows of his Subjects in more State, and with more Solemnity; whereas since that, he is content to employ more Agents and take more Pains himself too; now he runs up and down Hackney in the World, more like a Drudge than a Prince, and much more than he did then.

Hence all those Things we call Apparitions and Visions of Ghosts, Familiar-Spirits and Dealings with the Devil, of which there is so great a Variety in the World at this Time, were not so much known among the People, in those first Ages of the Devil's Kingdom; *in a Word*, the Devil seems to be put to his Shifts, and to fly to Art and Stratagem for the carrying on his Affairs, much more now than he did then.

One Reason for this may be, that he has been more discovered and exposed in these Ages, than he was before; then he could appear in the World in his own proper Shapes, and yet not be known; when the Sons of God appeared at the divine Summons, Satan came along with them; but now he has plaid so many scurvy Tricks upon Men, and they know him so well, that he is obliged to play quite out of sight and act in disguise; Mankind will allow nothing of his doing, and hear nothing of his saying, in his own Name; and if you propose any Thing to be done, and it be but said the *Devil* is to help in the doing it, or if you say of any Man he deals with the *Devil*, or the *Devil* has a Hand in it, every Body flies him and shuns him, as the most frightful Thing in the World.

Nay, if any Thing strange and improbable be done or related to be done, we presently say the *Devil* was at the doing it: Thus the great Ditch at *Newmarket Heath*, is called the *Devil's Ditch*; so the *Devil* built *Crowland* Abby, and the Whispering-Place in *Gloucester* Cathedral; nay, the Cave at *Castleton*, only because there's no getting to the farther End of it, is called the *Devil's* A—— and the like: The poor People of *Wiltshire*, when you ask them how the great Stones at *Stonehenge* were brought thither? they'll all tell you the *Devil* brought them: If any Mischief extraordinary befalls us, we presently say the *Devil* was in it, and the *Devil* would have it so; in a Word, the *Devil* has got an ill Name among us, and so he is fain to act more *in Tenebris*, more *incog.* than he used to do, play out of sight himself, and work by the Sap, as the Engineers call it, and not openly and avowedly in his own Name and Person, as formerly, though perhaps not with less Success than he did before; and this leads me to enquire more narrowly into the manner of the *Devil's* Management of his Affairs since the Christian Religion began to spread in the World, which manifestly differs from his Conduct in more ancient Times; in which if we discover some of the most consummate Fool's Policy, the most profound simple Craft, and the most subtle shallow Management of Things that can by our weak Understandings be conceived, we must only resolve it into this, that in short it is the Devil.

Chapter II

Of Hell as it is represented to us, and how the Devil *is to be understood, as being personally in Hell, when at the same Time we find him at Liberty ranging over the World*

It is true, as that learned and pleasant Author, the inimitable Dr. *Brown* says, the *Devil* is his own Hell; one of the most constituting Parts of his Infelicity is, that he cannot act upon Mankind *brevi Manu*, by his own inherent Power, as well as Rage; that he cannot unhinge this Creation, which, *as I have observed in its Place*, he had the utmost Aversion to from its Beginning, as it was a stated Design in the Creator to supply his Place in Heaven with a new Species of *Beings* called *Man*, and fill the Vacancies occasioned by his Degeneracy and Rebellion.

This filled him with Rage inexpressible, and horrible Resolutions of Revenge, and the Impossibility of executing those Resolutions torments him with Despair; this added to what he was before, makes him a complete *Devil*, with a Hell in his own Breast, and a Fire unquenchable burning about his Heart.

I might enlarge here, and very much to the Purpose, in describing spherically and mathematically that exquisite Quality called *a devilish Spirit*, in which it would naturally occur to give you a whole Chapter upon the glorious Articles of *Malice* and *Envy*, and especially upon that luscious, delightful, triumphant Passion called Revenge; how natural to Man, nay even to both Sexes; how pleasant in the very Contemplation, though there be not just at that Time a Power of Execution; how palatable it is in itself, and how well it relishes when dished up with its proper Sauces, such as Plot, Contrivance, Scheme, and Confederacy, all leading on to Execution: How it possesses a human Soul in all the most sensible Parts; how it empowers Mankind to sin in Imagination, as effectually to all future Intents and Purposes (Damnation) as if he had sinned actually: How safe a Practice it is too, as to Punishment in this Life, namely, that it empowers us to cut Throats clear of the Gallows, to slander Virtue, reproach Innocence, wound Honor and stab Reputation; and in a Word, to do all the wicked Things in the World, out of the Reach of the Law.

It would also require some few Words to describe the secret Operations of those nice Qualities when they reach the human Soul; how effectually they form a Hell within us, and how imperceptibly they assimilate and transform us into *Devils*, mere human Devils, as really *Devils* as Satan himself, or any of his Angels; and that therefore 'tis not so much out of the Way, as some imagine, to say, such a Man is an *incarnate* Devil; for as Crime made Satan a *Devil*, who was before a bright immortal Seraph, or Angel of Light; how much more easily may the same Crime make *the same* Devil, though every Way meaner and more contemptible, *of a Man or a* Woman either? But this is too grave a Subject for me at this Time.

The *Devil* being thus, I say, fired with Rage and Envy, in consequence of his Jealousy upon the Creation of Man, his Torment is increased to the highest by the Limitation of his Power, and his being forbid to act against Mankind by Force of Arms; this is, I say, part of his *Hell*, which, as above, is within him, and which he carries with him wherever he goes; nor is it so difficult to conceive of *Hell*, or of the *Devil*, either under this just Description, as it is by all the usual Notions that we are taught to entertain of them, by (the old Women) our Instructors; for every Man may, by taking but a common View of himself, and making a just Scrutiny into his own Passions, on some of their particular Excursions, see a *Hell* within himself, and himself a mere *Devil* as long as the Inflammation lasts; and that as really, and to all Intents and Purposes, as if he had the Angel (*Satan*) before his Face, in his Locality and Personality; that is to say, all Devil and Monster in his Person, and an immaterial but intense Fire flaming about and from within him, at all the Pores of his Body.

The Notions we receive of the Devil, *as a Person* being in Hell *as a Place*, are infinitely absurd and ridiculous; the first we are certain is not true in Fact, because he has a certain Liberty, (*however limited* that is not to the Purpose) is daily visible, and to be traced in his several Attacks upon Mankind, and has been so ever since his first Appearance in *Paradise*; as to his corporal Visibility that is not the present Question neither; 'tis enough that we can hunt him by the Foot, that we can follow him as Hounds do a Fox upon a hot Scent: We can see him as plainly by the Effect, by the Mischief he does, and more by the Mischief he puts us upon doing, *I say*, as plainly, as if we saw him by the Eye.

It is not to be doubted but the *Devil* can see us when and where we cannot see him: and as he has a Personality, though it be spirituous, he and his Angels too may be reasonably supposed to inhabit the World of Spirits, and to have free Access from thence to the Regions of Life, and to pass and repass in the Air, as really, though not perceptible to us, as the Spirits of Men do after their release from the Body, pass to the Place (wherever that is) which is appointed for them.

If the *Devil* was confined to a Place (*Hell*) as a Prison, he could then have no Business here; and if we pretend to describe *Hell*, as not a Prison, but that the Devil has Liberty to be there, or not be there as he pleased, then he would certainly never be there, or *Hell* is not such a Place as we are taught to understand it to be.

Indeed according to some, *Hell* should be a Place of Fire and Torment to the Souls that are cast into it, but not to the *Devils* themselves; who we make little more or less than keepers and Turnkeys to Hell, as a Goal; that they are sent about to bring Souls thither, lock them in when they come, and then away upon the Scent to fetch more: That one Sort of *Devils* are made to live in the World among Men, and to be busy continually debauching and deluding Mankind bringing them as it were to the Gates of *Hell*; and then another Sort are Porters and Carriers to fetch them in.

This is, *in short*, little more or less than the old Story of *Pluto*, of *Cerberus*, and of *Charon*; only that our Tale is not half so well told, nor the Parts of the Fable so well laid together.

In all these Notions of *Hell* and *Devil*, the Torments of the first, and the Agency of the last Tormenting, we meet with not one Word of the main and perhaps only Accent of Horror, which belongs to us to judge of about Hell, I mean the Absence of Heaven; Expulsion, and Exclusion from the Presence and Face of the chief Ultimate, the only eternal and sufficient Good; and this loss sustained by a sordid Neglect of our Concern in that excellent Part, in exchange for the most contemptible and justly condemned Trifles, and all this eternal and irrecoverable: These People tell us nothing of the eternal Reproaches of Conscience, the Horror of Desperation, and the Anguish of a Mind hopeless of ever seeing the Glory, which alone constitutes Heaven, and which makes all other Places dreadful, and even Darkness itself.

And this brings me directly to the Point in Hand, (*viz.*) the State of that Hell which we ought to have in view when we speak of the *Devil* as *in Hell*: This is the very Hell, which is the Torment of the *Devil*; in short, the *Devil* is in Hell, and Hell is in the *Devil*; he is filled with this unquenchable Fire, he is expelled the Place of Glory, banished from the Regions of Light, Absence from the Life of all Beatitude is his Curse, Despair is the reigning Passion in his Mind, and all the little Constituent Parts of his Torment, such as Rage, Envy, Malice, and Jealousy are consolidated in this, to make his Misery complete, (*viz.*) the Duration of it all, the Eternity of his Condition; that he is without Hope, without Redemption, without Recovery.

If anything can inflame this *Hell* and make it hotter, 'tis this only, and this does add an inexpressible Horror to the Devil himself; *namely*, the seeing Man (the only Creature he hates) placed in a State of Recovery, a glorious Establishment of Redemption formed for him in Heaven, and the Scheme of it perfected on Earth; by which *this Man*, though even the *Devil* by his Art may have deluded him, and drawn him into Crime, is yet in a State of

Recovery, which the Devil is not; and that it is not in his (*Satan's*) Power to prevent it: Now take the Devil as he is in his own Nature Angelic, a bright immortal Seraph, Heaven-born, and having tasted the eternal Beatitude, which these are appointed to enjoy; the Loss of that State to himself, the Possession of it granted to his Rival though wicked like and as himself; I say, take the Devil as he is, having a quick Sense of his own Perdition, and a stinging Sight of his Rival's Felicity, 'tis *Hell enough*, and more than enough, even for an Angel to support; nothing we can conceive can be worse.

As to any other Fire than this, such and so immaterially intense as to Torment a Spirit, which is itself Fire also; I will not say it cannot be, because to Infinite every Thing is possible, but I must say, I cannot conceive rightly of it.

I will not enter here into the Wisdom or Reasonableness of representing the Torments of Hell to be Fire, and that Fire to be a Commixture of *Flame* and *Sulfur*; it has pleased God to let the Horror of those eternal Agonies about *a lost Heaven*, be laid before us by those Similitudes or Allegories, which are most moving to our Senses and to our Understandings; nor will I dispute the Possibility; much less will I doubt but that there is to be a Consummation of Misery to all the Objects of Misery when the *Devil's* Kingdom in this World ending with the World itself, that Liberty he has now may be farther abridged; when he may be returned to the same State he was in between the Time of his Fall and the Creation of the World; with perhaps some additional Vengeance on him, such as at present we cannot describe, for all that Treason and those high Crimes and Misdemeanors which he has been guilty of here, in his Conversation with Mankind.

As his Infelicity will be then consummated and completed, so the Infelicity of that Part of Mankind, who are condemned with him, may receive a considerable Addition from those Words in their Sentence, to be tormented *with the Devil and his Angels*; for as the Absence of the Supreme Good is a complete Hell, so the hated Company of the Deceiver, who was the great Cause of his Ruin, must be a Subject of additional Horror, and he will be always saying, as a *Scots* Gentleman, who died of his Excesses, said to the famous Dr. P——, who came to see him on his Death-bed, but had been too much his Companion in his Life,

O tu fundamenta jecisti———

I would not treat the very Subject itself with any Indecency, nor do I think my Opinion of that *Hell*, which I say consists in the Absence of him, in whom is Heaven, one Jot less Solemn than theirs who believe it all *Fire* and *Brimstone*; but I must own, that to me nothing can be more ridiculous than the Notions that we entertain and fill our Heads with about *Hell*, and about the *Devil's* being there tormenting of Souls, broiling them upon

Gridirons, hanging them up upon Hooks, carrying them upon their Backs, and the like, with the several Pictures of *Hell*, represented by a great Mouth with horrible Teeth, gaping like a Cave on the Sides of a Mountain; suppose that appropriated to *Satan* in the *Peak*, which indeed is not much unlike it, with a Stream of Fire coming out of it, as there is of Water, and smaller Devils going and coming continually in and out, to fetch and carry Souls the Lord knows whither, and for the Lord knows what.

These Things, however intended for Terror, are indeed so ridiculous, that the *Devil* himself, to be sure, mocks at them, and a Man of Sense can hardly refrain doing the like, only I avoid it, because I would not give offence to weaker Heads.

However, I must not Compliment the Brains of other Men, at the Expense of my own, or talk Nonsense because they can understand no other; I think all these Notions and Representations of *Hell* and of the *Devil*, to be as prophane as they are ridiculous, and I ought no more to talk profanely than merrily of them.

Let us learn to talk of these Things then, as we should do; and as we really cannot describe them to our Reason and Understanding, why should we describe them to our Senses; we had, I think, much better not describe them at all, that is to say, not attempt it: The blessed Apostle St. *Paul* was, as he said himself, carried up, or caught up into the *third Heaven*, yet when he came down again, he could neither tell what he heard or describe what he saw; all he could say of it was, that what he heard was *unutterable*, and what he saw was *inconceivable*.

It is the same thing as to the State of the *Devil* in those Regions which he now possesses, and where he now more particularly inhabits; my present Business then is not to enter into those grave Things so as to make them ridiculous, as I think most People do that talk of them; but as the *Devil*, let his Residence be where it will, has evidently free Leave to come and go, not into this World only; (*I mean, the Region of our Atmosphere,*) but for ought we know, to all the other inhabited Worlds which God has made, where-ever they are, and by whatsoever Names they are or may be known or distinguished; for if he is not confined in one Place, we have no Reason to believe he is excluded from any Place, Heaven only excepted, from whence he was expelled for his Treason and Rebellion.

His Liberty then being thus ascertained, three Things seem to be material for us to give an Account of, in order to form this Part of his History.

1. What his Business is on this Globe of Earth which we vulgarly call the World, how he acts among us, what Affairs Mankind and he have together, and how far his Conduct here relates to Us, and Ours is, or may be influenced by him.

2. Where his Principal Residence is, and whether he has not a particular Empire of his own, to which he retreats upon proper Occasions; where he entertains his Friends when they come under his particular Administration; and where, when he gets any Victory over his Enemies, he carries his Prisoners of War.

3. What may probably be the great Business this black Emperor has at present upon his Hands, either in this World or out of it, and by what Agents he works?

As these Things may perhaps run promiscuously thro' the Course of this whole Work, and frequently be touched at under other Branches of the *Devil*'s History, so I do not propose them as Heads of Chapters or Particular Sections, for the Order of Discourse to be handled apart; for (by the way) as Satan's Actings have not been the most regular Things in the World, so in our Discourse about him, it must not be expected that we can always tie our selves down to Order and Regularity, either as to Time, or Place, or Persons; for Satan being *hic & oblique*, a loose ungoverned Fellow, we must be content to trace him where we can find him.

It is true, in the foregoing Chapter, I showed you the Devil entered into the Herd Ecclesiastic, and gave you some Account of the first successful Step he took with Mankind since the Christian Epoch; how having secretly managed both Temporal and Spiritual Power apart, and by themselves, he now united them in Point of Management, and brought the Church Usurpation and the Army's Usurpation together; the Pope to bless the General in deposing and murdering his Master the Emperor; and the General to recognize the Pope in dethroning his Master Christ Jesus.

From this time forward you are to allow the *Devil* a mystical Empire in this World; not an Action of Moment done without him, not a Treason but he has a Hand in it, not a Tyrant but he prompts him, not a Government but he has a —— in it; not a Fool but he tickles him, not a Knave but he guides him; he has a Finger in every Fraud, a Key to every Cabinet, from the *Divan* at *Constantinople*, to the *Mississippi* in *France*, and to the *South-Sea* Cheats at ———; from the first Attack upon the Christian World, in the Person of the *Romish* Antichrist, down to the Bull *Unigenitus*; and from the Mixture of St. *Peter* and *Confucius* in *China*, to the Holy Office in *Spain*; and down to the *Emlins* and *Dodwells* of the current Age.

How he has managed, and does manage, and how in all Probability he will manage till his Kingdom shall come to a Period, and how at last he will probably be managed himself, *Enquire within, and you shall know farther.*

Chapter III

Of the Manner of Satan's acting and carrying on his Affairs in this World, and particularly of his ordinary Workings in the dark, by Possession and Agitation

The Devil being thus reduced to act upon Mankind by Stratagem only, it remains to enquire how he performs, and which way he directs his Attacks; the Faculties of Man are a kind of a Garrison in a strong Castle, which as they defend it on the one hand under the Command of the reasoning Power of Man's Soul, so they are prescribed on the other hand, and can't sally out without Leave; for the Governor of a Fort does not permit his Soldiers to hold any Correspondence with the Enemy, without special Order and Direction. Now the great Enquiry before us is, How comes the Devil to a Parley with us? how does he converse with our Senses, and with the Understanding? How does he reach us, which way does he come at the Affections, and which way does he move the Passions? It's a little difficult to discover this treasonable Correspondence, and that Difficulty is indeed the *Devil's* Advantage, and, for ought I see, the chief Advantage he has over Mankind.

It is also a great Enquiry here, whether the *Devil* knows our Thoughts or no? If I may give my Opinion, I am with the negative; I deny that he knows anything of our Thoughts, except of those Thoughts which he puts us upon thinking, for I will not doubt but he has the Art to inject Thoughts, and to revive dormant Thoughts in us: It is not so wild a Scheme as some take it to be, that Mr. *Milton* lays down, to represent the *Devil* injecting corrupt Desires and wandering Thoughts into the Head of *Eve*, by Dreams, and that he brought her to Dream whatever he put into her Thoughts, by whispering to her vocally when she was asleep; and to this End, he imagines the Devil laying himself close to her Ear, in the Shape of a Toad, when she was fall asleep; I say, this is not so wild a Scheme, seeing even now, if you can whisper anything close to the Ear of a Person in a deep Sleep, so as to speak distinctly to the Person, and yet not awaken him, as has been frequently tried, the Person sleeping shall dream distinctly of what you say to him; nay, shall dream the very Words you say.

We have then no more to ask, but how the Devil can convey himself to the Ear of a sleeping Person, and it is granted then that he may have Power to make us dream what he pleases: But this is not all, for if he can so forcibly, by his invisible Application, cause us to dream, what he pleases, why can he not with the same Facility prompt our Thoughts, whether sleeping or waking? To dream, is nothing else but to think sleeping; and we have abundance of deep-headed Gentlemen among us, who give us ample Testimony that they dream waking.

But if the Devil can prompt us to dream, that is to say, to think, yet if he does not know our Thoughts, how then can he tell whether the Whisper had its Effect? The answer is plain, the Devil, like the Angler, baits the Hook, if the Fish bite he lies ready to take the Advantage, he whispers to the Imagination, and then waits to see how it works; as *Naomi* said to *Ruth*, Chap. iii. 5, 18. *Sit still, my Daughter, until thou know how the Matter will fall, for the Man will not be at rest until he have finished the thing.* Thus when the Devil had whispered to *Eve* in her Sleep, *according to Milton*, and suggested Mischief to her Imagination, he only sat still to see how the Matter would work, for he knew if it took with her, he should hear more of it; and then by finding her alone the next Day, without her ordinary Guard her Husband, he presently concluded she had swallowed the Bait, and so attacked her afresh.

A small deal of Craft, and less by far than we have reason to believe the *Devil* is Master of, will serve to discover whether such and such Thoughts as he knows he has suggested, have taken Place or no; the Action of the Person presently discovers it, at least to him that lies always upon the Watch, and has every Word, every Gesture, every Step we take subsequent to his Operation, open to him; it may therefore, for ought we know, be a great Mistake, and what most of us are guilty of, to tell our Dreams to one another in the Morning, after we have been disturbed with them in the Night; for if the *Devil* converses with us so insensibly as some are of the Opinion he does, *that is to say*, if he can hear as far as we can see, we may be telling our Story to him indeed, when we think we are only talking to one another.

This brings me most naturally to the important Enquiry, whether the *Devil* can walk about the World invisibly or no? The Truth is, this is no question to me; for as I have taken away his Visibility already, and have denied him all Prescience of Futurity too, and have proved he cannot know our Thoughts, nor put any Force upon Persons or Actions, if we should take away his Invisibility too, we should *undevil* him quite, to all Intents and Purposes, as to any Mischief he could do; nay, it would banish him the World, and he might even go and seek his Fortune somewhere else; for if he could neither be visible or invisible, neither act in public or in private, he could neither have Business or Being in this Sphere, nor could we be any way concerned with him.

The *Devil* therefore most certainly has a Power and Liberty of moving about in this World, after *some manner or another*; this is verified as well by way of Allegory, as by way of History, in the Scripture itself; and as the first strongly suggests and supposes it to be so, the last positively asserts it;

and, not to crowd this Work with Quotations from a Book which we have not much to do with in the *Devil's* Story, at least not much to his Satisfaction, I only hint his personal Appearance to our Saviour in the Wilderness, where it is said, *the Devil taketh him up to an exceeding high Mountain*; and in another Place, *the Devil departed from him.* What Shape or Figure he appeared in, we do not find mentioned, but I cannot doubt his appearing to him there, any more than I can his talking to our Saviour in the Mouths, and with the Voices of the several Persons who were under the terrible Affliction of an actual Possession.

These Things leave us no room to doubt of what is advanced above, namely, that he, (the *Devil*) has a certain Residence, or Liberty of residing in, and moving about upon the Surface of this Earth, as well as in the Compass of the Atmosphere, vulgarly called the Air, in some manner or other: That is the general.

It remains to enquire into the manner, which I resolve into two Kinds;

1. *Ordinary*, which I suppose to be his invisible Motions as a Spirit; under which Consideration I suppose him to have an unconfined, unlimited, unrestrained Liberty, as to the manner of acting; and this either in Persons, by Possession; or in Things, by Agitation.

2. *Extraordinary*; which I understand to be his Appearances in borrowed Shapes and Bodies, or Shadows rather of Bodies; assuming Speech, Figure, Posture, and Several Powers, of which we can give little or no Account; in which extraordinary manner of Appearances, he is either limited by a Superior Power, or limits himself politically, as being not the Way most for his Interest or Purpose, to act in his Business, which is more effectually done in his State of Obscurity.

Hence we must suppose the *Devil* has it very much in his own Choice, whether to act in one Capacity, or in the other, or in both; that is to say, of appearing, and not appearing, as he finds for his Purpose: In this State of Invisibility, and under the Operation of these Powers and Liberties, he performs all his Functions and Offices, as *Devil*, as Prince of Darkness, as God of this World, as Tempter, Accuser, Deceiver, and all whatsoever other Names of Office, or Titles of Honor he is known by.

Now taking him in this large unlimited, or little limited State of Action, he is well called, *the God of this World*, for he has very much of the Attribute of Omnipresence, and may be said, *either by himself or his Agents*, to be everywhere, and see everything; that is to say, everything that is visible; for I cannot allow him any Share of *Omniscience* at all.

That he ranges about everywhere, is *with us*, and sometimes *in us*, sees when he is not seen, hears when he is not heard, comes in without Leave, and goes out without Noise, is neither to be shut in or shut out, that when he runs *from us* we can't catch him, and when he runs *after us* we can't escape him, is seen when he is not known, and is known when he is not seen; all these things, and more, we have Knowledge enough about to convince us of the Truth of them; so that, as I have said above, he is certainly walking to and fro thro' the Earth, *etc..* after *some manner or other*, and in some Figure or other, visible or invisible, as he finds Occasion. Now in order to make our History of him complete, the next Question before us is, how, and in what manner he acts with Mankind? how his Kingdom is carried on, and by what Methods he does his Business, for he certainly has a great deal of Business to do; he is not an idle Spectator, nor is he walking about *incognito*, and clothed in Mist and Darkness, purely in Kindness to us, that we should not be startled at him; but 'tis in Policy, that he may act undiscovered, that he may see and not be seen, may play his Game in the dark, and not be detected in his Roguery; that he may prompt Mischief, raise Tempests, blow up Coals, kindle Strife, embroil Nations, use Instruments, and not be known to have his Hand in anything, when at the same time he really has a Hand in everything.

Some are of Opinion, *and I among the rest*, that if the *Devil* was personally and visibly present among us, and we conversed with him Face to Face, we should be so familiar with him in a little time, that his ugly Figure would not affect us at all, that his Terrors would not fright us, or that we should any more trouble our selves about him, than we did with the last great Comet in 1678, which appeared so long and so constantly without any particular known Event, that at last we took no more Notice of it than of the other ordinary Stars which had appeared before we or our Ancestors were born.

Nor indeed should we have much Reason to be startled at him, or at least none of those silly Things could be said of him which we now amuse our selves about, and by which we set him up like a Scare-Crow to fright Children and old Women, to fill up old Stories, make Songs and Ballads, and in a Word, carry on the low prized Buffoonery of the common People; we should either see him in his Angelic Form, as he was from the Original, or if he has any Deformities entailed upon him by the supreme Sentence, and in Justice to the Deformity of his Crime, they would be of a superior Nature, and fitted more for our Contempt as well as Horror, than those weak fancied Trifles contrived by our ancient Devil-raisers and Devil-makers, to feed the wayward Fancies of old Witches and Sorcerers, who cheated the ignorant World with a *Devil* of their own making, set forth, *in terrorem*, with Bat's Wings, Horns, cloven Foot, long Tail, forked Tongue, and the like.

In the next Place, be his frightful Figure what it would, and his Legions as numerous as the Host of Heaven, we should see him still, as the Prince of *Devils*, though monstrous as a Dragon, flaming as a Comet, tall as a Mountain, yet dragging his Chain after him equal to the utmost of his supposed Strength; always in Custody of his *Jailors* the Angels, his Power over-powered, his Rage cowed and abated, or at least awed and under Correction, limited and restrained; in a Word, we should see him a vanquished Slave, his Spirit broken, his Malice, though not abated, yet Hand-cuffed and overpowered, and he not able to work any Thing against us by Force; so that he would be to us but like the Lions in the Tower, encaged and locked up, unable to do the Hurt he wishes to do, and that we fear, or indeed any hurt at all.

From hence 'tis evident, that 'tis not his Business to be public, or to walk up and down in the World visibly, and in his own Shape; his Affairs require a quite different Management, as might be made apparent from the Nature of Things, and the Manner of our Actings, as Men, either with our selves or to one another.

Nor could he be serviceable in his Generation, as a public Person as now he is, or answer the End of his Party who employ him, and who, if he was to do their Business in public, as he does in private, would not be able to employ him at all.

As in our modern Meetings for the Propagation of Impudence and other Virtues, there would be no Entertainment and no Improvement for the Good of the Age, if the People did not all appear in Masque, and concealed from the common Observation; so neither could *Satan* (from whose Management those more happy Assemblies are taken as Copies of a glorious Original) perform the usual and necessary Business of his Profession, if he did not appear wholly in Covert and under needful Disguises; how, but for the Convenience of his Habit, could he call himself into so many Shapes, act on so many different Scenes, and turn so many Wheels of State in the World, as he has done? as a mere professed *Devil* he could do nothing.

Had he been obliged always to act the mere Devil in his own Clothes, and with his own Shape, appearing uppermost in all Cafes and Places, he could never have preached in so many Pulpits, presided in so many Councils, voted in so many Committees, sat in so many Courts, and influenced so many Parties and Factions in Church and State, as we have Reason to believe he has done in our Nation, and in our Memories too, as well as in other Nations and in more ancient Times. The Share Satan has had in all the weighty Confusions of the Times, ever since the first Ages of Christianity in the World, has been carried on with so much Secrecy, and so much with an Air of Cabal and Intrigue, that nothing can have been managed more subtly and closely, and in the same Manner has he acted in our Times, in order to conceal his Interest, and conceal the Influence he has had in the Councils of the World.

Had it been possible for him to have raised the Flames of Rebellion and

War so often in this Nation, as he certainly has done? Could he have agitated the Parties on both Sides, and inflamed the Spirits of three Nations, if he had appears in his own Dress, a mere naked Devil? It is not the Devil as a *Devil* that does the Mischief, but the *Devil* in Masquerade, *Satan* in full Disguise, and acting at the Head of civil Confusion and Distraction.

If History may be credited, the *French* Court at the Time of our old Confusions was made the Scene of Satan's Politics, and prompted both Parties in *England* and in *Scotland* also to quarrel, and how was it done? Will any Man offer to scandalize the *Devil* so much as to say, or so much as to suggest that *Satan* had no Hand in it all? Did not the *Devil*, by the Agency of Cardinal *Richlieu*, send 400000 Crowns at one Time, and 600000 at another, to the *Scots*, to raise an Army and march boldly into *England?* and did not the same *Devil* at the same time, by other Agents, remit 800000 Crowns to the other Party, in order to raise an Army to fall upon the *Scots*? nay, did not the *Devil* with the same Subtlety send down the Archbishop's Order to impose the Service-Book upon the People in *Scotland*, and at the same Time raise a Mob against it, in the great Church (at St. *Giles*'s)? Nay, did not he actually, in the Person of an old Woman (his favorite Instrument) throw the three-legged Stool at the Service-Book, and animate the zealous People to take up Arms for Religion, and turn Rebels for God Sake?

All these happy and successful Undertakings, though 'tis no more to be doubted they were done by the Agency of *Satan*, and in a very surprising Manner too, yet were all done in secret, by what I call Possession and Injection, and by the Agency and Contrivance of such Instruments, or by the *Devil* in the Disguise of such Servants as he found out fitted to be employed in his Work, and who he took a more effectual Care in concealing of.

But we shall have Occasion to touch all this Part over again, when we come to discourse of the particular Habits and Disguises which the *Devil* has made use of, all along in the World, the better to cover his Actions, and to conceal his being concerned in them.

In the mean Time the Cunning or Artifice the *Devil* makes use of in all these Things is in itself very considerable; 'tis an old Practice of his using, and he has gone on in diverse Measures, for the better concealing himself in it; which Measures, though he varies sometimes, as his extraordinary Affairs require, yet they are in all Ages much the same, and have the same Tendency; namely, that he may get all his Business carried on by the Instrumentality of Fools; that he may make Mankind Agents in their own Destruction, and that he may have all his Work done in such a Manner as that he may seem to have no Hand in it; nay he contrives so well, that the very Name *Devil* is put upon his opposite Party, and the Scandal of the black Agent lies all upon them.

In order then to look a little into his Conduct, let us enquire into the common Mistakes about him, see what Use is made of them to his Advantage, and how far Mankind is imposed upon in those Particulars, and to what Purpose.

Chapter IV

Of Satan's Agents or Missionaries, and their Actings upon and in the Minds of Men in his Name

Infinite Advantages attend the *Devil* in his retired Government, as they respect the Management of his Interests, and the carrying on his absolute Monarchy in the World; particularly as it gives him room to act by the Agency of his inferior Ministers and Messengers, called on many Occasions *his Angels*, of whom he has an innumerable *Multitude*, at his Command, enough, for ought we know, to spare one to attend every Man and Woman now alive in the World; and of whom, if we may believe our second sight Christians, the Air is always as full, as a Beam of the Evening Sun is of Insects, where they are ever ready for Business, and to go and come as their great Governor issues out Orders for their Directions.

These, as they are all of the same spirituous Quality with himself, and consequently invisible like him, *except as above*, are ready upon all Occasions to be sent to *and into* any such Person, and for such Purposes, *superior Limitations only excepted*, as the grand Director of *Devils*, (The *Devil* properly so called guides them;) and be the Subject or the Object what it will, *that is to say*, be the Person they are sent to, *or into, as above*, who it will, and the Business the Messenger is to do what it will, they are sufficiently qualified; for this is a Particular to Satan's Messengers or Agents, that they are not like us humane *Devils* here in the World, some bred up one Way, some another, some of one Trade, some of another, and consequently some fit for some Business, some for another, some good for something, and some good for nothing, but his People are everyone fit for every Thing, can find their Way everywhere, and are a Match for every Body they are sent to; in a Word, there are no *foolish Devils*, they are all fully qualified for their Employment, fit for anything he sets them about, and very seldom mistake their Errand or fail in the Business they are sent to do.

Nor is it strange at all, that the *Devil* should have such a numberless Train of Deputy *Devils* to act under him; for it must be acknowledged he has a great deal of Business upon his Hands, a vast deal of Work to do, abundance of public Affairs under his Direction, and an infinite Variety of particular Cases always before him; *for Example.*

How many Governments in the World are wholly in his Administration? how many Divans and great Councils under his Direction? nay, I believe, it would be hard to prove that there is or has been one Council of State in the World for many hundred Years past, down to the Year 1713, (we don't pretend to come nearer home) where the *Devil* by himself, or his Agents in one Shape or another, has not sat as a Member, if not taken the Chair.

And though some learned Authors may dispute this Point with me, by giving some Examples where the Councils of Princes have been acted by a better Hand, and where Things have been carried against *Satan's* Interest, and even to his great Mortification, it amounts to no more than this; namely, that in such Cases the *Devil* has been out-voted; but it does not argue but he might have been present there, and have pushed his Interest as far as he could, only that he had not the Success he expected; for I don't pretend to say that he has never been disappointed; but those Examples are so rare, and of so small Signification, that when I come to the Particulars, as I shall do in the Sequel of this History, you will find them hardly worth naming; and that, take it one Time with another, the *Devil* has met with such a Series of Success in all his Affairs, and has so seldom been baulked; and where he has met with a little Check in his Politics, has notwithstanding, so soon and so easily recovered himself, regained his lost Ground, or replaced himself in another Country when he has been supplanted in one, that his Empire is far from being lessened in the World, for the last thousand Years of the Christian Establishment.

Suppose we take an Observation from the Beginning of *Luther*, or from the Year 1420, and call the Reformation a Blow to the *Devil's* Kingdom, which before that was come to such a Height in Christendom, that 'tis a Question not yet thoroughly decided, whether that Medley of Superstition and horrible Heresies, that Mass of Enthusiasm and Idols called the Catholic Hierarchy, was a Church of God or a Church of the *Devil*; whether it was an Assembly of Saints or a Synagogue of Satan: I say, take that Time to be the *Epoch* of Satan's Declension and of Lucifer's falling from Heaven, that is, from the Top of his terrestrial Glory, yet whether he did not gain in the Defection of the *Greek* Church about that Time and since, as much as he lost in the Reformation of the *Roman*, is what Authors are not yet agreed about, not reckoning what he has regained since of the Ground which he had lost even by the Reformation, (*viz.*) the Countries of the Duke of *Savoy's* Dominion, where the Reformation is almost eaten out by Persecution; the whole *Valtoline* and some adjacent Countries; the whole Kingdom of *Poland* and almost all *Hungary*; for since the last War the Reformation, as it were, lies gasping for Breath, and expiring in that Country, also several large Provinces in *Germany*, as *Austria*, *Carinthia*, and the whole Kingdom of *Bohemia*, where the Reformation once powerfully planted, received its Death's Wound at the Battle of *Prague*, *Ann.* 1627, and languished but a very little while, died and was buried, and good King Popery reigned in its stead.

To these Countries thus regained to Satan's infernal Empire, let us add his modern Conquests and the Encroachments he has made upon the

Reformation in the present Age, which are, *however light we make of them*, very considerable (*viz.*) the Electorate of the *Rhine* and the *Palatinate*, the one fallen to the House of *Bavaria*, and the other to that of *Neuburgh*, both Popish; the Dutchy of *Deux Ponts* fallen just now to a popish Branch, the whole Electorate of *Saxony* fallen under the Power of popish Government by the Apostasy of their Princes, and more likely to follow the Fate of *Bohemia*, whenever the diligent *Devil* can bring his new Project in *Poland* to bear, as 'tis more than probable he will do so some time or other, by the growing Zeal as well as Power of (that House of Bigots) the House of *A——*.

But to sum up the dull Story; we must add in the Roll of the *Devil's* Conquests, the whole Kingdom of *France*, where we have in one Year seen, to the immortal Glory of the *Devil's* Politics, that his Measures have prevailed to the total Extirpation of the Protestant Churches without a War; and that Interest which for 200 Years had supported itself in spite of Persecutions, Massacres, five civil Wars and innumerable Battles and Slaughters, at last received its mortal Wound from its own Champion *Henry* IV. and sunk into utter Oblivion, by *Satan's* most exquisite Management under the Agency of his two prime Ministers Cardinal *Richlieu* and *Lewis* the XIV, whom he entirely possessed.

Thus far we have a melancholy View of the *Devil's* new Conquests, and the Ground he has regained upon the Reformation, in which his secret Management has been so exquisite, and his Politics so good, that could he bring but one Thing to pass, which by his own former Mistake, (for the *Devil* is not infallible) he has rendered impossible, he would bring the Protestant Interest so near its Ruin, that Heaven would be, *as it were*, put to the Necessity of working by Miracle to prevent it; *the Case is thus.*

Ancient Historians tell us, and from good Authority, that the Devil finding it for his Interest to bring his favorite *Mahomet* upon the Stage, and spread the victorious Half-Moon upon the Ruin of the Cross, having with great Success, raised first the *Saracen* Empire, and then the *Turkish* to such a Height, as that the Name of Christian seemed to be extirpated in those two Quarters of the World, which were then not the greatest only, but by far the most powerful, I mean *Asia* and *Africa*; having totally laid wast all those ancient and flourishing Churches of *Africa*, the Labors of St. *Cyprian*, *Tertullian*, St. *Augustine*, and 670 Christian Bishops and Fathers, who governed there at once, also all the Churches of *Smyrna*, *Philadelphia*, *Ephesus*, *Sardis*, *Antioch*, *Laodicea*, and innumerable others in *Pontus*, *Bithynia*, and the Provinces of the lesser *Asia*.

The *Devil* having, I say, finished these Conquests so much to his Satisfaction, began to turn his Eyes Northward, and though he had a considerable Interest in the *Whore of Babylon*, and had brought his Power by the Subjection of the *Roman* Hierarchy to a great Height, yet finding the Interest of *Mahomet* most suitable to his *devilish* Purposes, as most adapted to the Destruction of Mankind, and laying waste the World, he resolved to espouse the growing Power of the *Turk*, and bring him in upon *Europe* like a Deluge.

In order to this, and to make Way for an easy Conquest, like a true *Devil* he worked under Ground, and sapped the Foundation of the Christian Power, by sowing Discord among the reigning Princes of *Europe*; that so envying one another they might be content to stand still and look on while the *Turk* devoured them one by one, and at last might swallow them up all.

This *devilish* Policy took to his Heart's Content; the Christian Princes stood still, stupid, dozing, and unconcerned, till the Turk conquered *Thrace*, over-run *Servia, Macedonia, Bulgaria*, and all the Remains of the *Grecian* Empire, and at last the Imperial City of *Constantinople* itself.

Finding this politic Method so well answer his Ends, the *Devil*, who always improves upon the Success of his own Experiments, resolved from that time to lay a Foundation for the making those Divisions and Jealousies of the Christian Princes immortal; whereas they were at first only personal, and founded in private Quarrels between the Princes respectively; such as *Emulation* of one another's Glory, *Envy* at the extraordinary Velour, or other Merit of this or that Leader, or *Revenge* of some little Affront; for which notwithstanding, so great was the Piety of Christian Princes in those Days, that they made no Scruple to sacrifice whole Armies, yea, Nations, to their Piques and private Quarrels, *a certain Sign whose Management they were under.*

These being the Causes by which the Devil first sowed the Seeds of Mischief among them, and the Success so well answering his Design, he could not but wish to have the same Advantage always ready at his Hand; and therefore he resolved to order it so, that these Divisions, which, however useful to him, were only personal, and consequently temporary, like an Annual in the Garden, which must be raised anew every Season, might for the future be national, and consequently durable and immortal.

To this end it was necessary to lay the Foundation of eternal Feud, not in the Humors and Passions of Men only, but in the Interests of Nations: The Way to do this was to form and state the Dominion of those Princes, by such a Plan drawn in Hell, and laid out from a Scheme truly political, of which the *Devil* was chief Engineer; that the Divisions should always remain, being made a natural Consequence of the Situation of the Country, the Temper of their People, the Nature of their Commerce, the Climate, the Manner of living, or something which should forever render it impossible for them to unite.

This, I say, was a Scheme truly infernal, in which the *Devil* was as certainly the principal Operator, to illustrate great Things by small, as ever *John* of *Leyden* was of the High *Dutch* Rebellion, or Sir *John B———t* of the late Project, called the *South-Sea* Stock. Nor did this Contrivance of the *Devil* at all dishonor his Author, or the Success appear unworthy of the Undertaker; for we see it not only answer the End, and made the *Turk* victorious at the same Time, and formidable to *Europe* ever after, but it works to this Day, the Foundation of the Divisions remains in all the several Nations, and that to such a Degree that it is impossible they should unite.

This is what I hinted before, in which the *Devil* was mistaken, and is another instance that he knows nothing of what is to come; for this very Foundation of immortal Jealousy and Discord between the several Nations of *Spain*, *France*, *Germany*, and others, which the *Devil* himself with so much Policy contrived, and which served his Interests so long, is now the only Obstruction to his Designs, and prevents the entire Ruin of the Reformation; for though the reformed Countries are very Powerful, and some of them, as *Great Britain* and *Prussia* is particularly, more powerful than ever; yet it cannot be said that the Protestant Interests in general are stronger than formerly, or so strong as they were in 1623 under the victorious Arms of the *Swede*; On the other Hand, were it possible that the Popish Powers, to wit, of *France*, *Spain*, *Germany*, *Italy* and *Poland*, which are entirely Popish, could heartily unite their Interests, and should join their Powers to attack the Protestants, the latter would find it very difficult, if not impossible, to defend themselves.

But as fatal as such a Union of the Popish Powers would be, and as useful as it would be to the *Devil*'s Cause at this time, not the *Devil* with all his Angels are able to bring it to pass; no, not with all his Craft and Cunning; he divided them, but he can't unite them; so that even just as 'tis with Men, so 'tis with *Devils*, they may do in an Hour what they can't undo in an Age.

This may comfort those faint-hearted Christians among us, who cry out of the Danger of a religious War in *Europe*, and what terrible Things will happen when *France*, and *Spain*, and *Germany*, and *Italy*, and *Poland* shall all unite; let this Answer satisfy them, The *Devil* himself can never make *France* and *Spain*, or *France* and the Emperor unite; jarring Humors may be reconciled, but jarring Interests never can: They may unite so as to make Peace, *though that can hardly be long*, but never so as to make Conquests together; they are too much afraid of one another, for one to bear, that any Addition of Strength should come to the other. But this is a Digression. We shall find the *Devil* mistaken and disappointed too on several other Occasions, as we go along.

I return to Satan's Interest in the several Governments and Nations, by virtue of his Invisibility, and which he carries on by Possession; 'tis by this Invisibility that he presides in all the Councils of *foreign Powers*, (for we never mean our own, that we always premise;) and what though it is alleged by the Critics, that he does not preside, because there is always a President; I say, if he is not in the President's Chair, yet if he be in the President himself, the Difference is not much; and if he does not vote as a Counselor, if he votes in the Counselor, 'tis much the same; and here, as it was in the Story of *Ahab* the King of *Israel*, as he was a *lying Spirit* in the Mouths of *all his Prophets*, so we find him a Spirit of some particular evil Quality or other, in all the Transactions and Transactors on that Stage of Life we call the State.

Thus he was a dissembling Spirit in *Char*. IX. a turbulent Spirit in *Char*. V. Emperors; a bigoted Spirit of Fire and Faggot in our Queen *Mary*; an apostate Spirit in *Hen*. IV.; a cruel Spirit in *Peter* of *Castile*; a revengeful Spirit in *Ferdinand* II.; a *Phaeton* in *Lewis* XIV.; a *Sardanapalus* in *C——* — II.

In the Great Men of the World, take them a degree lower than the Class of Crowned Heads, he has the same secret Influence; and hence it comes to pass, that the greatest Heroes, and Men of the highest Character for Achievements of Glory, either by their Virtue or Valor, however they have been crowned with Victories, and elevated by human Tongues, whatever the most consummate Virtues or good Qualities they have been known by, yet they have always had some Devil or other in them to preserve *Satan*'s Claim to them uninterrupted, and prevent their Escape out of his Hands; thus we have seen a bloody Devil in a *D'Alva*; a profligate Devil in a *Buckingham*; a lying, artful, or politick Devil in a *Richlieu*; a treacherous Devil in a *Mazarin*; a cruel, merciless Devil in a *Cortez*; a debauched Devil in an *Eugene*; a conjuring Devil in a *Luxemburg*; and a covetous Devil in a *M————h*: In a word, tell me the Man, I tell you the Spirit that reigned in him.

Nor does he thus carry on his secret Management by Possession in Men of the first Magnitude only, but have you not had Evidences of it among ourselves? how has he been a *lying* Spirit in the Mouths of our Prophets, a factious Spirit in the Heads of our Politicians, a profuse *Devil* in a *B——s*, a corrupt Devil in *M——*, a proud Spirit in my Lord *Plausible*, a bullying Spirit in my Lord *Bugbear*, a talkative Spirit in his Grace the *D——* of *Rattle-hall*, a scribbling Spirit in my Lord *H———*, a run-away Spirit in my Lord *Frightful*; and so thro' a long Roll of Heroes, whose exceeding, and particular Qualifications proclaim loudly what Handle the *Devil* took them by, and how fast he held them; for these were all Men of ancient Fame, I hope you know that.

From Men of Figure, we descend to the Mob, and 'tis there the same thing; Possession, like the Plague, is *Morbus Plebaei*; not a Family but he is a Spirit of Strife and Contention among them; not a Man but he has a Part in him; he is a drunken *Devil* in one, a whoring *Devil* in another, a thieving

Devil in a third, a lying *Devil* in the fourth, and so on, to a thousand, and a hundred thousand, *ad infinitum*.

Nay, even the Ladies have their Share in the Possession; and if they have not the *Devil* in their Heads, or in their Tails, in their Faces or their Tongues, it must be some poor despicable She-devil that Satan did not think it worth his while to meddle with; and the Number of those that are below his Operation, I doubt is very small. But that Part I have much more to say to in its Place.

From Degrees of Persons, to Professions and Employments, 'tis the same; we find the *Devil* is a true Posture-master, he assumes any Dress, appears in any Shape, counterfeits every Voice, acts upon every Stage; here he wears a Gown, there a long Robe; here he wears the Jack-Boots, there the Small-Sword; is here an *Enthusiast*, there a *Buffoon*; on this Side he acts the *Mountebank*, on that Side the *Merry-Andrew*; nothing comes amiss to him, from the Great *Mogul*, to the *Scaramouch*; the *Devil* is in them, more or less, and plays his Game so well that he makes sure Work with them all: He knows where the *Common Foible* lies, which is Universal Passion, what Handle to take hold of every Man by, and how to cultivate his Interest so, as not to fail of his End, or mistake the Means.

How then can it be denied but that his acting thus *in tenebris*, and keeping out of the sight of the World, is abundantly his Interest, and that he could do nothing, comparatively speaking, by any other Method?

What would this public Appearance have signified? Who would have entertained him in his own proper Shape and Person? Even B—— B—— himself, though all the World knows him to have a foolish *Devil* in him, would not have been Fool enough to have taken him into his Service, if he had known him: And my Lord *Simpleton* also, who *Satan* has set up for a cunning Fool, seems to have it sit much better upon him now he passes for a Fool of Art, than it should have done if the naked Devil had come and challenged him for a Fool in Nature.

Infinite Variety illustrate the *Devil's* Reign among the Sons of Men; all which he manages with admirable Dexterity, and a Slight particular to himself, by the mere Advantage of his present concealed Situation, and which, had he been obliged to have appeared in Public, had been all lost, and he capable of just nothing at all, or at least of nothing more than the other ordinary Politicians of Wickedness could have done without him.

Now, Authors are much divided as to the manner how the *Devil* manages his proper Instruments for Mischief; for Satan has a great many Agents in the Dark, who neither have the Devil in them, nor are they much acquainted with him, and yet he serves himself of them, whether of their Folly, or of that other Frailty called Wit, 'tis all one, he makes them do his

Work, when they think they are doing their own; nay, so cunning is he in his guiding the weak Part of the World, that even when they think they are serving God, they are doing nothing less or more than serving the *Devil*; nay, 'tis some of the nicest Part of his Operation, to make them believe they are serving God, when they do his Work. Thus those who the Scripture foretold should persecute Christ's Church in the latter Days, were to think they do God *good Service*: Thus the Inquisition, (for Example,) it may be, at this time, in all the acts of Christian Cruelty which they are so famous for (if any of them are ignorant enough not to know that they are *Devils* incarnate) they may, for ought we know, go on for God's sake; torture, murder, starve to Death, mangle and macerate, and all for God, and God's Catholic Church; and 'tis certainly the *Devil's* Master-piece to bring Mankind to such a Perfection of Devilism as that of the *Inquisition* is; for *if the* Devil *had not been in them*, could they christen such a *Hell-fire* Judicature as the *Inquisition* is, by the Name of *the Holy Office*? And so in Paganism, how could so many Nations among the poor *Indians* offer human Sacrifices to their Idols, and murder thousands of Men, Women and Children, to appease this God of the Air, when he is angry, if the *Devil* did not act in them under the Visor of Devotion?

But we need not go to *America*, or to the Inquisition, not to Paganism or to Popery either, to look for People that are sacrificing to the *Devil*, or that give their Peace-offerings to him, while they are offered upon God's Altar; are not our Churches (ay, and Meeting-houses too, as much as they pretend to be more sanctified than their Neighbors) full of *Devil* Worshipers? Where do his Devotees gratulate one another, and congratulate him, more than at Church? where, while they hold up their Hands, and turn up their Eyes towards Heaven, they make all their Vows to Satan, or at least to the fair *Devils* his Representatives, which I shall speak of in their Place.

Do not the Sons of God make Assignations with the Daughters of Men in the very House of Worship? Do they not talk to them in the Language of the Eyes? And what is at the Bottom of it, while one Eye is upon the Prayer-book, and the other adjusting their Dress? Are they not sacrificing to *Venus* and *Mercury*, nay, and the very *Devil* they dress at?

Let any Man impartially survey the Church-Gestures, the Air, the Postures and the Behavior; let him keep an exact Roll, and if I do not show him two *Devil* Worshipers for one true Saint, then the Word *Saint* must have another Signification than I ever yet understood it by.

The Church (as a Place) is the Receptacle of the Dead, as well as the Assembly of the Living; what relates to those below, I doubt Satan, if he would be so kind, could give a better Account of than I can; but as to the Superficies, I pretend to so much Penetration as to tell you, that there are more Specters, more Apparitions always there, than you that know nothing of the matter may be aware of.

I happened to be at an eminent Place of God's most devout Worship the other Day, with a Gentleman of my Acquaintance, who, I observed, minded very little the Business he ought to come about; first I saw him always busy staring about him and bowing this Way and that Way, nay, he made two or three bows and Scrapes when he was repeating the Responses to the Ten Commandments, and assure you he made it correspond strangely, so that the Harmony was not so broken in upon as you would expect it should; thus; *Lord,* and a Bow to a fine Lady just come up to her Seat, *have Mercy upon us;* —— three Bows to a Throng of Ladies that came into the next Pew altogether, *and incline* —— then stopped to make a great Scrape to my Lord ——, *our Hearts,* just then the Hearts of all the Church were gone off from the Subject, for the Response was over, so he huddled up the rest in Whispers, for *God a Mighty* could hear him well enough, *he said,* nay, as well as if he had spoken as loud as his Neighbors did.

After we were come home, I asked him what he meant by all this, and what he thought of it?

How could I help it, *said he,* I must not be rude.

What, *says I,* rude to who?

Why, *says he,* there came in so many she *Devils* I could not help it.

What, *said I,* could not you help bowing when you were saying your Prayers?

O Sir! *says he,* the Ladies would have thought I had slighted them, I could not avoid it.

Ladies! *said I,* I thought you called them *Devils* just now.

Ay, ay, *Devils, said he,* little charming Devils, but I must not be rude to them however.

Very well, *said I,* then you would be rude to *God a Mighty,* because you could not be rude to the Devil?

Why that's true, *said he,* but what can we do? there's no going to Church as the Case stands now, if we must not worship the *Devil* a little between whiles.

This is the Case indeed, and Satan carries his Point on every Hand; for if the fair speaking World, and the fair looking World are generally *Devils*, that is to say, are in his Management, we are sure the foul speaking and the foul doing World are all on his Side, and you have then only the fair-doing Part of the World that are out of his Class, and when we speak of them, *O how few!*

But I return to the *Devil*'s managing our wicked Part, for this he does with most exquisite Subtlety; and this is one Part of it, (*viz.*) he thrusts our Vices into our Virtues, by which he mixes the Clean and the Unclean, and thus by the Corruption of the one, poisons and debauches the other, so that the Slave he governs cannot account for his own common Actions, and is fain to be obliged to his Maker to accept of the Heart without the Hands and Feet; to take, as we vulgarly express it, *the Will* for the *Deed*, and if Heaven was not so good to come into that half in half Service, I don't see but the *Devil* would carry away all his Servants: Here indeed I should enter into a long Detail of involuntary Wickedness, which in short, is neither more or less than the *Devil* in every Body, ay, in every one of you, (our Governors excepted) take it as you please.

What is our Language when we look back with Reflection and Reproach on past Follies? *I think I was bewitched,* I was *possessed, certainly the Devil was in me, or else I had never been such a Sot*: *Devil* in you, Sir! Ay, who doubts it; you may be sure the *Devil* was in you, and there he is still, and next Time he can catch you in the same Snare, you'll be just the same Sot that you say you were before.

In short, the *Devil* is too cunning for us, and manages us his own Way; he governs the Vices of Men by his own Methods; though every Crime will not make a Man a *Devil*, yet it must be owned that every Crime puts the Criminal in some Measure into the Devil's Power, gives him a Title to the Man, and he treats him magisterially ever after.

Some tell us every single Man, every individual has a *Devil* attending him, to execute the Orders of the (Grand Signior) Devil of the whole Clan; that this attending *evil Angel*, for so he is called, sees every Step you take, is with you in every Action, prompts you to every Mischief, and leaves you to do every Thing that is pernicious to yourself; they also allege that there is a good Spirit which attends him too, which latter is always accessory to every Thing that we do that is good, and reluctant to evil; If this is true, how comes it to pass that those two opposite Spirits do not quarrel about it when they are pressing us to contrary Actions, one good and the other evil? and why does the evil tempting Spirit so often prevail? Instead of answering this difficult Question, I shall only tell you, as to this Story of good and evil Angels attending every particular Person, 'tis a good Allegory indeed to represent the Struggle in the Mind of Man between good and evil Inclinations; but as to the rest, the best Thing I can say of it is, *that I think 'tis a Fib.*

But to take Things as they are, and only talk by way of natural Consequence, for to argue from Nature is certainly the best Way to find out the *Devil*'s Story; if there are good and evil Spirits attending us, that is to say, a good Angel and a *Devil*, then 'tis no unjust Reproach upon any Body to say, when they follow the Dictates of the latter, the *Devil* is in them; or they are *Devils*; nay, I must carry it farther still, namely, that as the Generality and greatest Number of People do follow and obey the evil Spirit and not the good, and that the predominate Power is allowed to be the nominating Power; you must then allow, that in short, the greater Part of Mankind has the Devil in them, and so I come to my Text.

To this Purpose give me leave to borrow a few Lines of a Friend on this very Part of the Devil's Management.

To Places and Persons he suits his Disguises,
And dresses up all his Banditti,
Who as Pickpockets flock to a Country Assizes,
Crowd up to the Court and the City.

They're at every Elbow and every Ear,
And ready at every call, Sir;
The vigilant Scout plants his Agents about,
And has something to do with us all, Sir.

In some he has Part, and in some he's the Whole,
And of some (like the Vicar of *Baddow*)
It can neither be said they have Body or Soul,
But only are *Devils* in Shadow.

The Pretty and Witty, are Devils in Masque,
The Beauties are mere Apparitions;
The homely alone by their Faces are known,
And the Good by their ugly Conditions.

The Beaus walk about like the Shadows of Men.
And wherever he leads them they follow,
But take them and shake them, there's not one in ten
But it is as light as a Feather and hollow.

Thus all his Affairs he drives on in Disguise,
And he tickles Mankind with a Feather:
Creeps in at our Ears, and looks out at our Eyes,
And jumbles our Senses together.

He raises the Vapors, and prompts the Desires,
And to every dark Deed holds the Candle;
The Passions enflames and the Appetite fires,
And takes every Thing by the Handle.

Thus he walks up and down in complete Masquerade,
And with every Company mixes,
Sells in every Shop, works at every Trade,
And every Thing doubtful perplexes.

How Satan comes by this governing Influence in the Minds and upon the Actions of Men, is a Question I am not yet come to, nor indeed does it so particularly belong to the Devil's History, it seems rather a Polemic, so it may pass at School among the Metaphysics, and puzzle the Heads of our Masters; wherefore I think to write to the learned Dr. *B——* about it, imploring his most sublime Haughtiness, that when his other more momentous Avocations of Pedantry and Pedagogism will give him an Interval from Wrath and Contention, he will set apart a Moment to consider human Nature Devilized, and give us a Mathematical Anatomical Description of it; with a Map of Satan's Kingdom in the Microcosm of Mankind, and such other Illuminations as to him and his Contemporaries —— and, —— *etc..* in their great Wisdom shall seem meet.

Chapter V

Of the Devil's Management in the Pagan Hierarchy by Omens, Entrails, Augurs, Oracles, and such like Pageantry of Hell; and how they went off the Stage at last by the Introduction of true Religion

I have adjourned, not finished, my Account of the *Devil's* secret Management by *Possession*, and shall reassume it, in its Place; but I must take leave to mention some other Parts of his retired Scheme, by which he has hitherto managed Mankind, and the first of these is by that Fraud of all Frauds called Oracle.

Here his Trumpet yielded an uncertain Sound for some Ages, and like what he was, and according to what he practiced from the Beginning, he delivered out Falsehood and Delusion by Retale: The Priests of *Apollo* acted this Farce for him to a great Nicety at *Delphos*; there were divers others at the same Time, and some, which to give the Devil his due, he had very little Hand in, as we shall see presently.

There were also some smaller, some greater, some more, some less famous Places where those Oracles were seated, and Audience given to the Enquirers, in all which the *Devil*, or some Body for him, *Permissu Superiorum*, for either vindictive or other hidden Ends and Purposes, was allowed to make at least a Pretension to the Knowledge of Things to come; but, as public Cheats generally do, they acted in Masquerade, and gave such uncertain and inconsistent Responses, that they were obliged to use the utmost Art to reconcile Events to the Prediction, even after things were come to pass.

Here the Devil was a *lying Spirit*, in a particular and extraordinary manner, in the Mouths of all the Prophets; and yet he had the Cunning to express himself so, that whatever happened, the Oracle was supposed to have meant as it fell out; and so all their Augurs, Omens and Voices, by which the Devil amused the World, not at that Time only, but since, have been likewise interpreted.

Julian the Apostate dealt mightily in these Amusements, but the Devil, who neither wished his Fall, or presaged it to him, evidenced that he knew nothing of *Julian's* Fate; for that, as he sent almost to all the Oracles of the

East, and summoned all the Priests together to inform him of the Success of his *Persian* Expedition, they all, like *Ahab's Prophets*, having a lying Spirit in them, encouraged him and promised him Success.

Nay, all the ill Omens which disturbed him, they presaged good from; *for Example*, he was at a prodigious Expense when he was at *Antioch* to buy up white Beasts, and white Fowls, for Sacrifices, and for predicting from the Entrails; from whence the *Antiochians*, in contempt, called him *Victimarius*; but whenever the Entrails foreboded Evil, the cunning Devil made the Priests put a different Construction upon them, and promise him Good: When he entered into the Temple of the *Genij* to offer Sacrifice, one of the Priests dropped down dead; this, had it had any Signification more than a Man falling dead of an Apoplectic, would have signified something fatal to *Julian*, who made himself a Brother Sacrist or Priest; whereas the Priests turned it presently to signify the Death of his Colleague, the Consul *Sallust* which happened just at the same Time, though eight hundred Miles off; so in another Case, *Julian* thought it ominous that he, who was *Augustus* should be named with two other Names of Persons, both already dead; the Case was thus, the Style of the Emperor was *Julianus Fœlix Augustus*, and two of his principal Officers were *Julianus* and *Fœlix*; now both *Julianus* and *Fœlix* died within a few Days of one another, which disturbed Him much, who was the third of the three Names; but his flattering *Devil* told him it all imported Good to him (*viz.*) that though *Julianus* and *Fœlix* should die, *Augustus* should be immortal.

Thus whatever happened, and whatever was foretold, and how much so ever they differed from one another, the lying Spirit was sure to reconcile the *Prediction* and the *Event*, and make them at least seem to correspond in Favor of the Person enquiring.

Now we are told Oracles are ceased, and the *Devil* is farther limited for the Good of Mankind, not being allowed to vent his Delusions by the Mouths of the Priests and Augurs, as formerly: I will not take upon me to say how far they are really ceased, more than they were before; I think 'tis much more reasonable to believe there was never any Reality in them at all, or that any Oracle ever gave out any Answers but what were the Invention of the Priests and the Delusions of the Devil; I have a great many ancient Authors on my Side in this Opinion, as *Eusebius, Tertullian, Aristotle*, and others, who as they lived so near the Pagan Times, and when even some of those Rites were yet in Use, they had much more Reason to know, and could probably pass a better Judgment upon them; nay *Cicero* himself ridicules them in the openest manner; again, other Authors descend to Particular and show how the Cheat was managed by the Heathen Sacrists and Priests, and in what enthusiastic manner they spoke; namely, by going into the hollow Images, such as the brazen Bull and the Image of *Apollo*, and how subtilly they gave out *dubious* and *ambiguous* Answers; that when the People did not find their Expectations answered by the Event, they might be imposed upon by the Priests, and confidently told they did not rightly understand the Oracle's Meaning: However, I cannot say but that indeed there are some Authors of good Credit too, who will have it that there was a real prophetic Spirit in the Voice or Answers given by the Oracles, and that oftentimes they were miraculously exact in those Answers; and they give that of the *Delphic* Oracle answering the Question which was given about *Crœsus* for an Example, *viz.* what *Crœsus* was doing at that time? *to wit*, that he was boiling a Lamb and the Flesh of a Tortoise together, in a brass Vessel, or Boiler, with a Cover of the same Metal; that is to say, in a Kettle with a brass Cover.

To affirm therefore, that they were all Cheats, a Man must encounter with Antiquity, and set his private Judgment up against an established Opinion; but 'tis no matter for that; if I do not see anything in that received Opinion capable of Evidence, much less of Demonstration, I must be allowed still to think as I do; others may believe as they list; I see nothing hard or difficult in the Thing; the Priests, who were always historically informed of the Circumstances of the Enquirer, or at least something about them, might easily find some ambiguous Speech to make, and put some double *Entendre* upon them, which upon the Event solved the Credit of the Oracle, were it one way or other; and this they certainly did, or we have room to think the Devil knows less of Things now than he did in former Days.

It is true that by these Delusions the Priests got infinite Sums of Money, and this makes it still probable that they would labor hard, and use the utmost of their Skill to uphold the Credit of their Oracles; and 'tis a full Discovery, as well of the Subtlety of the Sacrists, as of the Ignorance and Stupidity of the People, in those early Days of *Satan's* Witchcraft; to see what merry Work the *Devil* made with the World, and what gross Things he put upon Mankind: Such was the Story of the *Dordonian* Oracle in *Epirus, viz.* That two *Pigeons* flew out of *Thebes* (*N. B.* it was the *Egyptian Thebes*) from the Temple of *Belus*, erected there by the ancient Sacrists, and that one of these fled Eastward into *Libya*, and the Deserts of *Africa*, and the other into *Greece*, namely, to *Dordona*, and these communicated the divine Mysteries to one another, and afterwards gave mystical Solutions to the devout Enquirers; first the *Dordonian* Pigeon perching upon an Oak spoke audibly to the People there, that the Gods commanded them to build an Oracle, or Temple, to *Jupiter*, in that Place; which was accordingly done: The other Pigeon did the like on the Hill in *Africa*, where it commanded them to build another to *Jupiter Ammon*, or *Hammon*.

Wise *Cicero* contemned all this, and, as Authors tell us, ridiculed the Answer, which, as I have hinted above, the Oracle gave to *Crœsus* proving that the Oracle itself was a *Liar*, that it could not come from *Apollo*, for that *Apollo* never spoke *Latin*: In a Word, *Cicero* rejected them all, and *Demosthenes* also mentions the Cheats of the *Oracles*; when speaking of the Oracle of *Apollo*, he said, *Pithia Philippiz'd*; that is, that when the

Priests were bribed with Money, they always gave their Answers in favor of *Philip* of *Macedon*.

But that which is most strange to me is, that in this Dispute about the Reality of Oracles, the Heathen who made use of them are the People who expose them, and who insist most positively upon their being Cheats and Impostors, as in particular those mentioned above; while the Christians who reject them, yet believe they did really foretell Things, answer Questions, *etc.*. only with this Difference, that the Heathen Authors who oppose them, insist that 'tis all Delusion and Cheat, and charge it upon the Priests; and the Christian Opposers insist that it was real, but that the *Devil*, not the Gods, gave the Answers; and that he was permitted to do it by a superior Power, to magnify that Power in the total silencing them at last.

But, as I said before, I am with the Heathen here, against the Christian Writers, for I take it all to be a Cheat and Delusion: I must give my Reason for it, or I do nothing; my Reason is this, I insist Satan is as blind in Matters of Futurity, as we are, and can tell nothing of what is to come; these Oracles often pretending to predict, could be nothing else therefore but a Cheat formed by the Money-getting Priests to amuse the World, and bring Grist to their Mill: If I meet with anything in my Way to open my Eyes to a better Opinion of them, I shall tell it you as I go on.

On the other hand, whether the *Devil* really spoke in those Oracles, or set the cunning Priests to speak for him; whether they predicted, or only made the People believe they predicted; whether they gave Answers which came to pass, or prevailed upon the People to believe that what was said did come to pass, it was much at one, and fully answered the *Devil*'s End; namely, to amuse and delude the World; and as to do, or to cause to be done, is the same Part of Speech, so whoever did it, the *Devil*'s Interest was carried on by it, his Government preserved, and all the Mischief he could desire was effectually brought to pass, so that every way they were the *Devil*'s Oracles, that's out of the Question.

Indeed I have wondered sometimes why, since by this Sorcery the *Devil* performed such Wonders, that is, played so many Tricks in the World, and had such universal Success, he should set up no more of them; but there might be a great many Reasons given for that, too long to tire you with at present: It's true, there were not many of them, and yet considering what a great deal of Business they dispatched, it was enough, for six or eight Oracles were more than sufficient to amuse all the World: The chief Oracles we meet with in History are among the *Greeks* and the *Romans*, *viz.*

That of *Jupiter Ammon*, in *Libya*, as above.

The *Dordonian*, in *Epirus*.

Apollo Delphicus, in the Country of *Phocis* in *Greece*.

Apollo Clavius, in *Asia Minor*.

Serapis, in *Alexandria* in *Egypt*.

Trophomis, in *Bæotia*.

Sybilla Cumæa, in *Italy*.

Diana, at *Ephesus*.

Apollo Daphneus, at *Antioch*.

Besides many of lesser Note, in several other Places, as I have hinted before.

I have nothing to do here with the Story mentioned by *Plutarch*, of a Voice being heard at Sea, from some of the Islands called the *Echinades*, and calling upon one *Thamuz*, an *Egyptian* who was on board a Ship, bidding him, when he came to the *Palodes*, other Islands in the *Ionian* Seas, tell them there that the great God Pan was dead; and when *Thamuz* performed it, great Groanings, and Howlings, and Lamentation were heard from the Shore.

This Tale tells but indifferently, though indeed it looks more like *a Christian Fable*, than a Pagan; because it seems as if made to honor the Christian Worship, and blast all the Pagan Idolatry; and for that Reason I reject it, the Christian Profession needing no such fabulous Stuff to confirm it.

Nor is it true in fact, that the Oracles did cease immediately upon the Death of Christ; but, as I noted before, the Sum of the Matter is this; the Christian Religion spreading itself universally, as well as miraculously, and that too *by the Foolishness of Preaching*, into all Parts of the World, the Oracles ceased; that is to say, their Trade ceased, their Rogueries were daily detected, the deluded People being better taught, came no more after them, and being ashamed, as well as discouraged, they sneaked out of the World as well as they could; in short the Customers fell off, and the Priests, who were the Shopkeepers, having no Business to do, shut up their Shops, broke, and went away; the Trade and the Tradesmen were hissed off the Stage together; so that the *Devil*, who, it must be confessed, got infinitely by the Cheat, became bankrupt, and was obliged to set other Engines at work, as other Cheats and Deceivers do, who when one Trick grows stale, and will serve no longer, are forced to try another.

Nor was the *Devil* to seek in new Measures; for though he could not give out his delusive Trash as he did before, in Pomp and State, with the Solemnity of a Temple and a Set of Enthusiasts called Priests, who plaid a thousand Tricks to amuse the World, he then had Recourse to his old *Egyptian* Method, which indeed was more ancient than that of Oracles; and that was by Magic, Sorcery, Familiars, Witchcraft, and the like.

Of this we find the people of the *South*, that is, of *Arabia* and *Chaldea* were the first, from whence we are told of the Wise Men, that is to say, Magicians, were called *Chaldeans* and *Soothsayers*. Hence also we find *Ahaziah* the King of *Israel* sent to *Baalzebub* the God of *Ekron*, to enquire whether he should live or die? This some think was a kind of an Oracle, though others think it was only some over-grown Magician, who counterfeited himself to be a *Devil*, and obtained upon that Idol-hunting Age to make a Cunning Man of him; and for that Purpose he got himself made a Priest of *Baalzebub*, the God of *Ekron*, and gave out Answers in his Name. Thus those merry Fellows in *Egypt*, *Jannes* and *Jambres*, are said to mimick *Moses* and *Aaron*, when they worked the miraculous Plagues upon the *Egyptians*; and we have some Instances in Scripture that support this, such as the Witch of *Endor*, the King *Manasses*, who dealt with the *Devil* openly, and had a Familiar; the Woman mentioned *Acts* xvi. who had a Spirit of *Divination*, and who got Money by playing the Oracle; that is, answering doubtful Questions, *etc.*. which Spirit, or *Devil*, the Apostles cast out.

Now though it is true that the old Women in the World have filled us with Tales, some improbable, others impossible; some weak, some ridiculous, and that this puts a general Discredit upon all the graver Matrons, who entertain us with Stories better put together, yet 'tis certain, and I must be allowed to affirm, that the *Devil* does not disdain to take into his Service many Troops of good *Old Women*, and Old Women-Men too, who he finds 'tis for his Service to keep in constant Pay; to these he is found frequently to communicate his Mind, and oftentimes we find them such Proficients, that they know much more than the *Devil* can teach them.

How far our ancient Friend *Merlin*, or the grave Matron his (Satan's) most trusty and well-beloved Cousin and Counselor, Mother *Shipton*, were commissioned by him to give out their prophetic Oracles, and what degree of Possession he may have arrived to in them upon their Midnight Excursions, I will not undertake to prove; but that he might be acquainted with them both, as well as with several of our modern Gentlemen, I will not deny neither.

I confess it is not very incongruous with the *Devil*'s Temper, or with the

Nature of his Business, to shift hands; possibly he found that he had tried the World with Oracular Cheats; that Men began to be forfeited with them, and grew sick of the Frauds which were so frequently detected; that it was time to take new Measures, and contrive some new Trick to Bite the World, that he might not be exposed to Contempt; or perhaps he saw the Approach of new Light, which the Christian Doctrine bringing with it began to spread in the Minds of Men; that it would out-shine the dim burning *ignis fatuus*, with which he had so long cheated Mankind, and was afraid to stand it, lest he should be mobbed off the Stage by his own People, when their Eyes should begin to open: That upon this foot he might in Policy withdraw from those old Retreats the Oracles, and restrain those Responses before they lost all their Credit; for we find the People seemed to be at a mighty Loss for some time, for want of them, so that it made them run up and down to Conjurers, and *Man-Gossips*, to brazen Heads, speaking Calves, and innumerable simple Things, so gross that they are scarce fit to be named, to satisfy the Itch of having their Fortunes told them, as we call it.

Now as the Devil is very seldom blind to his own Interest, and therefore thought fit to quit his old way of imposing upon the World by his Oracles, only because he found the World began to be too wise to be imposed upon that way; so on the other hand, finding there was still a Possibility to delude the World, though by other Instruments, he no sooner laid down his Oracles, and the solemn Pageantry, magnificent Appearances, and other Frauds of his Priests and Votaries, in their Temples and Shrines; but he set up a new Trade, and having, as I have said, Agents and Instruments sufficient for any Business that he could have to employ them in, he begins in Corners, as the learned and merry Dr. *Brown* says, and exercises his minor Trumperies by way of his own contriving, lifting a great Number of new-found Operators, such as Witches, Magicians, Diviners, Figure-casters, Astrologers, and such inferior Seducers.

Now it is true, as that Doctor says, this was running into Corners, as if he had been expelled his more triumphant way of giving Audience in Form, which for so many Ages had been allowed him; yet I must add, that as it seemed to be the Devil's own doing, from a right Judgment of his Affairs, which had taken a new Turn in the World, upon the shining of new Lights from the Christian Doctrine, so it must be acknowledged the *Devil* made himself amends upon Mankind, by the various Methods he took, and the Multitude of Instruments he employed, and perhaps deluded Mankind in a more fatal and sensible manner than he did before, though not so universally.

He had indeed before more Pomp and Figure put upon it, and he cheated Mankind then in a Way of Magnificent and Splendor; but this was not in above eight or ten principal Places, and not fifty Places in all, public or private; whereas now fifty thousand of his Angels and Instruments, visible and invisible, hardly may be said to suffice for one Town or City; but in

166

short, as his invisible Agents fill the Air, and are at hand for Mischief on every Emergence, so his visible Fools swarm in every Village, and you have scarce a Hamlet or a Town but his Emissaries are at Hand for Business; and which is still worse, in all Places he finds Business; nay even where Religion is planted and seems to flourish; yet he keeps his Ground and pushes his Interest according to what has been said elsewhere upon the same Subject, that wherever Religion plants, the Devil plants close by it.

Nor, as I say, does he fail of Success, Delusion spreads like a Plague, and the Devil is sure of Votaries; like a true Mountebank, he can always bring a Crowd about his Stage, and that some Times faster than other People.

What I observe upon this Subject is this, that the World is at a strange Loss for want of the Devil; if it was not so, what's the Reason, that upon the silencing the Oracles, and Religion telling them that Miracles are ceased, and that God has done speaking by Prophets, they never enquire whether Heaven has established any other or new Way of Revelation, but away they ran with their Doubts and Difficulties to these Dreamers of Dreams, Tellers of Fortunes, and personal Oracles to be resolved; as if when they acknowledge the Devil is dumb, these could speak; and as if the wicked Spirit could do more than the Good, the *Diabolical* more than the *Divine*, or that Heaven having taken away the Devil's Voice, had furnished him with an Equivalent, by allowing Scolds, Termagants, and old weak and superannuated Wretches to speak for him; for these are the People we go to now in our Doubts and Emergencies.

While this Blindness continues among us, 'tis Nonsense to say that Oracles are silenced, or the *Devil* is dumb, for the *Devil* gives Audience still by his Deputies; only as *Jeroboam* made Priests of the meanest of the People, so he is grown a little humble, and makes use of meaner Instruments than he did before; for whereas the Priests of *Apollo*, and of *Jupiter*, were splendid in their Appearance, of grave and venerable Aspect, and sometimes of no mean Quality; now he makes use of Scoundrels and Rabble, Beggars and Vagabonds, old Hags, superannuated miserable Hermits, Gypsies and Strollers, the Pictures of Envy and ill Luck.

Either the *Devil* is grown an ill Master, and gives but mean Wages, that he can get no better Servants; or else Common Sense is grown very low prized and contemptible; that such as these are fit Tools to continue the Succession of Fraud, and carry on the *Devil's* Interest in the World; for were not the Passions and Temper of Mankind deeply pre-engaged in favor of this dark Prince, we could never suffer ourselves to accept of his Favors by the Hands of such contemptible Agents as these! How do we receive his Oracles from an old Witch of particular Eminence, and who we believe to be more than ordinarily inspired from Hell; I say, we receive the Oracle with Reverence; that is to say, with a kind of Horror, with regard to the Black Prince it comes from, and at the same time turn our Faces away from the Wretch that mumbles out the Answers, lest she should cast an *Evil Eye*, as we call it, upon us, and put a Devil into us when she plays the *Devil* before us? How do we listen to the Cant of those worst of Vagabonds the *Gypsies*, when at the same time we watch our Hedges and Hen-roosts for fear of their thieving?

Either the Devil uses us more like Fools than he did our Ancestors, or we really are worse Fools than those Ages produced, for they were never deluded by such low-prized *Devils* as we are; by such despicable *Bridewell* Devils, that are fitter for a Whipping-post than an Altar, and instead of being received as the Voice of an Oracle, should be sent to the House of Correction for Pick-pockets.

Nor is this accidental, and here and there one of these Wretches to be seen, but in short, if it has been in other Nations as it is with us, I do not see that the Devil was able to get any better People into his Pay, or at least very rarely: Where have we seen anything above a Tinker turn Wizard? and where have we had a Witch of Quality among us, Mother *Je———gs* excepted? and if she had not been more of something else than a Witch, 'twas thought she had never got so much Money by her Profession.

Magicians, Soothsayers, Devil-raisers, and such People, we have heard much of, but seldom above the Degree of the meanest of the mean People, the lowest of the lowest Rank: Indeed the Word *Wise Men*, which the *Devil* would fain have had his Agents honored with, was used a while in *Egypt*, and in *Persia*, among the *Chaldeans*, but it continued but a little while, and never reached so far Northward as our Country; nor, however the *Devil* has managed it, have many of our great Men, who have been most acquainted with him, ever been able to acquire the Title of Wise Men.

I have heard that in older Times, I suppose in good Queen *Bess*'s Days, or beyond, (for little is to be said here for anything on this Side of her time) there were some Counselors and Statesmen who merited the Character of *wise*, in the best Sense; that is to say, *good*, and *wise*, as they stand in Conjunction; but as to what has happened since that, or, as we may call it, from that Queen's Funeral to the late Revolution, I have little to say; but I'll tell you what honest *Andrew Marvel* said of those Times, and by that you may, if you please, make your Calculation or let it alone, 'tis all one.

"To see a white Staff-maker, a Beggar, a Lord,
"And scarce *a wise Man* at a long Council-Board.

But I may be told this relates to wise Men in another Constitution, or wise Men as they are opposed to Fools; whereas we are talking of them now under another Class, namely, as *Wisemen* or Magicians, South-sayers, *etc.*. such as were in former Times called by that Name.

But to this I answer, that take them in which Sense you please, it may be the same; for if I were to ask the *Devil* the Character of the best States-man he had employed among us for many Years past, I am apt to think that though Oracles are ceased, he would honestly, according to the old ambiguous Way, when I asked if they were Christians, answer they were (his) *Privy-Counselors*.

It is but a little while ago, that I happened (in Conversation) to meet with a long List of the Magistrates of that Age, in a neighboring Country, that is to say, the Men of Fame among them; and it was a very diverting Thing to see the Judgment which was passed upon them among a great deal of good Company; it is not for me to tell you how many white Staves, Golden Keys, Mareshals Batoons, Cordons Blue, Gordon Rouge and Gordon Blanc, there were among them, or by what Titles, as Dukes, Counts, Marquis, Abbot, Bishop, or Justice they were to be distinguished; but the marginal Notes I found upon most of them were (being marked with an Asterism) as follows.

Such a Duke, such eminent Offices added to his Titles (* in the Margin) — —— *No Saint.*

Such an Arch—— with the Title of Noble added, ——— *No Archangel.*

Such an eminent Statesman and prime Minister, ——— *No Witch.*

Such a Ribbon with a Set of great Letters added, ——— *No Conjurer.*

It presently occurred to me that though Oracles were ceased, and we had now no more double *Entendre* in such a Degree as before, yet that ambiguous Answers were not at an End; and that whether those Negatives were meant so by the Writers, or not, 'twas certain Custom led the Readers to conclude them to be Satyrs, that they were to be rung backwards like the Bells when the Town's on fire; though in short, I durst not read them backward anywhere, but as speaking of foreign People, for fear of raising the *Devil* I am talking of.

But to return to the Subject; to such mean Things is the Devil now reduced in his ordinary Way of carrying on his Business in the World, that his Oracles are delivered now by the Bellmen and the Chimney-Sweepers, by the meanest of those that speak in the Dark, and if he operates by them, you may expect it accordingly; his Agents seem to me as if the Devil had singled them out by their Deformity, or that there was something particular required in their Aspect to qualify them for their Employment; whence it is become proverbial, when our Looks are very dismal and frightful, to say, I look like a Witch, or in other Cases to say, as ugly as a Witch; in another Case to look as envious as a Witch; now whether there is any Thing particularly required in the Looks of the Devil's modern Agents, which is assisting in the Discharge of their Offices, and which make their Answers appear more solemn, this the *Devil* has not yet revealed, at least not to me; and therefore why it is that he singles out such Creatures as are fit only to fright the People that come to them with their Enquiries, I do not take upon me to determine.

Perhaps it is necessary they should be thus extraordinary in their Aspect, that they might strike an Awe into the Minds of their Votaries, as if they were Satan's true and real Representatives; and that the said Votaries may think when they speak to the Witches they are really talking to the *Devil*; or perhaps 'tis necessary to the Witches themselves, that they should be so exquisitely ugly, that they might not be surprised at whatever Figure the Devil makes when he first appears to them, being certain they can see nothing uglier than themselves.

Some are of the Opinion that the Communication with the *Devil*, or between the Devil and those Creatures his Agents, has something assimilating in it, and that if they were tolerable before, they are, *ipso facto*, turned into Devils by talking with him; I will not say but that a Tremor in the Limbs, a Horror in the Aspect, and a surprising Stare in the Eyes may seize upon some of them when they really see the Devil, and that the frequent Repetition may make those Distortions, which we so constantly see in their Faces becomes natural to them; by which if it does not continue always upon the Countenance, they can at least, *like the Posture-Masters*, cast themselves into such Figures and frightful Dislocations of the Lines and Features in their Faces, and so assume a Devil's Face suitable to the Occasion, or as may serve the turn for which they take it up, and as often as they have any use for it.

But be it which of these the Enquirer pleases, 'tis all one to the Case in Hand; this is certain, that such deformed *Devil-like* Creatures, most of those we call *Hags* and *Witches*, are in their Shapes and Aspects, and that they give out their Sentences and frightful Messages with an Air of Revenge for some Injury received; for Witches are famed chiefly for doing Mischief.

It seems the *Devil* has always picked out the most ugly and frightful old Women to do his Business; *Mother Shipton*, our famous *English* Witch or Prophetess, is very much wronged in her Picture, if she was not of the most terrible Aspect imaginable; and if it be true that *Merlin*, the famous *Welch* Fortune-Teller, was a frightful Figure, it will seem the more rational to believe, if we credit another Story, (*viz.*) that he was begotten by the Devil himself, of which I shall speak by itself: But to go back to the Devil's Instruments being so ugly; it may be observed, I say, that the Devil has always dealt in such sort of Cattle; the *Sybils*, of whom so many strange prophetic Things are recorded, whether true or no is not to the Question, are (if the *Italian* Painters may have any Credit given them) all represented as very old Women; and as if Ugliness were a Beauty to old Age, they seem to paint them out as ugly and frightful as (not they, the Painters) but even as the Devil himself could make them; not that I believe there are any original Pictures of them really extant; but it is not unlikely that the *Italians* might have some traditional Knowledge of them, or some remaining Notions of them, or particularly that ancient *Sybil* named *Anus*, who sold the fatal Book to *Tarquin*; 'tis said of her that *Tarquin* supposed she dotted with Age.

I had Thoughts indeed here to have entered into a learned Disquisition of the Excellency of old Women in all diabolical Operations, and particularly of the Necessity of having recourse to them for *Satan's* more exquisite Administration, which also may serve to solve the great Difficulty in the natural Philosophy of Hell; namely, why it comes to pass that the Devil is obliged for want of old Women, properly so called, to turn so many ancient Fathers, grave Counselors both of Law and State, and especially Civilians or Doctors of the Law into old Women, and how the extraordinary Operation is performed; but this, as a Thing of great Consequence in Satan's Management of humane Affairs, and particularly as it may lead us into the necessary History, as well as Characters of some of the most eminent of these Sects among us, I have purposely reserved for a Work by itself, to be published, if *Satan hinders not*, in fifteen Volumes in Folio, wherein I shall in the first Place define in the most exact Manner possible, what is to be understood by a *Male old Woman*, of what heterogeneous Kind they are produced, give you the monstrous Anatomy of the Parts, and especially those of the Head, which being filled with innumerable Globules of a sublime Nature, and which being of a fine Contexture without, but particularly hollow in the Cavity, defines most philosophically that ancient paradoxical Saying, (*viz.*) *being full of Emptiness*, and makes it very consistent with Nature and common Sense.

I shall likewise spend some Time, *and it must be Labor too, I assure you, when 'tis done*, in determining whether this new Species of Wonderfuls are not derived from that famous *old Woman Merlin*, which I prove to be very reasonable for us to suppose, because of the many several judicious Authors, who affirm the said *Merlin*, as I hinted before, to have been begotten by the *Devil*.

As to the deriving his Gift of Prophesy from the Devil, by that pretended Generation, I shall omit that Part, because, as I have all along insisted upon it, that Satan himself has no prophetic or predicting Powers of his own, it is not very clear to me that he could convey it to his Posterity, *nil dat quod not habet*.

However, in deriving this so much magnified Prophet in a right Line from the *Devil*, much may be said in favor of his ugly Face, in which it was said he was very remarkable, for it is no new Thing for a Child to be like the

Father; but all these weighty Things I adjourn for the present, and proceed to the Affair in Hand, namely, the several Branches of the *Devil's* Management since his quitting his Temples and Oracles.

Chapter VI

Of the extraordinary Appearance of the Devil, and particularly of the Cloven-Foot

Some People would fain have us treat this Tale of the *Devil's* appearing with a Cloven-Foot with more Solemnity than I believe the *Devil* himself does; for Satan, who knows how much of a Cheat it is, must certainly ridicule it, in his own Thoughts, to the last Degree; but as he is glad of any Way to hoodwink the Understandings, and bubble the weak Part of the World; so if he sees Men willing to take every Scarecrow for a Devil, it is not his Business to undeceive them; on the other Hand, he finds it his Interest to foster the Cheat, and serve himself of the Consequence: Nor could I doubt but the Devil, if any Mirth be allowed him, often laughs at the many frightful Shapes and Figures we dress him up in, and especially to see how willing we are first to paint him as black, and make him appear as ugly as we can, and then stare and start at the Spectrum of our own making.

The Truth is, that among all the Horribles that we dress up Satan in, I cannot but think we show the least of Invention in this of a Goat, or a Thing with a Goat's Foot, of all the rest; for though a Goat is a Creature made use of by our Saviour in the Allegory of the Day of Judgment, and is said there to represent the wicked rejected Party, yet it seems to be only on Account of their Similitude to the Sheep, and so to represent the just Fate of Hypocrisy and Hypocrites, and in particular to form the necessary Antithesis in the Story; for else, *our whimsical Fancies excepted*, a Sheep or a Lamb has a Cloven-Foot as well as a Goat; nay, if the Scripture be of any Value in the Case, 'tis to the *Devil's* Advantage, for the dividing the Hoof was the distinguishing Character or Mark of a clean Beast, and how the Devil can be brought into that Number is pretty hard to say.

One would have thought if we had intended to have given a just Figure of the *Devil*, it would have been more apposite to have ranked him among the Cat-kind, and given him a Foot (if he is to be known by his Foot) like a Lion, or like a *red Dragon*, being the same Creatures which he is represented by in the Text, and so his Claws would have had some Terror in them as well as his Teeth.

But neither is the *Goat* a true Representative of the Devil at all, for we do not rank the Goats among the Subtle or cunning Part of the Brutes; he is counted a fierce Creature indeed of his Kind, though nothing like those

173

other above-mentioned; and he is emblematically used to represent a lustful Temper, but even that Part does not fully serve to describe the Devil, whose Operation lies principally another Way.

Besides it is not the *Goat* himself that is made use of, 'tis the Cloven-Hoof only, and that so particularly, that the *Cloven Foot* of a Ram or a Swine, or any other Creature, may serve as well as that of a *Goat*, only that History gives us some Cause to call it the *Goat's Foot*.

In the next Place 'tis understood by us not as a bare Token to know *Satan* by, but as if it were a Brand upon him, and that like the Mark God put upon *Cain*, it was given him for a Punishment, so that he cannot get leave to appear without it, nay cannot conceal it whatever other Dress or Disguise he may put on; and as if it was to make him as ridiculous as possible, they will have it be, that whenever *Satan* has Occasion to dress himself in any humane Shape, be it of what Degree so ever, from the King to the Beggar, be it of a fine Lady or of an *old Woman*, (the Latter it seems he oftenest assumes) yet still he not only must have this *Cloven-Foot* about him, but he is obliged to show it too; nay, they will not allow him any Dress, whether it be a Prince's Robes, a Lord Cha—r's Gown, or a Lady's Hoop and long Petticoats, but the Cloven-Foot must be showed from under them; they will not so much as allow him an artificial *Shoe* or a *Jack-Boot*, as we often see contrived to conceal a *Club-Foot* or a *Wooden-Leg*; but that the *Devil* may be known wherever he goes, he is bound to show his Foot; they might as well oblige him to set a Bill upon his Cap, as Folks do upon a House to be let, and have it written in capital Letters, *I am the* Devil.

It must be confessed this is very particular, and would be very hard upon the *Devil*, if it had not another Article in it, which is some Advantage to him, and that is, that *the Fact is not true*; but the Belief of this is so universal, that all the World runs away with it; by which Mistake the good People miss the *Devil* many times where they look for him, and meet him as often where they did not expect him, and when for want of this Cloven-Foot they do not know him.

Upon this very Account I have sometimes thought, not that this has been put upon him by mere Fancy, and the Cheat of a heavy Imagination, propagated by Fable and Chimney-Corner Divinity, but that it has been a Contrivance of his own; and that, in short, the Devil raised this Scandal upon himself, that he might keep his Disguise the better, and might go a Visiting among his Friends without being known; for were it really so, that he could go nowhere without this particular Brand of Infamy, he could not come into Company, could not dine with my Lord Mayor, nor drink Tea with the Ladies, could not go to the Drawing-R—— at ———, could not have gone to *Fontainebleau* to the King of *France's* Wedding, or to the Diet of *Poland*, to prevent the Grandees there coming to an Agreement; nay, *which would be still worse than all*, he could not go to the Masquerade, nor to any of our Balls; the Reason is plain, he would be always discovered, exposed and forced to leave the good Company, or which would be as bad, the Company would all cry out the *Devil* and run out of the Room as if they were startled; nor could all the Help of Invention do him any Service, no Dress he could put on would cover him; not all our Friends at *Tavistock Corner* could furnish him with a Habit that would disguise or conceal him, this unhappy Foot would spoil it all: Now this would be a great a Loss to him, that I question whether he could carry on any of his most important Affairs in the World without it; for though he has access to Mankind in his complete Disguise, I mean that of his Invisibility, yet the Learned very much agree in this, that his corporal Presence in the World is absolutely necessary upon many Occasions, to support his Interest and keep up his Correspondences, and particularly to encourage his Friends when Numbers are requisite to carry on his Affairs; but this Part I shall have Occasion to speak of again, when I come to consider him as a Gentleman of Business in his Locality, and under the Head of visible Apparition; but I return to the *Foot*.

As I have thus suggested that the Devil himself has politically spread about this Notion concerning his appearing with *a Cloven-Foot*, so I doubt not that he has thought it for his Purpose to paint this *Cloven-Foot* so lively in the Imaginations of many of our People, and especially of those clear sighted Folks who see the *Devil* when he is not to be seen, that they would make no Scruple to say, nay and to make Affidavit too, even before *Satan* himself, whenever he sat upon the Bench, that they had seen his Worship's Foot at such and such a Time; this I advance the rather because 'tis very much for his Interest to do this, for if we had not many Witnesses, *viva voce*, to testify it, we should have had some obstinate Fellows always among us, who would have denied the Fact, or at least have spoken doubtfully of it, and so have raised Disputes and Objections against it, as impossible, or at least as improbable; buzzing one ridiculous Notion or other into our Ears, as if the Devil was not so black as he was painted, that he had no more a *Cloven-Foot* than a Pope, whose Apostolical Toes have so often been reverentially kissed by Kings and Emperors: but now alas this Part is out of the Question, not the Man in the Moon, not the Groaning-Board, not the speaking of Friar *Bacon*'s Brazen-Head, not the Inspiration of *Mother Shipton*, or the Miracles of Dr. *Faustus*, Things as certain as Death and Taxes, can be more firmly believed: The Devil not have a Cloven-Foot! I doubt not but I could, in a short Time, bring you a thousand old Women together, that would as soon believe there was no Devil at all; nay, they will tell you, he could not be a Devil without it, any more than he could come into the Room, and the Candles not burn blue, or go out and not leave a smell of Brimstone behind him.

Since then the Certainty of the Thing is so well established, and there are so many good and substantial Witnesses ready to testify that he has a Cloven-Foot, and that they have seen it too; nay, and that we have Antiquity on our Side, for we have this Truth confirmed by the Testimony of many Ages; why should we doubt it any longer? we can prove that many of our Ancestors have been of this Opinion, and divers learned Authors have left it upon Record, as particularly that learned Familiarist Mother *Hazel*, whose Writings are to be found in MS. in the famous Library at *Pye-Corner*; also the admired *Joan* of *Amesbury*, the History of the *Lancashire* Witches, and the Reverend Exorcist of the *Devil's* of *London*, whose History is extant among us to this Day; all these and many more may be quoted, and their Writings referred to for the Confirmation of the Antiquity of this Truth; but there seems to be no Occasion for farther Evidence, 'tis enough, *Satan* himself, if he did not raise the Report, yet tacitly owns the Fact, at least he appears willing to have it believed, and be received as a general Truth for the Reasons above.

But besides all this, and as much a Jest as some unbelieving People would have this Story pass for, who knows but that if *Satan* is empowered to assume any Shape or Body, and to appear to us visibly, as if really so shaped; I say, who knows but he may, by the same Authority, be allowed to assume the Addition of the Cloven-Foot, or two or four Cloven-Feet, if he pleased? and why not a *Cloven-Foot* as well as any other Foot, if he thinks fit? For if the *Devil* can assume a Shape, and can appear to Mankind in a visible Form, it may, I doubt not, with as good Authority be advanced that he is left at Liberty to assume what Shape he pleases, and to choose *what Case of Flesh and Blood he'll please to wear*, whether real or imaginary; and if this Liberty be allowed him, it is an admirable Disguise for him to come generally with his *Cloven-Foot*, that when he finds it for his Purpose, on special Occasions to come without it, as I said above, he may not be suspected; *but take this with you as you go*, that all this is upon a Supposition that the *Devil* can assume a visible Shape, and make a real Appearance, which however I do not yet think fit to grant or deny.

Certain it is, the first People who bestowed a *Cloven-Foot* upon the Devil, were not so despicable as you may imagine, but were real Favorites of Heaven; for did not *Aaron* set up the *Devil* of a Calf in the Congregation, and set the People a dancing about it for a God? Upon which Occasion, Expositors tell us, that particular Command was given, *Levit.* xvii. 7. *They shall no more offer their Sacrifices unto* Devils, *after whom they have gone a Whoring*; likewise King *Jeroboam* set up the two Calves, one at *Dan* and the other at *Bethel*, and we find them charged afterwards with setting up the Worship of *Devils* instead of the Worship of *God*.

After this we find some Nations actually sacrificed to the *Devil* in the Form of a Ram, and others of a Goat; from which, and that above of the Calves at *Horeb*, I doubt not the Story of the *Cloven-Foot* first derived; and it is plain that the Worship of that Calf at *Horeb* is meant in the Scripture quoted above, *Levit.* xvii. 7. *Thou shalt no more offer Sacrifices unto Devils*: The Original is *Seghnirim*; that is, rough and hairy *Goats* or *Calves*; and some think also in this Shape the *Devil* most ordinarily appeared to the *Egyptians* and *Arabians*, from whence it was derived.

Also in the old Writings of the *Egyptians*, I mean their hieroglyphic Writing, before the Use of Letters was known, we are told this was the Mark that he was known by; and the Figure of a *Goat* was the *Hieroglyphic* of the *Devil*; some will affirm that the *Devil* was particularly pleased to be so represented; how they came by their Information, and whether they had it from his own Mouth or not, Authors have not yet determined.

But be this as it will, I do not see that *Satan* could have been at a Loss for some extraordinary Figure to have bantered Mankind with, though this had not been thought of; but thinking of the *Cloven-Foot* first, and the Matter being indifferent, this took place, and easily rooted itself in the bewildered Fancy of the People, and now 'tis riveted too fast for the *Devil* himself to remove it if he was disposed to try; but as I said above, 'tis none of his Business to solve Doubts or remove Difficulties out of our Heads, but to perplex us with more, as much as he can.

Some People carry this Matter a great deal higher still, and will have the *Cloven-Foot* be like the great Stone which the *Brazilian Conjurers* used to solve all difficult Questions upon, after having used a great many monstrous and barbarous Gestures and Distortions of their Bodies, and cut certain Marks or magical Figures upon the Stone; so, *I say*, they will have this Cloven-Foot be a kind of a Conjuring-Stone, and tell us, that in former Times, when *Satan* drove a greater Trade with Mankind in public, than he has done of late, he gave this *Cloven-Foot* as a Token to his particular Favorites to work Wonders with, and to conjure by, and that Witches, Fairies, Hobgoblins, and such Things, of which the Ancients had several Kinds, at least in their Imagination, had all a *Goat's Leg* with a *Cloven-Foot* to put on upon extraordinary Occasions; it seems this Method is of late grown out of Practice, and so like the melting of Marble and the painting of Glass, 'tis laid aside among the various useful Arts which History tells us are lost to the World; what may be practiced in the Fairy World, if such a Place there be, we can give no particular Account at present.

But neither is this all, for other would-be-wise People take upon them to make farther and more considerable Improvements upon this Doctrine of the *Cloven-Foot*, and treat it as a most significant Instrument of Satan's private Operation, and that as *Joseph* is said to *Divine*, that is to say, to *conjure* by his Golden Cup which was put into *Benjamin*'s Sack, so the *Devil* has managed several of his secret Operations, and Possessions, and other hellish Mechanisms upon the Spirits as well as Bodies of Men, by the Medium or Instrumentality of the *Cloven-Foot*; accordingly it had a Kind of an hellish Inspiration in it, and a separate and magical Power by which he wrought his infernal Miracles; that the Cloven-Foot had a superior Signification, and was not only emblematic and significative of the Conduct of Men, but really guided their Conduct in the most important Affairs of Life; and that the Agents the Devil employed to influence Mankind, and to delude them and draw them into all the Snares and Traps that he lays continually for their Destruction, were equipped with this Foot in Aid of their other Powers for Mischief.

Here they read us learned Lectures upon the sovereign Operations which the Devil is at present Master of, in the Government of human Affairs; and how the Cloven-Foot is an Emblem of the true *double Entendre* or divided Aspect, which the great Men of the World generally act with, and by which all their Affairs are directed; from whence it comes to pass that there is no such Thing as a single hearted Integrity, or an upright Meaning to be found in the World; that Mankind, worse than the ravenous Brutes, preys upon his own Kind, and devours them by all the laudable Methods of Flattery, Whyne, Cheat and Treachery; *Crocodile like*, weeping over those it will devour, destroying those it smiles upon, and, in a Word, devours its own Kind, which the very Beasts refuse, and that by all the Ways of Fraud and Allurement that *Hell* can invent; holding out a cloven divided Hoof, or Hand, pretending to save, when the very Pretence is made use of to ensnare and destroy.

Thus the divided Hoof is the Representative of a divided double Tongue, and Heart, an Emblem of the most exquisite Hypocrisy, the most fawning and fatally deceiving Flattery; and here they give us very diverting Histories, though tragical in themselves, of the manner which some of the *Devil's* inspired Agents have managed themselves under the especial Influence of the *Cloven-Foot*; how they have made War under the Pretence of Peace, murdered Garrisons under the most sacred Capitulations, massacred innocent Multitudes after Surrenders to Mercy.

Again, they tell us the *Cloven-Foot* has been made use of in all Treasons, Plots, Assassinations, and secret as well as open Murders and Rebellions. Thus *Joab* under the Treason of an Embrace, showed how dexterously he could manage the *Cloven-Foot*, and struck *Abner* under the fifth Rib: Thus *David* played the Cloven-Foot upon poor *Uriah*, when he had a Mind to lie with his Wife: Thus *Brutus* played it upon *Cesar*; and to come nearer home, we have had a great many retrograde Motions in this Country by this magical Implement the *Foot*; Such as that of the Earl of *Essex's* Fate, beheading the Queen of *Scots*, and diverse others in Queen *Elizabeth's* Time: That of the Earl of *Shrewsbury* and Sir *Thomas Overbury*, *Gondamor* and Sir *Walter Raleigh*, and many others in King *James* the I.'s Time; in all which, if the Cloven-Foot had not been dexterously managed, those Murders had not been so dexterously managed, or the Murderers have so well been screened from Justice; for which and the imprecated Justice of Heaven unappeased, some have thought the innocent Branches of the Royal House of *Stuart* did not fare the better in the Ages which followed.

It must be confessed, the Cloven-Foot was in its full Exercise in the next Reign, and the Generation that rose up immediately after them, arrived to the most exquisite Skill for Management of it; here they fasted and prayed, there they plundered and murdered; here they raised War for the King, and there they fought against him, cutting Throats for *God's Sake*, and deposing both King and kingly Government according to Law.

Nor was the *Cloven-Foot* unemployed on all Sides, for 'tis the main Excellency of this Instrument of Hell, that it acts on every Side, it is its denominating Quality, and is for that Reason called a cloven or divided Hoof.

This mutilated Apparition has been so public in other Countries too, that it seems to convince us the Devil is not confined to *England* only, but that as his Empire extended to all the sublunary World, so he gives them all Room to see he is qualified to manage them his own Way.

What abundant Use did that Prince of Dissemblers, *Charles* V. make of this Foot? 'twas by the Help of this Apparition of the Foot that he baited his Hook with the City of *Milan*, and tickled *Francis* I. of *France* so well with it, that when he passed thro' *France*, and was in that King's Power, he let him go, and never get the Bait off of the Hook neither; it Seems the *Foot* was not on King *Francis's* Side at that Time.

How cruelly did *Philip* II. of *Spain* manage this Foot in the Murder of the Nobility of the *Spanish Netherlands*, the Assassination of the Prince of *Orange*, and at last: in that of his own Son *Don Carlos* Infant of *Spain*? and yet such was the *Devil's* Craft, and so nicely did he bestir his *Cloven-Hoof*, that this Monarch died consolated (though impenitent) in the Arms of the Church, and with the Benediction of the Clergy too, *those second best Managers of the said Hoof in the World.*

I must acknowledge, I agree with this Opinion thus far; namely, that the Devil acting by this Cloven-Foot, as a Machine, has done great Things in the World for the propagating his dark Empire among us; and History is full of Examples, besides the little low prized Things done among us; for we are come to such a Kind of Degeneracy in Folly, that we have even dishonored the *Devil*, and put this glorious Engine the Cloven-Foot to such mean Uses, that the *Devil* himself seems to be ashamed of us.

But to return a little to foreign History, besides what has been mentioned above, we find flaming Examples of most glorious Mischief done by this Weapon, when put into the Hands of Kings and Men of Fame in the World: How many Games have the Kings of *France* played with this *Cloven-Foot*, and that within a few Years of one another? First, *Charles* IX. played the *Cloven-Foot* upon *Gaspar Coligni* Admiral of *France*, when he caressed him, complimented him, invited him to *Paris*, to the Wedding of the King of *Navarre*, called him Father, kissed him, and when he was wounded sent his own Surgeons to take Care of him, and yet three Days after ordered him to be assassinated and murdered, used with a thousand Indignities, and at last thrown out of the Window into the Street to be insulted by the Rabble?

Did not *Henry* III. in the same Country, play the Cloven-Foot upon the Duke of *Guise*, when he called him to his Council, and caused him to be murdered as he went in at the Door? The *Guises* again plaid the same Game back upon the King, when they sent out a *Jacobin* Friar to assassinate him in his Tent as he lay at the Siege of *Paris*.

In a Word, this Opera of the *Cloven-Foot* has been acted all over the Christian World, ever since *Judas* betrayed the Son of God with a Kiss; nay, our Saviour says expressly of him, *One of you is a Devil*; and the sacred Text says in another Place, *The Devil entered into Judas*.

It would take up a great deal of Time and Paper too, to give you a full Account of the Travels of this *Cloven-Foot*; its Progress into all the Courts of *Europe*, and with what most accurate Hypocrisy *Satan* has made use of it upon many Occasions, and with what Success; but as in the elaborate Work of which I just now gave you a Specimen I design one whole Volume upon this Subject, and which I shall call, *The complete History* of the *Cloven-Foot*; I say, for that Reason, and diverse others, I shall say but very little more to it in this Place.

It remains to tell you, that this merry Story of the *Cloven-Foot* is very essential to the History which I am now writing, as it has been all along the great Emblem of the *Devil*'s Government in the World, and by which all his most considerable Engagements have been answered and executed; for as he is said not to be able to conceal this Foot, but that he carries it always with him, it imports most plainly, that the *Devil* would be no *Devil* if he was not a Dissembler, a Deceiver, and carried a *double Entendre* in all he does or says; that he cannot but say one Thing and mean another, promise one Thing and do another, engage and not perform, declare and not intend, and act like a true *Devil* as he is, with a Countenance that is no Index of his Heart.

I might indeed go back to Originals, and derive this *Cloven-Foot* from Satan's primitive State as a Cherubim or a celestial Being, which Cherubims, as *Moses* is said to have seen them about the Throne of God in Mount *Sinai*, and as the same *Moses*, from the Original represented them afterwards covering the Ark, had the Head and Face of a Man, Wings of an Eagle, Body of a Lion, and Legs and Feet of a Calf; but this is not so much to our present Purpose, for as we are to allow that whatever *Satan* had of heavenly Beauty before the Fall, he lost it all when he commenced *Devil*, so to fetch his Original so far up would be only to say, that he retained nothing but the *Cloven-Foot*, and that all the rest of him was altered and deformed, become frightful and horrible as the Devil; but his Cloven-Foot, as we now understand it, is rather mystical and emblematic, and describes him only as the Fountain of Mischief and Treason, and the Prince of Hypocrites, and as such we are now to speak of him.

It's from this Original all the hypocritic World copy, he wears the Foot on their Account, and from this Model they act: This made our blessed Lord tell them, *the Works of your Father ye will do*, meaning the *Devil*, as he had expressed it just before.

Nor does he deny the Use of the *Foot* to the meaner Class of his Disciples in the World, but decently equips them all upon every Occasion with a needful Proportion of Hypocrisy and Deceit; that they may hand on the Power of promiscuous Fraud thro' all his temporal Dominions, and wear *the Foot* always about them as a Badge of their professed Share in whatever is done by that Means.

Thus every Dissembler, every false Friend, every secret Cheat, every Bearskin-Jobber has a *Cloven-Foot*, and so far hands on the Devil's Interest by the same powerful Agency of Art, as the *Devil* himself uses to act when he appears in Person, or would act if he was just now upon the Spot; for this *Foot* is a Machine which is to be wound up and wound down, as the Cause it appears for requires; and there are Agents and Engineers to act in it by Directions of *Satan* (the grand Engineer) who lies still in his Retirement, only issuing out his Orders as he sees convenient.

Again, every Class, every Trade, every Shopkeeper, every Peddler, nay, that meanest of Tradesmen, that Church Peddler the Pope, has a Cloven-Foot, with which he *Paw wa's* upon the World, wishes them all well, and at the same time cheats them; wishes them all fed, and at the same time starves them; wishes them all in Heaven, and at the same time marches before them directly to the Devil, *alamode de Cloven-Foot*.

Nay, the very Bench, the everliving Foundation of Justice in the World; how often has it been made the Tool of Violence, the Refuge of Oppression, the Seat of Bribery and Corruption, by this Monster in Masquerade, and that every where (our own Country always excepted)? They had much better wipe out the Picture of justice blinded, and having the Sword and Scales in her Hand, which in foreign Countries is generally painted over the Seat of those who sit to do Justice, and place instead thereof a naked unarmed Cloven-Hoof, a proper Emblem of that Spirit that Influences the World, and of the Justice we often see administered among them; human Imagination cannot form an Idea more suitable, nor the *Devil* propose an Engine more or better qualified for an Operation of Justice, by the Influence of Bribery and Corruption; it is this magnipotent Instrument in the Hands of the Devil, which under the closest Disguise agitates every Passion, bribes every Affection, blackens every Virtue, gives a double Face to Words and Actions, and to all Persons who have any Concern in them, and in a Word, makes us all Devils to one another.

Indeed the Devil has taken but a dark Emblem to be distinguished by, for this of a Goat was said to be a Creature hated by Mankind from the beginning, and that there is a natural Antipathy in Mankind against them: Hence the Scape Goat was to bear the Sins of the People, and to go into the Wilderness with all that Burthen upon him.

But we have a Saying among us, in Defense of which we must enquire into the proper Sphere of Action which may be assigned to this Cloven-Foot, as hitherto described: The Proverb is this; *Every* Devil *has not a Cloven-Foot.* This Proverb, instead of giving us some more favorable Thoughts of the *Devil*, confirms what I have said already, that the *Devil* raised this Scandal upon himself; I mean, the Report that he cannot conceal or disguise his Devil's Foot, or Hoof, but that it must appear, under whatever Habit he shows himself; and the Reason I gave holds good still, *namely*, that he may be more effectually concealed when he goes abroad without it: For if the People were fully persuaded that the *Devil* could not appear without this Badge of his Honor, or Mark of his Infamy, *take it as you will*; and that he was bound also to show it upon all Occasions, it would be natural to conclude, that whatever frightful Appearances might be seen in the World, if the Cloven-Foot did not also appear, we had no Occasion to look for the *Devil*, or so much as to think of him, much less to apprehend he was near us; and as this might be a Mistake, and that the *Devil* might be there while we thought our selves so secure, it might on many Occasions be a Mistake of very ill Consequence, and in particular, as it would give the *Devil* room to act in the Dark, and not be discovered, where it might be most needful to know him.

From this short Hint, thus repeated, I draw a new Thesis, namely, That *Devil* is most dangerous that has no Cloven-Foot; or, if you will have it in Words more to the common Understanding, the *Devil* seems to be most dangerous when he goes without his Cloven-Foot.

And here a learned Speculation offers itself to our Debate, and which indeed I ought to call a Council of Casuists, and Men learned in the *Devil*'s Politics, to determine:

Whether is most hurtful to the World, the *Devil* walking about without his Cloven-Foot, or the Cloven-Foot walking about without the *Devil*?

It is indeed a nice and difficult Question, and merits to be well enquired into; for which Reason, and diverse others, I have referred it to be treated with some Decency, and as a Dispute of Dignity sufficient to take up a Chapter by itself.

Chapter VII

Whether is most hurtful to the World, the Devil walking about without his Cloven-Foot, or the Cloven-Foot walking about without the Devil?

In discussing this most critical Distinction of Satan's private Motions, I must, as the Pulpit Gentlemen direct us, explain the Text, and let you know what I mean by several dark Expressions in it, that I may not be understood to talk (as the *Devil* walks) in the dark.

1. As to the Devil's walking about.

2. His walking without his Cloven-Foot.

3. The Cloven-Foot walking about without the *Devil*.

Now as I study Brevity, and yet would be understood too, you may please to understand me as I understand myself, thus.

1. That I must be allowed to suppose the *Devil* really has a full Intercourse in, and through, and about this Globe, with Egress and Regress, for the carrying on his special Affairs, when, how, and where, to his Majesty, in his great Wisdom, it shall seem meet; that sometimes he appears and becomes visible, and that, like a Mastiff without his Clog, he does not always carry his Cloven-Foot with him. This will necessarily bring me to some Debate upon the most important Question of Apparitions, Hauntings, Walkings, *etc..* whether of *Satan* in human Shape, or of human Creatures in the *Devil's* Shape, or in any other manner whatsoever.

2. I must also be allowed to tell you that Satan has a great deal of Wrong done him by the general embracing vulgar Errors, and that there is a Cloven-Foot oftentimes without a *Devil*; or, in short, that Satan is not guilty of all the simple Things, no, or of all the wicked Things we charge him with.

These two Heads well settled will fully explain the Title of this Chapter, answer the Query mentioned in it, and at the same time correspond very well with, and give us a farther Prospect into the main and original Design of this Work, *namely, The History of the Devil*. We are so fond of, and pleased with the general Notion of seeing the *Devil*, that I am loath to disoblige my Readers so much as calling in question his Visibility would do. Nor is it my Business, any more than it is his, to undeceive them, where the Belief is so agreeable to them; especially since upon the whole 'tis not one Farthing matter, either on one Side or on the other, whether it be so or no, or whether the Truth of Fact be ever discovered or not.

Certain it is, whether we see him or no, here he is, and I make no doubt but he is looking on while I am writing this Part of his Story, whether behind me, or at my Elbow, or over my Shoulder, is not material to me, nor have I once turned my Head about to see whether he is there or no; for if he be not in the Inside, I have so mean an Opinion of all his extravasated Powers, that it seems of very little Consequence to me what Shape he takes up, or in what Posture he appears; nor indeed can I find in all my Enquiry that ever the *Devil* appeared (*Qua Devil*) in any of the most dangerous or important of his Designs in the World; the most of his Projects, especially of the significant Part of them, having been carried on another way.

However, as I am satisfied no Body will be pleased if I should dispute the Reality of his Appearance, and the World runs away with it as a received Point, and that admits no Dispute, I shall most readily grant the General, and give you some Account of the Particulars.

History is fruitful of Particulars, whether Invention has supplied them or not, I will not say, where the *Devil* is brought upon the Stage in plain and undeniable Apparition: The Story of *Samuel* being raised by the Witch of *Endor*, I shall leave quite out of my List, because there are so many Scruples and Objections against that Story; and as I shall not dispute with the Scripture, so on the other hand, I have so much Deference for the Dignity of the *Devil*, as not to determine rashly how far it may be in the Power of every old (*Witch*) Woman, to call him up whenever she pleases, and that he must come, whatever the Pretence is, or whatever Business of Consequence he may be engaged in, as often as 'tis needful for her to *Pa wa* for half a Crown, or perhaps less than half the Money.

Nor will I undertake to tell you, till I have talked farther with him about it, how far the *Devil* is concerned to discover Frauds, detect Murders, reveal Secrets, and especially to tell where any Money is hid, and show Folks where to find it; 'tis an odd thing that Satan should think it of Consequence to come and tell us where such a Miser hid a Strong Box, or where such an old Woman buried her *Chamber Pot* full of Money, the Value of all which is perhaps but a Trifle, when at the same time he lets so many Veins of Gold, so many unexhausted Mines, nay, Mountains of Silver, as, we may depend upon it, are hid in the Bowels of the Earth, and which it would be so much to the Good of whole Nations to discover, lie still there, and never say one Word of them to any Body. Besides, how does the *Devil's* doing Things so foreign to himself, and so out of his way, agree with the rest of his Character; namely, showing a kind of a friendly Disposition to Mankind, or doing beneficent Things? This is so beneath *Satan's* Quality, and looks so little, that I scarce know what to say to it; but that which is still more pungent in the Case is, these Things are so out of his Road, and so foreign to his Calling, that it shocks our Faith in them, and seems to clash with all the just Notions we have of him, and of his Business in the World. The like is to be said of those little merry Turns we bring him in acting with us, and upon us, upon trifling and simple Occasions, such as tumbling Chairs and Stools about House, setting Pots and Vessels Bottom upward, tossing the Glass and Crockery Ware about without breaking; and such like mean foolish Things, beneath the Dignity of the *Devil*, who, in my Opinion, is rather employed in setting the World with the Bottom upward, tumbling Kings and Crowns about, and dashing the Nations one against another; raising Tempests and Storms, whether at Sea, or on Shore; and, in a word, doing capital Mischiefs suitable to his Nature, and agreeable to his Name, *Devil*; and suited to that Circumstance of his Condition, which I have fully represented in the primitive Part of his exiled State.

But to bring in the *Devil* playing at Push-pin with the World, or like *Domitian* catching Flies, that is to say, doing nothing to the purpose; this is not only deluding our selves, but putting a Slur upon the *Devil* himself; and, I say, I shall not dishonor Satan so much as to suppose anything in it: However, as I must have a care too how I take away the proper Materials of Winter Evening Frippery, and leave the good Wives nothing of the Devil to fright the Children with, I shall carry the weighty Point no farther. No doubt the *Devil* and Dr. *Faustus* were very intimate; I should rob you of a very significant [5] Proverb, if I should so much as doubt it; no doubt the *Devil* showed himself in the Glass to that fair Lady who looked in it to see where to place her Patches; but then it should follow too that the *Devil* is an Enemy to the Ladies wearing Patches, and that has some Difficulties in it which we cannot so easily reconcile; but we must tell the Story, and leave out the Consequences.

But to come to more remarkable Things, and in which the *Devil* has thought fit to act in a Figure more suitable to his Dignity, and on Occasions consistent with himself; take the Story of the Appearance of *Julius Cesar*, or the *Devil* assuming that murdered *Emperor*, to the great *Marcus Brutus*, who notwithstanding all the good Things said to justify it, was no less than a King-killer and an Assassinator, which we in our Language call by a very good Name, and peculiar to the *English* Tongue, a *Ruffian*.

The Specter had certainly the Appearance of *Cesar*, with his Wounds bleeding fresh, as if he had just received the fatal Blow; he had reproached him with his Ingratitude, with a *Tu Brute! tu quoque, mi fili*: "What Thou *Brutus*! Thou, my adopted Son!" Now History seems to agree universally,

---

[5] *As great as the Devil and Doctor* Faustus. Vulg. Dr. *Foster*.

not only in the Story itself, but in the Circumstances of it; we have only to observe that the *Devil* had certainly Power to assume, not a human Shape only, but the Shape of *Julius Cesar* in particular.

Had *Brutus* been a timorous *Conscience-harried*, weak-headed Wretch, had he been under the Horror of the Guilt, and terrified with the Dangers that were before him at that time, we might suggest that he was over-run with the Vapors, that the Terrors which were upon his Mind disordered him, that his Head was delirious and prepossessed, and that his Fancy only placed *Cesar* so continually in his Eye, that it realized him to his Imagination, and he believed he saw him; with many other suggested Difficulties to invalidate the Story, and render the Reality of it doubtful.

But the contrary, to an Extreme, was the Case of *Brutus*; his known Character placed him above the Power of all Hypochondriacs, or fanciful Delusions; *Brutus* was of a true *Roman* Spirit, a bold Hero, of an intrepid Courage; one that scorned to fear even the *Devil*, as the Story allows: Besides, he gloried in the Action; there could be no Terror of Mind upon him; he valued himself upon it, as done in the Service of Liberty, and the Cause of his Country; and was so far from being startled at the *Devil* in the worst Shape, that he spoke first to him, and asked him, *What art thou?* and when he was cited to see him again at *Philippi*, answered, with a Gallantry that knew no Fear, *well I will see thee there.* Whatever the *Devil's* Business was with *Brutus*, this is certain, according to all the Historians who give us the Account of it, that *Brutus* discovered no Fear; he did not, *like Saul at Endor,* fall to the Ground in a Swoon, 1 *Sam.* xxviii. 20. *Then Saul fell all along upon the Earth, and there was no Strength in him, and was sore afraid.* In a word, I see no room to charge *Brutus* with being over-run with the *Hyppo,* or with Vapors, or with Fright and Terror of Mind; but he saw the *Devil,* that's certain, and with Eyes open, his Courage not at all daunted, his Mind resolute, and with the utmost Composure spoke to him, replied to his Answer, and defied his Summons to Death, which indeed he feared not, as appeared afterward.

I come next to an Instance as eminent in History as the other; this was in *Char.* VI. of *France,* surnamed, *The Beloved*; who riding over the Forest near *Mans,* a ghastly frightful Fellow (that is to say, the *Devil* so clothed in human Vizor) came up to his Horse, and taking hold of his Bridle, stopped him, with the Addition of these Words, *Stop King, whither go you? You are betrayed!* and immediately disappeared. It is true, the King had been distempered in his Head before, and so he might have been deceived, and we might have charged it to the Account of a whimsical Brain, or the Power of his Imagination; but this was in the Face of his Attendants, several of his great Officers, Courtiers, and Princes of the Blood being with him, who all saw the Man, heard the Words, and immediately, to their Astonishment, lost Sight of the Specter, who vanished from them all.

Two Witnesses will convict a Murderer, why not a Traitor? This must be the *Old Gentleman*, emblematically so called, or who must it be? nay, who else could it be? His Ugliness is not the Case, though *ugly as the Devil*, is a Proverb in his Favor; but vanishing out of sight is an Essential to a Spirit and to an evil Spirit in our Times especially.

These are some of the *Devil*'s Extra ordinaries, and it must be confessed they are not the most agreeable to Mankind, for sometimes he takes upon him to disorder his Friends very much on these Occasions, as in the above Case of *Cha.* VI. of *France*; the King, they say, was really demented ever after; that is, as we vulgarly, but not always improperly, express it, he was really *startled out of his Wits*. Whether the malicious *Devil* intended it so, or not, is not certain, though it was not so foreign to his particular Disposition if he did.

But where he is more intimate, we are told he appears in a manner less disagreeable, and there he is more properly *a familiar Spirit*; that is, in short, a *Devil* of their Acquaintance: It is true, the Ancients understand the Word, *a familiar Spirit*, to be one of the kinds of Possession; but if it serves our turn as well under the Denomination of an intimate *Devil*, or a *Devil* visitant, it must be acknowledged to be as near in the literal Sense and Acceptation of the Word, as the other; nay, it must be allowed 'tis a very great Piece of Familiarity in the *Devil* to make Visits, and show none of his Disagreeables, not appear formidable, or in the Shape of what he is, respectfully withholding his dismal Part, in Compassion to the Infirmities of his Friends.

It is true, *Satan* may be obliged to make different Appearances, as the several Circumstances of Things call for it; in some Cases he makes his public Entry, and then he must show himself in his Habit of Ceremony; in other Cases he comes upon private Business, and then he appears in Disguise; in some public Cases he may thing fit to be *incog.* and then he appears dressed *a la Masque*; so they say he appeared at the famous St. *Bartholomew* Wedding at *Paris*, where, he came in dressed up like a Trumpeter, danced in his Habit, sounded a *Levet*, and then went out and rung the Alarm-Bell (which was the Signal to begin the Massacre) half an Hour before the Time appointed, lest the King's Mind should alter, and his Heart fail him.

If the Story be not made upon him, (for we should not slander the *Devil*) it should seem, he was not thoroughly satisfied in King *Charles* IX.'s Steadiness in his Cause; for the King, it seems, had relaxed a little once before, and Satan might be afraid he would fall off again, and so prevent the Execution: Others say, the King did relent immediately after the ringing the *Alarm-Bell*, but that then it was too late, the Work was begun, and the Rage of Blood having been let loose among the People, there was no recalling the Order. If the *Devil* was thus brought to the Necessity of a secret Management, it must be owned he did it dexterously; but I have not Authority enough for the Story, to charge him with the Particulars, so I leave it *au croc*.

I have much better Vouchers for the Story following, which I had so solemnly confirmed by one that lived in the Family, that I never doubted the Truth of it. There lived, in the Parish of St. *Bennet Fynk*, near the *Royal Exchange*, an honest poor Widow Woman, who, *her Husband being lately dead*, took Lodgers into her House; that is, she let out some of her Rooms in order to lessen her own Charge of Rent; among the rest, she let her Garrets to a working Watchwheel-maker, or one some way concerned in making the Movements of Watches, and who worked to those Shop-keepers who sell Watches; as is usual.

It happened that a Man and Woman went up, to speak with this Movement-maker upon some Business which related to his Trade, and when they were near the Top of the Stairs, the Garret-Door where he usually worked being wide open, they saw the poor Man (the Watch-maker, or Wheel-maker) had hanged himself upon a Beam which was left open in the Room a little lower than the Pilaster, or Ceiling: Surprised at the Sight, the Woman stopped, and cried out to the Man who was behind her on the Stairs that he should run up, and cut the poor Creature down.

At that very Moment comes a Man hastily from another Part of the Room which they upon the Stairs could not see, bringing a Joint-Stool in his Hand, as if in great Haste, and sets it down just by the Wretch that was hanged, and getting up as hastily upon it pulls a Knife out of his Pocket, and taking hold of the Rope with one of his Hands, beckoned to the Woman and the Man behind her with his Head, as if to stop and not come up, showing them the Knife in his other Hand, as if he was just going to cut the poor Man down.

Upon this, the Woman stopped a while, but the Man who stood on the Joint-Stool continued with his Hand and Knife as if fumbling at the Knot, but did not yet cut the Man down; at which the Woman cried out again, and the Man behind her called to her. Go up, *says he*, and help the Man upon the Stool! supposing something hindered. But the Man upon the Stool made Signs to them again to be quiet, and not come on, as if saying, I shall do it immediately; then he made two Strokes with his Knife, as if cutting the Rope, and then stopped again; and still the poor Man was hanging, and consequently dying: Upon this, the Woman on the Stairs cried out to him. What ails you? Why don't you cut the poor Man down? And the Man behind her, having no more Patience, thrusts her by, and said to her. Let me come, I'll warrant you I'll do it; and with that runs up and forward into the Room to the Man; but when he came there, behold, the poor Man was there hanging; but no Man with a Knife, or Joint-Stool, or any such thing to be seen, all that was Specter and Delusion, in order, no doubt, to let the poor Creature that had hanged himself perish and expire.

The Man was so startled and surprised, that with all the Courage he had before, he dropped on the Floor as one dead, and the Woman at last was fain to cut the poor Man down with a Pair of Scissors, and had much to do to effect it.

As I have no room to doubt the Truth of this Story, which I had from Persons on whose Honesty I could depend. So I think it needs very little Trouble to convince us who the Man upon the Stool must be, and that it was the *Devil* who placed himself there in order to finish the Murder of the Man who he had, *Devil*-like, tempted before, and prevailed with to be his own Executioner. Besides, it corresponds so well with the *Devil's* Nature, and with his Business, *viz.* that of a *Murderer*, that I never questioned it; nor can I think we wrong the *Devil* at all to charge him with it.

> *N. B.* I cannot be positive in the remaining Part of this Story, *viz.* whether the Man was cut down soon enough to be recovered, or whether the *Devil* carried his Point, and kept off the Man and Woman till it was too late; but be it which it will, 'tis plain he did his Devilish Endeavour, and stayed till he was forced to abscond again.

We have many solid Tales well attested, as well in History as in the Reports of honest People, who could not be deceived, intimating the *Devil's* personal Appearance, some in one Place, some in another; as also sometimes in one Habit or Dress, and sometimes in another; and it is to be observed, that in none of those which are most like to be real, and in which there is least of Fancy and Vapor, you have any Mention of the *Cloven Foot*, which rather seems to be a mere Invention of Men (and perhaps chiefly of those who had a Cloven Understanding) I mean a shallow kind of Craft, the Effect of an empty and simple Head, thinking by such a well-meant, though weak Fraud, to represent the *Devil* to the old Women and Children of the Age, with some Addition suitable to the Weakness of their Intellects, and suited to making them afraid of him.

I have another Account of a Person who travelled upwards of four Years with the *Devil* in his Company, and conversed most intimately with him all the while; nay, if I may believe the Story, he knew most part of the Time that he was the *Devil*, and yet conversed with him, and that very profitably, for he performed many very useful Services for him, and constantly preserved him from the Danger of Wolves and wild Beasts, which the Country he travelled thro' was intolerably full of. Where, by the way, you are to understand, that the Wolves and Bears in those Countries knew the *Devil*, whatever Disguise he went in; or that the *Devil* has some Way to fright Bears and such Creatures, more than we know of. Nor could this *Devil* ever be prevailed upon to hurt him or any of his Company. This

Account has an innumerable Number of diverting Incidents attending it; but they are equal to all the rest in Bulk, and therefore too long for this Book.

I find too upon some more ordinary Occasions the *Devil* has appeared to several People at their Call: This indeed shows abundance of good Humor in him, considering him as a *Devil*, and that he was mighty complaints: Nay some, they tell us, have a Power to raise the *Devil* whenever they think fit; this I cannot bring the *Devil* to a Level with, unless I should allow him to be *Servus Servorum*, as another *Devil* in Disguise calls himself; subjected to ever old Wizard's Call; or that he is under a Necessity of appearing on such or such particular Occasions, whoever it is that calls him; which would bring the *Devil's* Circumstances to a pitch of Slavery which I see no Reason to believe of them.

Here also I must take Notice again, that though I say the *Devil*, when I speak of all these Apparitions, whether of a greater or lesser Kind, yet I am not obliged to suppose Satan himself in Person is concerned to show himself, but that some of his *Agents*, Deputies and Servants, are sent to that Purpose, and directed what Disguise of Flesh and Blood to put on, as may be suitable to the Occasion.

This seems to be the only Way to reconcile all those simple and ridiculous Appearances which not *Satan*, but his Emissaries, (which we old Women call Imps) sometimes make, and the mean and sorry Employment they are put to: Thus Fame tells us of a certain Witch of Quality, who called the *Devil* once to carry her over a Brook where the Water was swelled with a hasty Rain, and lashed him soundly with her Whip for letting her Ladyship fall into the Water before she was quite over. Thus also, as Fame tells us, she set the *Devil* to work, and made him build *Crowland* Abbey, where there was no Foundation to be found, only for disturbing the Workmen a little who were first set about it. So it seems another laborious *Devil* was obliged to dig the great Ditch cross the Country from the Fenn Country to the Edge of *Suffolk* and *Essex*; which whoever he has preserved the Reputation of, and where it crosses *New-Market* Heath, 'tis called *Devil's Ditch* to this Day.

Another Piece of Punishment no doubt it was, when the *Devil* was obliged to bring the Stones out of *Wales* into *Wiltshire*, to build *Stonehenge*: How this was ordered in those Days, when it seems they kept *Satan* to hard Labor, I know not; I believe it must be registered among the ancient Pieces of Art which are lost in the World, such as melting of Stone, painting of Glass, *etc.*. Certainly they had the *Devil* under Correction in those Days; that is to say, those lesser Sorts of *Devils*; but I cannot think that the *muckle Thief Devil*, as they call him in the *North*, the Grand Seignior *Devil* of all, was ever reduced to Discipline. What *Devil* it was that *Dunstan* took by the Nose with his red hot Tongs, I have not yet examined Antiquity enough to be certain of, any more than I can what Devil it was that St. *Francis* played so many warm Tricks with, and made him run away from him so often: However, this I take upon me to say, in the *Devil*'s Behalf, that it could not be our *Satan*, the Arch *Devil* of all *Devils*, of whom I have been talking so long.

Now is it unworthy the Occasion, to take notice that we really wrong the *Devil*, and speak of him very much to his Disadvantage, when we say of such a Great Lord, or of such a Lady of Quality, *I think the* Devil *is in your Grace*: No, no, Satan has other Business, he very rarely possesses F—ls: Besides, some are so far from having the *Devil* in them, that they are really transmigrated into the very Essence of the *Devil* themselves; and others again not transmigrated, or assimilated, but Indeed and in Truth show us that they are to have mere native *Devils* in every Part and Parcel of them, and that the rest is only Masque and Disguise. Thus if *Rage, Envy, Pride* and *Revenge* can constitute the Parts of a *Devil*, why should not a Lady of such Quality, in whom all those Extraordinaries abound, have a Right to the Title of being a *Devil* really and substantially, and to all Intents and Purposes, in the most perfect and absolute Sense, according to the most exquisite Descriptions of Devils already given by me or any Body else; and even just as *Joan* of *Arc*, or *Joan* Queen of *Naples* were, who were both sent home to their native Country, as soon as it was discovered that they were real *Devils*, and that *Satan* acknowledged them in that Quality.

Nor does my Lady D——ss's wearing sometimes a Case of Humanity about her, called *Flesh and Blood*, at all alter the Case; for so 'tis Evident, according to our present Hypothesis, *Satan* has been always allowed to do, upon urgent Occasions; ay, and to make his Personal Appearance as such, among even the Sons and Daughters of God too, as well as among the Children of Men; and therefore *her Grace* may have appeared in the Shape of a fine Lady, as long as she has been supposed to do, without any Impeachment of her just Claim to the Title of *Devil*; which being her true and natural Original, she ought not, nor indeed shall not, by me, be denied her Shapes of Honor, whenever she pleases to declare for a Re-assumption.

And farther, to give every Truth its due Illustration, this need not be thought so strange; and is far from being unjust; *her Grace* (as she, it may be, is now stilled) has not acted, at least that I never heard of, so unworthy her great and illustrious Original, that we should think she has lost anything by walking about the World so many Years in Apparition: But to give her the due Homage of her Quality, she has acted as consonant to the Essence and Nature of *Devil*, which she has such a Claim to, as was consistent with the needful Reserve of her present Disguise.

Nor shall we lead the Reader into any Mistake concerning this part of our Work, as if this was or is meant to be a particular Satyr upon the D——ss of —————, and upon her only, as if we had no Devils among us in the

191

Phenomena of fair Ladies, but this one: If Satan would be so honest to us as he might be (and it would be very ingenuous in him, that must be acknowledged, to give us a little of his Illumination in this Case) we should soon be able to un-masque a great many notable Figures among us, to our real Surprise.

Indeed 'tis a Point worth our further Enquiry, and would be a Discovery many ways to our Advantage, were we blessed with it, to see how many real *Devils* we have walking up and down the World in Masque, and how many Hoop-Petticoats complete the entire Masque that disguises the Devil in the Shape of that Thing called Woman.

As for the Men, Nature has satisfied herself in letting them be their own Disguise, and in suffering them to act the *old Women*, as old Women are vulgarly understood, in Matters of Council and Politics; but if at any time they have Occasion for the *Devil* in Person, they are obliged to call him to their Aid in such Shape as he pleases to make use of *pro hac vice*; and of all those Shapes, the most agreeable to him seems to be that of a Female of Quality, in which he has infinite Opportunity to act to Perfection, what Part so ever he is called in for.

How happy are those People who they say have the particular Quality, or acquired Habit, called the *Second Sight*; one Sort of whom they tell us are able to distinguish the *Devil*, in whatever Case or Outside of Flesh and Blood he is pleased to put on, and consequently could know the *Devil* wherever they met him? Were I blest with this excellent and useful Accomplishment, how pleasant would it be, and how would it particularly gratify my Spleen, and all that which I, in common with my fellow Creatures carry about me, called Ill-Nature, to stand in the *Mall*, or at the Entrance to any of our *Assemblies of Beauties*, and point them out as they pass by, with this particular Mark, That's a *Devil*; that fine young Toast is a *Devil*; There's a *Devil* drest in a new Habit for the Ball; There's a *Devil* in a Coach and Six, *cum aliis*. In short, it would make a merry World among us if we could but enter upon some proper Method of such Discriminations: but, *Lowered*, what a Hurricane would it raise, if, like ———, who they say scourged the *Devil* so often that he durst not come near him in any Shape whatever, we could find some new Method out to make the *Devil* unmask, like the Angel *Uriel*, who, Mr. *Milton* says, had an enchanted Spear, with which if he did but touch the *Devil*, in whatever Disguise he had put on, it obliged him immediately to start up, and show himself in his true original Shape, mere *Devil* as he was.

This would do nicely, and as I who am originally a Projector, have spent some Time upon this Study, and doubt not in a little Time to finish my Engine, which I am contriving, to screw the *Devil* out of every Body, or any Body; I question not when I have brought it to Perfection, but I shall make most excellent Discoveries by it; and besides the many extraordinary

Advantages of it to human Society, I doubt not but it will make good Sport in the World too; wherefore, when I publish my Proposals, and divide it into Shares, as other less useful Projects have been done, I question not, for all the severe Act lately passed against Bubbles, but I shall get Subscribers enough, *etc.*.

In a Word, a secret Power of discovering what Devils we have among us, and where and what Business they are doing, would be a vast Advantage to us all; that we might know among the Crowd of *Devils* that walk about Streets, who are *Apparitions*, and who are not.

Now I, you must know, at certain Intervals when the Old Gentleman's Illuminations are upon me, and when I have something of an *Eclaricissement* with him, have some Degrees of this discriminating *Second Sight*, and therefore 'tis no strange thing for me to tell a great many of my Acquaintance that they are really *Devils*, when they themselves know nothing of the Matter: Sometimes indeed I find it pretty hard to convince them of it, or at least they are very unwilling to own it, but it is not the less so for that.

I had a long Discourse upon this Subject one day, with a young beautiful Lady of my Acquaintance, who the World very much admired; and as the World judges no farther than they can see, (and how should they, you would say) they took her to be, as she really was, a most charming Creature.

To me indeed she discovered herself many Ways, besides the Advantage I had of my extraordinary Penetration by the magic Powers which I am vested with: To me, *I say*, she appeared a Fury, a Satyr, a fiery little Fiend as could possibly be dressed up in Flesh; in short, she appeared to me what really she was, a very Devil: It is natural to human Creatures to desire to discover any extraordinary Powers they are possessed of superior to others, and this Itch prevailing in me, among the rest, I was impatient to let this Lady know that I understood her Composition perfectly well, nay, as well as she did herself.

In order to this, happening to be in the Family once for some Days, and having the Honor to be very intimate with her and her Husband too, I took an Opportunity on an extraordinary Occasion, when she was in the Height of good Humor, to talk with her; You must note, that as I said, the Lady was in an extraordinary good Humor, and there had been a great deal of Mirth in the Family for some Days; but one Evening, Sir *E——* her Husband, upon some very sharp Turn she gave to another Gentleman, which made all the Company pleasant, run to her, and with a Passion of good Humor takes her in his Arms, and turning to me, says he, Jack, This Wife of mine is full of Wit and good Humor, but when she has a Mind to be smart, she is the keenest little *Devil* in the World: This was alluding to the quick Turn she had given the other Gentleman.

Is that the best Language you can give your Wife, says my Lady? O Madam, says I, such *Devils* as you, are all *Angels*; ay, ay, says my Lady, I know that, he has only let a Truth fly out that he does not understand: Look ye there now, *says Sir* Edward, could anything but such a dear *Devil* as this have said a thing so pointed? Well, well, adds he, *Devil* to a Lady in a Man's Arms, is a Word of divers Interpretations. Thus they rallied for a good while, he holding her fast all the while in his Arms, and frequently kissing her, and at last it went off, all in Sunshine and Mirth.

But the next Day, for I had the Honor to lodge in the Lady's Father's House, where it all happened; I say, the next Day my Lady begins with me upon the Subject, and that very smartly, so that first I did not know whether she was in jest or earnest: Ay, ay, *says she*, you Men make nothing of your Wives after you have them, *alluding to the Discourse with* Sir Edward *the Night before.*

Why Madam, says I, *we Men*, as you are pleased to term it, if we meet with good Wives worship them, and make Idols of them, what would you have more of us?

No, no, says she, before you have them they are Angels, but when you have been in Heaven, *adds she and smiled*, then they are Devils.

Why Madam, *says I*, Devils are Angels, you know, and were the highest Sort of Angels once.

Yes, *says she*, very smartly, all *Devils* are Angels, but all Angels are not *Devils*.

But Madam, *says I*, you should never take it ill to be called *Devil*, you know.

I know, *says she*, hastily, what do you mean by that?

Why Madam, *says I*, and looked very gravely and serious, I thought you had known that I knew it, or else I would not have said so, for I would not offend you; but you may depend I shall never discover it, unless you order me to do so for your particular Service.

Upon this she looked hard and wild, and bid me explain myself. I told her, I was ready to explain myself if she would give me her Word, she would not resent it, and would take nothing ill.

She gave me her word solemnly she would not, though like a true *Devil* she broke her Promise with me all at once.

Well however, being unconcerned whether she kept her Word or no, I began, by telling her that I had not long since obtained the second sight, and had some years studied Magic, by which I could penetrate into many things, which to ordinary Perception were invisible, and had some Glasses, by the Help of which I could see into all visionary or imaginary Appearances in a different Manner than other People did.

Very well, *says she*, suppose you can, what's that to me?

I told her it was nothing to her any further than that as she knew herself to be originally not the same Creature she seemed to be, but was of a sublime angelic Original; so by the Help of my recited Art I knew it too, and so far it might relate to her.

Very fine, says she, so you would make a *Devil* of me indeed.

I took that Occasion to tell her, I would make nothing of her but what she was; that I supposed she knew well enough God Almighty never thought fit to make any human Creature so perfect and completely beautiful as she was, but that such were also reserved for Figures to be assumed by Angels of one Kind or other.

She rallied me upon that, and told me that would not bring me off, for I had not determined her for anything Angelic, but a mere *Devil*; and how could I flatter her with being handsome and a *Devil* both at the same time?

I told her, as Satan, whom we abusively called *Devil*, was an immortal Seraph, and of an original angelic Nature, so abstracted from anything wicked, he was a most glorious Being; that when he thought fit to encase himself with Flesh, and walk about in Disguise, it was in his Power equally with the other Angels to make the Form he took upon himself be as he thought fit, beautiful or deformed.

Here she disputed the Possibility of that, and after charging me faintly with flattering her Face, told me the Devil could not be represented by anything handsome, alleging our constant picturing the *Devil* in all the frightful Appearances imaginable.

I told her we wronged him very much in that, and quoted St. *Francis*, to whom the *Devil* frequently appeared in the Form of the most incomparably beautiful naked Woman, to allure him, and what Means he used to turn the Appearance into a *Devil* again, and how he affected it.

She put by the Discourse, and returned to that of Angels, and insisted that Angels did not always assume beautiful Appearances; that sometimes they appeared in terrible Shapes, but that when they did not, it was at best only amiable Faces, not exquisite; and that therefore it would not hold, that to be handsome, should always render them suspected.

I told her the *Devil* had more Occasions to form Beauties than other Angels had, his Business being principally to deceive and ensnare Mankind. And then I gave her some Examples upon the whole.

I found by her Discourse she was willing enough to pass for an *Angel*, but 'twas the hardest thing in the World to convince her that she was a Devil, and she would not come into that by any means; she argued that I knew her Father, and that her Mother was a very good Woman, and was delivered of her in the ordinary Way, and that there was such and such Ladies who were present in the Room when she was born, and that had often told her so.

I told her that was nothing in such a Case as hers; that when the Old Gentleman had occasion to transform himself into a fine Lady, he could easily dispose of a Child, and place himself in the Cradle instead of it, when the Nurse or Mother were asleep; nay, or when they were broad awake either, it was the same thing to him; and I quoted *Luther* to her upon that Occasion, who affirms that it had been so. However I said, to convince her that I knew it, (for I would have it that she knew it already) if she pleased I would go to my Chamber and fetch her my Magic Looking-glass, where she should see her own Picture, not only as it was an angelic Picture for the World to admire, but a *Devil* also frightful enough to any Body but herself and me that understood it.

No, no, *said she*, I'll look in none of your conjuring Glasses; I know myself well enough, and I desire to look no otherwise than I am.

No, Madam, *says I*, I know that very well; nor do you need any better Shape than that you appear in, 'tis most exquisitely fine; all the World knows you are a complete Beauty, and that is a clear Evidence what you would be if your present appearing Form was reduced to its proper Personality.

Appearing Form! says she, why, what would you make an *Apparition* of me?

An *Apparition!* Madam, said I, yes, to be sure; why you know, you are nothing else but an *Apparition*; and what else would you be, when it is so infinitely to your Advantage?

With that, she turned pale and angry, and then rose up hastily, and looked into the Glass, (*a large Peer-glass being in the Room*) where she stood, surveying herself from Head to Foot, with Vanity not a little.

I took that Time to slip away, and running up into my Apartment, I fetched my *Magic Glass* as I called it, in which I had a hollow Case so framed behind a Looking-glass, that in the first; she would see her own Face only; in the second, she would see the *Devil*'s Face, ugly and frightful enough, but dressed up with a Lady's Head-Clothes in a Circle, the *Devil*'s Face in the Center, and as it were at a little Distance behind.

I came down again so soon that she did not think the Time long, especially having spent it in surveying her fair self; when I returned, I said, Come, Madam, do not trouble yourself to look there, that is not a Glass capable of showing you anything; come, take this Glass.

It will show me as much of myself, *says she, a little scornfully*, as I desire to see; so she continued looking in the Peer-glass; after some time more (for seeing her a little out of Humor, I waited to see what Observations she would make) I asked her if she had viewed herself to her Satisfaction? She said she had, and she had seen nothing of *Devil* about her. Come, Madam, said I, look here; and with that I opened the Looking-glass, and she looked in it, but saw nothing but her own Face; Well, *says she*, the Glasses agree well enough, I see no Difference; what can you make of it? With that I took it a little away; Don't you? *says I*, then I should be mistaken very much; so I looked in it myself, and giving it a Turn imperceptible to her, I showed it her again, where she saw the *Devil* indeed, dressed up like a fine Lady, but ugly, and *Devil* like as could be desired for a *Devil* to be.

She started, and cried out most horribly, and told me, she thought I was more of a *Devil* than she, for that she knew nothing of all those Tricks, and I did it to fright her, she believed I had raised the *Devil*.

I told her it was nothing but her own natural Picture, and that she knew well enough, and that I did not show it her to inform her of it, but to let her know that I knew it too; that so she might make no Pretences of being offended when I talked familiarly to her of a Thing of this Nature.

Very well; so, *says she*, I am a real frightful *Devil*, am I?

O, Madam, says I, don't say, *Am I?* why you know what you are, don't you? A *Devil*! ay, certainly; as sure as the rest of the World believes you a Lady.

I had a great deal of farther Discourse with her upon that Subject, though she would fain have beat me off of it, and two or three times she put the Talk off, and brought something else on; but I always found Means to revive it, and to attack her upon the Reality of her being a Devil, till at last I made her downright angry, and then she showed it.

First she cried, told me I came to affront her, that I would not talk so if Sir *Ed——* was by; and that she ought not to be used so. I endeavored to pacify her, and told her I had not treated her with any Indecency, nor I would not; because while she thought fit to walk Abroad *incog.* it was none of my Business to discover her; that if she thought fit to tell Sir *Ed——* anything of the Discourse, she was very welcome, or to conceal it, (*which I thought the wisest Course*) she should do just as she pleased; but I made no question I should convince Sir *E——* her Husband, that what I said was just, and that I was really so; whether it was for her Service or no for him to know it, was for her to consider.

This calmed her a little, and she looked hard at me a Minute without speaking a Word, when on a sudden she broke out thus: And you will undertake, *says she*, to convince Sir *Ed——* that he has married a *Devil*, will ye? A fine Story indeed! and what follows? why then it must follow that the Child I go with (for she was big with Child) will be a *Devil* too, will it? A fine Story for Sir *Ed——* indeed! isn't it?

I don't know that, Madam, said I, that's as you order it; by the Father's Side, *said I*, I know it will not, but what it may by the Mother's Side, that's a Doubt I can't resolve till the *Devil* and I talk farther about it.

You and the Devil talk together! *says she*, and looks ruefully at me; why do you talk with the *Devil* then?

Ay, Madam, *says I*, as sure as ever you did yourself; besides, said I, can you question that? Pray who am I talking to now?

I think you are mad, *says she*; why you will make *Devils* of all the Family, it may be, and particularly I must be with Child of a *Devil*, that's certain.

No, Madam, *said I*, 'tis not certain, as I said before, I question it.

Why you say I am the Devil, the Child, you know, has always most of the Mother in it, then that must be a Devil too I think, what else can it be, *says she*?

I can't tell that, Madam, *said I*; that's as you agree among your selves, this Kind does not go by Generation; that's a Dispute foreign to the present Purpose.

Then I entered into a Discourse with her of the Ends and Purposes for which the Devil takes up such beautiful Forms as hers, and why it always gave me a Suspicion when I saw a Lady handsomer than ordinary, and set me upon the Search to be satisfied whether she was really a Woman or an *Apparition*? a Lady or a Devil? allowing all along that her being a Devil was quite out of the Question.

Upon that very Foot, she took me up again roundly, and so, *says she*, you are very civil to me through all your Discourse, for I see it ends all in that, and you take it as a thing confessed, that I am a Devil! A very pretty piece of good Usage indeed! *says she; I thank you for it.*

Nay, Madam, *says I*, do not take it ill of me, for I only discover to you that I knew it; I do not tell it you as a Secret, for you are satisfied of that another way.

Satisfied of what? says she, that I am a Devil? I think the Devil's in you: *And so began to be hot.*

A Devil! yes, Madam, says I, without doubt a mere Devil; take it as you please, I can't help that: And so I began to take it ill that she should be disgusted at opening such a well-known Truth to her.

With that she discovered it all at once, for she turned *Fury*, in the very Letter of it; flew out in a Passion, railed at me, curst me most heartily, and immediately disappeared; which you know is the particular Mark of a Spirit or Apparition.

We had a great deal of Discourse besides this, relating to several other young Ladies of her Acquaintance, some of which, I said, were mere *Apparitions* like herself; and told her which were so, and which not; and the Reason why they were so, and for what Uses and Purposes, some to delude the World one way, and some another; and she was pretty well pleased to hear that, but she could not bear to hear her own true Character, which however, as cunning as she was, made her act the Devil at last, as you have heard; and then vanished out of my sight.

I have seen her in Miniature several Times since; but she proves herself still to be the Devil of a Lady, for she bears Malice, and will never forgive me, that I would not let her be an Angel; but like a very Devil as she is, she endeavors to kill me at a Distance; and indeed the Poison of her Eyes, (Basilisk-like) is very strong, and she has a strange Influence upon me; but I that know her to be a Devil, strive very hard with myself to drive the Memory of her out of my Thoughts.

I have had two or three Engagements since this, with other *Apparitions* of the same Sex, and I find they are all alike, they are willing enough to be thought Angels, but the Word Devil does not go down at all with them: But 'tis all one, whenever we see an *Apparition*, it is so natural to say we have seen the Devil, that there's no prevailing with Mankind to talk any other Language. A Gentleman of my Acquaintance, the other Day, that had courted a Lady a long time, had the Misfortune to come a little suddenly upon her, when she did not expect him, and found her in such a Rage at some of her Servants, that it quite disordered her, especially a Footman; the Fellow had done something that was indeed provoking, but not sufficient to put her into such a Passion, and so out of herself; nor was she able to restrain herself when she saw her Lover come in, but damned the Fellow, and raged like a Fury at him.

My Friend did his best to compose her, and begged the Fellow's Pardon of her, but it would not do; nay, the poor Fellow made all the Submissions that could be expected, but 'twas the same thing: And so the Gentleman, not caring to engage himself farther than became him, withdrew, and came no more at her for three Days, in all which time she was hardly cool.

The next Day my Friend came to me, and talking of it in Confidence to me, I am afraid, *says he*, I am going to marry a She *Devil*, and so told me the Story; I took no Notice to him, but finding out his Mistress, and taking proper Measures, with some of my particular Skill, I soon found out that it was really so, that she was a mere *Apparition*; and had it not been for that accidental Disorder of her Passions, which discovered her Inside, she might indeed have cheated any Man, for she was a lovely Devil as ever was seen; she talked like an Angel, sung like a Siren, did everything, and said everything that was taking and charming: But what then? it was all Apparition, for she was a mere *Devil*. It is true, my Friend married her, and though she was a *Devil* without doubt, yet either she behaved so well, or he was so good, I never could hear him find Fault with her.

These are particular Instances; but alas! I could run you a Length beyond all those Examples, and give you such a List of Devils among the gay Things of the Town, that would fright you to think of; and you would presently conclude, with me, that all the perfect Beauties are Devils, mere Apparitions; but Time and Paper fails, so we must only leave the Men the Caution, let them venture at their Peril. I return to the Subject.

We have a great many charming *Apparitions* of like kind go daily about the World in complete Masquerade, and, though we must not say so, they are in themselves mere *Devils*, wicked dangerous murdering Devils, that kill various Ways, some, Basilisk-like, with their Eyes; some Siren-like, with their Tongues; all *Murderers*, even from the *Beginning*: It is true, 'tis pity these pretty *Apparitions* should be Devils, and be so mischievous as they are; but since it is so, I can do no less than to advertise you of it, that you may shun the Devil in whatever Shape you meet with him.

Again, there are some half Devils, they say, like the *Sagittarian*, half Man, half Horse, or rather like the *Satyr*, who, *they say*, is half Devil, half Man; or, like my Lord Bishop, who, *they say*, was half-headed; whether they mean half-witted or no, I do not find Authors agreed about it: But if they had voted him such, it had been as kind a thing as any they could say of him, because it would have cleared him from the Scandal of being a Devil, or half a Devil, for we don't find the Devil makes any Alliance with F——ls.

Then as to merry Devils, there's my Master *G———*, he may indeed have the Devil in him, but it must be said, to the Credit of Possession in general, that Satan would have scorned to have entered into a Soul so narrow that there was not room to hold him, or to take up with so discording a Creature, so abject, so scoundrel, as never made a Figure among Mankind greater than that of a Thief, a *Moroder*, molded up into Quality, and a rapparee dressed up *a-la-Masque*, with a *Robe* and a *Coronet*.

Some little Dog-kennel Devil may indeed take up his Quarters in or near him, and so run into and out of him as his Drum beats a Call; but to him that was born a *Devil*, Satan, that never acts to no purpose, could not think him worth being possessed by anything better than a Devil of a dirty Quality; that is to say, a Spirit too mean to wear the Name of *Devil*, without some Badge or Addition of Infamy and Meanness to distinguish it by.

Thus what *Devil* of Quality would be confined to a *P————n*, who inheriting all the Pride and Insolence of his Ancestors, without one of their good Qualities; the Bully, the *Billingsgate*, and all the hereditary ill Language of his Family, without an Ounce of their Courage; that has been rescued five or six times from the Scandal of a Coward, by the Bravery, and at the Hazard of Friends, and never failed to be ungrateful; that if ever he committed a Murder, did it in cold Blood, because nobody could prove he ever had any hot; who possessed with a Poltroon *Devil*, was always wickeder in the Dark, than he durst be by Day-light; and who, after innumerable passive Sufferings, has been turned out of human Society, because he could not be kicked or cuffed either into good Manners or good Humor.

To say this was a *Devil*, an Apparition, or even a half *Devil*, would be unkind to *Satan* himself, since though he (the *Devil*) has so many Millions of inferior *Devils* under his Command, not one could be found base enough to match him, nor one *Devil* found but what would think himself dishonored to be employed about him.

Some merry good-for-nothing *Devils* we have indeed, which we might, if we had room, speak of at large, and divert you too with the Relation, such as my Lady *Hatt's Devil* in *Essex*, who upon laying a Joiner's Mallet in the Window of a certain Chamber, would come very orderly and knock with it all Night upon the Window, or against the Wainscot, and disturb the Neighborhood, and then go away in the Morning, as well satisfied as may be; whereas if the Mallet was not left, he would think himself affronted, and be as insufferable and terrifying as possible, breaking the Windows, splitting the Wainscot, committing all the Disorders, and doing all the Damage that he was able to the House, and to the Goods in it. And again, such as the Drumming *Devil* in the Well at *Oundle* in *Northamptonshire*, and such like.

A great many antic *Devils* have been seen also, who seemed to have little or nothing to do, but only to assure us that they can appear if they please, and that there is a Reality in the thing called Apparition.

As to Shadows of *Devils*, and imaginary Appearances, such as appear, and yet are invisible at the same time, I had thought to have bestowed a Chapter upon them by themselves, but it may be as much to the Purpose to let them alone, as to meddle with them; 'tis said our old Friend *Luther* used to be exceedingly troubled with such invisible Apparitions, and he tells us much of them, in what they call his Table-talk; but with Master *Luther*'s leave, though the *Devil* passes for a very great liar, I could swallow many things of his own proper making, as soon as some of those I find in a Book that goes by his Name, particularly the Story of the Devil in a Basket, the Child flying out of the Cradle, and the like.

In a word, the walking *Devils* that we have generally among us, are of the female Sex; whether it be that the *Devil* finds less Difficulty to manage them, or that he lives quieter with them, or that they are fitter for his Business than the Men, I shall not now enter into a Dispute about that; perhaps he goes better disguised in the fair Sex than otherwise; Antiquity gives us many Histories of She-Devils, such as we can very seldom match for Wickedness among the Men; such now as in the Text, *Lot*'s Daughters, *Joseph*'s Mistress, *Sampson*'s *Dalilah*, *Herod*'s *Herodias*, these were certainly *Devils*, or played the *Devil* sufficiently in their Turn; one Male Apparition indeed the Scripture furnishes you with, and that is *Judas*; for his Master says expressly of him, *One of you is a Devil*; not has the *Devil*, or is possessed of the Devil; but really is a Devil, or is a real Devil.

How happy is it, that this great Secret comes thus to be discovered to mankind? Certainly the World has gone on in Ignorance a long time, and at a strange rate, that we should have so many *Devils* continually walking about among us in humane Shape, and we know it not.

Philosophers tell us that there is a World of Spirits, and many learned Pieces of Guess-work they make at it, representing the World to be so near us, that the Air, as they describe it, must be full of Dragons and *Devils*, enough to fright our Imaginations with the very Thoughts of them; and if they say true, 'tis our great Felicity that we cannot see any farther into it than we do, which if we could, would appear as frightful as Hell itself; but none of those Sages ever told us, till now, that half the People who converse with us are *Apparitions*, especially of the Women; and among them especially this valuable Part, the Woman of Figure, the fair, the beautiful, or patched and painted.

This unusual Phenomenon has been seen but a little while, and but a little way, and the general Part of Mankind cannot come into the same Notions about it; nay, perhaps they will all think it strange; but be it as strange as it will, the Nature of the Thing confirms it, this lower Sphere is full of *Devils*; and some of both Sexes have given strange Testimonies of the Reality of their pre-existent *Devilism* for many Ages past, though I think it never came to that Height as it has now.

It is true, in former times Satan dealt much in old Women, and those, as I have observed already, very ugly, *Ugly as a Witch*, *Black as a Witch*, *I look like a Witch*, all proverbial Speeches, and which testified what Tools it was Satan generally worked with; and these old Specters, they tell us, used to ride thro' the Air in the Night, and upon Broomsticks too, all mighty homely Doings; some say they used to go to visit their Grand Seignior the *Devil*, in those Nocturnal Perambulations: But be that as it will, 'tis certain the *Devil* has changed hands, and that now he walks about the World clothed in Beauty, covered with the Charms of the Lovely, and he fails not to disguise himself effectually by it, for who would think a beautiful Lady could be a Masque to the Devil? and that a fine Face, a divine Shape, a heavenly Aspect, should bring the *Devil* in her Company, nay, should be herself an *Apparition*, a mere Devil.

The Enquiry is indeed worth our while, and therefore I hope all the enamored Beaus and Boys, all the Beauty-hunters and Fortune-hunters, will take heed, for I suppose if they get the *Devil*, they will not complain for want of a Fortune; and there's Danger enough, I assure you, for the World is full of Apparitions, *non rosa sine spinis*; not a Beauty without a *Devil*, the old Women Specters, and the young Women Apparitions; the ugly ones Witches, and the handsome ones *Devils*; Lord ha' Mercy, and a ✠ may be Set on the Man's Door that goes a courting.

Chapter VIII

Of the Cloven-Foot walking about the World without the Devil, (viz.) of Witches making Bargains for the Devil, and particularly of selling the Soul to the Devil

I have dwelt long upon the *Devil* in Masque as he goes about the World incog. and especially without his Cloven-Foot, and have touched upon some of his Disguises in the Management of his Interest in the World; I must say some of his Disguises only, for who can give a full account of all his Tricks and Arts in so narrow a Compass as I am prescribed to?

But as I said, that every *Devil* has not a Cloven-Foot, so I must add now for the present Purpose, that every Cloven-Foot is not the Devil.

Not but that wherever I should meet the Cloven-Hoof, I should expect that the *Devil* was not far off, and should be apt to raise the Posse against him, to apprehend him; yet it may happen otherwise, that's certain; every Coin has its Counterfeit, every Art its Pretender, every Whore her Admirer, every Error its Patron, and every Day has its Devil.

I have had some thought of making a full and complete Discovery here of that great Doubt which has so long puzzled the World, namely, whether there is any such Thing, as secret making Bargains with the Devil, and the first positive Assurance I can give you in the Case, is, that if there is not, 'tis not his Fault, 'tis not for want of his Endeavour, 'tis plain, if you will pardon me for taking so mean a Step, as that of quoting Scripture; I say, 'tis evident he would fain have made a Contract with our Saviour, and he bid boldly (*give him his due*) namely, *all the Kingdoms of the World for one bend of his Knee*: Impudent Seraph! To think thy Lord should pay thee Homage! How many would agree with him here for a less Price! They say, *Oliver Cromwell* struck a Bargain with him, and that he gave *Oliver* the Protectorship, but would not let him call himself King, which stuck so close to that *Furioso*, that the Mortification Spread into his Soul, and it is said, he dyad of a Gangreen in the Spleen. But take Notice and do *Oliver* Justice; I do not vouch the Story, neither does the Bishop say one Word of it.

Fame used to say, that the old famous Duke of *Luxemburg* made a Magic compact of this Kind; nay, I have heard many an (old Woman) Officer of the Troops, who never cared to see his Face, declare that he carried the

Devil at his Back. I remember a certain Author of a News Paper in *London* was once taken up, and they say, it cost him 50*l.* for printing in his News, that *Luxemburg* was *Humpbacked.* Now if I have resolved the Difficulty, namely, that he was not humped, only carried the *Devil* at his Back; I think the poor Man should have his 50*l.* again, or I should have it for the Discovery.

I confess, I do not well understand this compacting with such a Fellow as can neither write nor read; nor do I know who is the Scrivener between them, or how the Indenture can be executed; but that which is worse than all the rest is, that in *the first Place,* the *Devil* never keeps Articles; he will contract perhaps, and they say he is mighty forward to make Conditions; but who shall bind him to the Performance, and where is the Penalty if he fails? if we agree with him, he will be apt enough to claim his Bargain and demand Payment; nay, perhaps before it is due; but who shall make him stand to his.

Besides, he is a Knave in his Dealing, for he really promises what he cannot perform; witness his impudent Proposal to our Lord mentioned above. *All these Kingdoms will I give* thee! *Lying Spirit!* Why they were none of thine to give, no not one of them; for the Earth is the Lords and the kingdoms thereof, nor were they in his Power any more than in his Right: So (I have heard that) some poor dismal Creatures have sold themselves to the Devil for a Sum of Money, for so much Cash, and yet even in that Case, when the Day of Payment came, I never heard that he brought the Money or paid the Purchase, so that he is a Scoundrel in his Treaties, for you shall trust for your Bargain, but not be able to get your Money; and yet for your Part, he comes for you to an Hour: *Of which by itself.*

In a Word, let me caution you all, when you trade with the Devil, either get the Price or quit the Bargain; the *Devil* is a cunning Shaver, he will wriggle himself out of the Performance on his Side if possible, and yet expect you should be punctual on your Side. They tell you of a poor Fellow in *Herefordshire,* that offered to sell his Soul to him for a Cow, and though the *Devil* promised, and as they say, signed the Writings, yet the poor Countryman could never get the Cow of him, but still as he brought a Cow to him, some body or other came and challenged it, proving that it was lost or stolen from them; so that the Man got nothing but the Name of a Cow-stealer, and was at last carried to *Hereford* Goal, and condemned to be hanged for stealing two Cows, one after the other: The wicked Fellow was then in the greatest Distress imaginable, he summoned his *Devil* to help him out, but he failed him, as the *Devil* always will; he really had not stolen the Cows, but they were found in his Possession, and he could give no Account how he came by them; at last he was driven to confess the Truth, told the horrid Bargain he had made, and how the *Devil* often promised him a Cow, but never gave him one, except that several Times in the Morning early he found a Cow put into his Yard, but it always proved to belong to some of his Neighbors: Whether the Man was hanged or no, the

Story does not relate; but this Part is to my Purpose, that they that make Bargains with the *Devil*, ought to make him give Security for the Performance of Covenants, and who the Devil would get to be bound for him, I can't tell, they must look to that who make the Bargain: Besides, if he had not had a Mind to cheat or baffle the poor Man, what need he have taken a Cow so near home? if he had such and such Powers as we talk of, and as Fancy and Fable furnish for him, could not he have carried a Cow in the Air upon a Broom-stick, as well as an old Woman? Could he not have stole a Cow for him in *Lincolnshire*, and set it down in *Herefordshire*, and so have performed his Bargain, saved his Credit, and kept the poor Man out of Trouble? so that if the Story is True, as I really believe it is, either it is not the Devil that makes those Bargains, or the Devil has not such Power as we bestow on him, except on Special Occasions he gets a Permit, and is bid go, as in the Case of *Job*, the *Gadaren Hogs*, and the like.

We have another Example of a Man's selling himself to the *Devil*, that is very remarkable, and that is in the Bible too, and even in that, I do not find, what the *Devil* did for him, in Payment of the Purchase Price. The Person selling was *Ahab*, of whom the Text says expressly, *there was none like* him, *who did sell himself to work Wickedness in the Sight of the* Lord, 1 *Kings* xxi. 20, and the 25. I think it might have been rendered, if not translated *in Spite of the Lord*, or *in Defiance of God*; for certainly that's the Meaning of it; and now allowing me to preach a little upon this Text, my Sermon shall be very short. *Ahab* sold himself, who did he sell himself to? I answer that Question by a Question; who would buy him? who, *as we say*, would give any thing for him? and the Answer to that is plain also, you may judge of the Purchaser by the Work he was to do; he that buys a Slave in the Market, buys him to work for him, and to do such Business as he has for him to do: *Ahab* was bought to work wickedness, and who would buy him for that but the *Devil*?

I think there's no room to doubt but *Ahab* sold himself to the Devil; the Text is plain that he sold himself, and the Work he was sold to do points out the Master that bought him; what Price he agreed with the *Devil* for, that indeed the Text is silent in, so we may let it alone, nor is it much to our Purpose, unless it be to enquire whether the *Devil* stood to his Bargain or not, and whether he paid the Money according to Agreement, or cheated him as he did the Farmer at *Hereford*.

This buying and selling between the *Devil* and us, is, I must confess, an odd kind of Stock-jobbing, and indeed the *Devil* may be said to sell the *Bear-skin*, whatever he buys; but the strangest Part is when he comes to demand the transfer; for as I hinted before, whether he Performs or no, he expects his Bargain to a Tittle; there is indeed some Difficulty in resolving how and in what Manner Payment is made; the Stories we meet with in our Chimney-Corner Histories, and which are so many Ways made Use of to make the *Devil* frightful to us and our Heirs forever, are generally so foolish and ridiculous, as, if true or not true, they have nothing Material in them, are of no Signification, or else so impossible in their Nature, that they make no Impression upon anybody above twelve Years old and under seventy; or else are so tragical that Antiquity has fabled them down to our Taste, that we might be able to hear them and repeat them with less Horror than is due to them.

This Variety has taken off our Relish of the Thing in general, and made the Trade of Soul-selling, like our late more eminent Bubbles, be taken to be a Cheat and to have little in it.

However, to speak a little more gravely to it, I cannot say but that since, by the two eminent Instances of it above in *Ahab*, and in Christ himself, the Fact is evidently ascertained; and that the Devil has attempted to make such a Bargain on one, and actually did make it with the other. The Possibility of it is not to be disputed; but then I must explain the Manner of it a little, and bring it down, nearer to our Understanding, that it may be more intelligible than it is; for as for this selling the Soul, and making a Bargain to give the *Devil* Possession by Livery and Seisin on the Day appointed, that I cannot come into by any Means; no nor into the other Part, namely, of the Devil coming to claim his Bargain, and to demand the Soul according to Agreement, and upon Default of a fair Delivery, taking it away by Violence *Case and all*, of which we have many historical Relations pretty current among us; some of which, *for ought I know*, we might have hoped had been true, if we had not been sure they were false, and others we had Reason to fear were false, because it was impossible they should be true.

The Bargains of this Kind, according to the best Accounts we have of them, used to consist of two main Articles, according to the ordinary Stipulations in all Covenants; namely,

1. Something to be performed on the Devil's Part, buying.
2. Something to be performed on the Man's Part, selling.

1. The *Devil's* Part: This was generally some poor Trifle, for the Devil generally bought good Penny-worths, and oftentimes like a complete Sharper, agreed to give what he was not able to procure; that is to say, would bargain for a Price he could not pay, as in the Case of the *Hereford* Man and the Cow; for Example, 1. *Long Life*: This though the deluded Chapman has often had folly enough to contract for, the Devil never had Power to make good; and we have a famous Story, how true I know not, of a Wretch that sold himself to the Devil on Condition he, *Satan*, should assure him (1.) That he should never want Victuals; (2.) That he should never be a cold; (3.) That he should always come to him when he called him; and (4.) That he should let him live one and twenty Years, and then Satan was at Liberty to have him; that is, I suppose, to take him wherever he could find him.

It seems, the Fellow's desire to be assured of 21 Years Life, was chiefly, that during that Time, he might be as wicked as he would, and should yet be sure not to be hanged, nay, to be free from all Punishment; upon this Foot 'tis said he commenced Rogue, and committed a great many Robberies and other villanous Things; now it seems the *Devil* was pretty true to his Bargain in several of those things; particularly, that two or three times when the Fellow was taken up for petty Crimes, and called for his old Friend, he came and startled the Constables so, that they let the Offender get away from them: But at Length having done some capital Crime, a Set of Constables, or such like Officers, seized upon him, who were not to be startled with the *Devil*, in what Shape so ever he appeared; so that they carried him off, and he was committed to *Newgate* or some other Prison as effectual.

Nor could Satan with all his Skill unlock his Fetters, much less the Prison Doors; But he was tried, convicted, and executed. The Fellow in his Extremity, *they say*, expostulated with the *Devil* for his Bargain, the Term of 21 Years it seems not being expired. But the *Devil*, it is said, shuffled with him, told him a good while, he would get him out, bid him have Patience and stay a little, and thus led him on, till he came as it were within Sight of the Gallows, that is to say, within a Day or two of his Execution; when the *Devil* caviled upon his Bargain, told him, he agreed to let him live 21 Years, and he had not hindred him, but that he did not Covenant to cause him to live that Time; that there was a great deal of Difference between doing and suffering; that he was to suffer him to live, and that he did; but he could not make him live when he had brought himself to the Gallows.

Whether this Story were true or not, for you must not expect we Historians should answer for the Discourse between the *Devil* and his Chaps, because we were not privy to the Bargain: I say, whether it was true or not, the Inference is to our Purpose several Ways.

1. It confirms what I have said of the Knavery of the *Devil* in his Dealings, and that when he has Stock-jobbed with us on the best Conditions he can get, he very seldom performs his Bargain.

2. It confirms what I have likewise said, that the *Devil's* Power is limited; with this Addition, that he not only cannot destroy the Life of Man, but that he cannot preserve it; *in short*, he can neither prevent or bring on our Destruction.

I may be allowed, I hope, for the Sake of the present Discourse, to suppose that the *Devil* would have been so just to this wicked, though foolish Creature, as to have saved him from the Gallows if he could; but it seems, he at last acknowledged that it was not in his Power; nay, he could not keep him from being taken and carried to Prison, after he was gotten into the

Hands of a bold Fellow or two, that were not to be feared with his Bluster, as some foolish Creatures had been before.

And how simple, how weak, how unlike any Thing of an Angelic Nature, was it to attempt to save the poor Wretch, only by little Noises and sham Appearances, putting out the Candles, rushing and jostling in the Dark, *and the like*! If the *Devil* was that mighty Seraph, which we have heard of, if he is a God of this World, a Prince of the Air, a Spirit able to destroy Cities and make Havoc in the World; if he can raise Tempests and Storms, throw Fire about the World, and do wonderful Things, as an unchained *Devil* no Doubt could do; what need all this Frippery? and what need he try so many ridiculous Ways, by the Emptiness, nay, the silly nonsensical Manner, of which, he shows, that he is able to do no better, and that his Power is extinguished? *In a Word*, he would certainly act otherwise, if he could. *Sed caret pedibus*, he wants Power.

How weak a thing is it then, for any Man to expect Performance from the *Devil*? If he has not Power to do Mischief, which is his Element, his very Nature, and on many Accounts, is the very sum of his Desires; How should he have Power to do Good? how Power to deliver from Danger or from Death? which Deliverance would be in itself a Good, and we know it is not in his Nature to do Good to or for any Man?

In a Word, the *Devil* is strangely impudent, to think that any Man should depend upon him for the Performance of an Agreement of any Kind whatever, when he knows himself, that he is not able, if he was honest enough, to be as good as his Word.

Come we next to his expecting our Performance to him; though he is not so just to us, yet, it seems, he never fails to come and demand Payment of us at the very Day appointed: He was but a weak Trader in Things of this Nature, who having sold his Soul to the *Devil*, so our old Women's Tales call the Thing, and when the *Devil* came to demand his Bargain, put it off as a Thing of no Force, for that it was done so long ago, he thought he (*the Devil*) had forgot it. It was a better Answer, which they tell us, a *Lutheran* Divine gave the *Devil* in the Name of a poor Wretch, who had sold himself to the *Devil*, and who was in a terrible Fright about his coming for his Bargain, as he might well be indeed, if the *Devil* has such a Power, as really to come and take it by Force. *The Story (if you can bear a serious one) is this.*

The Man was in great Horror of Mind, and the Family feared he would destroy himself; at length they sent for a *Lutheran* Minister to talk with him, and who after some Labor with him, got out the Truth (*viz.*) that he had sold himself to the *Devil*, and that the Time was almost expired, when he expected the *Devil* would come and fetch him away, and he was sure he would not fail coming to the Time to a Minute; the Minister first endeavored to convince him of the horrid Crime, and to bring him to a true Penitence for that Part; and having as he thought made him a sincere Penitent, he then began to encourage him, and particularly, desired of him, that when the Time was come, that the *Devil* should fetch him away, he, the Minister, should be in the House with him; accordingly, to make the Story short, the Time came, the *Devil* came, and the Minister was present, when the *Devil* came; what Shape he was in, the Story does not say; the Man said he saw him, and cried out; the Minister could not see him, but the Man affirming he was in the Room, the Minister said aloud, *in the Name of the* living God, *Satan, what comest thou here for?* The *Devil* answered, *I come for my own*; the Minister answered, *He is not thy own, for Jesus Christ has redeemed him, and in his Name I charge thee to avoid and touch him not*; at which, says the Story, the *Devil* gave a furious Stamp (with his Cloven-Foot I suppose) and went away, and was never known to molest him afterward.

Another Story, though it be in itself a long one, I shall abridge (for your reading with the less Uneasiness) as follows.

A young Gentleman of ——*berg*, in the Elector of *Brandenburgh*'s (now the King of *Prussia*'s) Dominions, being deeply in Love with a beautiful Lady, but something above his Fortune, and whom he could by no Means bring to love him again, applied himself to an *old thing* called *a Witch*, for her Assistance, and promised her great Things, if she could bring the Lady to love him, or any how compass her, so as he might have his Will of her; nay, at last he told her he would give up his Soul to her, if she would answer his Desire.

The old Hag, it seems, having had some of his Money, had very honestly tried what she could do, but all to no Purpose, the Lady would not comply; but when he offered such a great Price, she told him, she would consider farther against such a Time, and so appointed him the next Evening.

At the Time appointed he comes, and the Witch made a long Speech to him upon the Nicety of the Affair; I suppose to prepare him not to be surprised at what was to come; for she supposed he was not so very desperately bent as he appeared to be; she told him it was a Thing of very great Difficulty; but as he had made such a great Offer, of *selling his Soul for it*, she had an Acquaintance in the House, who was better skilled (than she was) in such particular Things, and would treat with him farther, and she doubted not but that both together they might answer his End. The Fellow it seems was still of the same Mind, and told her, he cared not what he pawned or sold, if he could but obtain the Lady; well, says the old Hag, sit still a while, and with that she withdraws.

By and by she comes in again with a Question in her Mouth; pray, says she, do you seek this Lady for a Wife, or for a Mistress, would you marry her, or would you only lie with her? The young Man told her *no, no*, he did not expect she would lie with him, therefore he would be satisfied to marry her, but asks her the Reason of the Question; why truly, says the old Hag, my Reason is very Weighty; for if you would have her for your Wife, I doubt, we can do you no Service; but if you have a Mind to lie with her, the Person, I speak of, will undertake it.

The Man was surprised at that, only he objected that this was a transient or short Felicity, and that he should perhaps have her no more; the old Hag bid him not fear, but that if she once yielded to be his Whore, he might have her as often as he pleased; upon this he consents, for he was stark mad for the Lady; He having consented, she told him then, he should follow her, but told him, whoever he saw, he must speak to nobody but her, till she gave him leave, and that he should not be surprised, whatever happened, for no hurt should befall him; all which he agreed to, and the old Woman going out he followed her.

Being upon this led into another Room, where there was but very little Light, yet enough to let him see that there was no body in it but himself and the Woman, he was desired to sit down in a Chair next to a Table, and the old Woman clapping the Door too after her, he asked her why she shut the Door, and where was the Person she told him of? At which she answered *there he is*, pointing to a Chair at a little Distance: The young Gentleman turning his Head, saw a grave Kind of a Man sitting in an Elbow-Chair, though he said, he could have sworn there was no body in the Chair when the old Woman shut the Door; however, having promised not to speak to anybody but the old Woman, he said not a Word.

By and by the Woman making abundance of strange Gestures and Motions, and mumbling over several Things which he could not understand, on a sudden a large Wicker-Chair, which stood by the Chimney, removes to the other End of the Table which he sat by, but there was no body in the Chair; in about two Minutes after that the Chair removed, there appeared a Person sitting in that too, who, the Room being, as is said, almost dark, could not be so distinguished by the Eye, as to see his Countenance.

After some while, the first Man, and the Chair he sat in, moved, as if they had been one Body, to the Table also; and the old Woman and the two Men seemed to talk together, but the young Man could not understand any Thing they said; after some Time the old Witch turned to the young Gentleman, told him his Request was granted, but not for Marriage, but the Lady should love and receive him.

The Witch then gave him a Stick dipt in Tar at both Ends, and bid him hold it to a Candle, which he did, and instead of burning like a Stick it burnt out like a Torch; then she bid him break it off in the Middle, and light the other

End; he did that too, and all the Room seemed to be in a light Flame; then she said, deliver one Piece here, pointing to one only of the Persons, so he gave the first Fire-stick to the first Man or *Apparition*; now says she, deliver the other here, so he gave the other Piece to the other Apparition, at which they both rose up and spoke to him Words, which he said he understood not, and could not repeat, and immediately vanished with the Fire-sticks and all, leaving the Room full of Smoke: I do not remember that the Story says any Thing of Brimstone, or the Smell of it, but it says the Door continued fast locked, and no Body was left in the Room but the young Gentleman and the Witch.

Now the Ceremony being over, he asked the Witch if the Business was done? She said *yes*. Well, but says he, have I sold my Soul to the Devil? Yes, says she, you have, and you gave him Possession, when you delivered the two Fire-sticks to him. *To him!* says he, why, was that the *Devil*? Yes, says the old Hag. At which the young Man was in a terrible Fright for a while, but it went off again.

And what's next, says he, when shall I see the Lady for whose sake I have done all this? You shall know that presently, said she, and opening the Door, in the next Room she presents him with a most beautiful Lady, but had charged him not to speak a Word to her: She was exactly dressed like, and he presently knew her to be the Lady he desired; upon which he flew to her and clasped her in his Arms, but that Moment he had her fast, as he thought, in his Arms, she vanished out of his sight.

Finding himself thus disappointed, he upbraids the old Woman with betraying him, and flew out with ill Language at her, in a great Rage; the *Devil* often deluded him thus, after this, with Shows and Appearances, but still no Performance; after a while he gets an Opportunity to speak with the Lady herself in Reality, but she was as positive in her Denial as ever, and even took away all Hopes of his ever obtaining her, which put him into Despair; for now he thought he had given himself up to the *Devil* for nothing, and this brought him to himself; so that he made a penitent Confession of his Crime to some Friends, who took great Care of him, and encouraged him, and at last furnished him with such an Answer as put the *Devil* into a Fright, when he came for the Bargain.

For Satan, it seems, *as the Story says*, had the Impudence to demand his Agreement, notwithstanding he had failed in the Performance on his Part; what the Answer was I do not pretend to have seen, but it seems it was something like what is mentioned above, (*viz.*) that he was in better Hands, and that he durst not touch him.

I have heard of another Person that had actually signed a Contract with the *Devil*; and upon a Fast kept by some Protestant or Christian Divines, while they were praying for the poor Man, the Devil was obliged to come and throw the Contract in at the Window.

But I vouch none of these Stories, there may be much in them and much Use made of them, even whether exactly such in Fact, as they are related, or no; the best Use I can make of them, is this, if any wicked desperate Wretches have made Bargain and Sale with *Satan*, their only Way is to repent, if they know how, and that before he comes to claim them; then batter him with his own Guns; play Religion against Devilism, and perhaps they may drive the *Devil* out of their Reach; at least he will not come at them, which is as well.

On the other Hand, how many Stories have we handed about of the Devil's really coming with a terrible Appearance at the Time appointed, and powerfully or by violence carrying away those, that have given themselves thus up to him; nay, and sometimes a Piece of the House along with them, as in the famous Instance of *Sudbury*, *Anno* 1662. It seems he comes with Rage and Fury upon such Occasions, pretending he only comes to take his own, or as if he had leave given him to come and take his Goods, *as we say*, where he could find them, and would strike a Terror into all that should oppose him.

The greatest Part of the Terror we are usually in upon this Occasion, is from a Supposition, that when this *Hell-Fire Contract* is once made, God allows the *Devil* to come and take the wicked Creature, how and in what manner he thinks fit, as being given up to him by his own Act and Deed; but in my Opinion there's no Divinity at all in that; for as in our Law we punish a *Felo de se*, or Self-murderer, because, *as the Law suggests*, he had no Right to dismiss his own Life; that he being a Subject of the Common-wealth, the Government claims the *Ward* or Custody of him, and so 'twas not Murder only, but Robbery, and is a Felony against the State, robbing the King of his Liege-Man, as *'tis justly called*; so neither has any Man a Right to dispose of his Soul, which belongs to his Maker in Property and in Right of Creation: The Man then having no Right to sell, Satan has no Right to buy, or at best he has made a Purchase without a Title, and consequently has no just Claim to the Possession.

It is therefore a Mistake to say, that when any of us have been so mad to make such a pretended Contract with the Devil, that God gives him leave to take it as his Due; *'tis no such thing*; the *Devil* has bought, what you had no Right to sell, and therefore, as an unlawful Oath is to be repented of, and then broken; so your Business is to repent of the Crime, and then tell the *Devil*, you have better considered of it, and that you won't stand to your Bargain, for you had no Power to sell; and if he pretends to Violence after that, I am mistaken; I believe the *Devil* knows better.

It is true, our old Mothers and Nurses have told us other Things, but they only told us what their Mothers and Nurses told them, and so the Tale has been handed down from one Generation of old Women to another; but we have no Vouchers for the Fact other than Oral Tradition, the Credit of which, I confess, goes but a very little Way with me; nor do I believe it one Jot the more for all the frightful Addenda which they generally join to the Tale, for it never wants a great Variety of that Kind.

Thus they tell us the Devil carried away Dr. *Faustus* and took a Piece of the Wall of his Garden along with them: Thus at *Salisbury* the *Devil* as it is said, and publicly printed, carried away two Fellows that had given themselves up to him, and carried away the Roof of the House with them, *and the like*; all which I believe my Share of; besides, if these Stories were really true, they are all against the Devil's true Interest, *Satan* must be a Fool, which is indeed what I never took him to be in the Main; this would be the Way not to increase the Number of Desperadoes, who should thus put themselves into his Hand, but to make himself a Terror to them; and this is one of the most powerful Objections I have against the Thing, for the Devil, I say, is no Fool, that must be acknowledged; he knows his own Game, and generally plays it sure.

I might, before I quit this Point, seriously reflect here upon our *Beau mond* (*viz.*) the gay Part of Mankind, especially those of the Times we live in, who walk about in a Composure and Tranquility inexpressible, and yet as we all know, must certainly have all sold themselves to the Devil, for the Power of acting the foolishest Things with the greater Applause; it is true, to be a Fool is the most pleasant Life in the World, if the Fool has but the particular Felicity, which few Fools want, (*viz.*) to think themselves wise: The learned say, it is the Dignity and Perfection of Fools, that they never fail trusting themselves; they believe themselves sufficient and able for every Thing; and hence their want or waste of Brains is no Grievance to them, but they hug themselves in the Satiety of their own Wit; but to bring other People to have the same Notion of them, which they have of themselves, and to have their apish and ridiculous Conduct make the same Impression on the Minds of others, as it does on their own; this requires a general Infatuation, and must either be a Judgment from Heaven, or a Mist of Hell; nothing but the Devil can make all the Men of Brains applaud a Fool, and can any Man believe, that the Devil will do this for nothing? no, no, he will be well paid for it, and I know no other Way they have to compound with him, but this of Bargain and Sale.

It's the same thing with Rakes and Bullies, as 'tis with Fools and Beaus; and this brings me to the Subject of *buying* and *selling* itself, and to examine what is understood by it in the World, what People mean by such and such a Man selling himself to the Devil: I know the common Acceptation of it is, that they make some Capitulation for some Indulgence in Wickedness, on Conditions of Safety and Impunity, which the Devil promises them; though as I said above, he is a *Bite* in that too, for he can't perform the Conditions; however, I say, he promises boldly, and they believe him, and for this Privilege in Wickedness, they consent, that he shall come and fetch them for his own, at such or such a Time.

This is the State of the Case in the general Acceptation of it; I do not say 'tis really so, nay 'tis even an Inconsistency in itself; for one would think, they need not capitulate with the Devil to be so, and so, superlatively wicked, and give him such a Price for it, seeing, unless we have a wrong Notion of him, he is naturally inclined, as well as avowedly willing to have all Men be as superlatively wicked as possibly they can, and must necessarily be always ready to issue out his Licenses gratis, as far as his Authority will go in the Case; and therefore I do not see why the Wretches that deal with him, should article with him for a Price; but suppose, for Argument sake, that it is so, then the next Thing is, some capital Crime follows the Contract, and then the Wretch is forsaken, for the Devil cannot protect him, as he promised; so he is *Trust up*, and like *Coleman* at the Gallows, he exclaims that *there is no Truth in* Devils.

It may be true, however, that under the powerful Guard and Protection of the Devil, Men do sometimes go a great Way in Crime, and that perhaps farther in these our Days of boasted Morals than was known among our Fathers; the only Difference that I meet with between the Sons of *Belial* in former Days, and those of our Ages, seems to be in the Devil's Management, not in theirs; the Sum of which amounts to this, that Satan seems to act with more Cunning, and they with less; for in the former Ages of Satan's Dominion, he had much Business upon his Hands, all his Art and Engines, and Engineers also, were kept fully employed, to wheedle, allure, betray and circumvent People, and draw them into Crimes, and they found him, as we may say, a full Employment; I doubt not, he was called the Tempter on that very Account; but the Case seems quite altered now, the Tables are turned; then the Devil tempted Men to sin, *But now, in short*, they tempt the Devil; Men push into Crimes before he pushes them; they out shoot him in his own Bow, out run him on his own Ground, and, as we say of some hot Spurs who ride Post, they whip the Post-Boy; in a Word, the Devil seems to have no Business now but to sit still and look on.

This, I must confess, seems to intimate some secret Compact between the Devil and them; but then it looks, not as is they had contracted with the Devil for leave to sin, but that the Devil had contracted with them, that they should sin so and so, up to such a Degree, and that without giving him the Trouble of daily Solicitation, private Management, and artful screwing up their Passions, their Affections and their most retired Faculties, as he was before obliged to do.

This also appears more agreeable to the Nature of the Thing; and as it is a most exquisite part of Satan's Cunning, so 'tis an undoubted Testimony of his Success; if it was not so, he could never bring his Kingdom to such a height of absolute Power as he has done; this also solves several Difficulties in the Affair of the World's present Way of sinning, which otherwise it would be very hard to understand; as particularly how some eminent Men of Quality among us, whose upper Rooms are not extraordinary well furnished in other Cases, yet are so very witty in their Wickedness, that they gather Admirers by hundreds and thousands; who, however heavy, lumpish, slow and backward, even by Nature, and in force of Constitution in better things, yet in their Race Devil-wards they are of a sudden grown nimble, light of Foot, and outrun all their Neighbors; Fellows that are as empty of Sense as Beggars are of Honesty, and as far from Brains as a Whore is of Modesty; on a sudden you shall find them dip into *Polemics*, study *Michael Servetus, Socinus*, and the most learned of their Disciples; they shall reason against all Religion, as strongly as a Philosopher; blaspheme with such a Keenness of Wit, and satirize God and Eternity, with such a Brightness of Fancy, as if the soul of a *Rochester* or a *Hobbs* was transmigrated into them; in a little length of Time more they banter Heaven, burlesque the Trinity, and jest with every sacred thing, and all so sharp, so ready, and so terribly witty, as if they were born Buffoons, and were singled out by Nature to be Champions for the Devil.

Whence can all this come? how is the Change wrought? who but the Devil can inject Wit in Spite of natural Dullness, create Brains, fill empty Heads, and supply the Vacuities in the Understanding? and will Satan do all this for nothing? *No, no*, he is too wise for that; I can never doubt a secret Compact, if there is such a thing in Nature; when I see a Head where there was no Head, Sense in *Posse* where there is no Sense in *Esse*, Wit without Brains, and Sight without Eyes, 'tis all *Devil-Work*: Could *G——* write Satyrs, that could neither read *Latin* or spell *English*, like old Sir *William Read*, who wrote a Book of Opticks, which when it was printed, he did not know which was the right Side uppermost, and which the wrong? Could this eminent uninformed Beau turn Atheist, and make wise Speeches against that Being, which made him a Fool, if the Devil had not sold him some Wit in exchange for that Trifle of his, called Soul? Had he not bartered his Inside with that Son of the Morning, to have his Tongue tipped with Blasphemy, he that knew nothing of a God, but only to swear by him, could never have set up for a Wit, to burlesque his Providence and ridicule his Government of the World.

But the Devil, as he is God of the World, has one particular Advantage, and that is, that when he has Work to do he very seldom wants Instruments; with this Circumstance also, that the Degeneracy of human Nature supplies him; as the late King of *France* said of himself, when they told him what a Calamity was like to befal his Kingdom by the Famine: *Well*, says the King, then I shall not want Soldiers; *and it was so*, want of Bread supplied his Army with Recruits; so want of Grace supplied the *Devil* with Reprobates for his Work.

Another Reason why, I think, the *Devil* has made more Bargains of that

Kind we speak of, in this Age, is, because he seems to have laid by his Cloven-Foot; all his old Emissaries, the Tools of his Trade, the Engineers which he employed in his Mines, such as Witches, Warlocks, Magicians, Conjurers, Astrologers, and all the hellish Train or Rabble of human *Devils*, who did his Drudgery in former Days, seem to be out of Work: I shall give you a fuller Enumeration of them in the next Chapter.

These, I say, seem to be laid aside; not that his Work is abated, or that his Business with Mankind, for their Delusion and Destruction is not the same, or perhaps more than ever; but the *Devil* seems to have changed Hands; the Temper and Genius of Mankind is altered, and they are not to be taken by Fright and Horror, as they were then: The Figures of those Creatures was always dismal and horrible, and that is it which I mean by the *Cloven-Foot*; but now Wit, Beauty and gay Things, are the Sum of his Craft, he manages by the Soft and the Smooth, the Fair and the Artful, the Kind and the Cunning, not by the Frightful and Terrible, the Ugly and the Odious.

When the *Devil* for weighty Dispatches,
Wanted Messengers cunning and bold,
He passed by the beautiful Faces,
And picked out the *Ugly* and *Old*.

Of these he made *Warlocks* and *Witches*,
To run of his Errands by Night,
Till the over wrought Hag-ridden Wretches,
Were as fit as the *Devil*, to fright.

But whoever has been his Adviser,
As his Kingdom increases in Growth;
He now takes his Measures much wiser,
And Traffics with Beauty and Youth.

Disguised in the Wanton and Witty,
He haunts both the Church and the Court,
And sometimes he visits the City,
Where all the best Christians resort.

Thus dressed up in full Masquerade,
He the bolder can range up and down,
For he better can drive on his Trade,
In any one's Name than his own.

Chapter IX

Of the Tools the Devil works with, (viz.) Witches, Wizards or Warlocks, Conjurers, Magicians, Divines, Astrologers, Interpreters of Dreams, Tellers of Fortunes; and above all the rest, his particular modern Privy-Counselors called Wits and Fools

Though, as I have advanced in the foregoing Chapter, the *Devil* has very much changed Hands in his modern Management of the World, and that instead of the Rabble and long Train of Implements reckoned up above, he now walks about in Beaus, Beauties, Wits and Fools; yet I must not omit to tell you that he has not dismissed his former Regiments, but like Officers in Time of Peace, he keeps them all in half Pay, or like Extraordinary Men at the Custom-House, they are kept at a Call, to be ready to fill up Vacancies, or to employ when he is more than ordinarily full of Business; and therefore it may not be amiss to give some brief Account of them, from Satan's own Memoirs, their Performance being no inconsiderable Part of his History.

Nor will it be an unprofitable Digression to go back a little to the primitive Institution of all these *Orders*, for they are very ancient, and I assure you, it requires great Knowledge of Antiquity, to give a Particular of their Original; I shall be very brief in it.

In order then to this Enquiry, you must know that it was not for want of Servants, that Satan took this Sort of People into his Pay; he had, as I have observed in its Place, Millions of diligent *Devils* at his Call, whatever Business, and however difficult, he had for them to do; but as I have said above, that our modern People are forwarder than even the *Devil* himself can desire them to be; and that they come before they are called, run before they are sent, and crowd themselves into his Service; so it seems it was in those early Days, when the World was one universal Monarchy under his Dominion, as I have at large described in its Place.

In those Days the Wickedness of the World keeping a just Pace with their Ignorance, this inferior Sort of low prized Instruments did the *Devil's* work mighty well; they drudged on in his Black-Art so laboriously, and with such good Success, that he found it was better to employ them as Tools to delude and draw in Mankind, than to send his invisible Implements about, and oblige them to take such Shapes and Dresses as were necessary upon every trifling Occasion; which, perhaps, was more Cost than Worship, more Pains than Pay.

Having then a Set of these Volunteers in his Service, the true *Devil* had nothing to do but to keep an exact Correspondence with them, and communicate some needful Powers to them, to make them be and do something extraordinary, and give them a Reputation in their Business; and these, in a Word, did a great Part of, nay almost all the *Devil's* Business in the World.

To this Purpose gave he them Power, if we may believe old *Glanville*, *Baxter*, *Hicks*, and other learned Consultors of Oracles, to walk invisible, to fly in the Air, ride upon Broom-sticks, and other Wooden Gear, to interpret Dreams, answer Questions, betray Secrets, to talk (Gibberish) the universal Language, to raise Storms, sell Winds, bring up Spirits, disturb the Dead, and torment the Living, with a thousand other needful Tricks to amuse the World, keep themselves in Veneration, and carry on the *Devil's* Empire in the World.

The first Nations among whom these infernal Practices were found, were the *Chaldeans*; and that I may do Justice in earnest, as well as in jest, it must be allowed that the *Chaldeans*, or those of them so called, were not Conjurers or Magicians, only Philosophers and Studiers of Nature, wise, sober and studious Men at first, and we have an extraordinary Account of them; and if we may believe some of our best Writers of Fame, *Abraham* was himself famous among them for such Magic, as Sir *Walter Raleigh* expresses it, *Qui Contemplatione Creaturarum Cognovit Creatorem.*

Now granting this, it is all to my Purpose, namely, that the Devil drew these wise Men in, to search after more Knowledge than Nature could instruct them in; and the Knowledge of the true God being at that Time sunk very low, he debauched them all with Dreams, Apparitions, Conjurers, *etc.*. till he ruined the just Notions they had, and made *Devils* of them all, like himself.

The learned *Senensis*, speaking of this *Chaldean* Kind of Learning, gives us an Account of five Sorts of them; you will pardon me for being so grave as to go this Length back.

1. *Chascedin* or *Chaldeans*, properly so called, being Astronomers.

2. *Asaphim* or *Magicians*, such was *Zoroastres* and *Balaam* the Son of *Beor*.

3. *Chatumim* or Interpreters of Dreams and hard Speeches, Inchanters, *etc.*

4. *Mecasphim* or Witches, called at first Prophets, afterwards *Malefici* or *Venefici*, Poisoners.

5. *Gazarim* or *Auruspices*, and Diviners, such as divin'd by the Entrails of Beasts, the Liver in particular; mention'd in *Ezek.* or as others, called Augurs.

Now, as to all these, I suppose, I may do them no wrong, if I say, however justifiable they were in the Beginning, the *Devil* got them all into his Service at last, and that brings me to my Text again, from which the rest was a Digression.

1. The *Chascedin* or *Chaldean* Astronomers turned Astrologers, Fortune-Tellers, Calculators of Nativities, and vile Deluders of the People, as if the Wisdom of the holy God was in them, as *Nebuchadnezzar* said of *Daniel* on that very Account.

2. The *Asaphim* or Magi, or Magicians; *Sixtus Senensis* says, they were such as wrought by Covenants with Devils, but turned to it from their Wisdom, which was to study the practical Part of Natural Philosophy, working admirable Effects by the mutual Application of Natural Causes.

3. The *Chartumim* from being Reasoners or Disputers upon difficult Points in Philosophy, became Enchanters and Conjurers. So,

4. The *Mecasphim* or Prophets, they turned to be Sorcerers, Raisers of Spirits, such as wounded by an evil Eye, and by bitter Curses, and were afterwards famed for having familiar Converse with the *Devil*, and were called Witches.

5. The *Gazarim*, from the bare observing of the good and bad Omens, by the Entrails of Beasts, flying of Birds, *etc..* were turned to Sacrists or Priests of the Heathen Idols and Sacrificers.

Thus, I say, first or last the *Devil* engrossed all the Wise-Men of the East, for so they are called; made them all his own, and by them he worked Wonders, that is, he filled the World with lying Wonders, as if wrought by these Men, when indeed it was all his own, from Beginning to the End, and set on Foot merely to propagate Delusion, impose upon blinded and ignorant Men; the God of this World blinded their Minds, and they were led away by the Subtlety of the *Devil*, to say no worse of it, till they became *Devils* themselves, as to Mankind; for they carried on the Devil's Work upon all Occasions, and the Race of them still continue in other Nations, and some of them among ourselves, as we shall see presently.

The *Arabians* followed the *Chaldeans* in this Study, while it was kept within its due Bounds, and after them the *Egyptians*; and among the Latter we find that *Jannes* and *Jambres* were famous for their leading *Pharaoh* by their pretended magic Performances, to reject the real Miracles of *Moses*; and History tells us of strange Pranks the Wise-Men, the Magicians and the Southsayers plaid to delude the People in the most early Ages of the World.

But, as I say, now, the *Devil* has improved himself, so he did then; for the *Grecian* and *Roman* Heathen Rites coming on, they outdid all the Magicians and Southsayers, by establishing the *Devil's* lying Oracles, which, as a Master-Piece of Hell, did the *Devil* more Honor, and brought more Homage to him, than ever he had before, or could arrive to since.

Again, as by the setting up the Oracles, all the Magicians and Southsayers grew out of Credit; so at the ceasing of those Oracles, the *Devil* was fain to go back to the old Game again, and take up with the Agency of Witches, Divinations, Enchantments and Conjurings, as I hinted before, answerable to the four Sorts mentioned in the Story of *Nebuchadnezzar*, (viz.) *Magicians*, *Astrologers*, the *Chaldeans* and the *Southsayers*: How these began to be out of Request, I have mentioned already; but as the *Devil* has not quite given them over, only laid them aside a little for the present, we may venture to ask what they were, and what Use he made of them when he did employ them.

The Truth is, I think, as it was a very mean Employment for anything that wears a human Countenance to take up, so I must acknowledge, I think, 'twas a mean low prized Business for *Satan* to take up with; below the very *Devil*; below his Dignity as an Angelic, though condemned Creature; below him even as a *Devil*; to go to talk to a parcel of ugly, deformed, spiteful, malicious old Women; to give them Power to do Mischief, who never had a Will, after they entered into the State of *old Woman-Hood*, to do anything else: Why the *Devil* always chose the ugliest old Women he could find; whether *Wizardism* made them ugly, that were not so before, and whether the Ugliness, as it was a Beauty in Witchcraft, did not increase according to the meritorious Performance in the Black-Trade? These are all Questions of Moment to be decided, (if human Learning can arrive to so much Perfection) in Ages to come.

Some say the evil Eye and the wicked Look were Parts of the Enchantment, and that the Witches, when they were in the height of their Business, had a powerful Influence with both; that by looking upon any Person they could bewitch them, and make the *Devil*, *as the Scots express it*, ride through them booted and spurred; and that hence came that very significant Saying, *to look like a Witch*.

The strange Work which the *Devil* has made in the World, by this Sort of his Agents called Witches, is such, and so extravagantly wild, that except our Hope that most of those Tales happen not to be true, I know not how anyone could be easy to live near a Widow after she was five and fifty.

All the other Sorts of Emissaries which Satan employs, come short of these Ghosts; and Apparitions sometimes come and show themselves, on particular Accounts, and some of those Particulars respect doing Justice, repairing Wrongs, preventing Mischief; sometimes in Matters very considerable, and on Things so necessary to public Benefit, that we are tempted to believe they proceed from some vigilant Spirit who wishes us well; but on the other Hand, these Witches are never concerned in anything but Mischief; nay, if what they do portends good to one, it issues in hurt to many; the whole Tenor of their Life, their Design in general, is to do Mischief, and they are only employed in Mischief, and nothing else: How far they are furnished with Ability suitable to the horrid Will they are vested with, remains to be described.

These Witches, 'tis said, are furnished with Power suitable to the Occasion that is before them, and particularly that which deserves to be considered, as Prediction, and foretelling Events, which I insist the Author of Witchcraft is not accomplished with himself, nor can he communicate it to any other: How then *Witches* come to be able to foretell Things to come, which, 'tis said, the *Devil* himself cannot know, and which, as I have shown, 'tis evident he does not know himself, is yet to be determined; that Witches do foretell, is certain, from the Witch of *Endor*, who foretold Things to *Saul*, which he knew not before, namely, that he should be slain in Battle the next Day, which accordingly came to pass.

There are, however, and notwithstanding this particular Case, many Instances wherein the *Devil* has not been able to foretell approaching Events, and that in Things of the utmost Consequence, and he has given certain foolish or false Answers in such Cases; the Devil's Priests, which were summoned in by the Prophet *Elija*, to decide the Dispute between God and *Baal*, had the *Devil* been able to have informed them of it, would certainly have received Notice from him, of what was intended against them by *Elija*; that is to say, that they would be all cut in pieces; for Satan was not such a Fool as not to know that *Baal* was a Non-Entity, a Nothing, at best a dead Man, perished and rotting in his Grave; for *Baal* was *Bell* or *Belus*, an ancient King of the *Assyrian* Monarchy, and he could no more answer by Fire to consume the Sacrifice, than he could raise himself from the dead.

But the Priests of *Baal* were left of their Master to their just Fate, namely, to be a Sacrifice to the Fury of a deluded People; hence I infer his Inability, for it would have been very unkind and ungrateful in him not to have answered them, if he had been able. There is another Argument raised here most justly against the *Devil*, with Relation to his being under Restraint, and that of greater Eminence than we imagine, and it is drawn from this very Passage, thus; 'tis not to be doubted but that *Satan*, who has much of the Element put into his Hands, as Prince of the Air, had a Power, or was able potentially speaking, to have answered *Baal's* Priests by Fire; Fire being in Virtue of his airy Principality a Part of his Dominion; but he was certainly *withheld* by the Superior Hand, which gave him that Dominion, I mean *withheld* for the Occasion only: So in another Case, it was plain that *Balaam*, who was one of those Sorts of *Chaldeans* mentioned above, who dealt in *Divinations* and *Enchantments*, was withheld from cursing Israel.

Some are of Opinion that *Balaam* was not a Witch or a Dealer with the *Devil* because 'tis said of him, or rather he says it of himself, that he saw the Visions of God, *Numb.* xxiv. 16. *He hath said, who heard the Words of* God, *and knew the Knowledge of the most High, which saw the Visions of the Almighty, falling into a* Trance, *but having his Eyes open*: Hence they alledge he was one of those Magi, which St. *Augustin* speaks of, *de Divination*, who by the Study of Nature, and by the Contemplation of created Beings came to the Knowledge of the Creature; and that *Balaam's* Fault was, that being tempted by the Rewards and Honors that the King promised him, he intended to have cursed *Israel*; but when his Eyes were opened, and that he saw they were God's own People, he durst not do it; they will have it therefore, that except, *as above*, *Balaam* was a good Man, or at least that he had the Knowledge of the true God, and the Fear of that God upon him, and that he honestly declares this, *Numb.* xxii. 18. *If* Balak *would give me his House full of Silver and Gold, I cannot go beyond the Word of the Lord* my God: Where though he is called a false Prophet by some, he evidently owns God, and assumes a Property in him, as other Prophets did; my God, and I cannot go beyond his Orders; but that which gives me a better Opinion of *Balaam* than all this is, his plain Prophesy of Christ, Chap. xxiv. 17. where he calls him the Star of *Jacob*, and declares, *I shall see him, but not now, I shall behold him, but not nigh; there shall come a Star out of* Jacob, *and a Scepter shall rise out of* Israel, *and shall smite the Corners of* Moab, *and destroy all the Children of* Seth, all which express not a Knowledge only, but a Faith in Christ; but I have done preaching, this is all by the by, I return to my Business, which is the History.

There is another Piece of dark Practice here, which lies between Satan and his particular Agents, and which they must give us an Answer to, when they can, which I think will not be in haste; and that is about the obsequious *Devil* submitting to be called up into Visibility, whenever an old Woman has her Hand crossed with a white Six-pence, *as they Call it*: One would think that instead of these vile Things called Witches, being sold to the *Devil*, the *Devil* was really sold for a Slave to them; for how far so ever Satan's Residence is off of this State of Life, they have Power, it seems, to fetch him from home, and oblige him to come at their Call.

I can give little Account of this, only that indeed so it is; nor is the Thing so strange in its self, as the Methods to do it are mean, foolish, and ridiculous;

as making a Circle and dancing in it, pronouncing such and such Words, saying the Lord's Prayer backward, and the like; now is this agreeable to the Dignity of the Prince of the Air or Atmosphere, that he should be commended forth with no more Pomp or Ceremony than that of muttering a few Words, such as the old Witches and he agree about? or is there something else in it, which none of us or themselves understand?

Perhaps, indeed, he is always with those People called Witches and Conjurers, or at least some of his *Camp Volant* are always present, and so upon the least call of the Wizard, it is but putting off the misty Cloak and showing themselves.

Then we have a Piece of mock Pageantry in bringing those Things called witches or Conjurers to Justice, that is, first to know if a Woman be a Witch, throw her into a Pond, and if she be a Witch, she will swim, and it is not in her own Power to prevent it; if she does all she can to sink herself, it will not do, she will swim like a Cork. Then that a Rope will not hang a Witch, but you must get a With, a green Osyer; that if you nail a Horse-Shoe on the Sill of the Door, she cannot come into the House, or go out, if she be in; these and a thousand more, too simple to be believed, are yet so vouched, so taken for granted, and so universally received for Truth, that there is no resisting them without being thought atheistical.

What Methods to take to know, who are *Witches*, I really know not; but on the other Side, I think there are variety of Methods to be used to know who are not; *W—— G——*, Esq; is a Man of Fame, his Parts are great, because his Estate is so; he has threescore and eight Lines of *Virgil* by rote, and they take up many of the Intervals of his merry Discourses; he has just as many witty Stories to please Society; when they are well told, *once over*, he begins again, and so he lives in a round of Wit and Learning; he is a Man of great Simplicity and Sincerity; you must be careful not to mistake my Meaning, as to the Word Simplicity; some take it to mean Honesty, and so do I, only that it has a Negative attending it, in his particular Case; in a Word, *W—— G——* is an honest Man, and no *Conjurer*; a good Character, I think, and without Impeachment to his Understanding, he may be a Man of Worth for all that; take the other Sex, there is the Lady *H——* is another Discovery; bless us! what Charms in that Face! How bright those Eyes! How flowing white her Breasts! How sweet her Voice? add to all, how heavenly, divinely good her Temper! How inimitable her Behavior! How spotless her Virtue! How perfect her Innocence! and to sum up her Character, we may add, the Lady *H——* is no *Witch*; sure none of our Beau Critics will be so unkind now as to censure me in those honest Descriptions, as if I meant that my good Friend *W—— G——* Esq; or my adored Angel, the bright, the charming Lady *H——* were Fools; but what will not those Savages, called Critics, do, whose barbarous Nature enclines them to trample on the brightest Characters, and to cavil on the clearest Expressions?

It might be expected of me, however, in justice to my Friends, and to the bright Characters of abundance of Gentlemen of this Age, who, by the Depth of their Politics, and the Height of their Elevations might be suspected, and might give us Room to charge them with Subterranean Intelligence; I say, it might be expected that I should clear up their Fame, and assure the World concerning them, even by Name, that they are no *Conjurers*, that they do not deal with the *Devil*, at least, not by the Way Witchcraft and Divination, such as Sir *T——k, E—— B——*, Esq; my Lord *Homily*, Coll. *Swagger, Jeoffry Well with*, Esq; Capt. *Harry Go Deeper*, Mr. *Wellcome Woollen*, Citizen and Merchant Taylor of *London*, *Henry Cadaver*, Esq; the D—— of *Caerfilly*, the Marquess of *Sillyhoo*, Sir *Edward Thro' and Thro'* Bart. and a World of fine Gentlemen more, whose great Heads and Weighty Understandings have given the World such Occasion to challenge them with being at least descended from the *Magi*, and perhaps engaged with old Satan in his Politics and Experiments; but I, that have such good Intelligence among *Satan's* Ministers of State, as is necessary to the present Undertaking, am thereby well able to clear up their Characters: and I doubt not, but they will value themselves upon it, and acknowledge their Obligation to me, for letting the World know the *Devil* does not pretend to have had any Business with them, or to have enrolled them in the List of his Operators; *in a Word*, that none of them are *Conjurers*: Upon which Testimony of mine, I expect they be no longer charged with, or so much as suspected of having an unlawful Quantity of Wit, or having any Sorts of it about them, that are contraband or prohibited, but that for the future they pass unmolested, and be taken for nothing but what they are, (*viz.*) very honest worthy Gentlemen.

Chapter X

Of the various Methods the Devil takes to converse with Mankind

Having spoken something of Persons, and particularly of such as the *Devil* thinks fit to employ in his Affairs in the World, it comes next of course to say something of the Manner how he communicates his Mind to them, and by them to the rest of his Acquaintance in the World.

I take the *Devil* to be under great Difficulties in his Affairs on his Part, especially occasioned by the Bounds which are set him, or which Policies oblige him to set to himself, in his Access to the conversing with Mankind; 'tis evident he is not permitted to fall upon them with Force and Arms, that is to say, to muster up his infernal Troops, and attack them with Fire and Sword; if he was not loose to act in this Manner as he was able, by his own seraphic Power to have destroyed the whole Race, and even the Earth they dwelt upon, so he would certainly, and long ago have effectually done it; his particular Interests and Inclinations are well enough known.

But in the next Place, as he is thus restrained from Violence, so Prudentials restrain him in all his other Actings with Mankind; and being confined to Stratagem, and soft still Methods, such as Persuasion, Allurement, feeding the Appetite, prompting, and then gratifying corrupt Desires, and the like; he finds it for his Purpose not to appear in Person, except very rarely, and then in Disguise; but to act all the rest in the Dark, under the Visor of Art and Craft, making Use of Persons and Methods concealed, or at least not fully understood or discovered.

As to the Persons whom he employs, I have taken some Pains you see to discover some of them; but the Methods he uses with them, either to inform and instruct, and give Orders to them, or to converse with other People by them, these are very particular, and deserve some Place in our Memoirs, particularly as they may serve to remove some of our Mistakes, and to take off some of the frightful Ideas we are apt to entertain in Prejudice of this great Manager; as if he was no more to be matched in his Politics, than he would be to be matched in his Power, if it was let loose; which is so much a Mistake, that on the contrary, we read of several People that have abused and cheated the *Devil*, a Thing, which I cannot say, is very honest nor just, notwithstanding the old Latin Proverb, *Fallere fallentem non est fraus*, (which Men construe, or rather render, by way of Banter Upon Satan) 'tis no Sin to cheat the *Devil*, which for all that, upon

226

the whole I deny, and alledge, that let the *Devil* act how he will by us, we ought to deal fairly by him.

But to come to the Business, without Circumlocutions; I am to enquire how Satan issues out his Orders, gives his Instructions and fully delivers his Mind to his Emissaries, of whom I have mentioned some in the Title to Chap. IX. In order to this, you must form an Idea of the *Devil* sitting in great State, in open Campaign, with all his Legions about him, in the height of the Atmosphere; or if you will, at a certain Distance from the Atmosphere, and above it, that the Plan of his Encampment might not be hurried round its own Axis, with the Earth's diurnal Motion, which might be some Disturbance to him.

By this fixed Situation, the Earth performing its Rotation, he has every Part and Parcel of it brought to a direct Opposition to him, and consequently to his View once in twenty four Hours: The last time I was there, if I remember right, he had this Quarter of the World, which we call Christendom, just under his Eye; and as the Motion is not so swift, but that his piercing Optics can take a strict View of it *en passant*; for the Circumference of it being but twenty one thousand Miles, and its circular Motion being full twenty four Hours performing, he has something more than an Hour to view every thousand Miles, which, to his supernatural Penetration, is not worth naming.

As he takes thus a daily View of all the Circle, and an hourly View of the Parts, he is fully Master of all Transactions, at least such as are done above Board by all Mankind; and then he dispatches his Emissaries or *Aid du Camps* to every Part with his Orders and Instructions: Now these Emissaries, you are to understand, are not the *Witches* and *Diviners*, who I spoke of above, for I call them also Emissaries; but they are all *Devils* or (as you know they are called) *Devil's* Angels; and these may, perhaps, come and converse personally with the Sub-emissaries I mentioned, to be ready for their Support and Assistance on all Occasions of Business: These are those *Devils* which the Witches are said to raise; for we can hardly suppose the Master *Devil* comes himself, at the Summons of every ugly old Woman.

These run about into every Nook and Corner, wherever Satan's Business calls them, and are never wanting to him; but are the most diligent *Devils* imaginable; like the *Turkish Chaiux*, they no sooner receive their Errand, but they execute it with the utmost Alacrity; and as to their Speed, it may be truly written as a Motto, upon the Head of every individual *Devil*,

Non indiget calcaribus

These are those, who they tell us our Witches, Sorcerers, Wizards, and such Sorts of Folks converse freely with, and are therefore called their *Familiars*; and as they tell us, come to them in human Shapes, talk to them with articulate plain Voices, as if Men, and that yet the said Witches, *etc.*. know them to be *Devils*.

History has not yet enlightened us in this Part of useful Knowledge, or at least not sufficiently for a Description of the Persons or Habits of these Sorts of Appearances; as what Shapes they take up, what Language they speak, and what particular Works they perform, so we must refer it to farther Enquiry; but if we may credit History, we are told many famous Stories of these Appearances; for Example, the famous Mother *Lakland*, who was burnt for a Witch at *Ipswich, Anno* 1646, confessed at the Time of her Execution, or a little before it, that she had frequent Conversation with the *Devil* himself; that she being very poor, and withal of a devilish passionate, cruel and revengeful Disposition before, used to wish she had it in her Power to do such and such mischievous Things to some that she hated; and that the *Devil* himself, who, it seems, knew her Temper, came to her one Night as she lay in her Bed, and was between sleeping and waking, and speaking in a deep hollow Voice, told her; if she would serve him in some Things he would employ her to do, she should have her Will of all her Enemies, and should want for nothing: That she was much afraid at first, but that he soliciting her very often, bad her not be afraid of him, and still urged her to yield, and as she says, struck his Claw into her Hand, and though it did not hurt her, made it bleed, and with the Blood wrote the Covenants, that is to say, the Bargain between them: being asked what was in them, and whether he required her to curse or deny God or Christ? She said no.

N. B. I do not find she told them whether the *Devil* wrote it with a Pen, or whether on Paper or Parchment, nor whether she signed it or no, but it seems he carried it away with him. I suppose, if Satan's Register were examined, it might be found among the Archives of Hell, the Rolls of his *acta Publica*; and when his Historiographer Royal publishes them, we may look for it among them.

Then he furnished her with three *Devils*, to wait upon her (I suppose) for she confessed they were to be employed in her Service; they attended in the Shapes of two little Dogs and a Mole: The first she bewitched was her own Husband, by which he lay a while in great Misery and died; then she sent to one Captain *Beal* and burnt a new Ship of his just built, which had never been at Sea; these and many other horrid Things she did and confessed, and having been twenty Years a Witch, at last the *Devil* left her, and she was burnt as she deserved.

That some extraordinary Occasions may bring these Agents of the *Devil*, nay, sometimes the *Devil* himself, to assume human Shapes, and appear to other People we cannot doubt; he did thus in the Case of our Savior *as a Tempter*, and some think he did so to *Manasses* as a Familiar, who the Scripture charges with Sorcery, and having a Familiar or Devil; Fame tells us that St. *Dunstan* frequently converts with him, and finally, took him by the Nose; and so of others.

But in these modern Ages of the World, he finds it much more to his Purpose to work under Ground as I have observed, and to keep upon the Reserve; so that we have no authentic Accounts of his personal Appearance, but what are very ancient or very remote from our Faith, as well as our Enquiry.

It seems to be a Question that would bear some debating, whether all Apparitions are not *Devils* or from the *Devil*; but there being so many of those Apparitions which we call Spirits, which really assume Shapes and make Appearances in the World, upon such Accounts as we know *Satan* himself scorns to be employed in, that I must dismiss the Question in favor of the *Devil*; assuring them, that as he never willingly did any good in his Life, so he would be far from giving himself the Trouble of setting one Foot into the World, on such an Errand; and for that Reason we maybe assured those certain Apparitions, which we are told came to detect a Murder in *Gloucestershire*, and others who appeared to prevent the ruining an Orphan for want of finding a Deed, that was not lost, was certainly some other Power equally concerned, and not the *Devil*.

On the other Hand, neither will it follow that *Satan* never appears in human Shape; for though every Apparition may not be the *Devil*, yet it does not follow that the *Devil* never makes an Apparition: All I shall say to it is, as I have mentioned before, that generally speaking, the *Devil* finds it more for his Purpose, to have his Interest in the World propagated another Way; namely, in private, and his personal Appearances are reserved for Things only of extraordinary Consequence, and, as I may say, of evident Necessity, where his Honor is concerned, and where his Interest could be carried on no other Way; not forgetting to take Notice that this is very seldom.

It remains to enquire, what then those Things are which we make so much stir about, and which are called *Apparitions*, or Spirits assuming human Shapes, and showing themselves to People on particular Occasions? whether they are evil Spirits or good? and though, indeed, this is out of my Way at this Time, and does not relate at all to the *Devil*'s History, yet I thought it not amiss to mention it; (1.) Because, as I have said, I do not wholly exclude Satan from all Concern in such Things; and (2.) Because I shall dismiss the Question with so very short an Answer, namely, that we may determine which are and which are not the *Devil*'s, by the Errand they come upon; everyone to his own Business; if it comes of a good Errand, you may certainly acquit the *Devil* of it, conclude him innocent, and that he has no hand in it; if it comes of a wicked and devilish Errand, you may even take him up upon Suspicion, 'tis ten to one but you find him at the Bottom of it.

Next to Apparitions, we find Mankind disturbed by abundance of little odd reserved Ways which the *Devil* is shrewdly suspected of having a Hand in, such as *Dreams, Noises, Voices*, etc.. smells of Brimstone, Candles burning blue, and the like.

As to Dreams, I have nothing to say in Satan's Prejudice at all there; I make no Question but he deals very much in that Kind of Intelligence, and why should he not? we know *Heaven* itself formerly converst very often with the greatest of Men, by the same Method, and the *Devil* is known to mimic the Methods, as well as the Actions of his Maker; whether Heaven has not quite left off that Way of working, we are not certain; but we pretty well know the *Devil* has not left it, and I believe some Instances may be given where his Worship has been really seen and talked to in sleep, as much as if the Person had been awake with his Eyes open.

These are to be distinguished too, pretty much by the Goodness or Badness of the Subject; how often have Men committed Murder, Robbery and Adultery in a Dream, and at the same time except an extraordinary Agitation of the Soul, and expressed by extraordinary Noises in the Sleep, by violent Sweating and other such Ways, the Head has never been removed from the Pillow, or the Body so much as turned in the Bed?

Whether in such Cases, the Soul with all the Passions and Affections being agitated, and giving their full assent to the Facts, of whatever Kind so ever, the Man is not as guilty as if the Sins so dreamed of his committing, had been actually committed? though it be no Doubt to me, but that it is so, yet as it is foreign to the present Affair, and not at all relating to the *Devil's* History, I leave it to the Reverend Doctors of the Church, as properly belonging to them to decide.

I knew a Person who the *Devil* so haunted with naked Women, fine beautiful Ladies in Bed with him, and Ladies of his Acquaintance too, offering their Favors to him, and all in his Sleep; so that he seldom slept without some such Entertainment; the Particulars are too gross for my Story, but he gave me several long Accounts of his Night's *Amours*, and being a Man of a virtuous Life and good Morals, it was the greatest Surprise to him imaginable; for you cannot doubt but that the cunning *Devil* made everything be acted to the Life with him, and in a manner the most wicked; he owned with Grief to me, that the very first Attack the *Devil* made upon him, was with a very beautiful Lady of his Acquaintance, who he had been really something freer than ordinary within their common Conversation; This Lady he brought to him in a Posture for Wickedness, and wrought up his Inclination so high in his Sleep, that he, as he thought, actually went about to debauch her, she not at all resisting; but that he walked in the very Moment, to his particular Satisfaction.

He was greatly concerned at this Part, namely, that he really gave the

Consent of his Will to the Fact, and wanted to know if he was not as guilty of Adultery, as if he had lain with her; indeed he decided the Question against himself, so forcibly, that I, who was of the same Opinion before, had nothing to say against it; however, I confirmed him in it, by asking him these Questions.

1. Whether he did not think the *Devil* had the chief Hand in such a Dream? he answered, it could certainly be nobody else, it must be the *Devil*.

2. I then asked him what Reason the *Devil* could have for it, if his Consent to the Fact in Sleep had not been criminal? *That's true indeed*, says he, *I am answered*: But then he asked another Question, which, I confess, is not so easy to answer, namely, How he should prevent being served so again.

Nor could all my Divinity or his own keep the *Devil* from attacking him again; on the other Hand, as I have said, he worried him to that Degree, that he injured his Health, bringing naked Women to him, sometimes one, sometimes another, sometimes in one Posture of Lewdness, sometimes in another, sometimes into his very Arms, sometimes with such Additions as I am not merry enough, and sometimes such as I am not wicked enough to put into your Heads; the Man, indeed, could not help it, and so the *Devil* was more Faulty than he; but as I hinted to him, he might bring his Mind to such a stated Habit of Virtue, as to prevent its assenting to any wicked Motion, even in Sleep, and that would be the Way to put an End to the Attempt; and this Advice he relished very well, and practiced, I believe, with Success.

By this same Method, the same *Devil* injects powerful Incentives to other Crimes, provokes Avarice, by laying a great Quantity of Gold in your View, and nobody present, giving you an Opportunity to steal it, or some of it, at the same time, perhaps, knowing your Circumstances to be such as that you are at that Time in a great want of the Money.

I knew another, who being a Tradesman, and in great Distress for Money in his Business, dreamed that he was walking all alone in a great Wood, and that he met a little Child with a Bag of Gold in its Hand, and a fine Necklace of Diamonds on its Neck, upon the Sight, his Wants presently dictated to him to rob the Child; the little innocent Creature, (just so he dreamed) not being able to resist; or to tell who it was, accordingly he consented to take the Money from the Child, and then to take the Diamond Necklace from it too, and did so.

But the *Devil*, (a full Testimony, as I told him, that it was the *Devil*, not contented with that, hinted to him, that perhaps the Child might some time or other know him, and single him out, by crying or pointing, or some such Thing, especially if he was suspected and showed to it, and therefore it would be better for him to kill the Child, prompting him to kill it for his own Safety, and that he need do no more but twist the Neck of it a little, or crush it with his Knee; He told me he stood debating with himself, whether he should do so or not; but that in that Instant his Heart struck him with the Word Murder, and he entertained a Horror of it, refused to do it, and immediately waked.

He told me, that when he waked, he found himself in so violent a Sweat as he never had known the like; that his Pulse beat with that Heat and Rage, that it was like a Palpitation of the Heart to him, and that the Agitation of his Spirits was such, that he was not fully composed in some Hours; though the Satisfaction and Joy that attended him, when he found it was but a Dream, assisted much to return his Spirits to their due Temperament.

It is neither my Business or Inclination to turn Divine here, nor is the Age I write to sufficiently Grave to relish a Sermon, if I was disposed to preach, though they must allow the Subject would very well bear it; but I shall only ask them, if they think this is not the *Devil*, what they think it is? If they believe it is the *Devil*, they will act accordingly I hope, or let it alone, as Satan and they can agree about it.

I should not oblige the *Devil* over much, whatever I might do to those that read it; if I should enter here upon a Debate of Interests, (*viz.*) to enquire whether the *Devil* has not a vast Advantage upon Mankind this Way, and whether it is not much his Interest to preserve it; and if I prove the Affirmative, I leave it to you to enquire whose Interest it is to disappoint and supplant him.

In short, I take Dreams to be the second Best of the Advantages the *Devil* has over Mankind; the first, I suppose, you all know (*viz.*) the Treachery of the Garrison within; by Dreams he may be said to get into the Inside of us without Opposition; here he opens and locks without a Key, and like an Enemy laying siege to a fortified City, Reason and Nature, the Governor of the City, keep him out by Day, and keep the Garrison true to their Duty; but in the Dark he gets in and parlees with the Garrison (the Affections and Passions) Debauches their Loyalty, stirring up them to Disloyalty and Rebellion, so they betray their Trust, Revolt, Mutiny, and go over to the Besieger.

Thus he manages his Interest, I say, and insinuates himself into the Inside of us, without our Consent, nay, without our Knowledge; for whatever Speculation may do, 'tis evident Demonstration does not assist us to discover which Way he gets Access to the Soul, while the Organ tied up, and dozed with Sleep has locked it up from Action; that it is so is clear, but how he does it is a Secret which I do not find the Ancients or Moderns have yet made a Discovery of.

That Devil of a Creature, Mother *Lakland*, whose Story I mentioned above, acknowledged that the first Time the *Devil* attempted to draw her in to be a Witch was in a Dream, and even when she consented, she said, she was between sleeping and waking; that is, she did not know whether she was awake or asleep, and the cunning Devil it seems was satisfied with her Assent given so, when she was asleep, or neither asleep or awake, so taking the Advantage of her Incapacity to act rationally.

The Stories of her bewitching several People, and the manner in which they died, are so formidable and extravagant, that I care not to put any one's Faith to the stretch about them, though published by Authority, and testified by Abundance of Witnesses; but this is recorded in particular, and to my Purpose, whether from her own Mouth or not, I do not say, namely, the Description of a Witch, and the Difference between Witches, and those other of Satan's Acquaintance who act in his Name.

1. They have consulted and covenanted with a Spirit or *Devil*.

2. They have a Deputy *Devil*, sometimes several to serve and assist them.

3. These they employ as they please, call them by Name, and command their Appearance in whatever Shape they think fit.

4. They send them abroad to or into the Persons who they design to bewitch, who they always torment, and often murder them, as Mother *Lakland* did several.

As to the Difference between the several Devils that appear, it relates to the Office of the Persons who employ them; as Conjurers, who seem to command the particular *Devil* that waits upon them with more Authority, and raise them and lay them at Pleasure, drawing Circles, casting Figures, and the like; but the Witch, in a more familiar manner, whispers with the Devil, keeps the *Devil* in a Bag or a Sack, sometimes in her Pocket, and the like, and like Mr. *Faux* shows Tricks with him.

But all these Kinds deal much in Dreams, talk with the Devil in their Sleep, and make other People talk with him in their Sleep too; and 'tis on this Occasion I mention it here; in short, the Devil may well take this Opportunity with Mankind, for not half the World that came into his Measures would comply, if they were awake; but of that hereafter.

And yet his thus insinuating himself by Dream, does not seem sufficient, in my Opinion, to answer the *Devil*'s End, and to carry on his Business; and therefore we must be forced to allow him a Kind of actual Possession, in particular Cases, and that in the Souls of some People, by different Methods from others; *Luther* is of the Opinion that the *Devil* gets a

Familiarity with some Souls just at, or rather before their being embodied; as to the Manner and Method how he gets in, that is another Question, and may be spoken of by itself; besides, why may not he, that at Satan's Request to enter into the Herd of Swine, said *go*, give the same Commission to possess a sort of Creatures so many Degrees below the Dignity of the *Gaderenian* Swine, and open the Door too? but as for that, when our Lord said *go*, the *Devil* never enquired which Way he should get in.

When then I see Nations, or indeed Herds of Nations set on Fire of Hell, and as I may say, enflamed by the *Devil*; when I see Towns, Parties, Factions and Rabbles of People visibly possessed; 'tis enough to me that the great Master of the Devils has said to him, go; there's no need to enquire which Way he finds open, or at what postern Gate he gets in; as to his appearing, 'tis plain he often gets in without appearing, and therefore the Question about his appearing still remains a Doubt, and is not very easy to be resolved.

In the Scripture we have some Light into it, and that is all the Help I find from Antiquity, and it goes a great Way to solve the Phenomena of Satan's appearing; what I mean by the Scripture giving some Light to it, is this; 'tis said in several Places, and of several Persons, God came to them in a Dream, *Gen.* xx. 3. *God came to* Abimelech *in a Dream by Night*, Gen. xxxi. 24. *And God came to* Laban *the* Syrian *in a Dream*, Matt. ii. 13. *The Angel of the Lord appeared to* Joseph *in a Dream*; short Comments are sufficient to plain Texts, applying this to my Friend when he wanted to be satisfied about the How, relating to his Dream (*viz.*) how he should come to Dream such wicked Things? I told him, in short, the Case was plain, *the Devil came to him in a Dream by Night*: How and in what manner he formed the wicked Representations, and spread debauched Appearances before his Fancy, by real Whispers and Voice, according to *Milton*, or by what other Methods, the Learned are not arrived to any Certainty about it.

This leads me necessarily to enquire whether the *Devil* or some of his Agents are not always in our Company, whether they make any visible Appearances or no? For my Part I make no Question of it, how else could he come at the Knowledge of what we do; for as I can allow him no Prescience at all, as for many Reasons I have observed already, he must be able to see and know us, and what we are about when we know nothing of him, or else he could know nothing of us and our Affairs, which yet we find otherwise; and this gives him infinite Advantage to Influence our Actions, to judge of our Inclinations, and to bring our Passions to clash with our Reason, as they often do, and get the better of it too.

All this he obtains by his being able to walk about invisible, and see when he is not seen, of which I have spoken already; hence that most wise and solid Suggestion, that when the Candles burn blue the *Devil* is in the

Room, which great Secret in Nature, that you may more fully be convinced of its imaginary Reality, I must tell you the following Story which I saw in a Letter directed to a particular Friend, take it Word for Word as in the Letter; because I do not make myself accountable for the Facts, but take them *ad referendum*.

Sir,

We had one Day, very early in the Morning, and for the most Part of the Day a great deal of Rain with a high Wind, and the Clouds very thick and dark all Day.

In the Evening the cloudy thick Weather continued, though not the Rain, when being at a Friend's House in —— Lane *London*, and several Ladies and some Gentlemen in the Room, besides two or three Servants (for we had been eating) the following Interlude happened for our Entertainment: When the Cloth was taken away, two large Candles were brought upon the Table and placed there with some Bottles and Glasses for the Gentlemen, who, it seems, were intending to drink and be very merry; two large Wax-Candles were also set on another Table, the Ladies being going to Cards, also there were two large Candles in Sconces over or near the Chimney, and one more in a Looking-Glass Sconce, on a Peer by the Window.

With all this *Apparatus*, the Company separating sat down, the Gentlemen at their Table, and the Ladies at theirs, to play *as above*; when after some time the Gentleman of the House said hastily to a Servant, *what a P——ails the Candles*? and turning to the Servant raps out an Oath or two, and bids him snuff the Candles, for they burnt as if the Devil was in the Room.

The Fellow going to snuff one of the Candles, snuffs it out, at which his Master being in a Passion the Fellow lights it again immediately at the other Candle, and then being in a little hurry, going to snuff the other Candle snuffed that out too.

The first Candle that was relighted (as is usual in such Cases) burned dim and dull for a good while, and the other being out, the Room was much darker than before, and a Wench that stood by the Ladies Table, bawls out to her Mistress, *Law Madam!* the Candles *burn blue*; an old Lady that sat by says, *ay Betty!* so they do; upon this one of the Ladies starts up, *Mercy upon us*, says she, *what is the Matter!* In this unlucky Moment another Servant, without Orders, went to the great Peer Sconce, and because, *as he thought*, he would be sure to snuff the Candle well, he offers to take it down, but very unhappily, I say, the Hook came out and down falls the Sconce Candle and all, and the Looking-Glass broke all to pieces, with a horrible Noise; however, the Candle falling out of the Sconce did not go out, but lay on the Floor burning dully, and as it is usual on such Cases, all on one Side, *Betty* cries out again, *Law Madam*, that Candle burns blue too; the very Moment she said this, the Footman that had thrown down the Sconce, says to his fellow Servant, that came to his Assistance, I *think* the Devil *is in the Candles to Night*, and away he run out of the Room, for fear of his Master.

The old Lady, who, upon the Maid *Betty*'s Notion of the Candles burning blue, had her Head just full of that old *Chimney-Corner Story*, the Candles *burn blue when the Spirits are in the Room*, heard the Footman Say the Word *Devil*, but heard nothing else of what he said; upon this she rises up in a terrible Fright, and cries out that the Footman said the *Devil was in the Room*; as she was, indeed, startled out of her Wits, she startled the Ladies most terribly, and they all starting up together, down goes the Card Table, and put the Wax-Candles out.

Mrs. *Betty*, that had startled them all, runs to the Sconce next the Chimney, but that having a long Snuff, she cried out it burnt blue too, and she durst not touch it; in short, though there were three Candles left still burning in the Room, yet the Ladies we're all so startled, that they and the Maids too run out of the Parlor screaming like mad Folks. The Master in a Rage kicked his first Man out of the Room, and the second Man was run out to avoid, as I said before, the like, so that no Servant was to be had, but all was in Confusion.

The two other Gentlemen, who were sitting at the first Table, kept their Seats composed and easy enough, only concerned to see all the House in such a fright; it was true, they said, the Candles burnt dim and very oddly, but they could not perceive they *burnt blue*, except one of those over the Chimney, and that on the Table, which was relighted after the Fellow had snufft it out.

However, the Maid, the old Lady and the Footman that pulled down the Sconce, all insist that the Candles *burnt blue*, and all pretend that the Devil was certainly in the Room, and was the Occasion of it; and they now came to me with the Story, to desire my Opinion of it.

This put me upon Enquiry into the Notion of Candles *burning blue* when Spirits are in a Room, which upon all the Search into Things, that I am able to make, amounts to no more than this; that upon any extraordinary Emission of sulphureous or of nitrous Particles, either in a close Room, or in any not very open Place, if the Quantity be great, a Candle or Lamp, or any such little Blaze of Fire will seem to be, or to *burn blue*; and if then they can prove that any such Effluvia attends or is emitted from a Spirit, then when Satan is at Hand it may be so.

But then 'tis begging the Question grossly, because no Man can assure us that the Devil has any sulphureous Particles about him.

It is true, the Candles burn thus in Mines and Vaults, and damp Places; and 'tis as true that they will do so upon Occasion of very damp, stormy and moist Air, when an extraordinary Quantity of Vapors are supposed to be dispersed abroad, as was the Case when this happened; and if there was any Thing of that in it on that *Monday* Night, the Candles might, perhaps, burn blue upon that Occasion; but that the *Devil* was abroad upon any extraordinary Business that Night, that I cannot grant, unless I have some better Testimony than the *old Lady* that heard the Footman's out-cry but by halves, or than Mrs. *Betty*, who first fancied the Candles *burnt blue*; so I must suspend my Judgment till I hear farther.

This Story however may solve a great many of those Things which pass for Apparitions in the World, and which are laid to the Devil's Charge, though he really may know nothing of the Matter; and this would bring me to defend *Satan* in many Things, wherein he may truly be said to suffer wrongfully; and if I thought it would oblige him, I might say something to his Advantage this Way; however, I'll venture a Word or two for an injured *Devil*, take it as you will.

First, it is certain, that as this Invisibility of the *Devil* is very much to our Prejudice, so the Doctrine of his Visibility is a great Prejudice to him, as we make Use of it.

By his Invisibility he is certainly vested with infinite Advantages against us; while he can be present with us, and we know nothing of the Matter, he informs himself of all our Measures, and arms himself in the best and most suitable manner to injure and assault us, as he can counteract all our secret concerted Designs, disappoint all our Schemes, and except when Heaven apparently concerns itself to over-rule him, can defeat all our Enterprises, break all our Measures, and do us Mischief in almost every Part of our Life, and all this, because we are not privy to all his Motions, as he is to ours.

But now for his Visibility and his real Appearance in the World, and particularly among his Disciples and Emissaries, such as Witches and Wizards, Demonists, and the like: Here, I think Satan has a great deal of Loss, suffers manifest Injury, and has great Injustice done him; and, that therefore I ought to clear this Matter up a little, if it be possible, to do Justice to Satan, and set Matters right in the World about him, according to that useful old Maxim of setting the Saddle upon the right Horse, or *giving the* Devil *his due.*

First, *as I have said*, we are not to believe every idle Head, who pretends even to converse Face to Face with the *Devil*, and who tells us, they have thus seen him, and been acquainted with him every Day: Many of these Pretenders are manifest Cheats; and, however, they would have the Honor of a private Interest in him, and boast how they have him at their Beck, can call him this Way, and send him that, as they please, raise him and lay him when and how, and as often as they find for their Purpose; I say, whatever Boasts they make of this Kind, they really have nothing of Truth in them.

Now the Injuries and Injustice done to the *Devil*, in these Cases, are manifest; namely, that they entitle the *Devil* to all the Mischief they are pleased to do in the World; and if they commit a Murder or a Robbery, fire a House, or do any Act of Violence in the World, they presently are said to do it by the Agency of the *Devil*, and the *Devil* helps them; so Satan bears the Reproach, and they have all the Guilt; this is, (1.) a grand Cheat upon the World, and (2.) a notorious Slander upon the *Devil*; and it would be a public Benefit to Mankind, to have such would-be-Devils as these turned inside out, that we might know when the *Devil* was really at work among us, and when not; what Mischiefs were of his doing, and which were not; and that these Fellows might not slip their Necks out of the Halter, by continually laying the Blame of their Wickedness upon the *Devil*.

Not that the *Devil* is not very willing to have his Hand in any Mischief, or in all the Mischief that is done in the World; but there are some low prized Rogueries that are too little for him, beneath the Dignity of his Operation, and which 'tis really a Scandal to the *Devil* to charge upon him. I remember the *Devil* had such a Cheat put upon him in *East-Smithfield* once, where a Person pretended to converse with the *Devil* Face to Face, and that in open Day too, and to cause him to tell Fortunes, foretell Good and Evil, *etc.*. discover stolen Goods, tell where they were who stole them, and how to find them again, nay, and even to find out the Thieves; but *Satan* was really slandered in the Case, the Fellow had no more to do with the *Devil* than other People, and perhaps not so much neither: This was one of those they called Cunning-Men, or at least he endeavored to pass for such a one, but 'twas all a Cheat.

Besides, what had the *Devil* to do to detect Thieves, and restore stolen Goods? Thieving and Robbing, Trick and Cheat, are part of the Craft of his Agency, and of the Employments which it is his Business to encourage; they greatly mistake him, who think he will assist any Body in suppressing and detecting such laudable Arts and such diligent Servants.

I won't say, but the *Devil*, to draw these People we call *Cunning-Men*, into a Snare, and to push on his farther Designs, may encourage them privately, and in a manner that they themselves know nothing of, to make use of his Name, and abuse the World about him, till at last they may really believe they do deal with the *Devil*, when indeed 'tis only he deals with them, and they know nothing of the Matter.

In other Cases he may encourage them in these little Frauds and Cheats, and give them leave, as above, to make use of his Name to bring them afterwards, and by Degrees to have a real Acquaintance with him; so bringing the Jest of their Trade into Earnest, till at length prompting them to commit some great Villany, he secures them to be his own, by their very Fear of his leaving them to be exposed to the World; thus he puts a *Jonathan Wild* upon them, and makes them be the very Wretches they only pretended to be before: So old *Parsons* of *Clithroe*, as Fame tells, was twenty five Years a *Cunning-man*, and twenty two Years a Witch; that is to say, for five and twenty Years, he was only pretending to deal with the *Devil*, when Satan and he had no manner of Acquaintance, and he only put his *Leger-de-main* upon the People in the *Devil*'s Name, without his leave; but at length the *Devil*'s Patience being tired quite out, he told the old Counterfeit, that in short, he had been his stalking Horse long enough, and that now, if he thought fit to enter himself, and take a Commission, well and good; and he should have a Lease to carry on his Trade for so many Years more, to his Heart's content; but if not, he would expose his Knavery to the World, for that he should take away his Peoples Trade no longer; but that he (Satan) would set up another in his Room, that should make a mere Fool of him, and carry away all his Customers.

Upon this, the old Man considered of it, took the *Devil*'s Counsel, and listed in his Pay; so he, that had plaid his Pranks twenty five Years as a Conjurer, when he was no Conjurer, was then forced really to deal with the Devil, for fear the People should know he did not: Till now he had *ambo dexter*, cheated the Devil on one Hand, and the People on the other; but the *Devil* gained his Point at last, and so he was a real Wizard ever after.

But this is not the only way the Devil is injured neither, for we have often found People pretend upon him in other Cases, and of nearer Concern to him a great deal, and in Articles more Weighty, as in particular, in the great Business of Possession; it is true this Point is not thoroughly understood among Men, neither has the Devil thought fit to give us those Illuminations about it, as I believe he might do; particularly that great and important Article, is not, for ought I can see, rightly explained, namely; whether there are not two several Kinds of Possession, (*viz.*) some wherein the Devil possesses us, and some in which we really possess the Devil; the Nicety of which I doubt this Age, with all its Penetration, is not qualified to explain, and a Dissertation upon it being too long for this Work, especially so near its Conclusion, I am obliged to omit, as I am also all the practical Discourses upon the Usefulness and Advantages of real Possession, whether considered one Way or other to Mankind, all which I must leave to hereafter.

But to come back to the Point in Hand, and to consider the Injustice done to the Devil, in the various Turns and Tricks which Men put upon him very often in this one Article (*viz.*) pretending to Possession, and to have the Devil in them, when really it is not so; certainly the Devil must take it very ill, to have all their demented, lunatic Tricks charged upon him; some of which, nay, most of which are so gross, so simple, so empty, and so little to the Purpose, that the *Devil* must be ashamed to see such Things pass in his Name, or that the World should think he was concerned in them.

It is true, that Possession being one of the principal Pieces of the Devil's Artifice in his managing Mankind, and in which, with the most exquisite skill he plays the Devil among us, he has the more Reason to be affronted when he finds himself invaded in this Part, and angry that any Body should pretend to possess, or be possessed without his leave, and this may be the Reason for ought we know, why so many Blunders have been made, when People have pretended to it without him, and he has thought fit not to own them in it; of which we have many Examples in History, as in *Simon Magus, the Devil of* London, *the fair Maid of* Kent, and several others, whose History it is not worthwhile to enlarge upon.

In short, Possessions, as I have said, are nice Things, as it is not so easy to mimic the *Devil* in that Part, as it may be in some other; designing Men have attempted it often, but their manner has been easily distinguished, even without the Devil's Assistance.

Thus the People of *Salem* in *New-England* pretended to be bewitched, and that a black Man tormented them by the Instigation of such and such, whom they resolved to bring to the Gallows: This black Man they would have be the *Devil*, employed by the Person who they accused for a Witch: Thus making the *Devil* a Page or a Footman to the Wizard, to go and torment whoever the said Wizard commanded, till the *Devil* himself was so weary of the foolish Part, that he left them to go on their own Way, and at last they over-acted the murdering Part so far, that when they confessed themselves to be Witches, and possessed, and that they had Correspondence with the Devil, *Satan* not appearing to vouch for them, no Jury would condemn them upon their own Evidence, and they could not get themselves hanged, whatever Pains they took to bring it to pass.

Thus you see the *Devil* may be wronged, and falsely accused in many Particulars, and often has been so; there are likewise some other sorts of counterfeit *Devils* in the World, such as *Gypsies, Fortune-Tellers,* Foretellers of good and bad Luck, Sellers of Winds, Raisers of Storms, and many more, some practiced among us, some in foreign Parts, too many almost to reckon up; nay I almost doubt whether the Devil himself knows all the Sorts of them; for 'tis evident he has little or nothing to do with them, I mean not in the Way of their Craft.

These I take to be Interlopers, or with the *Guinea* Merchants leave, separate Traders, and who act under the Screen and Protection of Satan's Power, but without his License or Authority; no doubt these carry away a great deal of his Trade, that is to say, the Trade which otherwise the *Devil* might have carried on by Agents or his own; I cannot but say, that while these People would fain be thought *Devils*, though they really are not, it is but just they should be really made as much *Devils* as they pretended to be, or that *Satan* should do himself Justice upon them, as he threatened to do upon old *Parsons* of *Clithroe* above-mentioned, and let the World know them.

Chapter XI

Of Divination, Sorcery, the Black-Art, Pawawing, and such like Pretenders to Devilism, and how far the Devil is or is not concerned in them

Though I am writing the History of the *Devil*, I have not undertaken to do the like of all the Kinds of People, Male or Female, who set up for *Devils* in the World: This would be a Task for the *Devil* indeed, and fit only for him to undertake, for their Number is and has been prodigious great, and may, with his other Legions be ranked among the Innumerable.

What a World do we inhabit! where there is not only with us a great *Roaring-Lyon-Devil* daily seeking whom of us he may devour, and innumerable Millions of lesser Devils hovering in the whole Atmosphere over us, nay, and for ought we know, other Millions always invisibly moving about us, and perhaps in us, or at least in many of us; but that have, besides all these, a vast many counterfeit *Hocus Pocus Devils*; human *Devils*, who are visible among us, of our own Species and Fraternity, conversing with us upon all Occasions; who like Mountebanks set up their Stages in every Town, chat with us at every Tea-Table, converse with us in every Coffee-House, and impudently tell us to our Faces that they are Devils, boast of it, and use a thousand Tricks and Arts to make us believe it too, and that too often with Success.

It must be confessed there is a strong Propensity in Man's Nature, especially the more ignorant part of Mankind, to resolve every strange Thing, or whether really strange or no, if it be but strange to us, into Devilism, and to say every Thing is the Devil, that they can give no Account of.

Thus the famous Doctors of the Faculty at *Paris*, when *John Faustus* brought the first printed Books that had then been seen in the World, or at least seen there, into the City, and sold them for Manuscripts: They were surprised at the Performance, and questioned *Faustus* about it; but he affirming they were Manuscripts, and that he kept a great many Clarks employed to write them, they were satisfied for a while.

But looking farther into the Work, they observed the exact Agreement of every Book, one with another, that every Line stood in the same Place, every Page a like Number of Lines, every Line a like Number of Words; if a

Word was mis-spelt in one, it was miss-spelt also in all, nay, that if there was a Blot in one, it was alike in all; they began again to muse, how this should be? in a Word, the learned Divines not being able to comprehend the Thing (and that was always sufficient) concluded it must be the *Devil*, that it was done by Magic and Witchcraft, and that in short, poor *Faustus* (who was indeed nothing but a mere Printer) dealt with the *Devil*.

> N. B. *John Faustus* was Servant, or Journeyman, or Compositor, or what you please to call it, to *Koster* of *Harlem*, the first inventor of Printing; and having printed the Psalter, sold them at *Paris* as Manuscripts; because as such they yielded a better Price.

But the learned Doctors not being able to understand how the Work was performed, concluded as above, it was all *the Devil*, and that the Man was a *Witch*; accordingly they took him up for a *Magician* and a *Conjurer*, and one that worked by the *Black Art*, that is to say, by the help of the *Devil*; and in a Word, they threatened to hang him for a Witch, and in order to it, commenced a Process against him in their criminal Courts, which made such a Noise in the World as raised the Fame of poor *John Faustus* to a frightful Height, till at last he was obliged, for fear of the Gallows, to discover the whole Secret to them.

> N. B. This is the true original of the famous Dr. *Faustus* or *Foster*, of whom we have believed such strange Things, as that it is become a Proverb, *as great as the* Devil *and Dr.* Foster: Whereas poor *Faustus* was no Doctor, and knew no more of the *Devil* than another Body.

Thus the Magistrates of *Bern* and *Switzerland*, finding a Gang of *French* Actors of Puppet-show opened their Stage in the Town, upon hearing the surprising Accounts which the People gave of their wonderful Puppets, how they made them speak, answer Questions, and discourse, appear and disappear in a Moment, pop up here, as if they rise out of the Earth, and down there, as if they vanished, and Abundance more Feats of Art, censured them as Demons; and if they had not packed up their Trinkets, and disappeared almost as dexterously as their Puppets, they had certainly condemned the poor Puppets to the Flames for *Devils*, and censured, if not otherwise punished their Masters. See *the Count de Rochfort's Memoirs*, p. 179.

Wonderful Operations astonish the Mind, especially where the Head is not over-burdened with Brains; and Custom has made it so natural to give the *Devil* either the Honor or Scandal of every Thing, that we cannot otherwise Account for, that it is not possible to put the People out of the Road of it.

The *Magicians* were, in the *Chaldean* Monarchy, called the Wisemen; and though they are joined with the Sorcerers and Astrologers in the same Place, *Dan.* ii. 4. yet they were generally so understood among those

People; but in our Language we understand them to be People that have an Art to reveal Secrets, interpret Dreams, foretell Events, *etc..* and that use Enchantments and Sorceries, by all which we understand the same Thing; which now in a more vulgar Way we express by one general coarse Expression, *Dealing with the* Devil.

The Scripture speaks of a Spirit of *Divination, Acts* xvi. 16. and a Wench that was possessed by this Spirit *brought her Master much Gain by Southsaying*, that is to say, according to the Learned, by *Oracling* or answering Questions; whence you will see in the Margin, that this southsaying *Devil* is there called *Python*, that is, *Apollo*, who is often called *Python*, and who at the Oracle of *Delphos* gave out such Answers and *double Entendres*, as this Wench possibly did; and hence all those Spirits which were called Spirits of Divination, were in another Sense called *Pythons*.

Now when the Apostle St. *Paul* came to see this Creature, this Spirit takes upon it to declare that *those Men*, meaning St. *Paul* and *Timotheus, were the Servants of the most high God, which showed unto them the Way of Salvation*; this was a good turn of the *Devil*, to preserve his Authority in the possessed Girl; she brought them Gain by Southsaying, that is to say, resolving difficult Questions, answering Doubts, interpreting Dreams, *etc..* Among these Doubts, he makes her give Testimony to *Paul* and *Timotheus*, to wheedle in with the new Christians, and perhaps (though very ignorantly) even with *Paul* and *Timotheus* themselves, so to give a Kind of Credit and Respect to her for speaking.

But the *Devil*, who never speaks Truth, but with some sinister End, was discovered here and detected; his flattering Recognition not accepted, and he himself unkenneled as he deserved; there the *Devil* was over-shot in his own Bow again.

Here now was a real Possession, and the evil Spirits who possessed her, did stoop to sundry little Acts of Servitude, that we could give little or no Reason for, only that the Girl's Master might get Money by her; but perhaps this was a particular Case, and, prepared to honor the Authority and Power the Apostles had over evil Spirits.

But we find these Things carried a great Way farther in many Cases, that is to say, where the Parties are thus really possessed; namely, the *Devil* makes Agents of the possessed Parties to do many Things for the propagating his Interest and Kingdom, and particularly for the carrying on his Dominion in the World: But I am for the present not so much upon the real Possession as the pretended, and particularly we have had many that have believed themselves possessed, when the *Devil* never believed it of them, and perhaps knew them better; some of these are really poor *Devils* to be pitied, and are what I call *Diables Imaginaire*; these have notwithstanding done the *Devil* good Service, and brought their Masters good Gain by Southsaying.

We find Possessions acknowledged in Scripture to be really and personally the *Devil*, or according to the Text, Legions of *Devils* in the Plural. The *Devil* or *Devils* rather, which possessed the Man among the Tombs, is positively affirmed to be the *Devil* in the Scripture; all the Evangelists agree in calling him so, and his very Works show it; namely, the Mischief he did, as well to the poor Creature among the Tombs, who was made so fierce, that he was the Terror of all the Country, as to the Herd of Swine and to the Country in the Loss of them.

I might preach you a Lecture here of the *Devil*'s Terror upon the Approach of our Saviour, the Dread of his Government, and how he acknowledged that there was a Time for his Torment, which was not yet come: *Art thou come to torment us before our Time?* It is evident the Devil apprehended that Christ would chain them up before the Day of Judgment; and therefore some think the Devil here, being, as it were, caught out of his due Bounds, possessing the poor Man in such a furious manner, was afraid, and petitioned Christ not to chain him up for it, and as the Text says, *They besought him to suffer them to go away*, etc.. that is to say, when they say, art thou come to torment us before the Time? the Meaning is, they begged he would not cast them into Torment before the Time, which was already fixed; but that if he would cast them out of the Man, he would let them go away, *etc.*.

The Evangelist St. *Luke* says, the *Devil besought him that he would not command them to go out into the Deep*: Our learned Annotators think that part is not rightly rendered; adding, that they do not believe the *Devil* fears drowning; but with Submission, I believe the meaning is, that they would not be confined to the vast Ocean, where no Inhabitants being to be seen, they would be effectually imprisoned and tied down from doing Mischief, which would be a Hell to them; as to their going into the Swine, that might afford us some Allegory; but I am not disposed to jest with the Scripture, no nor with the *Devil* neither, farther than needs must.

It is evident the *Devil* makes Use of very mean Instruments sometimes, such as the Damsel possessed with a Spirit of Divination, and several others.

I remember a Story, how true I know not, of a weak Creature next Door to an Idiot, who was established in the Country for an Oracle, and would tell People strange Things that should be, long before they came to pass; when People were sick, would tell them whether they should live or die; if People were married, tell how many Children they should have; and a hundred such Things as filled the People with Admiration, and they were the easier brought to believe that the Girl was possessed; but then they were divided about her too, and that was the finest spun Thread the Devil could work, for he carried a great Point in it; some said she had a good Spirit, and some a bad, some said she was a Prophetess, and some that she was the *Devil*.

Now had I been there to decide the Question, I should certainly have given it for the latter; if it were only upon this Account, namely, that the Devil has often found Fools very necessary Agents for the propagating his Interest and Kingdom, but we never knew the good Spirits do so; on the other Hand, it does not seem likely that Heaven should deprive a poor Creature of its Senses, and as it were take her Soul from her, and then make her an Instrument of Instruction to others, and an Oracle to declare his Decrees by; this does not seem to be rational.

But as far as this kind of Divination is in Use in our Days, yet I do not find room to charge the Devil with making any great Use of Fools, unless it be such as he has particularly qualified for his Work, for as to *Idiots* and *Naturals*, they are perfectly useless to him; but a sort of Fools called the Magi, indeed, we have some Reason to think he often works with.

We are not arrived to a certainty yet, in the settling this great Point, namely, what Magic is? whether a diabolical Art or a Branch of the Mathematics? Our most learned *Lexicon Technicum* is of the latter Opinion, and gives the *Magic Square* and the *Magic Lantern*, two Terms of Art.

The *Magic Square* is when Numbers in *Arithmetical Proportion* are disposed into such Parallels or equal Ranks, as that the Sums of each Row as well *Diagonally* as *Laterally* shall be all equal; for Example, 2, 3, 4, 5, 6, 7, 8, 9, 10. Place these Nine in a Square of three, they will *directly* and *diagonally* make 18. Thus,

5	10	3
4	6	8
9	2	7

This he calls the *Magic Square*, but gives no Reason for the Term, nor any Account of what infernal Operations are wrought by this Concurrence of the Numbers; neither do I see that there can be any such Use made of it.

The *Magic Lantern* is an optic Machine, by the Means of which are represented, on a Wall in the Dark, many Phantasms and terrible Appearances, *but no* Devil *in all this*, only that they are taken for the Effects of Magic, by those that are not acquainted with the Secret.

All this is done by the help of several little painted Pieces of Glass, only so and so situated, placed in certain Oppositions to one another, and painted with different Figures, the most formidable being placed foremost, and such as are most capable of terrifying the Spectators; and by this all the Figures may be represented upon the opposite Wall, in the largest Size.

I cannot but take Notice, that this very Piece of optic Delusion seems too much akin to the mock Possessions and infernal Accomplishments, which most of the Possessionists of this Age pretend to, so that they are most of them mere Phantasms and Appearances, and no more; Nor is the Spirit of Divination, the Magic, the Necromancing, and other Arts which were called Diabolical, found to be of any Use in modern Practice, at least, in these Parts of the World; but the Devil seems to do most of his Work himself, and by shorter Methods; for he has so complete an Influence among those that he now Lists in his Service, that he brings all the common Affairs of Mankind into a narrower Compass in his Management, with a Dexterity particular to himself, and by which he carries on his Interest silently and surely, much more to the Detriment of Virtue and good Government, and consequently much more to his Satisfaction, than ever he did before.

There is a Kind of *Magic* or *Sorcery*, or what else you may please to call it, which, though unknown to us, is yet, it seems, still very much encouraged by the *Devil*; but this is a great Way off, and in Countries where the politer Instruments, which he finds here, are not to be had; namely, among the *Indians* of *North-America*; This is called *Pawawing*, and they have their Divines, which they call *Pawaws* or Witches, who use strange Gestures, Distortions, horrid Smokes, Burnings, and Scents, and several such Things which the Sorcerers and Witches in ancient Times are said to use in casting Nativities, in Philtres, and in determining, or as they pretended, directing the Fate of Persons; by burning such and such Herbs and Roots, such as *Helebore, Wormwood, Storax, Devilwort, Mandrake, Nightshade,* and Abundance more such, which are called noxious Plants, or the Product of noxious Plants; also melting such and such Minerals, Gums, and poisonous Things, and by several hellish Mutterings and Markings over them, the like do these *Pawaws*; and the *Devil* is pleased, it seems, (or is permitted) to fall in with these Things, and as some People think, appears often to them for their Assistance upon those Occasions.

But be that as it will, he is eased of all that Trouble here; he can *Pawaw* here himself, without their aid, and having laid them all aside, he negotiates much of his Business without Ambassadors; he is his own Plenipotentiary, for he finds Man so easy to come at, and so easy when he is come at, that he stands in no need of secret Emissaries, or at least not so much as he used to do.

Upon the whole, as the World, within the Compass of a few passed Years is advanced in all Kinds of Knowledge and Arts, and every useful Branch of what they knew before improved, and innumerable useful Parts of Knowledge, which were concealed before are discovered; why should we think the *Devil* alone should stand at a stay, has taken no Steps to his farther Accomplishment, and made no useful Discoveries in his Way? That he alone should stand at a Stay, and be just the same unimproved Devil that he was before? No, no, as the World is improved every Day, and every Age is grown wiser and wiser than their Fathers; so, no doubt, he has bestirred himself too, in order to an increase of Knowledge and Discovery, and that he finds every Day a nearer Way to go to work with Mankind than he had before.

Besides, as Men in general seem to have altered their manner, and that they move in a higher and more exalted Sphere, especially as to Vice and Virtue; so the *Devil* may have been obliged to change his Measures, and alter his Way of working; particularly, those Things which would take in former Times, and which a stupid Age would come easily into, won't go down with us now: As the taste of Vice and Virtue alters, the *Devil* is forced to bait his Hook with new Compositions; the very Thing called Temptation is altered in its Nature, and that which served to delude our Ancestors, whose gross Conceptions of Things caused them to be manageable with less Art, will not do now; the Case is quite altered; in some Things, perhaps, as I hinted above, we come into Crime with ease, and may be led by a Finger; but when we come to a more refined Way of sinning, which our Ancestors never understood, other and more refined Politics must be made Use of, and the *Devil* has been put upon many useful Projects and Inventions, to make many new Discoveries and Experiments to carry on his Affairs; and to speak impartially, he is strangely improved either in Knowledge or Experiment, within these few Years; he has found out a great many new Inventions to shorten his own Labor, and carry on his Business in the World currently, which he never was master of before, or at least we never knew he was.

No wonder then that he has changed Hands too, and that he has left of pawawing in these Parts of the World; that we don't find our Houses disturbed as they used to be, and the Stools and Chairs walking about out of one Room into another, as formerly; that Children don't vomit crooked Pins and rusty stub Nails, as of old, the Air is not full of Noises, nor the Church-Yard full of Hobgoblins; Ghosts don't walk about in Winding-Sheets, and the good old scolding Wives visit and plague their Husbands after they are dead, as they did when they were alive.

The Age is grown too wise to be agitated by these dull scare-crow Things which their Fore-Fathers were tickled with; *Satan* has been obliged to lay by his Puppet-shows and his Tumblers, those things are grown stale; his morrice-dancing Devils, his mountebanking and quacking won't do now; those Things, as they may be supposed to be very troublesome to him, (and but that he has Servants enough would be chargeable too) are now of no great Use in the new Management of his Affairs.

In a Word, Men are too much Devils themselves, in the Sense that I have called them so, to be startled with such little low prized Appearances as these; they are better acquainted with the old Arch-Angel than so, and they seem to tell him they must be treated after another manner, and that then, as they are good-natured and tractable, he may deal with them upon better Terms.

Hence the *Devil* goes to work with Mankind a much shorter Way; for instead of the Art of Wheedling and Whining, together with the laborious Part of Tricking and Sharping, Hurrying and Driving, Freighting and Terrifying, all which the *Devil* was put to the Trouble of before; in short, he acts the Grand Manner as the Architects call it (I don't know whether our Free-Masons may understand the Word) and therefore I may hereafter explain it, as it is to be Diabolically as well as mathematically understood.

At present my meaning is, he acts with them immediately and personally by a magnificent Transformation, making them mere *Devils* to themselves, upon all needful Occasions, and *Devils* to one another too, whenever he (Satan), has Need of their Service.

This Way of embarking Mankind in the *Devil's* particular Engagement, is really very modern; and though the Devil himself may have been long acquainted with the Method, and as I have heard, began to practice it towards the Close of the *Roman* Empire, when Men began to act upon very polite Principles, and were capable of the most refined Wickedness, and afterwards with some Popes, who likewise were a kind of Church Devils, such as Satan himself could hardly expect to find in the World; yet I do not find that he was ever able to bring it into Practice, at least, not so universally as he does now: But now the Case is altered, and Men being generally more expert in Wickedness than they were formerly; they suffer the smaller Alteration of the Species, in being transmigrated; in a Word, they turn into *Devils*, with no trouble at all hardly, either to the *Devil* or to themselves.

This Particular would want much the less Explanation, could I obtain a License from Sir *Hellebore Wormwood*, Bart. or from my Lord *Thwartover*, Baron of *Scoundrel Hall* in the Kingdom of *Ireland*, to write the true History of their own Conduct; and how early, and above all, how easily they commenced *Devils*, without the least Impeachment of their

Characters, as wise Men, and without any Diminution of that Part of their Denomination which established them for Fools.

How many mad Fellows appear among us every Day in the critical Juncture of their Transmigration, just when they have so much of the Man left as to be known by their Names, and enough of the *Devil* taken up to settle their Characters? This Easiness of the *Devil's* access to these People, and the great Convenience it is to him in his general Business, is a Proof to me that he has no more Occasion of Diviners, Magicians, Sorcerers, and whatever else we please to call those People who were formerly so great with him; for what Occasion has he to employ *Devils* and Wizards to confound Mankind, when he is arrived to such a Perfection of Art as to bring Men, at least in these Parts of the World, to do it all themselves; upon this Account we do not find any of the old Sorcerers and Diviners, Magicians or Witches appear among us; not that the *Devil* might not be as well able to employ such People as formerly, and qualify them for the Employment too, but that really there is no need of them hereabout, the *Devil* having a shorter Way, and Mankind being much more easily possessed; not the old *Herd of Swine* were sooner agitated, though there was full 2000 of them together; Nature has opened the Door, and the *Devil* has egress and regress at Pleasure, so that Witches and Diviners are quite out of the Question.

Nor let any Man be alarmed at this Alteration, in the Case as it stands between Mankind and the *Devil*, and think the *Devil* having gained so much Ground, may in time, by Encroachment, come to a general Possession of the whole Race, and so we should all come to be *Devils* incarnate; I say, let us not be alarmed, for Satan does not get these Advantages by Encroachment, and by his infernal Power or Art, no not at all; but 'tis the Man himself does it by his Indolence and Negligence on one Hand, and his Complaisance to the *Devil* on the other; and both Ways he, as it were, opens the Door to him, beckons him with his very Hand to come in, and the Devil has nothing to do but enter and take Possession: Now if it be so, and Man is so frank to him; you know the *Devil* is no Fool not to take the Advantage when 'tis offered him, and therefore 'tis no wonder if the Consequences which I have been just now naming follow.

But let no Man be discouraged by this, from reaffirming his natural and religious Powers, and venturing to shut the *Devil* out; for the Case is plain he may be shut out; the Soul is a strong Castle, and has a good Garrison placed within to defend it; if the Garrison behave well, and do their Duty, it is impregnable, and the cowardly *Devil* must raise his Siege and be gone; nay, he must fly, or, as we call it, make his Escape, lest he be laid by the Heels, that is, lest his Weakness be exposed, and all his Lurking, lying in Wait, ambuscade-Tricks; this Part would bear a great Enlargement, but I have not room to be witty upon him, so you must take it in the Gross, the Devil lies at *Blye Bush*, as our Country People call it, to watch your coming out of your Hold; and if you happen to go abroad unarmed he seizes upon and masters you with ease.

Unarmed, you'll say, what Arms should I take? what Fence against a Flail? What Weapons can a Man take to fight the *Devil*? I could tell you what to fight him with, and what you might fright him with, for the *Devil* is to be startled with several Things besides *Holy Water*; but 'tis too serious for you, and you'll tell me I am a preaching and a canting, and the like; so I must let the *Devil* manage you rather than displease you with talking Scripture and Religion.

Well, but may not the *Devil* be fought with some of his own Weapons? Is there no dealing with him in a Way of human Nature? This would require a long answer, and some Philosophy might be acted, or at least imitated, and some Magic, perhaps; for they tells us there are Spells to draw away even the Devil himself; as in some Places they nail Horse-Shoes upon the Threshold of the Door, to keep him out; in other Places old pieces of Flint, with so many Holes and so many Corners, and the like: But I must answer in the Negative, I don't know what *Satan* might be scared at in those Days, but he is either grown cunninger since or bolder, for he values none of those Things now; I question much whether he would value St. *Dunstan* and his red hot Tongs, if he was to meet him now, or St. *Francis* or any of the Saints, no not the Host itself in full Procession; and therefore, though you don't care I should preach, yet in short, if you are afraid he should charge upon you and attack you, if you won't make Use of those Scripture Weapons I should have mentioned, and which you may hear of, if you enquire at *Eph*. vi. 16. you must look for better where you think you can find them.

But to go on with my Work, the Devil, I say, is not to be feared with Maukins, nor does he employ his old Instruments, but does much of his Work himself without Instruments.

And yet I must enter a Caveat here too, against being misunderstood in my saying the Devil stands in no need of Agents; for when I speak so, I am to be taken in a limited Sense; I don't say he needs them nowhere, but only that he does not need them in those polite Parts of the World which I have been speaking of, and perhaps not much here; but in many remote Countries 'tis otherwise still; the *Indians* of *America* are particularly said to have Witches among them, as well in those Countries where the *Spaniards* and the *English* and other Nations have planted themselves, as amongst those where the *European* Nations seldom come: *for Example*, the People of *Canada*, that is, of the Countries under the *French* Government of *Quebec*, the Equimeaux, and other Northern Climates, have Magicians, Wizards and Witches, who they call *Pilloatas* or *Pillotoas*; these pretend they speak intimately and familiarly with the Devil, and receive from him the Knowledge of Things to come; all which, by the Way,

I take to be little more than this; that these Fellows being a little more cunning than the rest, think, that by pretending to something more than human, they shall make the stronger Impressions on the ignorant People; as *Mahomet* amused the World with his Pigeon, using it to pick Peas out of his Ear, and persuaded the People it brought him superior Revelations and Inspirations from Paradise.

Thus these *Pillotoas* gaining an Opinion among the People, behave like so many Mountebanks of Hell, pretending to understand dark Things, cure Diseases, practice Surgery, Physic and Necromancy altogether; I will not say, but *Satan* may pick out such Tools to work with, and I believe does in those Parts, but I think he has found a nearer Way to the Wood with us, and that is sufficient to my present Purpose.

Some would persuade me the *Devil* had a great Hand in the late religious Breaches in *France*, among the Clergy, (*viz.*) about the Pope's Constitution *Unigenitus*, and that he made a fair Attempt to set the Pope and the *Gallican* Church together by the Ears, for they were all just upon the Point or breaking out into a Church War, that for ought we knew might have gone farther than the *Devil* himself cared it should; now I am of the quite contrary Opinion, I believe the *Devil* really did not make the Breach, but rather healed it, for fear it should have gone so far among them as to have set them all in a Flame, and have opened the Door to the Return of the *Hugonots* again, which it was in a fair Way to have done.

But be it one Way or the other, the historical Part seems to be a little against me; for 'tis certain, the *Devil* both wanted and made Use of Legions of Agents, as well human as infernal, visible and invisible in that great and important Affair, and we cannot doubt but he has innumerable Instruments still at work about it.

Like as in *Poland*, I make no Question but the *Devil* has thousands of his Banditti at work at this Time, and in another Country not far from it, perhaps, preparing Matters for the next General Diet, taking care to prevent giving any Relaxation to the Protestants, and to justify the moderate Executions at *Thorn*, to excite a Nation to quarrel with every Body who are able to fight with no body; to erect the Apostate Race of *S——y* upon a Throne which they have no Title to, and turn an elective Throne into an hereditary, in favor of Popery.

I might anticipate all your Objections, by granting the busy *Devil* at this Time employing all his Agents and Instruments (for I never told you they were idle and useless) in striving to enflame the Christian World, and bring a new War to overspread *Europe*; I might, perhaps, point out to you some of the Measures he takes, the Provocatives which his State Physicians administer to the Courts and Counselors of Princes, to foment and ferment the Spirits, and Members of Nations, Kingdoms, Empires and States in the

World, in order to bring these glorious Ends of Blood and War to pass; for you cannot think but he that knows so much of the *Devil's* Affairs, as to write his History, must know something of all these Matters more than those that do not know so much as he.

But all this is remote to the present Case, for this is no Impeachment of Satan's new Methods with Mankind, in this Part of the World, and in his private and separate Capacity; all this only signifies that in his more general and national Affairs, the *Devil* acts still by his old Methods; and when he is to seduce or embroil Nations, he, like other Conquerors, subdues them by Armies, employs mighty Squadrons of *Devils*, and sends out strong Detachments, with Generals and Generalissimos to lead them, some to one Part of the World, some to another; some to influence one Nation, some to manage and direct another, according as Business presents, and his Occasions require, that his Affairs may be carried on currently, and to his Satisfaction.

If it were not thus, but that the *Devil* by his new and exquisite Management, of which I have said so much, had brought Mankind in general to be the Agents of their own Mischiefs, and that the World were so at his Beck, that he need but command them to go and fight, declare War, raise Armies, destroy Cities, Kingdoms, Countries and People; the World would be a Field of Blood indeed, and all Things would run into Confusion presently.

But this is not the Case at all, Heaven has not let go the Government of the Creation to his subdued Enemy, the Devil; that would overturn the whole System of God, and give Satan more Power, than ever he was or will be vested with; when, therefore, I speak of a few forward Wretches in our Day, who are so warm in their Wickedness, that they anticipate the Devil, save him the Trouble to tempt, turn Devils to themselves, and gallop Hellward faster than he drives; I speak of them as single Persons, and acting in their own personal and private Capacity, but when I speak of Nations and Kingdoms, there the Devil is obliged to go on in the old Road, and act by Stratagem, by his proper Machinery, and to make use of all his Arts, and all his Agents, just as he has done in all Ages, from the beginning of his politic Government to this Day.

And if it was not thus too, what would become of all his numberless Legions, of which all Ages have heard so much, and all Parts of the World have had so much fatal Experience? They would seem to be quite out of Employment, and be rendered useless in the World of Spirits, where it is to be supposed they reside; not the Devil himself could find any Business for them, which by the Way, to busy and mischievous Spirits, as they are, would be a Hell to them, even before their Time; they would be, as it were, doomed to a State of Inactivity, which we may suppose was one Part of their Expulsion from Blessedness and the Creation of Man; or as they were for the surprising Interval between the Destruction of Mankind by the Deluge and *Noah*'s coming out of the Ark, when indeed they might be said to have nothing at all to do.

But this is not Satan's Case, and therefore let me tell you too, that you may not think I treat the Case with more Levity than I really do, and than I am sure I intend to do; though it is too true that our modern and modish Sinners have arrived to more exquisite Ways of being wicked, than their Fathers, and really seem, as I have said, to need no Devil to tempt them; nay, that they do Satan's Work for him as to others also, and make themselves Devils to their Neighbors, tempting others to crime even faster than the Devil desires them, running before they are sent, and going of the *Devil*'s Errands *gratis*; by which Means Satan's Work is, as to them, done to his Hand, and they may be said to save him a great deal of Trouble; yet after all, the Devil has still a great deal of Business upon his Hands, and as well himself as all his Legions, find themselves a full Employment in disturbing the World, and opposing the Glory and Kingdom of their great Superior, whose Kingdom it is their whole Business, however vain in its End, to overthrow and destroy, if they were able, or at least to endeavor it.

This being the Case, it follows of course that the general Mischiefs of Mankind, as well national and public, as family Mischiefs, and even personal, (except as before excepted) lie all still at the *Devil*'s Door, as much as ever, let his Advocates bring him off of it if they can; and this brings us back again to the manner of the Devil's Management, and the Way of his working by human Agents, or if you will, the Way of human Devils, working in Affairs of low Life, such as we call Divination, Sorcery, Black-Art, Necromancy, and the like; all which I take to consist of two material Parts, and both very necessary for us to be rightly informed of.

1. The Part which Satan by himself or his inferior *Devils* empowers such People to do, as he is in Confederacy with here on Earth; to whom he may be said, like the Master of an Opera or Comedy, to give their Parts to act, and to qualify them to act it; whether he obliges them to a Rehearsal in his Presence, to try their Talents, and see that they are capable of performing, that indeed I have not enquired into.

2. That Part which these empowered People do volunteer or beyond their Commission, to show their Diligence in the Service of their new Master, and either (1.) to bring Grist to their own Mill, and make their Market of their Employment in the best manner they can; or (2.) to gain Applause, be admired, wondered at, and applauded, as if they were ten Times more *Devils* than really they are.

In a Word, the Matter consists of what the *Devil* does by the Help of these People, and what they do in his Name without him; the Devil is sometimes cheated in his own Business; there are Pretenders to Witchcraft and Black-

Art, who Satan never made any Bargain with, but who he connives at, because at least they do his Cause no harm, though their Business is rather to get Money, than to render him any Service, of which I gave you a remarkable Instance before.

But to go back to his real Agents, of which I reckon two.

1. Those who act by Direction and Confederacy, as I have said already many do.

2. Those whom he acts in and by, and they (perhaps) know it not, of which Sort History gives us plenty of Examples, from *Machiavelli*'s first Disciple —— to the famous Cardinal *Alberoni*, and even to some more modern than his Eminence, of whom I can say no more till farther Occasion offers.

1. Those who act by immediate Direction of the Devil, and in Confederacy with him; these are such as I mentioned in the beginning of this Chapter, whose Arts are truly black, because really infernal; it will be very hard to decide the Dispute between those who really act thus in Confederacy with the *Devil*, and those who only pretend to it; so I shall leave that Dispute where I find it; but that there are, or at least have been, a Set of People in the World, who really are of his Acquaintance, and very intimate with him; and though, as I have said, he has much altered his Schemes and changed Hands of late; yet that there are such People, perhaps of all Sorts; and that the Devil keeps up his Correspondence with them; I must not venture to deny that Part, lest I bring upon me the whole Posse of the conjuring and bewitching Crew, Male and Female, and they should mob me for pretending to deny them the Honor of dealing with the *Devil*, which they are so exceeding willing to have the Fame of.

Not that I am hereby obliged to believe all the strange Things the Witches and Wizards, who have been allowed to be such, nay, who have been hanged for it, have said of themselves; nay, that they have confessed of themselves, even at the Gallows; and if I come to have an Occasion to speak freely of the Matter, I may perhaps convince you that the Devil's possessing Power is much lessened of late, and that he either is limited, and his Fetter shortened more than it has been, or that he does not find the old Way (as I said before) so fit for his Purpose as he did formerly, and therefore takes other Measures, but I must adjourn that to a Time and Place by itself: But we are told that there are another Sort of People, and, perhaps, a great many of them too, in whom and by whom the Devil really acts, and they know it not.

It would take up a great deal of Time and Room, too much for this Place, so near the Close of this Work, to describe and mark out the involuntary *Devils* which there are in the World; of whom it may be truly said, that really the *Devil* is in them, and they know it not: Now, though the *Devil* is cunning and managing, and can be very silent where he finds it for his Interest not to be known; yet it is very hard for him to conceal himself, and to give so little Disturbance in the House, as that the Family should not know who lodged in it; yet, I say, the Devil is so subtle and so mischievous an Agent, that he uses all manner of Methods and Craft to reside in such People as he finds for his Purpose, whether they will or no, and which is more, whether they know it or no.

And let none of my Readers be angry or think themselves ill used, when I tell them the Devil may be in them, and may act them, and by them, and they not know it; for I must add, it may, perhaps, be one of the greatest Pieces of human Wisdom in the World, for a Man to know when the Devil is in him, and when not; when he is a Tool and Agent of Hell, and when he is not; in a Word, when he is doing the Devil's Work, and under his Direction, and when not.

It is true, this is a very weighty Point, and might deserve to be handled in a more serious Way than I seem to be talking in all this Book; but give me leave to talk of Things my own way, and withall, to tell you, that there is no Part of this Work so seemingly ludicrous, but a grave and well weighed Mind may make a serious and solid Application of it, if they please; nor is there any Part of this Work, in which a clear Sight and a good Sense may not see that the Author's Design is, that they should do so; and as I am now so near the End of my Book, I thought it was meet to tell you so, and lead you to it as far as I can.

I say, 'tis a great Part of human Wisdom to know when the *Devil* is acting in us and by us, and when not; the next and still greatest Part would be to prevent him, put a Stop to his Progress, bid him go about his Business, and let him know he should carry on his Designs no farther in that manner; that we will be his Tools no longer; in short, to turn him out of Doors, and bring a stronger Power to take Possession; but this, indeed, is too solid a Subject, and too great to begin with here.

But now, as to the bare knowing when he is at work with us, I say this, though it is considerable, may be done, nor is it so very difficult; *for Example*, you have no more to do but look a little into the Microcosm of the Soul, and see there how the Passions which are the Blood, and the Affections which are the Spirit, move in their particular Vessels; how they circulate, and in what Temper the Pulse beats there, and you may easily see who turns the Wheel; if a perfect Calm possesses the Soul; if Peace and Temper prevail, and the Mind feels no Tempests rising; if the Affections are regular and exalted to virtuous and sublime Objects, the Spirits cool, and the Mind sedate, the Man is in a general Rectitude of Mind, he may be truly said to be *his own Man*; Heaven shines upon his Soul with its benign Influences, and he is out of the Reach of the evil Spirit; for the divine Spirit is an Influence of Peace, all calm and bright, happy and sweet like itself, and tending to every Thing that is good both present and future.

But on the other Hand, if at any Time the Mind is ruffled, if Vapours rise, Clouds gather, if Passions swell the Breast, if Anger, Envy, Revenge, Hatred, Wrath, Strife; if these, or any of these hover over you, much more if you feel them within you; if the Affections are possessed, and the Soul hurried down the Stream to embrace low and base Objects; if those Spirits, which are the Life and enlivening Powers of the Soul, are drawn off to Parties, and to be engaged in a vicious and corrupt manner, shooting out wild and wicked Desires, and running the Man headlong into Crime, the Case is easily resolved, the Man is possessed, the *Devil* is in him; and having taken the Fort, or at least the Counterscarp and Out-Works, is making his Lodgment to cover and secure himself in his Hold, that he may not be dispossessed.

Nor can he be easily dispossessed when he has got such hold as this; and 'tis no wonder, that being lodged thus upon the Out-Works of the Soul he continues to sap the Foundation of the rest, and by his incessant and furious Assaults, reduces the Man at last to a Surrender.

If the Allegory be not as just and apposite as you would have it be, you may, however, see by it in a full View, the State of the Man, and how the *Devil* carries on his Designs; nothing is more common, and I believe there are few thinking Minds but may reflect upon it in their own Compass, than for our Passions and Affections to flow out of the ordinary Channel; the Spirits and Blood of the Soul to be extravagated, the Passions grow violent and outrageous, the Affections impetuous, corrupt and violently vicious: Whence does all this proceed? from Heaven we can't pretend it comes; if we must not say 'tis the *Devil*, whose Door must it lie at? Pride swells the Passions; Avarice moves the Affections; and what is Pride, and what is Avarice, but the *Devil* in the Inside of the Man? ay, as personally and really as ever he was in the Herd of Swine.

Let not any Man then, who is a Slave to his Passions, or who is chained down to his Covetousness, pretend to take it ill, when I say he has the *Devil* in him, or that he is a *Devil*: What else can it be, and how comes it to pass that Passion and Revenge so often dispossess the Man of himself, as to lead him to commit Murder, to lay Plots and Snares for the Life of his Enemies, and so to thirst for Blood? How comes this but by the Devil's putting those Spirits of the Soul into so violent a Ferment, into a Fever? that the Circulation is precipitated to that Degree, and that the Man too is precipitated into Mischief, and at last into Ruin; 'tis all the *Devil*, though the Man does not know it.

In like manner Avarice leads him to rob, plunder and destroy for Money, and to commit sometimes the worst of Violences to obtain the wicked

Reward. How many have had their Throats cut for their Money, have been murdered on the Highway, or in their Beds, for the Desire of what they had? It is the same Thing in other Articles, every Vice is the Devil in a Man; Lust of Rule is the *Devil* of great Men, and that Ambition is their *Devil* as much as whoring is Father ———'s *Devil*, one has a *Devil* of one Class acting him, one another, and every Man's reigning Vice is a *Devil* to him.

Thus the *Devil* has his involuntary Instruments, as well as those who act in Confederacy with him; he has a very great Share in many of us, and acts us, and in us, unknown to our selves though we know nothing of it, and indeed though we may not suspect it of our selves; like *Hazael* the *Assyrian*, who when the Prophet told him how he would act the *Devil* upon the poor *Israelites*, answered with Detestation, *is thy Servant a Dog that he should do this Thing*, and yet he was that Dog, and did all those cruel Things for all that; the *Devil* acting him, or acting in him, to make him wickeder than ever he thought it was possible for him to be.

CONCLUSION

Of the Devil's last Scene of Liberty, and what may be supposed to be his End, with what we are to understand of his being tormented forever and ever

As the *Devil* is a Prince of the Power of the Air, his Kingdom is mortal, and must have an End; and as he is called the God of this World, that is, the great Usurper of the Homage and Reverence which Mankind ought of right to pay to their Maker, so his Usurpation also, like the World itself, must have an End: Satan is called the God of the World, as Men too much prostrate and prostitute themselves to him, yet he is not the Governor of this World; and therefore the Homage and Worship he has from the World is an Usurpation; and this will have an End, because the World itself will have an End; and all Mankind, as they had a beginning in Time, so must expire and be removed before the End of Time.

Since then the *Devil*'s Empire is to expire and come to an End, and that the *Devil* himself and all his Host of *Devils* are immortal Seraphs, Spirits that are not embodied and cannot die, but are to remain in being; the Question before us next will be, what is to become of him? what is his State to be? whether is he to wander, and in what Condition is he to remain to that Eternity to which he is still to exist?

I hope no Man will mistake me so much in what I have said as to Spirits, which are all Flame, not being affected with Fire, as if I supposed there was no Place of Punishment for the *Devil*, nor any Kind of Punishment that could affect them; and so of our Spirits also when transformed into Flame.

I must be allowed to speak there of that material Fire, by which, as by an Allegory, all the Terrors of an eternal State are represented to us in Scripture, and in the Writings of the learned Commentators, and by which the Pain of Sense is described; this, perhaps, I do not understand as they seem to do, and therefore have said,

When we're all Flame (that is all Spirit) we shall all Fire (that is, all such Fire as this) despise. And thus I claim to be understood.

It does not follow from hence, neither do I suggest, or so much as think that infinite Power cannot form a something (though inconceivable to us here) which shall be as tormenting, and as insupportable to a Devil, an

258

apostate Seraph, and to a Spirit, though exalted, unembodied and rarified into *Flame*, as Fire would be to other Bodies; in which I think I am orthodox, and do not give the least Occasion to an Enemy to charge me with profane Speaking, in those Words, or to plead for thinking prophanely himself.

It must be Atheistical to the last Degree to suggest, that whereas the *Devil* has been heaping up and amassing Guilt ever since the Creation of Man, increasing in hatred of God and Rebellion against him, and in all possible endeavor to dethrone and depose the Majesty of Heaven; that yet Heaven had not prepared, or could not prepare a just Penalty for him; and that it should not all end in God's entire Victory over Hell, and in Satan's open Condemnation: Heaven could not be just to its own Glory, if he should not avenge himself upon this Rebel, for all his superlative Wickedness in his modern as well as ancient Station; for the Blood of so many millions of his faithful Subjects and Saints whom he has destroyed; and if nothing else offered itself to prove this Part, it would appear undoubted to me; but this, I confess, does not belong to Satan's History, and therefore I have reserved it to this Place, and shall also be the shorter in it.

That his Condition is to be a State of Punishment, and that by Torment, the *Devil* himself has owned, and his calling out to our blessed Lord when he cast him out of the furious Man among the Tombs, is a Proof of it, *What have we to do with thee*, and *art thou come to torment us before the Time?* Luke viii. 28. where the *Devil* acknowledges four Things, and three of them are directly to my present Purpose, and if you won't believe the Word of God, I hope you will believe the *Devil*, especially when 'tis an open Confession against himself.

1. He confess Christ to be the *Son of God* (that by the Way) and *no Thanks to him*, for that does not want the *Devil*'s Evidence.

2. He acknowledges he may be tormented.

3. He acknowledges Christ was able to torment him.

4. He acknowledges that there is a Time appointed when he shall be tormented.

As to *how*, in *what Manner*, and by *what Means*, this tormenting the Devil is to be performed or executed, that I take to be as needless to us as 'tis impossible to know, and being not at present inclined to fill your Heads and Thoughts with weak and imperfect Guesses, I leave it where I find it.

It is enough to us that this Torment of the *Devil* is represented to us by Fire, it being impossible for our confined Thoughts to conceive of Torment by any Thing in the World more exquisite; whence I conclude, that *Devils* shall at last receive a Punishment suitable to their Spirituous Nature, and as exquisitely Tormenting as a burning Fire would be to our Bodies.

Having thus settled my own Belief of this Matter, and stated it so, as I think will let you see 'tis rightly sounded, the Matter stands thus.

Satan having been let loose to play his Game in this World, has improved his Time to the utmost; he has not failed on all Occasions to exert his Hatred, Rage, and Malice at his Conqueror and Enemy, *namely, his Maker*; he has nor failed, from Principles of mere Envy and Pride, to pursue Mankind with all possible Rancor, in order to deprive him of the Honor and Felicity which he was created for, namely, to succeed the *Devil* and his Angels in the State of Glory from which they fell.

This Hatred of God and Envy at Man, having broken out in so many several Ways in the whole Series of Time from the Creation, must necessarily have greatly increased his Guilt; and as Heaven is righteous to judge him, must terminate in an increase of Punishment, adequate to his Crime, and sufficient to his Nature.

Some have suggested, that there is yet a Time to come, when the *Devil* shall exert more Rage, and do more Mischief than ever yet he has been permitted to do; whether he shall break his Chain, or be unchained for a Time, they cannot tell, nor I neither; and 'tis happy for my Work, that even this Part too does not belong to his History; if ever it shall be given an Account of by Mankind, it must be after it is come to pass, for my Part is not Prophesy of foretelling what the Devil shall do, but History of what he has done.

Thus, good People, I have brought the History of the Devil down to *your own Times*; I have, as it were, *raised him* for you, and set him in your View, that you may know him and have a Care of him.

If any cunninger Men among you think they are able now to *lay him* again, and so dispose of him out of your Sight, that you shall be troubled no more with him, either here or hereafter, let them go to work with him their own Way; you know Things future do not belong to an Historian, so I leave him among you, wishing you may be able to give no worse an Account of him for the Time to come, than I have done for the Time past.

www.ingramcontent.com/pod-product-compliance
Lightning Source LLC
Chambersburg PA
CBHW030005290326
41934CB00005B/226